THE HOLD LIFE HAS

THE HOLD LIFE HAS

COCA AND CULTURAL IDENTITY IN AN ANDEAN COMMUNITY

SECOND EDITION

CATHERINE J. ALLEN

SMITHSONIAN BOOKS   Washington

Copy editor: Laura Starrett
Production editor: Duke Johns

Library of Congress Cataloging-in-Publication Data

Allen, Catherine J.
    The hold life has : coca and cultural identity
in an Andean community / Catherine J. Allen.—
2nd ed.
            p.   cm.
    Includes bibliographical references and index.
    ISBN 978-1-58834-032-0 (alk. paper)
    1. Quechua Indians—Rites and ceremonies.
    2. Quechua Indians—Social life and customs.
    3. Coca—Social aspects—Peru. 4. Sonco
    (Peru)—Social life and customs. I. Title.
    F2230.2.K4 A45 2002
    305.898'323—dc21   2002021013

British Library Cataloguing-in-Publication Data
available

Manufactured in the United States of America
15 14 13 12 11   4 5 6 7 8

♾ The paper used in this publication meets the
minimum requirements of the American National
Standard for Information Sciences—Permanence
of Paper for Printed Library Materials ANSI
Z39.48-1984.

For permission to reproduce illustrations appearing in this book, please correspond directly with
the owners of the works, as listed in the individual
captions (uncredited photos are the author's). The
Smithsonian Books does not retain reproduction
rights for these illustrations individually, or
maintain a file of addresses for photo sources.

To Rufina's children

O chestnut-tree, great-rooted blossomer,
Are you the leaf, the blossom or the bole?
O body swayed to music, O brightening glance,
How can we know the dancer from the dance?

—W. B. Yeats

For a complete man to be expressed,
individuals must hold hands in a chain of ceremony,
each giving deferentially with proper demeanor
to the one on the right what will be received
deferentially from the one on the left.

—Erving Goffman

Contents

Illustrations

Figures

Photographs

Preface to the Second Edition

As one can never step into the same river twice, I have resisted the temptation to tinker extensively with the text in preparing this second edition of *The Hold Life Has*. Beyond correcting some errors and making a few emendations, I have left the text pretty much alone. I have expanded the endnotes and updated the bibliography (although I cannot claim to have included every relevant publication published since 1988, and I regret any inadvertent omissions). I dropped a superfluous diagram and revised Appendix B to include changes in kinship terminology.

Nevertheless, my motivation for preparing a second edition was to update the material. The book continues to read as "ethnographic present," yet that present is rapidly dwindling into the past, and the hold that life has in 2002 is not the same as it was in 1985. To incorporate new material into the old text was impossible without a massive (and probably pointless) rewriting, so I opted to write a new chapter based on visits I paid to Sonqo in 1995 and 2000. It is included as an Afterword.

I found the new chapter difficult to write. It took far longer than I expected, and I thank Scott Mahler and other staff members at the Smithsonian Institution Press for their patience. My thanks also go to Enrique Mayer, Bruce Mannheim, András Sándor, Gary Urton, Frank Salomon, John Cohen, and Maria Eugenia Ulfe, all of whom commented on drafts of the new chapter, and to David Edwards who shared with me his video tapes and observations of a visit to Sonqo in 1999. The responsibility for any errors is, of course, my own.

I am gratified that my book continues to be read, and I thank the many readers and reviewers who have offered feedback over the years. Thanks are due as well to the George Washington University, which funded my research trip in 2002. I am grateful to colleagues in Peru, particularly Antonia Miranda, Jorge Flores, Mariana Mould de Pease and Jean-Jacques Decoster for their cordial and supportive reception during the trip. Percy Alvaro was generous in sharing his insight and experience as a development specialist in Sonqo. Madeleyne Gutierrez accompanied me part of the time in Sonqo; I thank her, and her brother Eldder, for their affectionate assistance.

Finally, I am deeply grateful to the friends in Sonqo who greeted me with open arms when I reappeared unexpectedly after many years. This second edition is dedicated to them.

Preface to the First Edition

"Haven't you finished that book?" asks Don Erasmo when I show up yet again in Sonqo. "I know it's hard work," he says, searching in his coca bundle for the best leaves to offer me. "We work hard in our potato fields, and you work hard at your desk. But you're taking too long!"

Being a kind of shaman, Erasmo appreciates the kind of work one does at a desk. The idea of a book about his community piques his interest, and he has been waiting for it since I first came to Sonqo in 1975. At that time I intended to do the usual stint of fieldwork leading first to a dissertation and then to a book, after which I planned to embark upon new projects in other communities and possibly other parts of the world. That first fieldwork did lead to my dissertation, bits and pieces of which surface in this book. But the episode never really closed; out of a mixture of inertia and fascination, my "follow-up" visits to Sonqo have continued for over a decade. Each time I return, I find that the community is changing rapidly in many ways. Children I knew in 1975 are now married and have children of their own, and some familiar faces are gone forever.

My own perspective has changed as well. Contemporary ethnography had originally been a secondary interest in the service of my research on pre-Columbian iconography. But after I came to know the *Runakuna* of Sonqo as living people in the twentieth century, my priorities reversed. The *Runakuna's* continual transformation and reinterpretation of their culture within new contexts have become endless sources of interest and admiration. With each visit

xiii

to Sonqo I find myself and my ideas changing, and with each return to the United States the work of writing seems to begin anew. Any stopping place is arbitrary.

Some of my perceptions have remained constant. My own socialization into *Runa* life began with *hallpay* (rather crudely translated as coca chewing), which *Runakuna* consider one of their most characteristic and meaningful activities. *Hallpay* continues to be my window onto Andean beliefs and values, and I have used it as such in writing about Andean culture. My focus on coca, the source of cocaine, has also forced me to confront American society's problematic relationship with Andean society and culture.

Foreigners have special advantages and disadvantages in observing another culture. I hope that the Peruvians who read this book will accept it as being offered in good will and affection, whatever they think of my perspective and interpretations. To Don Luis and to the other *Runakuna* of Sonqo I owe a great debt of gratitude. I have used the stuff of their lives in this book, and there is no way I can repay them (or atone) adequately.

Many people and organizations helped me bring this book to completion. The Henry and Grace Doherty Foundation, the National Science Foundation, the Wenner-Gren Foundation for Anthropological Research, the George Washington University Committee on Research, and the Columbian College of Arts and Sciences have all provided financial support at various times, and the Instituto Nacional de la Cultura Peruana provided me with the credentials I needed to travel and to conduct research in the countryside. I received invaluable cooperation and encouragement from the staffs of the Archeological Museum in Cuzco and of the various archives I consulted, as well as from the schoolteachers in Sonqo and Colquepata.

R. Tom Zuidema of the University of Illinois guided my initial fieldwork in Sonqo and continues to be an invaluable critic and a supportive friend. I also owe much to other teachers who guided my graduate work. Among them, the late Joseph Casagrande shared his practical wisdom with me and encouraged me to develop a personal style of ethnographic writing. Donald Lathrap taught me about the relationship between discipline and imagination.

Rick Wagner accompanied me to Sonqo in 1975. His presence and willing participation in *Runa* life was a major factor in my acceptance by the community; he contributed greatly to my research in many ways. Gary Urton and Deborah Poole visited me in Sonqo and made sensitive comparisons between Sonqo and other communities. Deborah was my companion on the Qoyllur Rit'i pilgrimage of 1980, when I suffered from altitude sickness and depended on her good-humored support. Peter Getzels introduced me to the community of Q'eros and shared his insights into religion and ritual in the province of Paucartambo. Many other colleagues have shared their ideas and friendship both "in the field" and at home, among them Harriet Gordon, Julia Meyerson, Ed Franquemont, Irene Silverblatt.

Many Peruvian ethnologists and historians have acted as an interested sounding board for my ideas and have given me practical help as well. They include Juan Núñez del Prado Bejar, who suggested I work in Sonqo; his father, the venerable Oscar Núñez del Prado; Jorge Flores Ochoa; Juan Ossio; Enrique Mayer; Manuel Burga; and Jaime Pantigoso, who tutored me in Quechua and transcribed many of my tapes. Henrique Urbano and other members of the Centro de Estudios Rurales Andinos in Cuzco generously allowed me to use their facilities. In Cuzco, the Gutierrez, Miranda, and Lau families fed me many meals and helped to raise my sometimes low spirits. Enrique Mayer and Helaine Silverman never failed to make room for me when I landed on their doorstep in Lima.

Many colleagues and friends—more than I can mention here—have offered specific suggestions regarding content and writing style. I have relied greatly on conversations with fellow Andeanists for inspiration and criticism. Among them, Billie Jean Isbell and Bruce Mannheim read and commented on drafts of various chapters. Janet Benton and my father, Augustine Allen, plowed through an early version of the manuscript and made editorial comments that led to major revisions. My colleagues in the anthropology department and the Latin American studies program at the George Washington University have provided a supportive environment in which to work. Catherine Griggs gave me generous critical and secretarial help as well as moral support. Nate Garner of the department of performing arts—together with our students in an interdisciplinary anthropology/drama class—read the manuscript and prodded me to clarify many points.

Final responsibility for any factual and interpretive errors rests, of course, with me. Translations from the Quechua are my own unless otherwise indicated. Pseudonyms are used for some personal names.

I am grateful to series editor William Merrill's special ability to provide incisive criticism in a warm and supportive manner. My other editors have been most generous with their time and interest as well, including Daniel Goodwin, editorial director of the Smithsonian Institution Press. Debra Bertram proved to be a careful reader and an exacting editor who nudged me to polish the manuscript one last time.

The insistence of my husband, András Sándor, that I should take a stand relative to Andean culture channeled this work into a different, and I think stronger, direction. He has carefully and insightfully commented upon many versions of this book over several years and urged me to forge ahead when I was on the verge of giving up. He also spent many hours in the darkroom converting my color slides to black-and-white prints and helped with the final editing of the manuscript. It is in large part due to him that I can finally deliver the goods on my next trip to Sonqo.

Introduction

Prelude: Sonqo 1976

It started to drizzle again. The four Quechua peasants pulled their hats over their ears, shrank into their ponchos, and pulled their small blankets over their legs. At 3,500 meters in the Peruvian Andes there is a penetrating chill, even in the summer rains of January.

It was Monday, late in the afternoon. The previous Tuesday, Rufina Quispe had died and been hurried into the ground. Now, prior to the ceremony of the Eighth Day, her male relatives had come to repack the grave, "her new house," as they called it. After covering the grave with flat stones and a small adobe marker, the men rested. As they sat on the old headstones, their sandaled feet sank into the damp weeds, and the adobes crumbled under them. The cemetery is not considered a healthy place, and no one returns to tidy up the graves. Four or five years later a communal work party would dig up Rufina's grave, mixing the bones and dirt to make room for the more recently dead.

Don Luis groped around for his coca bundle. As the dead woman's husband and therefore the host, he was obliged to give out frequent gifts of coca leaf. He stood up and began distributing small handfuls to each of his three companions, who received them with both hands cupped together, murmuring thanks. His eighteen-year-old son José, on leave from the Peruvian army, passed out a round of *trago* (cane alcohol) in a shot glass. He was crying qui-

1

This is rugged country where scattered houses and cultivated fields cling to the mountainsides.

etly. Luis's sister's son, Alcides, shuffled uneasily in the evil wind while old Don Idilio sat hunched over his coca.

At this point I entered the graveyard with another of Don Luis's sons, fourteen-year-old Bernardo, home from Cuzco, where he worked as a domestic servant. It was unusual for a woman to come to a grave on the Eighth Day, but I pleaded that I had missed the burial—having been on the coast seeing my husband off to the States—and Luis agreed to my coming. We had lived for the previous ten months in Luis's storeroom, and I felt strongly attached to his family. Returning after nearly a month's absence, I felt intrusive in the face of his grief—finding the competent and humorous man reduced, in his words, to a piece of ch'uño (dehydrated potato).[1]

Luis stepped forward to greet me. His eyes were swollen but dry, his round features set in a kind of blank composure. A blob of mud fell off his old felt hat and trickled down his poncho. We were all soaking wet. My hair straggled around my face and into my eyes.

He offered me a handful of coca, which I accepted with thanks, both hands outstretched. José poured me a glass of trago, which I downed after shifting my coca to one hand. Alcides, never one to be left out, jumped up and gave me a cigarette. Somehow I managed to accept the cigarette while returning the empty shot glass and holding on to my coca leaves. I sat down on an old grave, knowing that I should pray but having to do something with my coca first. I stuffed it in my jacket pocket and tried to retrieve the precious leaves I had spilled on the ground.

Finally I got myself together and went, suitably hatless, to the grave. I was moved by how carefully they had fixed it up and, knowing no prayers, I cried stealthily behind my hair. As I turned back I could see that the men were startled by my tears, and it surprised—nearly angered—me that Luis would think I could live with them for months and not grieve for his wife. Yet I had not wanted to cry for fear of wrecking Luis's composure.

As I sat down again I was given more *trago*. We all shared *k'intus* (small offerings of coca leaves). We blew on the *k'intus* to share them with Mother Earth, the Sacred Places around us, and the souls of the ancestral dead. There was some subdued conversation. "Haven't we made her a nice house? . . . Do you approve of our customs?" asked Alcides, proudly and nervously. I wondered how long it would take this grave to sink like the others into the mud and weeds. The malevolent *Machu Wayra,* Wind of the Old Ones, blew hard on us, and we all began to feel the dread and unhealthiness of the place. Alcides began to mutter about witchcraft: a toad had jumped out of the grave while they were working on it—right at Don Luis; there could hardly be a worse omen. At this Don Idilio glanced uneasily at me and at Luis, who was starting to look scared.

"We'd better finish up," he said, somewhat annoyed.

Alcides picked up two small boards nailed together in a cross. Luis began to rummage for the red gladiolus and marigolds in his bundle. "No *qantus*," he remarked sadly. Red, bell-shaped *qantus,* consecrated to the dead since pre-Spanish times, are a dry-season, cold-weather flower. Idilio smiled and quietly tumbled a heap of *qantus* out of his own bundle.

There was a flash of surprise and interest. *Maypichá!* Who knows where, in what out-of-way place, he found them. It was a lot of trouble for sure. José pulled a second weatherbeaten cross off an old grave and everyone, happy for a moment, set to work twining the flowers onto the crosses.

Alcides and Idilio put the finishing touches on the crosses, Alcides insisting on a single white flower among the red and orange ones. White was unsuitable for burials but it looked nice, and after some discussion they let it stay. We got up stiffly in our soaked clothing. Alcides set the crosses in the mound so that they stood over the grave. The men removed their hats, and we knelt together in the grass, trying to avoid the thistles. Alcides, who had been trained as a catechist, prayed from the Mass in Quechua as he stuck the crosses into the grave mound. Luis and Idilio trailed off into their own whispered prayers. We crossed ourselves and stood up.

Returning to our seats on the gravestones, we shared another round of coca and *trago*. Luis distributed small handfuls from his coca bundle, beginning with me and proceeding in order to Idilio, Alcides, José, and Bernardo. The two boys were not used to being treated as adults and accepted their portion gingerly. To chew coca was a new privilege for them—a privilege that back in Cuzco was denigrated as a nasty Indian habit.

But here in his natal community, José accepted his father's coca and offered him back a neat *k'intu* of three shiny, unbroken leaves placed one on top of the other.

"Hallpakusunchis, Taytáy" ("Let us chew coca together, Father"), he said.

Luis accepted with thanks. He blew over the *k'intu* before putting it in his mouth, calling quietly on *Pacha*, the Earth; on *Tirakuna*, the Places; and on *Machula Aulanchis*, the Old Grandfathers.

The rest of us exchanged *k'intus* as well, blowing over each one before adding it to the wad of leaves in our mouths. José served us each a shot of *trago*, beginning with me and going on to his father, Idilio, Alcides, and poor Bernardo, who tried not to choke and splutter. We sat quietly for a while. Luis gave me more coca, telling me not to be so sad.

José stood up to start another round of *trago* and exclaimed in surprise, for a woman stood at the entrance of the cemetery calling to us. Luis went to greet her as she tentatively moved forward. She was from another community, and I had never seen her before. Tall and thin, she had a look of dry humor and common sense that reminded me of Luis's recently buried wife.

The newcomer took off her *montera* (flat fringed hat) and went directly to the grave, where she knelt down and prayed, dry eyed and composed. Then she stood up and stretched out her hands to the grave, keening in a high-pitched wail, loudly but without tears.

"Where have you gone? Why did you leave us? How could you leave your husband and children? What will they do without you?"

She turned away from the grave and approached us, still calling to the dead woman.

"Where have you gone, my sister? How shall I find you now? Your children are crying for you."

At this Don Luis began to sob. Yes, what was he going to do? The children were calling for their mother, and he was alone and helpless.

He greeted Doña Leonora, his wife's cousin from neighboring Chocopía, with the requisite handful of coca, the tears running down his face and over his chin. He took the *trago* from José and served Leonora himself; then he asked her to sit down. She sat on the ground like a proper woman, protected by her four heavy skirts.

Luis leaned toward me, explaining eagerly that Leonora, like myself, was from another town and was here now because she had missed the burial. We were alike, he said, with a gesture that took in both of us. Leonora looked doubtful.

She stood up again and carried her glass of *trago* to the grave, pouring out libations on the four corners and the center of the mound while speaking quietly to her dead cousin. Upon her return she launched into a formal Quechua thank-you, intoning the words rapidly in a high falsetto, *"Gracias, urpicháy, taytáy, yusulpayki urpicháy, urpicháy, sonqóy, taytáy, sonqollay, taytáy, diospagarasunki urpicháy"* ("Thank you, my dove, my father, thank you my dove, my dove, my heart, my father, my own heart, my father, may God repay you my dove").

She felt self-conscious in a foreign community.

The men responded quietly in a chorus, looking down at their feet or off

Luis and Rufina pose in front of their house a few weeks before Rufina's death in January 1976. Rufina holds their prized transistor radio; Luis displays his wristwatch on one hand and keeps a firm grip on little Cirilo with the other. Three-year-old Inocencia stands at her mother's side.

into space. The thanking duly finished, Leonora took off her bundle, replaced her hat, and settled down into the grass. She neatly transferred her coca from the folds of her skirt to her coca cloth. José restlessly started another round of *trago*, which young Bernardo tried to avoid.

Leonora turned urgently to Don Luis. How did it happen? The news reached her only yesterday and then in fragments.

"Ay!" exclaimed old Idilio. "She was healthy! Healthy! And then she died." He cried, his head in his hands.

Luis drew a shaky breath and began to tell of his wife's death.

Rufina had been forty-five years old and pregnant for the thirteenth time. It was hard on her, for she hadn't been well—just skin and bones—to start with. He'd considered turning down the presidency of the community because of her health, for a man's *cargo* (community office) weighs heavily on his wife. But she wouldn't hear of it.

Once she was pregnant she just kept getting worse, and nothing helped: not the injections of the *sanitario* (paramedic) in the district capital, or the massages of a local midwife, or the anthropologist's vitamin pills. She felt awful and had blinding headaches. Sometimes he even had to cook breakfast in the morning. She remarked that she was dying, but he didn't listen.

A week ago Saturday he'd been called, as president of the community, to a provincial assembly. He didn't get home before one o'clock in the morning, and she was in labor when he arrived. He found her naked, crazy from the

5

pain, staggering around the room, bumping into walls, and stumbling in the fireplace.

"What are you doing running around naked?" he scolded her. "Go to bed and I'll take care of you."

He was frightened, but after all, she'd lived through childbirth before.

She calmed down and he heated some *trago,* two little glasses for her and one (he admitted sheepishly) for himself. The labor continued until the next afternoon.

The baby boy was born alive, their seventh living child. Rufina slept with the infant, and he'd thought the worst was over. He fed the other children and nearly fell asleep himself.

Late in the afternoon, she woke up in terrible pain—her insides hurt! She was in agony! He didn't call anyone; there was no one he trusted. He still didn't believe she would die.

Here Luis broke down in tears again. What was he going to do? He'd had to give the baby to relatives he didn't like, and there were still four little ones at home.

He wept freely without wiping away the tears. José also broke down and gave the *trago* bottle to Bernardo, who turned away from us. Alcides laid his hand on Idilio's arm, and the two men wept together. I had to keep blowing my nose. My vision swam from rain, tears, and *trago.*

Doña Leonora sat looking out over the valley, chewing her coca thoughtfully.

Our Mother's Fragrance

The landscape that met Leonora's gaze is a high mountain tundra. It is rugged country where scattered houses and cultivated fields cling to the mountainsides, for there is no flat land. Precipitous ridges rise for hundreds of meters from narrow creek beds and then fall away, on their other sides, to other creeks or rivers. One of these ridges is named Sonqo. This ridge rises to a crest of jagged and—so I'm told—malevolent peaks that drop away on their opposite sides to the warmer and more fertile valley of the Vilcanota, which was sacred to the Incas. The almost treeless *puna* (high grassland moor also called *loma*) is brown and parched from June through August, but it begins to turn green with the rains that start in September and increase through February, when shafts of sunlight fall in a golden-green haze on fields of potato plants. For me, this is the most beautiful time—*poqoy* in Quechua, the season of maturation. By May the green fades again into brown, and we enter *chirawa*—the clear dry season of warm days and brilliant nights when, they say, the stars send down layers of frost, coating the brown grass and even covering the springs with a skin of ice.

Looking northeast from this ridge called Sonqo, across a small river valley one sees the scattered houses of Miskawara, a neighboring *ayllu* (commu-

Luis and Balvina relax on a sunny afternoon in July 1980. Balvina composes a *k'intu* from her coca leaves while Luis pours a cup of *chicha*. The plastic bag near Luis's foot contains his supply of coca leaves.

nity) in the same district. Another range of hills rises above it. Beyond these hills the footpaths descend through valleys and across ridges toward the jungle, passing through the provincial capital of Paucartambo, which is approximately a six-hour walk. These tropical lowlands exert a powerful fascination on the people of Sonqo as a repository of shamanistic power and the legendary hiding place of the last ancestral Incas.

From the closer and higher regions of this jungle come the green elliptical leaves of the coca bush, used for centuries by native Andean people as a mild stimulant and anesthetic; as a medicine; as a token of friendship and mutual cooperation; as a vehicle, in ritual, for religious revelation. *Hallpay* (coca chewing)[2] was invented, they say, when *Santísima María,* Our Mother, lost her child. Wandering aimlessly in her grief, she absentmindedly plucked some coca leaves, chewed on them, and discovered that this eased her pain. Andean people have chewed coca ever since. For life is hard, especially in the *puna.* Coca helps alleviate life's pain and draws people together in mutual support. It is, they say, "Our Mother's fragrance" (*"Mamanchispa q'apaynin"*).

It would never occur to mourners to visit a grave without coca leaves. They say coca protects them from the sickening wind of the dead, and that it comforts them in their grief. Chewing coca together, they are drawn as a group into a shared communion with the Earth, with the Sacred Places, and with the ancestral dead.

One May afternoon, as I sat chewing coca with Don Luis in the courtyard of his house, his thirteen-year-old daughter snitched some leaves from his coca bundle and mischievously shared them with her younger brother and sister.

"Do children chew coca?" I asked in surprise.

"Oh, they play at it," Luis replied, "but they don't understand it."

His eyes twinkled ironically as he turned his gaze back on me, sitting there in my blue jeans and L. L. Bean walking shoes. If the children were playing at chewing coca, what was I doing?

A decade later I am still trying to understand what it means to chew coca. *Hallpay* (coca chewing) carries a way of life with it. To do *hallpay* properly, according to traditional ceremony, is to be a *Runa,* a "real person." To chew coca leaves is to affirm the attitudes and values—the habits of mind and body—that are characteristic of indigenous Andean culture.

Such affirmation is possible only in terms of a particular worldview. Younger people, like Luis's son José, stand between Indian and Mestizo culture, with a foot, as it were, in each. They feel ambivalent about coca chewing, rejecting the practice scornfully in town but accepting it in their home communities. They exhibit an uneasiness toward coca chewing that expresses their own ambivalent cultural identity.

The Hold Life Has

"We have to study man," writes Malinowski, "and we must study what concerns him most intimately, that is, the hold which life has on him."[3]

In the memory-work that follows and precedes fieldwork, thinking about coca has helped me understand "the hold which life has" on the small Peruvian community of Quechua-speaking peasants with whom I lived for approximately eleven months in 1975–76, accompanied for much of that time by Rick Wagner, my former husband. Over the last decade I have returned alone four times (in 1978, 1980, 1984, and 1985) for shorter visits.[4] The Sonqueños are used to my comings and goings by this time. They put up with me, laugh at me bemusedly, exploit me shamelessly. With outsiders they seem rather proud of their resident gringa, but I suspect that most of them are glad when I leave. A few are genuinely fond of me, and I of them.

The individuals described in the opening pages are (as far as I know) going about their lives, unaware that I have appropriated their now decade-old grief in writing for my own purposes. Luis, Idilio, and Leonora carry on in the repeating cycles of potato planting and harvest. Luis sees little of them, for he remarried within a year of Rufina's death, built a new house in a different neighborhood of Sonqo, and forged another set of social bonds. At forty, Alcides is the head of a relatively prosperous extended family. The responsibility seems to irritate him; he resents the fact that, unlike his younger brothers, he never had the opportunity to work and live outside the community.

Luis and Alcides have looked at me quizzically more than once and asked why I keep coming back to them. They seem to recognize that in this curious activity of traveling, visiting, and remembering they see something of the hold which life has on *me*. True enough. As an ethnographer, I share the compulsions characteristic of my own cultural tradition. In Sontag's words, "modern thought is pledged to a kind of applied Hegelianism: seeking its Self in its Other"[5]—a quest that finds expression in travel, colonialism, and ethnography.

Malinowski instructed us that the ethnographer's goal is "to grasp the native's point of view, his relation to life, to realize *his* vision of *his* world."[6] But this is clearly impossible. No one can enter another person's consciousness to share that other subjective experience of life. What one can enter is a shared intersubjectivity that is created when communication takes place.[7] My

8

memory-work is carried along by this intersubjectivity, mine and theirs; by the moments I have felt that genuine communication took place: the moment Luis told me with amusement that his children only played at coca chewing; the moment the men stared at me crying in the graveyard. I can enter not so much into their world as, in Dennis Tedlock's phrase, into an "understanding of the *differences between* [our] two worlds."[8]

I have not tried to abstract my study of Sonqo from the personal relationships and experiences in which it took place. Nevertheless, as this is an ethnography and not a memoir, my focus is on the Sonqo *Runakuna*, the People of Sonqo.[9] I am in the book because I have to be—because I think about the *Runakuna* in terms of my experience of them, which was of course shaped by their experience of me.

Seen from this perspective, coca is a particularly good vehicle for exploring the hold life has on my acquaintances in Sonqo, for coca chewing provides the context par excellence in which communication takes place. Social activities—from casual chats, to council meetings, to funeral wakes, to carnival—all take place in this context. The newcomer to a gathering is offered coca leaves, as I was when I entered the graveyard. The offering of coca leaves draws one into social interaction and participation in the activities at hand. This social interaction includes not only the other persons present, but entities immanent in the living Earth as well: Mother Earth, the Mountain Lords, the ancient dead. Understanding the nature of this communicative bond, forged by coca chewing, means exploring an attitude in which land is experienced as animate, powerful, and imbued with consciousness—a parallel society of Earth Persons with whom one is in constant interaction.

Runakuna communicate with the land via coca and often via alcohol as well. Through coca, the individual is simultaneously connected with the land and with his or her *ayllu* (community) of fellow *Runakuna*. My book is devoted to the nature of this dual connection—how it is forged, maintained, reproduced (or, sometimes, not reproduced). In this way, I will explore how the *ayllu* coheres as a social entity.

Colquepata

In conversations Sonqueños often define themselves as *Runakuna* in opposition to the *Mistikuna* (Mestizos) who neither chew coca nor live in *ayllus*. From early colonial times, they have coexisted with the Mestizos who live in Colquepata, the district capital. Colquepata is a village of about five hundred people, located about 70 kilometers by road northeast of the departmental capital of Cuzco, a city numbering (in 2001) 278,590 souls. Cuzco is well-known to tourists and archaeologists as the capital of the Inca Empire, which fell to the Spanish in 1532. The route linking Colquepata to Cuzco travels through the crossroads town of Huambutio and, after crossing a pass, branches off the main highway at the community of Mica (see Figure 1). The highway, a one-lane dirt road built in 1927, continues on to Paucartambo and the tropical low-lands to the east. A rugged and dangerous route that can bear traffic in only one direction at a time, the Paucartambo highway is nevertheless a major thor-oughfare linking Cuzco with the lowlands and is seldom closed during the rainy season.

A fine two-lane paved road, built to accommodate tourist traffic, links Cuzco with the town of P'isaq in the Vilcanota Valley to the northeast. From there a new dirt road, built in the mid-1970s, climbs the steep range dividing the districts of P'isaq and Colquepata. Crossing the pass, the road descends through Sonqo to Colquepata and then continues to the town of Paucartambo. During the dry season an occasional car, motorbike, or vanload of tourists can be seen moving along this new road, and some of Sonqo's younger men ride to Sunday market on newly acquired bicycles. But during the rainy season this new road is simply impassable. Even though it provides a shorter route to Cuzco, truck traffic has stayed with the more secure, if longer, road to Cuzco via Mica and Huambutio.[10]

Situated at 3,079 meters, the town of Colquepata sits in the lower part of the district's barren territory. The indigenous *ayllus* are located higher and mainly to the west and south. As one descends from Sonqo to Colquepata, ap-proaching the end of a one- to two-hour's walk, the town appears as a clus-ter of roofs—some made of red tile, most of corrugated aluminum, and a few of thatch. As the path descends further, the roofs disappear from view; a few minutes later the footpath joins the road and enters town by the main street, running downhill, past the new marketplace to the town plaza. The street of packed and rutted earth is lined on both sides by two-story houses.[11] To pass through this canyon of houses after a long stay in the *puna* creates a sudden sense of having come to town, of entering a new and different kind of world.

On Sunday, Colquepata's shops are busy; the doors of its houses are open and many of its approximately fifteen hundred inhabitants meander through the streets and market. Occasionally a priest from Cuzco comes to hold Mass in the beautiful but dilapidated colonial church, which has not had a resident curate since the mid-1800s. Weekdays are quite different: the streets are de-serted and most of the shops and houses are locked. Their owners are either working in their fields or are off plying their commercial trade in the city of Cuzco. Several families send their children to private schools in Cuzco; the mother usually accompanies them, so the family spends more time in Cuzco than in Colquepata for much of the year.

When the trucks (numbering from one to three, depending on the sea-son) lumber down the main street late Monday, Wednesday, and Friday af-ternoons, Colquepata awakens for a brief period. On these days, shopkeepers unload their cargo, and elected officials look after supplies brought for public projects. The streets are active again in the early daylight hours on Tuesday, Thursday, and Saturday as the trucks are loaded with produce and passengers destined for Cuzco. But Sunday is the biggest day. Late in the morning, trucks

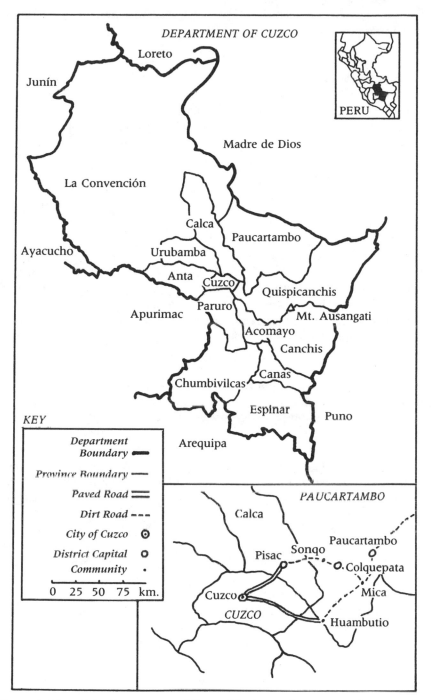

Figure 1. Map of the department of Cuzco. The insert shows routes between the city of Cuzco and the community of Sonqo. (Drawing by Robyn Johnson-Ross)

arrive from Cuzco laden down for the market and leave in midafternoon loaded with produce from the outlying *ayllu*s.

When Colquepata was built in the late 1500s, the plaza with its graceful church must have been the center of population and social activity. Now the wealthier families prefer to live above the plaza on the main street where the trucks enter town. The more prosperous dry-goods shops, the headquarters of the *guardia civil* (police), the new paved market with its aluminum roof, and the few houses built of concrete rather than adobe are located along this street.

Until 1975 Sunday market was held in the central plaza. The bustle of traffic must have been more evenly distributed then, but now virtually all market-day traffic is concentrated on the one main street. The town's other narrow streets, lined with single-story adobe dwellings, are nearly deserted. Below the plaza the road continues for a short distance past the primary school, which is quiet and empty on Sundays.

On the left side of the plaza stands the *consejo municipal*, or town hall, which also houses the medical post. Until the 1950s each of the district's *ayllu*s kept a small receiving house on this spot to shelter its officials when they came to Colquepata on business or for religious festivals. No trace remains of this complex, which was razed to make way for the town hall.

When I mention my research in Colquepata, Cuzqueños sometimes turn to me with sympathy and disbelief. How cold! How desolate! And the food! *"Puro ch'uño con papa!"* ("Nothing but *ch'uño* [dehydrated potatoes] with potatoes!").[12]

Indeed, the district's major product is potatoes, although barley and oats are increasingly raised as cash crops, and an occasional sheep is sold for its mutton. The exclamation *"Puro ch'uño con papa!"* is sometimes modified by the comment *"Pero hay carne bastante"* ("But there's plenty of meat").

Colquepata is not a wealthy town. Before the agrarian reform most of the district's few small *haciendas* (landed estates) were owned by churchmen and lawyers, and the townspeople themselves were never large landowners. They live from a mixture of agriculture and commerce, transporting the district's produce to Cuzco and returning with produce from lower altitudes, like corn, chili peppers, coca, and fruit, as well as supplies for their dry-goods shops like candles, kerosene, soap, and *trago*. But this commerce provides only a marginal living, and Mestizo families also work land for their own subsistence. Sonqo *Runakuna* sometimes point out that, in spite of their superior pose, the *Mistikuna* have to work their fields "the same as us."

The townspeople struggle to maintain their status as *gente civilizada* or *educada* (civilized or educated people), as they like to call themselves. This status is precarious, for the divide between *Runa* and *Misti* is neither wide nor impassable and may be crossed in either direction by individuals who succeed in adopting the other's social code (or, ipso facto, who fail to maintain their own). Nevertheless, members of both groups define themselves in mutual opposition to the other: to be *Runa* is to be not *Misti* and vice versa.

Runa and *Misti*

The Indians live dispersed in communities called "ayllus"; their huts are distant from each other, are unhygienic and very primitive. They do not use beds, or if they do these are made of some filthy llama or sheep hides . . . The Indians have not formed neighborhoods, much less small towns. Their isolation contributes considerably to their unsociability and makes for a sullen character.[13]

To be *gente civilizada* means to live in town and to involve oneself in commerce. It means that one sells but does not chew coca (at least not publicly), and that one speaks and usually writes Spanish even if Quechua is spoken within the home. The passage above is excerpted from a term paper written in 1959 by a young Colquepata Mestizo attending the University of Cuzco. The passage reveals his distaste for the Indians' way of living in dispersed rather than nucleated settlements and his conviction of the evil consequences of such living conditions: Indians are unsociable, withdrawn, and dirty, and do not even sleep in beds. A few pages earlier he writes:

Salient Characteristics of the Colquepata Indian: Like all Indians he is timid and skeptical; he expects nothing of anyone, and distrusts everything and everybody. His responses are always hesitant; he observes and waits without altering his features in moments of danger. He seems insensible, without physiological needs; he endures pain and the cruelest punishments with amazing stoicism. He suffers misfortune in his normal occupations with indifference. He seems to hold his life of little value; nevertheless, he loves nothing so intensely as his bit of earth. The Indian is not simply suicidal: he hates the Mestizo to eternal torment. In mass rebellion he is ferocious, cruel and bloodthirsty.[14]

Townspeople seldom visit the "primitive unhygienic huts" of the *ayllu*s with their "withdrawn" but potentially "bloodthirsty" inhabitants. Indians, on the other hand, frequently visit Colquepata for the Sunday market, and there they enter the shops and homes of the Mestizo "patrons" to whom they are related by ties of *compadrazgo* (godparenthood—see Chapter 2). Indian-Mestizo interactions are stylized, with language and demeanor emphasizing the power and superiority of the Mestizo and the subservence of the Indian. The Mestizo, for example, calls the Indian *"hijito,"* equivalent to "sonny" or "boy"; whereas the Indian, head bowed and shoulders bent, addresses the Mestizo as *"patrón," "señor,"* or *"wiraqocha"* ("sir").

My own nonconformity to this code of interaction has made for a rather strained relationship with the Colquepata Mestizos. It must seem incomprehensible to them that I actually prefer the space and solitude of the *puna* and enjoy the company of its reserved inhabitants. Even apart from my preference for open spaces, venturing into town and walking the tightrope between *Runa* and *Misti* is an ordeal I have avoided perhaps more than I should, thus introducing an inevitable bias into my fieldwork.

With time in Colquepata, I probably would have mastered the tightrope and learned much about the relationship between *Runa* and *Misti,* as well as Sonqo's place in the districtwide political system. But this is not how I have chosen to spend my time. I have stayed for the most part in Sonqo itself, immersed in the daily routine and the occasional ritual "blast."

During my first and longest stay in Sonqo, my relations with Colquepata were affected by the Velasco agrarian reform, which was then in full swing. The local *haciendas* had been expropriated by the government and were in the process of collectivization. Although independent indigenous communities like Sonqo were not profoundly affected as far as landholding was concerned, they were subject to various kinds of administrative reorganization. Government agents entrusted with the realization of these reforms were living in Colquepata, and when Rick Wagner and I suddenly appeared on the scene they viewed us with understandable, though unfounded, suspicion.

The *promotor* (chief agent) masked his suspicion under a show of hospitality, and we accepted several invitations to spend the night in his house before we learned that he was simultaneously maneuvering to have us expelled from the district. Although we successfully countered his maneuvers, we stopped visiting Colquepata in order to avoid him. The presence of agrarian reform agents made it difficult for me to investigate anything touching on agriculture and land tenure. The *promotor* managed to keep well-informed about the subjects I was investigating, and I discovered that even my queries about the classification of potatoes raised suspicions as far away as the provincial capital. Since land tenure was not my main interest anyway, I simply refrained from inquiring about it. Avoiding the *promotor* meant limiting my contact with the townspeople as well, so I simply adjusted to remaining in Sonqo. Like the *Runakuna,* I visited Colquepata mainly on Sundays—to attend the market, chat with shopkeepers, greet the mayor and police chief, and pay a visit to the *sanitario* who runs the local medical post.[15]

Given that the commercial role is not only their economic mainstay but central to their self-definition as well, it is not surprising that the townspeople have been ruthless in their control of the district's commerce, a control facilitated by the postwar commercialization of Peruvian agriculture.[16] Prior to the agrarian reform of the 1970s, Indians seldom traveled as far as the Cuzco market, as they were obliged by various means to sell their produce to Colquepata Mestizos who then marketed it for a profit.[17]

Shopkeepers in Colquepata easily drew Indians, particularly those related to them by *compadrazgo* (godparenthood), into debt-peonage by agreeing to sell the Indians scarce goods and alcohol on credit. Since Indians also relied on Mestizo *compadres* to help them with bureaucratic and legal problems, the Indians' illiteracy and limited access to money obviously increased the Mestizos' leverage. Thus, while the inhabitants of the "free" communities never found themselves in the serflike position of *hacienda* Indians, they were strongly dominated by local townspeople. This domination accounted for their "hatred

14

of the Mestizo to eternal torment"—a hatred that the Mestizos themselves recognized and feared. *Runakuna* hated *Mistikuna* with a mixture of envy and disgust; Mestizos despised Indians with a mixture of disgust and fear.

This situation persists in the late 1980s. Perhaps overly optimistic, I used the past tense in the previous paragraph because the dominance of the townspeople was somewhat altered and weakened during the period of agrarian reform in the 1970s. Spurred by governmental programs encouraging their participation in the market, the *indígenas* (natives), now officially relabeled *campesinos* (peasants), began bypassing the Mestizo middlemen and traveling to Cuzco to market their own produce. In spite of these changes, Mestizos have managed to maintain control of the district's commerce by manipulating traditional ties of *compadrazgo* to control the peasants' access to fertilizer, improved seed, and technical knowledge.[18] Since 1984 the presence of a police station has helped Mestizos maintain their fragile position of authority by enforcing traditionally subservient behavior on the part of Indian peasants.[19]

Nevertheless, now that the *haciendas* are gone and opportunities to travel and engage in commerce have increased, the *Runakuna*'s stubborn defensiveness is easing. The *ayllus* are not tied to Colquepata as they once were. The districtwide system of *ayllus* was once symbolized by the complex of receiving houses on the plaza, which recapitulated the organization of the district as a whole; and by a fiesta system in which each *ayllu* carried the image of its patron saint to Colquepata's church and back. But today's social forces are centrifugal, and Colquepata's hold has loosened: the *Runakuna* look to Cuzco as their economic center, and each *ayllu* celebrates its saints independently.[20]

Since 1975 the amount of land in Sonqo devoted to cash crops has increased dramatically. Most of Sonqo's barley is now destined for sale to the Cuzco brewery, and while the oats grown in Sonqo are fine for animals, they are not fit for human consumption. For the first time, the people of Sonqo are putting major amounts of land and energy into crops they cannot eat. The increase in cash cropping and the completion of the road brought about a major demographic shift in the early 1980s, and the distribution of Sonqo's population is quite different from what I first saw in 1975. Rapidly, Sonqo is being transformed.

Our Land, "Legally and Really"

This will not be Sonqo's first transformation. Throughout its history, Sonqo has developed and maintained its identity as an *ayllu* (community) in spite of opposing forces that have threatened to expropriate and destroy it. Although in Sonqo we encounter a way of life with roots in the pre-Spanish period of Andean civilization, *Runakuna* are not simply obstinate survivals of a lost past. The cultural identity of Sonqo *Runakuna* has developed over the last four centuries through complex interactions with Spanish-speaking Criollos and Mestizos (whose cultural identities are of course also historical products, in their own way equally Andean). The *ayllu* as it is today originated in colonial society after the Spanish Conquest of the Incas.[21]

In 1595, sixty-three years after the conquest, the population of the whole district was forcibly resettled in the town of Colquepata "in order that they may sustain and pay their taxes and fulfill other obligations that may be necessary." So states the document describing the *reducción* (reduction, i.e., resettlement) of the native population, part of Viceroy Toledo's grand plan to expedite the imposition of Spanish administration and missionization.[22]

The document contains a detailed list of the district's thirteen *ayllus*.The names of these *ayllus* coincide only partially with those now in existence, and do not include an *ayllu* called Sonqo.[23] I am inclined to think that in 1595 the *ayllus* were not localized in the same sense that they are today and that a major transformation took place between 1595 and 1658, the year that Fray Domingo de Lartaún Cabrera, "Inspecting Judge and Distributor of Lands for His Majesty the King of Spain," legally recognized Sonqo as a community with its current name and territory.[24]

From 1658 onward, Sonqo appears in various tax lists and church records. From these documents it is not clear, however, how early the *Runakuna* managed to move from their *reducción* in the district capital back to their current dispersed settlement, where they live spread out in small neighborhoods, some separated from each other by a half hour's walk or more.

Over the centuries, Sonqo has had to defend its right to exist as a free and independent community. Its success is impressive. During the nineteenth century several of the neighboring communities were incorporated into *haciendas*. In 1845 haciendas outnumbered *ayllus* thirty-one to seventeen.[25] Peons on these landed estates were required to spend as many as five days out of the week working the landlord's fields or tending his herds in return for the "privilege" of working the small plots allotted to them in the time remaining. The peons had to transport *hacienda* goods to market on their own pack animals as well as having to provide services in the manor house.

Sonqo managed to remain free during this period, and Sonqueños take great pride in their long history of independence. Legal documents pressing Sonqo's claims in a border dispute with neighboring Sipaskancha Alta, formerly a *hacienda*, refer proudly to "our community which has existed, legally and really, for three hundred and twenty-one years, and earlier still existed in the time of the Incas."[26]

"We are Incas!" *Runakuna* sometimes exclaim in conversation. They see themselves as the Incas' descendants, left to eke out a living on hard, intractable land. But at least this land is theirs, "legally and really."

Over the centuries, as the people of Sonqo held out against the encroachments of landlords, tax collectors, and missionaries, their bond with the land has developed into a paramount religious focus—more so than during the Incaic period according to the ethnohistorical studies of Duviols. The Sacred Places absorbed and retained the generative and protective power of the ancestral mummies and shrines of pre-Columbian times, which had been burned, smashed, and scattered by the "extirpators of idolatries."[27] The landscape became the last indestructible religious icon—the symbol of the *ayllu* itself. The Indians' legal battle to retain their land became part of their cultural and religious struggle to remain a separate people with an independent way of life.

The Plan of the Book

This book is about the practices, in particular the ritual practices, through which the people of Sonqo connect themselves with the land and, in the process, define and express their cultural identity as *Runakuna*. The land is many correlated things: it bears their crops, feeds their animals, and supplies mud bricks for their houses. It is also a legal unit, a bounded territory that they have defended for centuries. It is, moreover, a land*scape,* a constellation of familiar topographical features that serve as reference points in time as well as space. To *Runakuna,* these topographical features are sacred places called *Tirakuna;* they are experienced as a parallel society of animate and powerful personalities. The ritual use of coca brings about an integration of these two parallel societies, and by connecting *Runakuna* and *Tirakuna,* coca effectively binds the people to their land.

The ritual maintenance of this bond between people and land is a constant process, carried on in the daily routine as well as in the more intensified context of religious rites. Coca is the major vehicle for this ritual "work" (although other substances such as alcohol, cooked food, and cigarettes may be used as well). The ubiquitous ceremony of *hallpay* (coca chewing) helps to bring the *Runakuna* together as a community by sustaining their common relationship with the *Tirakuna.*

To an observer like myself, coca appears and reappears in virtually every aspect of *Runa* life like a leitmotif signifying the presence of social and spiritual bonds. Coca functions as a kind of leitmotif in this book as well. The reader will find coca reappearing in different contexts here, just as it does in the lives of *Runakuna.*

I begin by describing a cosmology communicated to me by my acquaintances in Sonqo. In this perspective, human society is embedded in a larger cosmic society. In Chapter 1, I explore the conceptual underpinnings of this cosmos: Andean ideas of time and space, matter and energy, body and soul, death and generation.

Chapter 2 turns to a smaller social order, the household, whose organization in many ways parallels that of the cosmos. Here I focus on routine activities that sustain and reproduce the household through the generations, and I trace the multiple social threads tying the household into an intricate network of mutual aid, duty, friendship, and hostility.

In this chapter I try to give the reader a feeling for the *Runakuna's* daily routine—for the styles of behavior and the attitudes that characterize their daily activities. My aim is to grasp their "habitus," to use Bourdieu's term.[28] The *Runa*'s cultural self develops through practices carried out routinely and unreflectingly in the process of living. Their worldview informs these routine practices; and their worldview, in turn, is informed by this activity.

Bateson speaks of the "process whereby knowledge (or 'habit'—whether of action, perception, or thought) sinks to deeper and deeper levels of the mind," adding that "the unconsciousness associated with habit is an economy both of thought and of consciousness."[29] Through routine activities, habitually carried out, a cultural identity takes shape: the sense of the self as *Runa*.

(Ethnographers, of course, arrive on the scene with their own habitus, and try to learn the new one from scratch—a slow process that meets with partial success at best, for it is carried on without benefit of a child's flexibility and receptivity. Like adults learning a new language, ethnographers pay attention to aspects of behavior that are second nature to the people themselves. Here the anthropologist has much in common with an actor preparing a role.)[30]

Much of the ritual as well as the utilitarian work bonding *Runakuna* to their land is of this habitual kind—carried out almost automatically and without reflection. Most coca chewing takes place in this routine context, and is carried out with careful but habitual ceremony.

As adults, most *Runakuna* arrive at a conscious understanding of coca's significance in their lives and learn to use coca in more intensified ritual contexts like divination and the preparation of burnt offerings. A few individuals (like Don Erasmo, who makes his appearance in Chapter 1) become ritual specialists and spend a good part of their adult lives contemplating coca leaves. But this reflective and conscious understanding of coca's significance develops during the years spent watching and playing at *hallpay* (coca chewing) as children and, once developed, such understanding continues to have as its foundation the unreflective use of coca in everyday life.

From the household's daily routine, Chapter 3 moves up an order of magnitude to the *ayllu* (community) itself, which has its basis in the connection between people and their land. Sonqo *Runakuna* are bound together as a group by their common connection to Sonqo's territory. They define themselves as an *ayllu* in opposition to people who do not share this common bond: other *Runakuna* who comprise other *ayllus*, bonded to other land; and the *Mistikuna*, who have no such connection. "Only *Runakuna* live in *ayllus*," they say.

The *ayllu* is maintained by various kinds of work: by collective labor on communal land, irrigation canals, the road, and the small church; by the people's decision-making duties in communal assemblies; by the elected officials' informal constitution of consensus and their tricky and difficult representation and defense of the *ayllu*'s interests to governmental agencies and law courts. And then there is the ritual work, carried out unceasingly to maintain the *Runakuna*'s bond with the land. From the land the *ayllu*'s leaders learn wisdom and discipline; the people's moral health, as well as their physical well-being, comes from the land. To recapitulate, to live in an *ayllu* implies, for the people of Sonqo, a particular kind of connection with the land: the communicative connection forged via coca.

This brings us back to the sacred leaf and to the center of the book,where my attention focuses specifically on this ritual work. In Chapter 4, I analyze coca chewing etiquette, those routine ritual forms that come into play whenever coca is chewed. These involve the making and sharing of *k'intus* (offerings of coca leaves) with prescribed phrases of invitation and thanks, including invocations to sacred Earth Persons. For mourners to share coca in the graveyard, for example, is simply an instance of normal *hallpay* etiquette, carried out with more emphasis and deliberation than usual owing to the seriousness and intensity of the situation. From this routine etiquette, the chapter moves to more specialized uses of coca in divination and curing, activities performed by ritual specialists.

Although coca is the essential ingredient of all ritual activities in Sonqo, its use is often accompanied by the consumption and libation of alcohol. On important ritual occasions, coca and alcohol are an indispensable pair. At Rufina's graveside, for example, we mourners not only shared coca leaves but were served coarse, low-grade cane alcohol called *trago*. Fermented corn liquor, called *chicha* or *aha*, is prepared for major holy days such as *San Juan P'unchay* (Feast of St. John, 24 June). As corn does not grow in Sonqo, *chicha* is prepared for only the most important feasts, and *trago*, purchased with money in the district capital, is the more common alcoholic beverage.

In Chapter 5, I explore the role of alcohol in the lives of the *Runakuna* and analyze the ritual forms with which it is shared, consumed, and offered to sacred beings. In ritual terms, the functions of alcoholic beverages are very similar to those of coca leaves. Libations of *chicha* or *trago* maintain communication with the land, and the sharing of drinks expresses social bonds.

But coca differs from alcohol in certain respects. The physiological effects are different; coca is a stimulant while alcohol is a depressant. The two also have different significance for Indian identity. Coca signifies Indian-ness. "Only *Runakuna* chew coca." Alcohol does not carry this meaning. To hide one's Indian origins one must foreswear chewing coca, but no such stigma is attached to drinking alcohol. As the *Runa* identity is left behind drinking continues, although some of the drinking patterns change; *Mistikuna* tend to prefer commercial beer to *chicha*.

In Chapters 6 and 7, I describe and analyze religious rites in which coca and alcohol together provide the vehicle for ritual action. Chapter 6 explores the ways in which each household maintains a positive relationship with the Earth, the Sacred Places, and the Ancestors by performing private rituals to ensure the well-being of family members, herds, and stores. Chapter 7 describes and analyzes community festivals that express the *ayllu*'s unity and continuity by stressing the connection between the people of Sonqo and their land.

During Carnival week, for example, *Runakuna* saturate their landscape as well as themselves with alcohol and coca. They feel that people and places dance together. Shortly before Corpus Christi, the major pilgrimage of the year integrates Sonqo *ayllu* within a regional set of *ayllu*s, all of which share a common religious focus: the range of sacred snow-covered peaks called Qoyllur Rit'i, Star Snow.

In a seeming paradox, ritual often achieves this integration of individuals, groups, and Sacred Places through competitive and violent encounters like the *tinku* (ritual battle). In Chapter 8, I analyze the nature of this ritual violence and relate it to dialectical tendencies inherent in Andean culture. Ritual provides a limiting and controlling context for the expression of these oppositional tendencies—whether in peaceful collaboration or in violent battle.

In times of rapid social change, these moderating ritual "frames" may be easily lost. For example, the pervasive ceremony of coca chewing, which draws participants into peaceful communication in the presence of deity, is progressively more difficult to maintain. Drug control programs aimed at cocaine traffickers have made it difficult to obtain and transport coca leaves. Moreover, the new opportunities to enter urban markets as independent agents propel *Runakuna* into situations in which coca chewing, the signifier of Indian-ness, is unacceptable. I turn to these issues in Chapter 9, the book's conclusion.

Coca and Cultural Identity

During the postconquest period, coca became the signifier par excellence of indigenous culture within a culturally mixed Andean world. Although Spanish colonists and their descendants cultivated coca as a market item, they rejected the practice of coca chewing. Soon after the conquest, missionaries were inveighing against coca use, thus creating in coca a symbol of cultural resistance. Coca chewing began to mark the developing boundary between *Runa* and *Misti*.

Today that boundary is changing, and the meaning of coca chewing is changing with it. As the town of Colquepata, the district's center, loosens its hold, *Runa* and *Misti* are no longer so tightly bound in their relationship of interdependence and mutual antagonism. The younger generation in Sonqo is now learning Spanish, putting on Western-style clothing, engaging in commerce, and spending more time in towns and cities, and the old distinction is beginning to lose its meaning. Thus the cultural definitions developed through the colonial dialectic of domination and resistance are undergoing transformation.

The meaning of two central terms in this book—*Runa* and *ayllu*— will change rapidly and perhaps drastically in the next twenty years. *Runakuna* no longer view the national society strictly in negative terms. The marked increase of cash crops reflects this more open and positive attitude, and many young people in their teens and twenties seem obsessed with the quest for money, which gives access to radios, bicycles, wristwatches, loudspeakers, and petromax lanterns. Most young men and some young women work for at least a few years outside the community. In addition, many young men are drafted into the army. Often, like Luis's son José, they prefer to settle in the city rather than to return home. Nevertheless, José's ties with Sonqo are strong; he returns to harvest the potato fields his father has set aside for him, and he knows he has a place there if he fails in the city. Sonqo remains José's safety net, but he prefers not to fall.

Some young men do fall, and they return to live in Sonqo; others are called back for family reasons. Alcides's two younger brothers, Vicente and Marcelino, for example, returned to Sonqo in 1981 after years of city life to help care for their aging father. In 1976 I met Marcelino in Cuzco, where he made every effort, in dress, language, and manner, to conceal his origins. Now, resigned to live in Sonqo, he appears fully *Runa*. From watching him at work in his fields, chewing coca and speaking Quechua, one would not suspect that Marcelino had lived in a city and was learning successfully to put himself across as a *Misti*. For men in this younger generation, to be *Runa* or to be *Misti* is like changing a suit of clothes (or to use an analogy more painfully apt, like repeatedly shedding a layer of skin).

In this time of flux and cultural transformation, coca epitomizes the conflict young men like José, Vicente, and Marcelino experience between their *Runa* selves and their identification with the national society. The ceremony of *hallpay* symbolizes the choices they must make about who they are.

That coca symbolizes this choice is ironic, for on one hand coca is among the oldest of the Andes' cultivated plants, trade items, and ritual symbols; on the other hand, coca is the source, in a completely altered form, of Peru's latest "boom" on the world market. In a new transformation of meaning, coca epitomizes the way native Andeans are entangled in the meshes of an international economy whose politics and morality affect their lives in ways they can neither imagine nor resist.

The irony extends to myself. I looked to the theme of coca as a way of exploring Andean culture, but I find its path leading to the back alleys and penthouses of my own country. Is this "finding my Self in the Other"? It seems that *"Runa-and-Misti"* is not the only dichotomy whose edges grow indistinct.

I will return to this subject in my conclusion. But until then I want to stay in Sonqo, with its rocky potato fields, its high marshy pastureland, its graveyard where José shared his father's coca—with the *Runakuna* as I know them, standing at the brink of their next transformation.

Chapter One

~~~~~~~~~~~~~~~~~~~~~~~~~~

Water, Stones, and Light
A Cosmology

In the Mind's Eye

As a temporary member of Don Luis's household, I participated in the daily rounds of work and rest. I learned how to harvest potatoes and to herd sheep. At night I sometimes lay awake in the pitch dark listening to the children's deep sleeping while their parents dozed shallowly, attuned to every rustle in the nearby corral. But to participate in activities is one thing, and to grasp the meaning they hold for the people involved in them is quite another. Out in the fields I could see and feel (and later taste) the potatoes; I could observe the methods of hoeing them out and the kinds of teamwork involved. But I could not observe the Earth's resentment of the hoes cutting into her, nor was it obvious to me that the surrounding hills and ridges watched us with critical eyes. These experiences are part of potato harvesting, but they can be seen only through the mind's eye. They had to be explained to me, or I had to infer them from the behavior of my companions, who invoked the Earth and the Places placatingly as they chewed their coca leaves.

Nevertheless, factors such as these—that the material world is experienced as animate, powerful, and responsive to human activity—constitute the scaffolding on which (to use the Weberian metaphor adopted by Geertz) *Runakuna* hang their webs of significance, webs they spin in the process of living and "in which they are themselves suspended."[1] I could learn about this mental and emotional scaffolding only by talking to people, by seeking out "informants" who were willing to explain what was obvious to them and invisible to me.

"Informant" is a terrible word to have to use. It sounds like "informer" and makes ethnography sound uncomfortably like spying. Yet ethnographers are hard put to know what else to call the people they learn from. Sometimes "consultant" is an apt choice, but it implies collaboration and a shared under-

22

standing of the ethnographer's purposes, an understanding that is not always present. What about "friends" and "teachers"? Again, these can be accurate descriptions, or they can reflect sentimentality and wishful thinking.

Nevertheless, I have learned the most (and I think this is true of most fieldworkers) from a few individuals whom I can genuinely call friends and teachers, and who see themselves in this light. I did not actually choose these people as informants; we became friends because we enjoyed each other's company. With Luis, Erasmo, and Basilia, "hanging out" coincided with my most profitable fieldwork, not to mention my happiest moments in Sonqo— which were spent with them sorting seed potatoes, squeezing *ch'uño,* cooking, or just chewing coca and talking. In these moments, my friends spoke to me about the powerful and peevish Mountain Lords who surrounded us. They told me about Mother Earth, the Saints, and the Old Ones who had built small, round houses on the hill Antaqaqa, and who come back to life on moonlit nights.

In the course of my fieldwork I had to make an effort to seek out other informants. My friendships were a trap in some respects because they provided refuge from the reticence and suspicion I encountered from many of the *Runakuna.* To stay in this refuge obviously would have limited my fieldwork, for our conversations focused on my friends' interests, often to the exclusion of the interests of others.

I recall, for example, how I tried to engage Erasmo in a conversation about *chakra ayni* (reciprocal aid in agricultural labor). A bored expression fell over his usually mobile and irregular features, as if to say, "Why are we talking about this?" As conversation lagged, he stared off into the sky and asked abruptly, "If I turned myself into a condor, could I fly to your country?"

I was riveted. "Can you turn yourself into a condor?"

"Can you?" he teased. "Some people can . . ."

I took the bait. So much for *chakra ayni.*

Erasmo

Erasmo is a cagey character. I still don't know whether he can turn himself into a condor, though I do know that he thinks a lot about the possibility. Maybe he can. He is a *paqo,* a religious specialist and practitioner. He knows how to talk to the Sacred Places through the medium of coca leaves and how to cure and cause illness with carefully composed burnt offerings. He knows a great deal of herbal lore and enjoys puttering in a small sheltered garden behind his house where he coaxes plants from lower altitudes to grow behind windbreaks. He calls himself a *hampiq* (medicine-doer), and many of his neighbors call him a *layqa* (sorcerer). In Sonqo, as in other Andean communities, people tend to seek out curers in other localities and avoid the ones nearby.

I was slow to get acquainted with Erasmo because the director of the local school, a Mestizo woman from Cuzco, warned me to keep away from him. She

Erasmo (left) sews a ritual tassel onto his horse's ear during the Feast of Santiago (25 July). His son, Hipolito, looks on.

considered him unreliable because she had contracted with him to supply her with milk, and he failed to keep up his end of the bargain.

She quite correctly perceived Erasmo to be socially marginal in the community. He had left Sonqo for several years to live with his wife in her native *hacienda* near Paucartambo. Although he disliked working for an *hacendado* (landlord), he preferred the warmer climate and the kind of labor involved in growing corn and beans rather than potatoes. He dislikes Sonqo's barren terrain, and potato farming bores and depresses him. In 1975 he specialized in beans and ocas (a sweetish white tuber); in 1984 I found him proudly and laboriously harvesting potatoes from the six-foot-deep furrows of a marsh he had drained. Other Sonqo *Runakuna* looked on aghast, for the marsh was known to be *saqra* (demonic) and liable to swallow people or to make them sick. When I suffered a migraine headache after visiting Erasmo, Luis was sure the swamp was to blame. But Erasmo and his family suffered no ill effects.

Erasmo is intensely involved with the public and ritual life of his community. He participates as musician, dancer, and spectator, and goes every year on the arduous pilgrimage to Qoyllur Rit'i, which many Sonqueños make no more than two or three times in their lives. At the age of forty-five, he has only recently given up dancing *ukuku,* the bear dance suitable for adolescents and young men. His somewhat ambiguous prestige in the community derives from his reputation as a diviner, curer, musician, and storyteller.

It was through his storytelling that I finally became friends with Erasmo, after duly avoiding him for nearly five months. As the *Runakuna* became more comfortable with my tape recorder and I began to collect myths and stories, I was constantly referred to Erasmo as the local expert. Erasmo concurred unabashedly in this opinion and took to the project enthusiastically. When I returned to Sonqo, we began again where we left off, settling down in the firelight with the coca bundle, the bottle of *trago,* and the tape recorder. In 1984 he listened to tapes we had made in 1975 and commented seriously that his stories would survive his death. It was, I think, as much a request as a comment.

Watchers

Erasmo likes to sit in front of his house watching the world. In this he is not unlike his fellow *Runakuna,* although he does it even more than most. Watching is one of Sonqo's favorite activities. Nothing seems more interesting to *Runakuna* than to be situated in a high, sheltered spot watching what happens.

Sonqo and its neighboring high *puna* communities are sparsely but fairly evenly settled. Only the high passes can be called truly unpopulated, and even there a grazing horse or a shepherd with alpacas may break the solitude. Wherever you are the view is panoramic, and every time you change your position the view changes. As you pass over the ridge on a hill—or even shift to the other side of your sheltering rock—new peaks, boulders, ravines, and houses come into view.

From my first few days in Sonqo, I was impressed with how easily and accurately *Runakuna* recognize each other from a long way off—including the women, who at a distance look alike (to me) in their almost identical black skirts and flat fringed hats. They recognize each other not through appearance but through mannerisms—Luis's lopsided walk, the way Eusevio swings his hands. On my return to Sonqo in 1984 Erasmo mentioned that he had immediately recognized me at a distance, not from my clothes but from the way I pick up my feet. They notice and speculate about one another's comings and goings, and if someone has a new acquisition too big to conceal, a good part of the community knows about it before the purchaser reaches home.

Watching is not merely a pastime, it is a form of communication among people acutely attuned to the nonverbal sign. For the watching is reciprocal; everybody watches everybody else. The clothes one wears, the things one carries, the animals one leads—or the routes taken and the schedules followed—can all be intended and interpreted as messages. Individuals who seldom meet or speak to each other directly may nevertheless see each other daily, passing at a distance on the way to fields or pastures, and know they are being watched and discussed.

It is not only people who are being watched. The landscape, too, has its changing aspects. Its features change as the sun passes in its course, as clouds cover the high peaks, as a hail storm gathers across the valley, as mist rises at night from lakes and ravines. *Runakuna* have an intimate knowledge of their landscape; every wrinkle in the Earth's physiognomy—every hill, knoll, plain, ridge, rock outcrop, or lake—possesses a name and a personality. Every child knows a vast number of these place names before the age of ten, for *Runakuna* orient themselves spatially in terms of landmarks rather than through abstract cardinal points. In the southern hemisphere, where no equivalent of the North Star provides a fixed reference point in the sky, the movements of celestial bodies, too, are calculated relative to landmarks.[2]

And the Places themselves are watchers—the greatest watchers, against whom there is no concealment, who know and remember one's every move. Their moods and reactions can be known only indirectly, for although it is said that the Incas could speak directly with rocks and mountains, their descendants realize that they have lost this ability and must receive these communications indirectly through signs: configurations of coca leaves, dreams, unusual events, and the state of one's luck and health.

These great watchers are called *Tirakuna*, the Places. The highest snowy mountains, who overlook the region and can be seen over a large area, are addressed as *apu*, a title of respect meaning lord. Collectively they are often called *taytakuna*, the fathers. Every aspect of the topography distinctive enough to be called a landmark in our terms has a specific and individual name and selfhood for the *Runakuna*. *Tirakuna* are not spirits who inhabit the places, but the Places themselves, who live, watch, and have ways of interacting with the human beings, plants, and animals that live around and upon them. Because of their power and liveliness, *Tirakuna* are described as *santu*, sacred or holy. The great *Apukuna* are so sacred that it can be dangerous to look directly at them, and during the annual pilgrimage to Qoyllur Rit'i they are approached with an intensity of emotion startling to behold. The lower hills, ravines, and *pampas* where one lives are more familiar characters, and *Runakuna* interact with them on a more regular basis.[3]

The Places—as Don Luis explained, his face lighting up at the thought—are *"uywaqninchiskuna,"* "our nurturers." They are nurturers in a moral as well as a biological sense, in the sense of bringing up a child into adulthood. They observe the life of the community; everything that happens concerns them. Affronts to group harmony and social well-being anger them, and they can bring down poor health on herds and their owners in punishment for moral lapses. Like parents, the *Tirakuna* can protect and chastise, and through the medium of coca leaves they can be asked for guidance.

The day I first arrived in Sonqo, Doña Basilia presented me with a handful of coca leaves, telling me to "blow" them to Antaqaqa, a prominent hill whose nearly bald top is covered with ruins. When I sent a couple of leaves sailing off in the wind she collapsed into gales of incredulous laughter; I was supposed to blow *on* the leaves before I chewed them, not blow them away! She showed me how to do a proper *phukuy* (ritual blowing), admonishing me to take care with Antaqaqa, who was sure to feel ill disposed toward me, a foreign interloper, with big, clumpy shoes no less! He wasn't going to like the way it felt when I walked on him.

Knowing the *Tirakuna*'s individual personalities can be as important as knowing the personalities of one's neighbors. When I visited him in Towlakancha, Julian instructed me that my *phukuy* should not neglect Ixchhinu, a neighboring pinnacle of rock. Towlakancha and Ixchhinu went together, he explained, and if I mentioned only one the other would feel insulted. Similarly, Panapunku, a high pass between the districts of Colquepata and San Salvador, is known as *millay* (nasty) and is prone to send bad weather. In general, local *Tirakuna* are more capricious and more directly concerned with the *Runakuna* of Sonqo than are the great regional *Apukuna*. These local Places continually demand coca and libations of alcohol. Neglect may bring on all sorts of accidents, major and minor—a stumble on the path, falling rocks, drowned sheep, and so forth. Attending to the *Tirakuna*'s wants, on the other hand, should assure one's well-being *(allin kawsay)*. The two communities of *Runakuna* and local *Tirakuna* are closely bound together by these ties of ongoing reciprocity, for without the *Runakuna*'s offerings, the Places are hungry and sad, and without the care and support of the Places, the *Runakuna* are poor and unhealthy.

At the head of the Colquepata valley stands Wanakawri, the ancient pass between Paucartambo and the Vilcanota River drainage. *Runakuna* say that a person who stands in the Inca ruins on Wanakawri can look back over the whole Colquepata valley. A mountain pass of the same name overlooks Cuzco, and in some versions of Cuzco's origin myth it was from this Wanakawri that the ancestral Inca, Manco Capac, first looked on the Cuzco valley. In Sonqo a different myth is told—a myth, not of origin, but of termination. They say that as the last Incas fled from the Spanish, they crossed Wanakawri and passed through Colquepata on their way to Paititi, their hidden jungle city. When—or if—they ever return, it will be by the same route.

Erasmo only nodded and chuckled when I told him that I intended to walk from Sonqo to P'isaq by this ancient route. Almost at the very moment I set out, rain began to pour down in torrents, and although I eventually managed to fumble my way across the pass, I was hemmed in by clouds on all sides. Later Erasmo caught up with me and slyly asked about the view from Wanakawri. "I knew you wouldn't see anything," he said. "Wanakawri never lets you see anything the first time you cross."

Antaqaqa, Ixchhinu, and other local promontories are like elders in Sonqo's family of Places. For Sonqo *Runakuna*, they are a focus of almost constant attention, whereas from the perspective of a more distant community they are small hills of no particular importance. The great snowy mountains, on the other hand, hold equal sway over a much larger area. These regional *Apukuna* are the *kamachikuqkuna*, the authorities (literally, the ones who make something happen, the actualizers). As we might expect of powers concerned with social well-being, the *Tirakuna* have their own internal social hierarchy. The great snowy mountains have the highest rank and the most power; lower mountains like Wanakawri are lower in the hierarchy; small hills that hold only local importance are of a lower order still.[4]

Chief of them all is Ausangati, whose squarish white peak, over 6,830 meters high, is visible over much of the department of Cuzco, providing widely separated localities with a regional orientation. It is Ausangati whom the highest level diviner, the *altumisayuq*, calls upon—and it is Ausangati who, in turn, orders the other Places to answer his questions.

To the east, hidden in the forested Andean foothills, is Apu Qañaqway, a *pacha urqo* (earth mountain) whose round top is devoid of snow. He specializes in clearing the sky of clouds, whereas Pitana, another mountain farther inside the tropical forest, is said to summon the rain.Qañaqway is also a great cattle herder. Wild and unapproachable bulls graze on his slope that sometimes mate with favored individuals' herds, producing fine and fertile offspring.[5]

Ausangati and Qañaqway lie roughly to the south and east of Sonqo. To the west towers the double peak of Sawasiray-Pitusiray, visible virtually everywhere in Sonqo. Although Sawasiray-Pitusiray is the closest of the snowy mountains, Sonqo *Runakuna* seem more focused on Ausangati and Qañaqway in their libations, invocations, and general conversation. This preference probably reflects the Sonqueños' ethnic identification with the provinces of Paucartambo and Quispikanchis, where Ausangati and Qañaqway are located, and their lack of identification with Calca, the province of Sawasiray-Pitusiray.

Luis feels a special tie to Apu Qolqepunku, another snow-covered peak near Ausangati, for during an *altumisa* (a divination session of the highest order), Qolqepunku addressed Luis directly, calling him "my child." During the same session, he heard the deep, growling voice of Apu Salkantáy, whose great peak dominates the landscape in Apurimac, far to the west. Few Sonqueños have seen this *Apu*, but they recognize his power nonetheless.

Some individuals establish special ties with Places closer to home. Luis's second wife, Doña Balvina, has a close bond with Picchu, a high hill overlooking the town of Colquepata. As a child, she played on Picchu's slopes, and one day the *Apu* gave her an *istrilla* (from Spanish *estrella*, star; a small found-object, in this case a colonial coin) that she considers the source of her well-being and insight.

Another important *Apu* not visible from Sonqo is Pachatusan, a jagged crest of rock jutting into the sky near Cuzco. Although he figures in their invocations, *Runakuna* are unwilling to discuss Pachatusan and become nervous at the mention of his name.

Thus the vigilant *Tirakuna* provide an orientation that is both emotional and cognitive, for space is experienced and organized in terms of this ever-widening circle of landmarks. The mountainous landscape provides an immediate and unique orientation relative to an individual's position at any given moment, an orientation that shifts as the individual moves. The landscape provides a local orientation to Sonqo's territory through Antaqaqa and the other Places of Sonqo, an orientation shared by the members of the *ayllu* (community); and the landscape further provides an ever-widening regional orientation in terms of the peaks of progressively higher mountains—shared by the *Runakuna* throughout much of the department of Cuzco.[6]

Mother House, Mother Earth

Of all the Places, the most familiar and immediate is *Wasitira* (House-Earth), a term encompassing the adobe house itself as well as the courtyard and its immediate environs. Each house lives because she is formed out of the living Earth, ritually enlivened during the *wasichayay* (house-raising) and warmed by the fires of her internal stove, the *q'uncha*. There is absolutely no escaping *Wasitira*'s vigilance. Nothing takes place in or around the house that she does not see. If a house is robbed, the diviner asks Ausangati to summon its *Wasitira*, who would have seen what took place and can describe the culprit.[7]

Wasitira is a localized expression of *Pacha*, the Earth, whose qualities she shares. "World" may be a more accurate translation than "Earth," for *Pacha* is simultaneously temporal and spatial, referring to the Earth's extension and materiality at a particular moment in time. Unlike the *Tirakuna*, who are discrete entities participating in a social hierarchy, *Pacha* is a generalized entity. She is everywhere. I say "she," because *Pacha* is personified as more female than male, whereas the *Tirakuna* are more male than female. As a female, *Pacha* is addressed as *Mama*—*Pacha Mama*, Mother Earth. *Pacha Mama* is primarily benevolent, although she is also capricious and easily angered.

"We owe our lives to her," Basilia told me, gesturing out over the potato fields. "She nurses the potatoes lying on her breast, and the potatoes nourish us."

I asked whether *Pacha Mama* teaches women their female skills—cooking, spinning, weaving.

"The *mamachakuna* [literally, little mothers; female saints] teach us those things," Basilia answered. "*Pacha Mama* doesn't teach us anything. She nourishes us. She nurses us."

Basilia went on to describe how *Pacha Mama* watches us, how she may rebuke and punish us, and how in divinaton rituals, *Pacha Mama* rises up as a woman and speaks directly to us.

Basilia

I have never been present at an *altumisa* (divination ritual). What I know about Salkantáy's growling voice or *Pacha Mama* rising up from the floor I know from my friends' descriptions. I imagine the scene, of course, based on these descriptions. But in the *altumisa* of the mind's eye it is Basilia who rises up in front of me. Basilia—a tiny, skinny woman in her fifties whose homely features seem always on the verge of laughter—stands there chattering away at a great rate, her prominent teeth glinting in the firelight. Her small frame carries a remarkable weight in woven clothing; in fact, she looks a little like a textile cone carried on legs like weathered leather sticks.

Basilia (right) poses in the doorway with her friend Josefa and Josefa's children. Both women display their weaving skill in their shawls and skirt borders. Their hats and ribbons were purchased at provincial markets, as was Basilia's vest. Josefa has substituted a factory-made sweater for the traditional vest. Dressed in her finest *Runa p'acha* (traditional Quechua clothing), Basilia proudly holds her transistor radio, the antenna raised and ready to receive "Radio Tawantinsuyu."

Basilia was an expert weaver and wore her handiwork proudly and in quantity. She persuaded me to replace my blue jeans with the heavy burlap skirts worn by Sonqo's women, taking it upon herself to make a skirt for me to dance in during Carnival. I remember her delight when I appeared laden with skirts and covered by a *lliklla* (woven shawl). With ribbons in my hat and my hair swinging in braids, I began to look like part of the community.

"*Comadre*, you could pass for a *Runa warmi* (*Runa* woman)," she exclaimed, giggling. "Just keep your mouth shut!"

Decked out like this I discovered that for a *wira warmi* (fat, substantial woman)—a term of high praise—it is the clothes that provide the substance. The layers of skirts hanging around the waist and swishing grandly below the knees—*chhaaq, chhaaq, chhaaq*—instill a feeling of weightiness and necessitate a rolling gait that *Runakuna* find womanly and dignified. More than two of these skirts tires me out and hurts my stomach, but Basilia wore a minimum of three—and at fiestas five. Her shawls were woven in difficult motifs that young women no longer attempt to learn. Basilia loved to weave and complained that even in her fifties she was still too bogged down with child care and herding to have enough time for it.

30

Living in Luis's household, it was inevitable that I would become acquainted with Basilia, for she and her brother Luis enjoyed each other's company, and her oldest son, Alcides, was Luis's godchild through marriage sponsorship. What was not inevitable was the affection we felt for each other. More than anyone else, she seemed able to see through my foreignness to a fellow human being; she extended a sympathy the genuineness of which I never doubted and the loss of which I feel whenever I return to Sonqo. I last saw her in Cuzco when she traveled in to say goodbye before I left in 1978. We sat up most of the night talking and drinking apricot brandy, which she found marvelously good.

Basilia was apparently tireless—tireless in talking as in every other activity. She was a great complainer, and when she carried on about fatigue and chest pains I dismissed it as hypochondria. All her intense worries, irritations, and amusements spilled out as they occurred to her, and she found a willing listener in me. I think her family was relieved to have me around in this capacity. For me there was always something interesting in her talk, and I never left her without feeling that I had learned something worthwhile. I would go home with a sense of well-being, and my journal entries were longest on the days I spent with her.

As for Basilia, she enjoyed socializing me, for she took it upon herself to turn me, a strange quasi-hermaphroditic schoolteacher-type, into a regular *Runa warmi* (woman). She wanted me not only to wear skirts, but to spin, cook, dance, and sing like a proper woman. She was determined that I should develop enough command of ritual comportment to keep the *Tirakuna* from rolling rocks at me or hailing incessantly. The project was hopeless, of course, but we made some progress and enjoyed the attempt. I did learn to wear *Runa p'acha* (*Runa* clothing), to spin after a fashion, and to blow coca leaves properly.

Unlike Erasmo, Basilia was not at all marginal to her community. The idea! I can see her bridling at the very suggestion. Her unpropitious start in life made Basilia all the more determined to be a woman of substance. Her father died in their house at Towlakancha when she was about five years old. She remembered two-year-old Luis climbing on the corpse, pummeling it playfully and telling it to wake up.

Their mother remarried, and their stepfather threw the three youngest children—Basilia, Luis, and Juana—out of the house to live in a pig hutch. Twelve-year-old María was allowed to stay, apparently because her labor was useful, and she managed to feed her siblings surreptitiously. Nevertheless, even as little children the three raised and prepared much of their own food. Basilia boasted of having used the *chakitaklla* (man's foot plow) until Luis grew big enough to handle it. To this day Luis harbors an intense resentment that extends to his stepfather's kindred and speaks little of his brutal childhood. Basilia was more vocal and apparently less bitter.

The three children survived the pig hutch and grew up to marry and come into their inheritance. Basilia told me that as teenagers she and her husband Gabriel "understood each other" because he too had grown up with an oppressive stepfather. His widowed mother remarried in the neighboring community of Sipaskancha Baja, but as a young man Gabriel returned to live in Sonqo, and he settled down with Basilia. When I met him in 1975 he was close to sixty—a handsome, taciturn man who had achieved elder status in the community, having led the pilgrimage to Qoyllur Rit'i the previous year. He nominated Luis as his successor, and Basilia enthusiastically helped out as her younger brother "came along behind." With her husband and brother finished with their *cargos* (community offices), she had a few years' respite, but when I returned in 1978, she was already losing sleep over Alcides's term the next year as *alcalde* (mayor), the decisive *cargo* in a man's life.

Basilia obviously felt that her prestige and self-esteem hinged on her family's performance of the *cargos*. She was determined that when the *Runakuna* gathered at her house there would be piles of food, endless *chicha*, and lots of dancing—and that everyone would see her swishing about in her many skirts, laughing, witty, and in command. Everybody should look at Basilia and say that, yes, *there* was a good woman, a substantial woman.

That the men in her family should pass their *cargos* well—I think this meant more to her than anything else in life. As it turned out, right before Carnival when Alcides's duties were heaviest, Basilia did the worst possible thing. She dropped dead.

Pacha Tira

The Earth is not always benign. She cracks open; she collapses; she withdraws her life-sustaining fertility. Individuals stricken with wasting illnesses like tuberculosis are described as *pachaq hap'isqan* (seized by the Earth). When the *Runakuna* cut into her with their foot plows, they speak apprehensively of *Pacha Tira* and blow their coca leaves especially to her lest in anger she put them to sleep and suck out their vital force.

The phrase *Pacha Tira* emphasizes the perverse aspect of *Pacha*'s complex nature. This phrase seems redundant at first, since *tira* is derived from the Spanish *tierra*, which means earth. But *pacha* and *tierra* are not true synonyms; *pacha* denotes a temporal dimension that *tierra* lacks. The word *tira* stresses the materiality of the world, whereas the word *pacha* refers to the world existing in time. Although some students of Andean religion have understood *Pacha Mama* and *Pacha Tira* to be two distinct members of a kind of Quechua pantheon, this is not how I found the terms used in Sonqo, where they differentiate aspects of *Pacha*'s complex nature.[8]

The word *Tirakuna*, which I translate as Places, might be more literally translated as "Earth Beings" or "Earth Ones." In conversations, some *Runakuna* emphasized to me that *Pacha* and the *Tirakuna* are essentially identical. Others made a qualified distinction, explaining that *Pacha* is *"hallpa, pampa"* ("soil, flat ground"), whereas the *Tirakuna* are hills. Analytically minded Erasmo told me that *Pacha Mama* and the *Tirakuna* are essentially the same; the important distinction, he said, is between *Pacha Mama/Tirakuna* and the *Machula Aulan-chis* (Ancestors). *Pacha Mama/Tirakuna* make the potatoes grow, whereas the *Machula Aulanchis* make them grow big.

The *Tirakuna,* then, seem to be localizations of the vitality animating the material Earth as a whole. Although the generalized Earth is female, the plural and hierarchically organized *Tirakuna* assume a male aspect. As a class, they display masculine qualities, and the most powerful of them—like the great snowy mountains of Qoyllur Rit'i—are called *Taytakuna* (Fathers).[9]

Considered from this perspective, maleness and femaleness do not stand in rigid opposition to each other. A given entity may be considered male in some contexts and female in others, according to the qualities it manifests. Thus, the Sacred Places *(Tirakuna)* may be identified as "Fathers" on the one hand and as manifestations of Mother Earth on the other. As localized expressions of *Pacha Mama*, the Places are nurturing guardians; as plural *Taytakuna*, they manifest principles of social hierarchy and enforce social order. The world, when viewed as singular (that is, without internal differentiations), is female and biologically nourishing. However, this singular world contains plurality; she is internally differentiated into parts that are organized to make up the whole. These differentiated parts are conceptualized as being male and social.

The Animated Cosmos

As the ultimate source of everything the *Runakuna* eat, drink, and wear, the Earth and the Places watch human consumption jealously and demand their part in it. *"La Tierra nos castiga"* ("The Earth disciplines us"), remarked José, home from the army and showing off his Spanish, as his father burned the first leaves of a new purchase of coca.

While the coca leaves burned, their *sami*, or animating essence, passed to the Earth. An offering of *sami*, called *samincha*, is also blown from the leaves in the ritual act of *phukuy*. It passes from alcoholic beverages as the liquid is poured onto the ground or flicked into the air. One directs the *samincha* to the proper recipient by calling out the relevant name: *"Pacha Mama!"* *"Antaqaqa!"* and so forth. The nourishing essence of food is shared in the aroma of its cooking; likewise, the *samincha* of beer passes spontaneously through its bubbles and foam. In 1978 Luis learned from a renowned diviner that soft drinks, with their lively bubbling, are acceptable offerings for the Mountain Lords as well.[10]

Anything displaying an inherent, internally generated liveliness or power is described as *samiyuq* (*sami* plus possessive suffix *-yuq*), possessing *sami*. Humans who have special abilities and talents beyond the ordinary are said to be *samiyuq*, particularly those gifted as singers, musicians, and public speakers. And like *sami* in beer, which can bubble away and be lost, *sami* in humans can leave and may need to be renewed from time to time. Erasmo, a talented musician from his youth, felt that he no longer played as well as he once did and worried that the *sami* was leaving him. Manufactured objects, like musical instruments and houses, can also possess the *sami*. When I brought Erasmo a harmonica, he told me of his plans to leave it at midnight in a hole leading to an underground stream, where a *sirena* (siren) would play it, endowing the instrument with *sami*.[11]

The word *samiyuq* is similar to another one, *santuyuq* (from Spanish *santo* plus *-yuq*), which applies to a person who has mastered a skill. Basilia happily proclaimed that I was *santuyuq* when I learned to spin passably. The word *santuyuq* means possessing the Saints, which, Basilia explained, refers to the Saints responsible for inventing the skill. For example, Santa Rosa and Santa Inés invented spinning and weaving, San Isidro invented plowing, and Santisima María invented coca chewing.[12] Learning takes place through imitation rather than through didactic instruction. After a long trial-and-error process, one comes into possession of the relevant Saints.

The polyglot Spanish-Quechua *santuyuq* is possibly a postconquest rendition of a Quechua word that is no longer used in Sonqo—the word *kamayuq*, derived from *kamay*, to create. According to dictionaries from the colonial period, a *kamayuq* was a person with special skills: a maker of *qeros* (ritual drinking vessels) was a *qero kamayuq*; an accountant who used the knotted strings called *qhipu* was a *qhipu kamayuq*. *Kamay* refers to creation not in the sense of making something from nothing, but in the sense of controlling *how* something happens, of directing its mode of existence.[13]

Samiyuq connotes a kind of genius or joyous, ebullient spirit, whereas *santuyuq* connotes mastery and control. Although the *sami* and the *santu* (saint) dwell within an individual, their source lies without, and both can be passed on to someone or something else. While everything that has material existence is alive, the intensity of a thing's liveliness varies and can be controlled, at least to some extent. This flow of enlivening spirit, inherent in all matter, bears conceptual similarities both to our ideas of energy and divine grace. Andean ritual works at holding, controlling, and directing the flow of *sami*.

God, Water, and Light

The most tangible manifestations of *sami*, without which the Earth would lie dormant and unproductive, are water and light. In the dry Andean highlands water is chronically scarce, and the welfare of the community depends on the arrival of rains in August and their departure by early May. They should begin slowly and build up to their greatest intensity in January. Heavy rains can be as destructive as the lack of rain; rain during *chirawa*, the dry season, ruins the *ch'uño* beds and the grain crops.

While the *Tirakuna* may affect local manifestations of the weather, God (called *Taytanchis*, Our Father; *Diosninchis*, Our God; and *Dios Tayta*, Father God) is the ultimate source of rain. In August the parched Earth opens to receive it.

"Can't you see how dry she is?" Basilia asked me as we sat in her courtyard one day in August, sorting seed potatoes and watching the gathering clouds. "All this dust! And you can see how in places she's even cracked open. That's to let the water in."

Pacha is full of water, Basilia explained, like a crust covering a great internal lake. She put her shawl over her hand in illustration: the cloth was the Earth, her hand the water. This internal water breaks through the surface in marshes, springs, and lakes, all places where the streams flowing over the Earth's surface originate.

Although he sustains the world, God is a distant being whose lack of direct involvement in human affairs contrasts strikingly with *Pacha Mama*'s immediacy, vigilance, and sensitivity. Rufina—pregnant, sick, and cold—commented, "*Taytanchis* sends the rain. He doesn't care. He's sitting up there nice and warm while we're down here freezing."

As far as I know, God is never offered the *samincha;* apparently he neither wants nor needs it. Nor have I heard prayers or invocations directed to him. He is involved in this world as the source of the water and light upon which all life depends. Only in death does one approach him—and on this subject many *Runakuna* express doubts.

Basilia's outspoken friend, Doña Josefa, remarked, "Where do we go when we die? They say we go right to Our Father's side [*Taytanchispa* larun], but who really knows?"

Balvina described heaven, or *hanan pacha* (literally, superior world) as a kind of great *hacienda* where the souls of the dead work, eat, get tired, and fall ill the way they do here. *Taytanchis* makes them work, and he takes care of them when they get sick. As a kind of big Landlord-in-the-Sky, how could God be anything but impersonal and distant—especially in a free community whose inhabitants have defended themselves for generations against the predations of *hacendados* and labor recruiters; a community that has never had a resident priest and whose small adobe church is called *Mamachaq Wasin*, Little Mother's House. Life in *kay pacha* (this world) may be harder and more insecure than life in the *hanan pacha hacienda,* but at least Sonqo *Runakuna* are alive and independent.

The *Runakuna* only half believe in this afterlife anyway. In a less individualized form, the dead remain closely associated with Sonqo's territory. Furthermore, *Runakuna* say that their Ancestors *"unupin purin"* ("travel/go around in water"), whereas the souls of the damned are doomed to wander in ice and snow. The two alternatives—that the dead join God in heaven, and that the dead reside in water and ice—are conceptually linked, for God is the source of the water that permeates and sustains the Earth, and that forms as ice and snow on mountain peaks.

The *Runakuna*'s relationship with God expresses the ambiguity and multifacetedness of their historical, social, and cultural situation. Imposed on a traumatized population after the Spanish Conquest, the Catholic God, modeled on the Hispanic *patrón*, epitomizes Hispanic domination. He has nothing to do with the *Runakuna,* yet they live and die according to his beneficence. Probably this sense of God's detachment even precedes the conquest and originated in the Inca nobility's association with the divine Sun, *Inti,* whereas *Pacha* was associated with the lower, agricultural classes.[14] *Runakuna,* contemporary descendants of this rural lower class, often motion or nod in the direction of the Sun when speaking of God. They address the Sun as *Hesu Kristu* (Jesus Christ) or *Wayna Qhapaq* (Young Lord or Powerful Youth; also the name of the twelfth Inca ruler). Thus God and the Sun, both celestial deities, are conceptualized in similar ways.

The Sun, too, gives the world light and water. He warms the Earth with his rays, and he draws terrestrial water into the air in order to send it back down as rain. Through water and light, the *sami* circulates through the world. *Runakuna* relate to these manifestations of the celestial deity in a straightforward way, uncomplicated by their ambivalent attitudes toward the Catholic ritual and the *Mistikuna* they both admire and hate. As the *sami*'s source, the celestial deity receives no ritual offerings. It would be illogical to offer the *sami* to itself, or to speak to anything so impersonal.

The *Sami*'s Flow

Rivers and streams provide a tangible manifestation of the *sami*'s flow, and they are conceptualized in terms of a vast circulatory system that distributes water throughout the cosmos. Rivers that flow out of highland lakes into the jungle are believed to return underground to their places of origin.[15] Water flows through the heavens through the great celestial *Mayu* (River), the Milky Way.[16]

K'uychi (Rainbow) facilitates the distribution of water on a local level. *K'uychi* is an *amaru* (great subterranean serpent) who lives in springs. Filled with water after a rain, he flies out of the spring and arches across the sky. Burying his head in a second spring, he siphons water through his body from one spring to the other.

Wayra (Wind) is also conceptualized as a localized circulatory agent of subterranean energy. He is said to rush out of his "house"—a high inaccessible cave—to flow like a river of air through the atmosphere before returning home.

The daily presence of the Sun's light and heat is felt to be intimately connected to normal social life and to the very existence of the human race. The previous world-age, inhabited by a race of giants, was lit only by the moon. Only when our Sun was created did the human race come into existence. If our age is succeeded by another, this new era will have a different sun and a different race of beings.

The margins between night and day are marked ritually in daily behavior. The household ends its day when the door is closed and the candle lit in its wall niche. Then the family members remove their hats, cross themselves, and greet each other courteously: *"Bwenos noches Mamáy"* ("Good evening

Mother!") *"Bwenos noches Taytáy!"* ("Good evening Father!") and so on. It can be a lengthy process.

In the morning, each member ritually observes his or her first passage over the threshold between the dark house and the daylight outside. Many times I awakened to see Balvina or Luis standing hatless before the open door, making the sign of the cross and quietly asking *Inti Tayta* for a good day before turning to greet each sleepy child or visitor.

On certain ritual occasions, like the Feast of Saint John (24 June), the moment of sunrise or sunset takes on special importance. On the morning of *San Juan P'unchay* (St. John's Day), the first rays of the rising Sun convert the waters of the streams and lakes to *hampi*. Usually translated as medicine, *hampi* refers to substances with special healing properties.

The most powerful manifestation of concentrated light is *Rayu* (Lightning). Erasmo encountered *Rayu* in his early twenties while walking along a high footpath. It was then that he received his vocation as a diviner and began to study coca leaves and the dreams *Rayu* sent to him. *Rayu* still brings him dreams, but Erasmo has not encountered him again directly. The highest grade diviner must encounter *Rayu* three times.

Lightning is a hazard in the high *puna*, and many people who encounter *Rayu* do not survive. A place known to have been struck by lightning is called *qhaqha* and receives offerings of coca and alcohol. A person or animal killed by lightning is also described as *qhaqha* and must be buried on the spot, joining the *Tirakuna*. *Rayu* is sometimes personified as Apu Qhaqha (Lord Qhaqha), who zigzags across the fields to steal potatoes. The plants grow beautifully, but once Apu Qhaqha has passed, the tubers underneath never develop.[17]

Objects that concentrate special generative powers in themselves are called *illas* (from *illariy*, to shine out). Each family has its *illas*, tiny models of animals or house compounds, which are kept carefully hidden as the repositories of household well-being. Personal power objects bestowed by *Rayu* or the *Tirakuna* are called *istrilla*. This word is obviously a Quechua version of Spanish *estrella* (star), which probably came to be applied to power objects because it contains the Quechua root *illa*. *Istrillas* may be pebbles, coins, or beads; they do not shine, nor do they necessarily fall from the sky. Balvina received hers from the hill Apu Picchu, where she played as a child. *Runakuna* use the Quechua words *qoyllur* and *ch'aska* when they talk about stars in the sky, reserving *istrilla* for power objects. Many of them know that *istrilla* means star in Spanish, but seem to feel no contradiction between the Spanish and Quechua usages.

Just as the Sacred Places are localizations of *Pacha's* inherent energy, so too lightning, stars, and power objects are localizations of the Sun's energy. Human beings derive their existence from the Sun, the most intense and concentrated light of all. In the light of a different sun there would be a different world and a different kind of people.

The Living and the Dead

In Sonqo and its neighboring communities, the highest hilltops are dotted with small, round ruined towers called *chullpa*s. No more than three to five feet in diameter, they are too small to have been dwellings and, as many contain ancient bones, they were probably tombs.[18] *Runakuna* say they were built by the *Machukuna* (Old Ones), a gigantic race who lived by moonlight in an age before the current Sun existed: "Our Moon was their Sun." They are also called *Ñawpa Machu* (Previous or Ancient Old Ones) and *Ñawpakuna* (Predecessors).

Although the *Machukuna* figure largely in Sonqueños' conversations, it took some effort to cajole Don Luis into talking about them for the tape recorder. This is what he said, in his own words, followed by my translation.

Ñawpa Timpu Runakuna kasqa. Machulakuna tiyasqa, llaqtakuna kasqa. Machu llaqta kunan kashan chaypi. Hinaspas, chaymanta, chay Machu Runakuna tiyaran, riki. Ñawpa Machukuna—runakuna noqanchis hinayá!

Hinaspas, tiyasqaku, chakrata ruwasqaku allintan. Hinaspas, chaymanta munaycha karanku. Askha runakuna!

Hinaspas, chaymanta, tukupunan hinanchá, yachakurankuchá, chay Intiq lloqsimunanta. Intis lloqsimusqa. Hinaspa willanakuranku, riki: "Intis lloqsimunqa!" nispa.

Hinaspan, astakusqa huq laruchakunapi, chay llaqtankuta saqispanku.Wasichata ruwasqaku, tichuchata ima ruwasqaku, riki. Chaypi askha muntunsi tullukuna kashan riki, q'ochashanku, riki: alkadi varayuq ima warminkunapis wawa oqllasqa—hina ch'akishanku, riki. Chayqa anchaypis pakakusqaku, hinaspas Inti lloqsirampusqa. Chay Inti ch'akirachipusqa chaykunata.

Chayqa, chaypi kawsaq Machuchakuna kashanku kunanpas. Hinaspa ch'akipusqanku Inti lloqsimpusqa. Hinaspas, chay Intipiqa huqñataq runakuna karanku.

They say there were people in the Previous Age—the Old Ones—and they had towns [indicating Antaqaqa]. That's their old town over there. Well, then those Old Ones lived there y'see, those Ancient Old Ones—people, people like us!

Well, they lived there, worked their fields well, and so they did very nicely—all those people! And well, this is how they came to an end: they must have realized the Sun was going to come up. Yes. It seems the Sun was going to come up, and so they spoke among themselves: "The Sun's going to come up!" they said.

So they left their town and moved to some hiding places. They made some little houses, complete with thatched roofs, y'see. That's where there are all those piles of bones, y'see, drying in the sunlight: their mayor with his staff, and their women, too, with babies in their arms—they're just drying up, y'see. They hid themselves over there when the sun came out, and the Sun dried them up.

So, the little Old Ones are alive over there, even now. They dried up when the Sun came up. And then, in that Sun, there existed another kind of people.[19]

Why did the Sun come up? The *Runakuna* answer that *Taytanchis* made it come up. And why did *Taytanchis* do that? According to some, he just felt like it. According to others, it was for the sake of the human race: "*Noqanchispaq Inti lloqsin"* ("The Sun came up for our sakes"). But everyone agrees that the *Machukuna* are envious *(invidiusu)* and embittered against the human race that displaced them.

The *Machukuna* are said to have lived by the light of the Moon. On bright moonlit nights, their bones are reanimated and they emerge exclaiming, *"Kunan p'unchay kashan!"* ("It's day now!"). The *Machukuna* visit each other and work their fields, which are "just where ours are." They call to each other in booming voices. Basilia imitated them, *"Yaw Alfo-onsu! Maytan rishanki?"* ("Hey Alfo-onso! Where're you going?").

Basilia's attitude mixed fear with familiarity, for she could not imagine Sonqo without the *Machukuna*. Every community has its own *Machukuna*, she explained. *"Sonqo Machukuna, Sipaskancha Machukuna, Chikchiqmarca Machukuna."* She pointed out their *chullpas* on the respective hilltops.

The remnants of a displaced race, *Machukuna* visit disease and disaster on the human race. An evil wind blows from the *chullpas* bringing chills and respiratory ailments; sometimes, in fact, the *chullpas* seem to have a life of their own. *Machukuna* also seduce vulnerable individuals in erotic dreams, causing miscarried pregnancies and birth defects. Understandably, these dreams leave people frightened and depressed.[20]

María, sister of Basilia and mother of Erasmo, died in 1975 after a long, lingering illness. During her illness I described her symptoms of vomiting, intense feelings of cold, and swelling of the limbs and stomach to the Colquepata *sanitario* who guessed her illness to be a liver ailment and gave me some pills (although he never came to check his diagnosis, nor did María's family seek him out). Basilia blamed it all on the *chullpa wayra*, for the wind blowing from the ruined towers had attacked María with a series of bad dreams.

Erasmo disagreed. He could have handled *Machukuna* or the *chullpa wayra* by assembling a burnt offering to satisfy their malevolent appetites—but the coca told him otherwise. Reading the leaves' configuration, he saw his mother's inevitable death; she was dying, the leaves told him, not from *Machukuna*, not even from a *qhaqha*, but "just from illness." When he announced this to his family, his stepfather sought out another *paqo* to prepare the futile burnt offering—another *paqo* "who prepared it just for the money," Erasmo says with unrelenting bitterness. María died while the offering was burning—"at that very moment."

Machukuna occupy a shadowy world. Normally their world parallels ours like a dark mirror, but in dreams, wind, and moonlight the two worlds intersect. The *Machukuna's* potato fields are "just where ours are"—and yet they are not the same fields. Their nocturnal labor (nocturnal for us; diurnal for them) makes the potatoes grow large in the *Runakuna's* fields, and the *chullpa's* wind, though it makes humans sick, is described as *wanu* (fertilizer) for the potatoes.

In October of 1975, as Luis planted some fields located fairly high on the slopes of Antaqaqa, his companions seemed anxious about the proximity of the *chullpas* and chewed coca to ward off the wind and keep *Pacha Tira* from putting them to sleep. But the oldest nodded approvingly, remarking that a hard *chullpa wayra* was good for the potatoes. In spite of risks to the farmers' personal health, the slopes of Antaqaqa are a fine place for potato fields.

In this fertilizing aspect, the *Machukuna* are usually addressed as "*Machula Aulanchis*" ("Our Old Grandfathers"). Erasmo explained that while the *Machukuna* belong to a different humanity, from another *timpu* (age), *Machula Aulanchis* are the *Runakuna*'s own ancestors: "our grandfathers and their fathers." Basilia, on the other hand, insisted that the *Machukuna* and *Machula Aulanchis* are different terms for the same beings, and when I pressed Luis on this point he waffled: "Yes, they're the same . . . but they're different . . . different . . . but the same . . ."

Both *Machula Aulanchis* and the *Machukuna* are said to live in the ruins on Antaqaqa. Both are described as fertilizing the potatoes and making them big, and both are identified with Sonqo as a community. In invocations over coca leaves, the words *Machukuna, chullpakuna, Machula Aulanchis,* and *Antaqaqa* are interchangeable.

Displaced creatures from a previous age, *Machukuna* pervert the normal course of human life, producing disease, birth defects, and false sexuality. In contrast, the ancestral *Machula Aulanchis* exert a life-supporting influence. Like *Pacha Mama* and the *Tirakuna,* who are equated as well as distinguished from each other, *Machukuna* and *Machula Aulanchis* seem to be different aspects of the same ancestral category. From their home on Antaqaqa these ancestral dead continue to exist and to affect this living world through indirect means.

Body and Soul

The cemetery shares some of the *chullpas*' characteristics; there one is subject to the ambivalent sickening/fertilizing *machu wayra,* and *Machukuna* are said to frequent the place. Sonqo's small church, originally located next to the cemetery, was relocated in 1983 because (among other reasons) people dislike attending religious celebrations so close to the graveyard. The graves are untended and left to the weeds and weather. An annual work party turns under the older graves, and workers joke over the jumbled bones, trying them on for size in drunken black humor. Ultimately, they know, their own bones will join this communal heap.

Runakuna usually refer to the bones of the dead as *alma,* Spanish for soul. When graves are turned under, the *almakuna* receive offerings of *trago.* In 1975, the workers brought four bottles for adult *almakuna* and two for those of children, consuming the alcohol themselves as they fulfilled their unpleasant task.[21]

Incas and pre-Incaic peoples before them placed great emphasis upon preserving the bodies of their dead. Royal mummies were kept in the Temple of the Sun in Cuzco, where they were dressed in fine textiles and carefully attended. In the smaller communities mummies were kept in caves and probably *chullpas* where, like the mummies in Cuzco, they received offerings of food, coca, and *chicha* and were dressed in special garments. Felipe Guaman Poma de Ayala, an indigenous Andean chronicler of the late sixteenth century, depicted the Inca offering *chicha* to the remains of his ancestors, which are indicated by the skeleton in a *chullpa*-like tomb (see Figure 2).[22] Ancestral mummies were considered vital to their community's well-being and in fact were so strongly identified with the locality that it was forbidden to remove them. The Inca term *waka* could refer both to Sacred Places and to the mummies kept in these places. This close association between the ancestral dead and their place of interment persists in Sonqo, for today the *chullpas* and the bones of the *Machukuna* are so closely identified as to be interchangeable terms in ritual invocations.

The zealous missionaries in the sixteenth and seventeenth centuries launched a major campaign to destroy these mummies and to institute Christian burial practices. In a macabre tug-of-war, indigenous Andeans often robbed their relatives' bodies out of Christian cemeteries to inter them properly in caves.[23] Sonqo still feels the effects of this missionization. While *Runakuna* bury their dead in the cemetery, conceptually they locate their ancestors—"our grandfathers and their fathers"—in the *chullpas* of their sacred hill.

The idea that the spiritual identity and power of the dead is located in their desiccated physical remains is a very old one in the Andes, and Sonqo *Runakuna* seem to have difficulty in reconciling these indigenous Andean beliefs with Christian ideas about the afterlife. While the newly deceased are said to go far away to *hanan pacha, Machula Aulanchis* on Antaqaqa are a more general and less personal category of ancestor; they have been dead much longer and lack individuality, like the bones mixed together in the communal pile of the cemetery.

Occasionally *Runakuna* save the bones of their dead. A skull sitting in a storeroom's wall niche is said to *khuyay* (care for, protect) its contents. "Some people keep their *machulas* [grandparents]," Don Luis commented, "and some people don't."

What can we make of this? How can a skull "protect" a storeroom? A partial answer lies in other objects also said to *khuyay*. Among them are small stone power objects representing domestic animals that have been handed down from generation to generation, and carved stone tablets that stand for the household with its stores and livestock. These *enqas*, also called *enqaychus* and *illas*, are brought out from their hiding place n the storeroom on the eves of Carnival week, August First (when the Earth "opens"), and the Feast of Saint John (24 June), when the *Runakuna* chew coca and drink libations of *trago* or *chicha*. The personal *istrilla*, too, emerges from hiding on these occasions. All of these objects are described lovingly as *khuyaqkuna*, caring protectors, and as *kawsaqkuna*, living ones (from *kawsay*, to live). They are the source of the health and fertility of the livestock, the crops, and the family members themselves.[24]

Cuzco's archaeological museum houses numerous beautifully carved In-

Figure 2. An Inca pours a libation of *chicha* to the dead while simultaneously drinking from a *qero*. A tomb resembling a *chullpa* is in the background.

caic *enqas*. My friends from Sonqo were greatly impressed and disturbed by the sight of them, as they walked past case after case of *kawsaqkuna*.[25] At one point, Basilia stopped in front of a large carved penis and remarked, *"Kawsaq kikin!"* ("The living one itself!") Her comment, implying that the *illas'* protective and living power is a kind of sexual potency, amplifies the word's meaning an intense concentration of light: vivifying energy originating in Father God.

This explained why Luis referred to the skull as *machula* and said that it protected the storeroom.[26] *Machula Aulanchis* on Antaqaqa have certain *illa*-like qualities. They are always described as male; their wind is fertilizer for the potatoes, which are considered to be female plants.[27] As "our old grandfathers," they are progenitors of the living *Runakuna* as well. Creatures of the past, the ancestral dead store the potential for Sonqo's future. They are a subterranean aspect of the *sami*, the flow of life manifested openly in water and light.[28]

Animu refers to a spiritual essence closer to the Christian idea of the soul than is the concept of *alma*. The *animu* can leave the living body to animate a hummingbird and travel to far-off relatives, usually as an omen of death. In August of 1975, a hummingbird suddenly appeared in my room. It hovered just inside the doorway, vibrating in the air for a moment before it left so suddenly it seemed almost to dematerialize. Later in the day, I mentioned this visitation to a group of women peeling potatoes for a house-raising dinner. A nervous silence fell over the group before someone changed the subject. Only later, when I asked old Doña Isabel about hummingbird visits in the abstract, did I learn the event's significance. A few weeks afterward, when we learned that my grandmother had died around this time, Luis immediately reminded me about the hummingbird's visit.

Unlike the Christian idea of the soul, however, neither *alma* nor *animu* is the seat of a person's essential individuality and will. After death the *alma* hovers around its home for eight days, and no matter how well-beloved the deceased, the *alma's* influence is felt to be malevolent and dangerous. The *alma* of the recently dead carries an evil, sickening influence called *qayqa* that peaks eight days after death. The word also applies to the wind from the *chullpas* and to the malevolent influence of angry *Tirakuna*.

The *alma* causes other mischief too; during her funeral wake, Rufina's *alma* caused sticky anisette liquor to spill on my tape recorder, which I had firmly put away under the ritual table, tired of hearing the same tapes played over and over with exhausted batteries.

"I told you so!" Basilia exclaimed after Alcides poured an immense libation that leaked onto the machine. "The *alma* did it."

"Why would Rufina want to ruin my tape recorder?"

"Because you turned it off, stupid. The *alma* liked the music."

Ironically, in 1980 I was to have a similar conversation with Luis about Basilia's *alma*. He was recalling how two years earlier I became violently ill at my *despedida*, a goodbye party that left me groaning in the corner for close to twenty-four hours, too sick to leave on schedule. This alarmed and puzzled Luis and his family, for *Runakuna* seldom get sick from drinking. But when I came back two years later, Luis told me that he had figured out the cause of my problem: Basilia had died within a year of my departure, and it was her *alma* that made me sick.

This struck me as very strange, and I asked why Basilia—of all people!— would want to make me sick.

"You don't understand," replied Luis. "It wasn't Basilia, it was her *alma.*"

He went on to explain that a year before a person dies, the *alma* begins to leave the body, spreading *qayqa* in the process. Early in 1979, he and Basilia sat up one night drinking together and both became inexplicably ill. Sure enough, two weeks later she died. Her departing *alma qayqa*-ed them both.

This deindividualized concept of *alma* coexists with the Christian idea that the soul is associated with the person's essential self. The personal *alma* goes off "to Our Father's Side" in *hanan pacha,* the *hacienda*-like place separated from this world by a River of Blood, *Yawar Mayu.*[29] The deceased person's dog—if it is black, brown, or spotted—carries the soul across the *Yawar Mayu.* Occasionally, through some strange twist of fortune, a living *Runa* visits the afterlife and returns to tell of it. Basilia told me of such an event:[30]

There was a foolish girl who talked to strange men, and during the night her head flew off. This happens to the sexually promiscuous; their heads fly off during the night. Well, when this head came back it found the door to the house closed, and since it had to find a body, it slammed into the shoulder of a passing *Runa* who was then blighted with two heads. Meanwhile, the girl's headless body died. But her dog recognized his mistress' head on the *Runa*'s shoulders and carried him over the *Yawar Mayu,* where the head leapt back to its owner's shoulders. The dog drank—lap, lap, lap—from the Blood River and then carried the *Runa* safely back to *kay pacha,* this world.

To summarize; the word *alma* is used in at least three senses: (1) the bones or corpse of the dead; (2) a deindividualized spirit normally localized in the body; and (3) the individual's personality, which continues to exist independently of the body after death (although the reunion of the girl's head and body shows that even in *hanan pacha* this separation of soul from body is not quite conceivable).

The soul's nature and fate after death is a domain of belief in which Christian ideas are essentially incompatible with indigenous Andean ones; *Runakuna* hold contradictory beliefs simultaneously and employ them in different contexts. The essential incompatibility between Christianity and indigenous beliefs lies in the different understandings of the relationship between body and soul. The Andean worldview does not accommodate the Western dualism of body and soul; for Andeans, all matter is in some sense alive, and conversely, all life has a material base.

At death, the relationship between body and soul changes—or better put, once the ancestral bones are cleansed of flesh, the body enters a new mode of existence. A sinful individual is unable to accomplish this transformation and continues to animate its rotting body, becoming a *kukuchi* condemned to wander among the glaciers of the Qoyllur Rit'i range, where "it goes around eating people" *("Purin, runata mikhuspa")*. A *kukuchi* feels an unmasterable compulsion to eat the flesh of humans, including its own relatives, and for this purpose it may return to haunt its own community.

A *kukuchi* is said to be weighted down by *hucha* (sin), a burden that the soul must cast off before it can leave this life properly. Alcides explained, "They rise from their graves along with their bodies. They die in vain" *("Pampasqa-manta lloqsinku kwerpontin. Yanqalla wañun")*. At night *Runakuna* sometimes hear these green, foul-smelling, zombielike creatures howling in pain from their rotting bodies. Driven by their appetite for human flesh, they beguile un-suspecting individuals to their deaths. There is a story about a woman who left her children for a few minutes in the care of a greenish-skinned stranger who ate them in her absence.

Hucha entails the improper disposition of one's energies—as in adultery, quarrelsomeness, and the failure to reciprocate help. The worst sin is incest, broadly defined to include second cousins, *compadres,* and the children of *compadres.*

The loss of even a hair from one's head is a *hucha,* and *Runakuna* carefully save and burn their fallen hairs to avoid having to search for them after death. Hair, growing spontaneously from our bodies, is another manifestation of the life force and should not be discarded indiscriminantly. Basilia and Josefa were horrified when they noticed me tossing away my hair.

"You'll have a mighty long trip back here from your country!" Basilia scolded.

(Indeed, I sometimes wondered as I combed my hair in the morning how anyone avoided becoming a *kukuchi.*)

The *kukuchi* bears some similarities to the *machu.* Both are a kind of ani-mated dead who attack the living at night, and both are surrounded by *qayqa* (the evil atmosphere surrounding a corpse)—for the wind from the *chullpas* is a kind of *qayqa,* and *qayqa* emanates from the *kukuchi's* rotting body. Both are connected with misdirected sexuality, for the *machu* harms its victims through erotic dreams, and the *kukuchi* is mentioned in connection with in-cest (perhaps expressed symbolically by its urge to eat its own relatives).

But physically the two are quite different. *Machukuna* are dry bones or desiccated mummies, whereas the *kukuchi* is described as putrid flesh with never a mention of bones. A *kukuchi* is unable to rid itself of its rotting body; in contrast, *Machukuna* are dried up bones who long for their flesh. The bones on Antaqaqa are even said to suck out the blood of humans.

Flesh should merge again with the Earth, leaving clean bones behind. Nei-ther *machu* nor *kukuchi* can achieve the proper separation of flesh and bone after death. The *Machukuna* are sun-dried bones who want their flesh and blood back, and the *kukuchi* is a rotting, zombielike creature with an insatiable appetite for human flesh. In contrast to both, *Machula Aulanchis* are dry bones whose flesh has been properly washed away by water and absorbed by the Earth. As *khuyaqkuna* (caring ones) they have a protective influence, and as

45

grandfathers who fertilize the potato crops, they exert a seminal influence as well. Sexual progenitors when alive, *Machula Aulanchis* continue in death to generate life through new channels, fertilizing potato fields rather than human beings.

When *Runakuna* die, then, they do not cease to exist but exist in a less immediate state than the living—a parallel world from which they indirectly influence this one. Small whirring birds, especially hummingbirds, are recognized as *almas* because they cannot be seen distinctly. A fast-moving blur, hummingbirds hover between worlds. *Machukuna* come out in moonlight and in dreams, and they too may be disembodied. The voices in radios and the images on photo negatives are described as *Machukuna*, and Luis once remarked about a dust dervish blowing across a field, "That's a *machu* and he wants *trago!*"

While walking with me in Cuzco, Josefa and Crisologo looked warily at a stone statue. They found it eerie and disturbing—a *machu!* Initially this struck me as a curious contrast to disembodied *Machukuna* manifested as radio voices or photo negatives, for to my Western habits of thought, the immateriality of radio voices, dreams, and dust dervishes opposes the hard materiality of bones and statues.

From an Andean perspective, the compact hardness of stones, bones, and statues implies not a lack of animation, but a different state of animation—life crystallized, as it were. Hard, unusual stones (such as *illas* and *isrillas*) and bare bones (like the skull kept for *khuyay*) are felt to be the most potent sources of energy. They are intimately connected with lightning and sunlight, whose power they absorb and condense (see Chapter 6). Water is most powerful and sacred in its crystallized form, and thus the glaciers of Qoyllur Rit'i are the focus of the year's most important and emotionally charged pilgrimage. Similarly, the most powerful *Apukuna* are those covered with snow and ice. And so, in the statue Josefa and Crisologo apparently saw a quality of petrified but potential humanity. This is what made it a *machu*—together with ancient bones, mummies, dream visitors, and disembodied voices.

Time and the World

Time and matter are signified simultaneously by a single term. While the word *Pacha* means Earth, it also refers to a moment in time.

*Pacha*s, or worlds, replace each other. Every world begins in the cataclysmic destruction of the previous world, and will itself end in a cataclysm. The destruction of the *Machukuna* was a *pachakuti* (world reversal), and when a future apocalypse destroys the *Mistikuna* and ushers back the reign of the Incas that, too, will be a *pachakuti*. Then, they say, Antaqaqa will burst open. Huge serpentine monsters *(amarukuna)* and enormous felines *(leonkuna)* will come roaring out, and there will be earthquakes, lightning, and hail.

Just as the Spanish *tierra* has been adopted to indicate the material aspect of *Pacha*, so the Spanish *tiempo*, as *timpu*, refers to her temporal aspect. A previous world-age can be termed *pacha,* but is more often called *timpu;* thus in his narration Don Luis calls the *Machukuna "Ñawpa Timpu Runakuna"* ("People of the Previous Age").

Runakuna conceptualize time as discontinuous, as a series of stages punctuated by apocalyptic interruptions. Nevertheless, when a given world "turns around" and is finished, it does not cease to exist. Previous *timpus* continue to exist in a different but less immediate state than the present, and they can affect this world indirectly.

In its temporal aspect the word *pacha* connotes complete immediacy: *"Chay pacha"* ("At that *very* moment"). A world is a particular state of immediacy. Human beings live out their lives in a given world, and on the grandest scale nothing *happens* in this *pacha* or *timpu.* Nevertheless, human beings do not live in immediacy alone but also in memory and anticipation; from the perspective of individuals living their lives plenty happens, and therefore any *timpu* is subdivided into numerous sub*timpus.* For an adult, "my time" *("noqaq timpuy")* stretches back about twenty years, even for people well into middle age. This is preceded by "my parents' time" *("taytamamaypa timpun").* *Timpus* are infinitely divisible; for on the microscale they end and begin with any significant change in the order of things. For example, the 1975 change in governmental regimes serves as a demarcation, or discontinuity, in time: "That happened in Velasco's *timpu;* this is Morales Bermudez's *timpu.*" Sonqo *Runakuna* felt that the expropriation of *haciendas* during Velasco's agrarian reform had been a fundamental change in the order of things, a *timpu* that ended with Velasco's ouster.

The year itself is subdivided by the alternation of wet and dry seasons, which are in turn subdivided by Catholic feast days. As the most important of these religious observances involves the veneration of Sacred Places as well as Saints, this annual cycle integrates the passage of time with places in the landscape.[31] Through feast days and pilgrimages, the pantheon of Catholic saints is integrated within the animated cosmos of indigenous Andean culture, for each community and its important *Tirakuna* is associated with specific Saints.

Sonqo's church houses two images of female Saints as well as two crosses and a small icon of Christ crucified. On feast days they are carefully dressed, reminiscent of the Incaic practice of clothing ancestral mummies. The similarity is heightened by the Sonqueños' assertion that if the *mamachas* (female Saints) are improperly dressed, the dead cannot return for their annual meal on the Day of the Dead. The guardianship of these clothes is one of the community's most important *cargos* and is entrusted to the *mayordomo,* a respected elder.

Basilia said that the Saints lived in a previous *timpu* during which they invented all the skills necessary to human life. The mastering of skill, during which one comes to "possess the Saint" *("santuyuq"),* involves the incorporation of potency and knowledge from a different dimension of time.

Basilia also located *condenados* (souls of the damned, virtually synonymous with *kukuchis*) like the Saints, in a different *timpu,* the *Condenado Timpu.* That *timpus* coexist simultaneously is illustrated by the fact that many *Runakuna* are convinced that they can and sometimes do encounter both saints and *conde-nados* in their own lives. Such meetings occur when the *timpu*s interpenetrate each other. Events occurring in "our own *timpu*" are described as existing *sut'ipi* (in clarity); other *timpu*s are, for us, out of focus. On the microscale, our own *timpu* ends daily with the setting of the Sun. Then *Runakuna* close their doors and avoid going out, leaving this world to the *Machukuna*, who exclaim "It's day now!" and come out to work their fields, "which are just where ours are." Their day ends as ours begins.

Certain Sacred Places are themselves believed to be petrified beings from another age. As the trucks lumber along the rough road toward Colquepata, passengers point out Pariqaqa (Priest Rock). At a distance of several kilometers sits Sipasqaqa (Girl Rock), and across the lake stand several rocky pinnacles that were once a wedding party. The priest, girl, and wedding party turned to stone when the lake swallowed up their city and their *timpu* came to an end. The city still sits underneath the lake, and during the dark of the moon one can hear its church bells ringing. If only that city hadn't been drowned, it would have been Cuzco, Sonqo *Runakuna* say regretfully.

The Incas, too, left their marks on the landscape as they fled to their hidden city, Paititi. An Inca's daughter turned to stone as she stopped to urinate at a *tinku*, a confluence of two or more streams. Nearby is Layqa Pampana, the Sorcerer's Burial, a dangerous spot where one may fall asleep never to awaken. An Inca enchanted the place to keep the Spanish from following him.

The saints, as well, may exist in this world as petrified landmarks. The Lord of Qoyllur Rit'i, for example, disappeared into a massive rock, leaving his miraculous imprint.

This tale shows that the potency of other *timpu*s is inherent in the material earth itself. The phrases *ukhu pacha* (inner world), *kay pacha* (this world), and *hanan pacha* (upper world) refer not simply to a three-layered cosmos, but to different dimensions or states of existence. The *Tirakuna*, the *Machukuna*, *Machula Aulanchis*, and Saints exist in an interior dimension of experience. They hold the generative and destructive power of the inner world.

The power of the inner world is the inverse, a kind of crystallization, of the power emanating from the upper world. We human beings live at the interface, in this world, where exchange and transformation take place.

Chapter Two

The Web of Reciprocity

Wasi-Familia: The Household

There is no way for strangers to break naturally into a community like Sonqo. The *ayllu's* social fabric consists of a close-knit web of reciprocity—defined initially through kinship and marriage, then expanded through formalized bonds of *compadrazgo* (spiritual kinship). As outsiders with no claim on anyone's hospitality and resources, Rick and I were well received only because we arrived armed with documents. The director of the primary school accepted our letters of introduction from the board of education in Cuzco, put us up overnight in the school, and then turned us over to Sonqo's president of administration.[1]

So there was Don Luis, stuck with a couple of strange gringos. He later admitted that he did his best to find someone else to put us up, but nobody wanted us. He was too polite to turn us away, and open rejection was out of the question anyway, because we were *dokumentuyuq* (possessed of documents). So he cleared out one of his two storerooms, and our second night in Sonqo was spent among the heaps of potatoes, *ullucus*, and dried sheep droppings. It was supposed to be a temporary arrangement but, as it turned out, we got along fine with Luis, and Rufina was willing to put up with us—so we stayed in these "temporary" lodgings for close to a year.

The arrangement worked well for us, providing some privacy without isolating us from family life. The Sonqo *Runakuna* were amused, for our situation resembled that of many young couples who share their parents' house compound for the first few years of married life. Luis jokingly called us his *churi* and *qhachun,* son and daughter-in-law.

An alternative fiction was to imagine that I was a new incarnation of Luis's and Rufina's firstborn child, Catalina, who had died years before at the age of six. In that version, we were his *ususi* and *qatay,* daughter and son-in-law. Al-

49

though it is more common for a young couple to move in with the man's parents, uxorilocal residence (when the couple moves in with the woman's parents) is not uncommon, especially if the wife's family is wealthier than the groom's.

The family grew accustomed to us and enjoyed exchanging bowls of potato soup for the oatmeal we cooked every morning on our primus stove. (Luis still thinks that oatmeal is the favored dish of all gringos.) They looked forward to the sugar we brought them from Cuzco and got used to my barging into their house at all hours.

An early morning in June, for example, found me standing by the door of their adobe house—a single rectangular room about ten feet wide and twenty feet long, covered by a thatched roof supported by an A-frame of eucalyptus poles. A gray wisp of smoke streamed out of the vent in the roof above the fireplace, indicating that Rufina was awake and preparing breakfast. She had been up late the night before, for they had been celebrating Luis's successful sponsorship of the rituals associated with Corpus Christi.

I bent down and called through the low doorway, "*Hamusayki, Mamáy! Visitamusayki!*" ("Here I come, Mother! I'm coming to visit you!").

"*Ha-ampu!*" ("Come in!"), replied the lady of the house.

I duck-waddled through the door to find Rufina sitting bleary-eyed by the fireplace peeling potatoes, removing each peel on one long spiral. She rose stiffly to find me a shawl to sit on, and settled down again.

As woman of the house, the stove (*q'uncha*) was Rufina's territory. The adobe seat across from the door, and the bench placed perpendicular to it in front of the bed, demarcated the area where men sat to talk and chew coca. The bed—a platform of poles, hides, and straw mats on adobe supports—was the family's territory. Luis was curled up at one end under a blanket; next to him the children were snuggled in a heap like a litter of kittens. Tools, blankets, fleece, balls of yarn, and a sheep carcass hung from the rafters. Earthenware and metal bowls and pots surrounded the stove. The wall niches in the cooking area were stuffed with herbs and produce from the Colquepata market. Other wall niches were full of things: toys and copybooks, festival ribbons for Rufina's hat, spindles with their half-spun fleece and yarn, Luis's identification papers, and packets of paper holding the sacred ingredients for the *despacho* (a ritual offering bundle). As I came in, the ten or so guinea pigs (*kuyes*) scavenging the potato peelings ran burbling and squeaking back to their nest under the bed.

Rufina was tired.

"I can hardly move!" she exclaimed. "We danced 'til two in the morning when the *trago* ran out. Look how slow I'm peeling the potatoes, my hands are so stiff. (No, don't you try to peel them! You never learned how in your country. Here, peel the *ch'uño*, that's easier.) That *trago*'s nasty stuff. You won't catch me out with the alpacas today, in that wind! What a bother those animals are! And look at my old man over there on the bed! *He* won't do much today, that's for sure."

Luis snorted and rolled over to sleep on his other side. The children were beginning to stir, and lay watching me over the side of the bed, their chins propped on their hands. Esteban, a boy of eight, obviously wanted to get up and pee out the door but, being naked, was embarrassed by my presence.

I offered to go out for water. Taking the heavy ceramic water jar, I crossed the courtyard where the family cow mooed pleadingly. Clambering up the low bank above the courtyard, I trudged across the frosty grass to the stream, past the stone corral where the herd of sheep, llamas, and alpacas was beginning to mill about restlessly. From the pig hutch came the sound of impatient snorting.

I filled the jug and returned slowly, listening to the bleating of the sheep and the curious high-pitched sob of the llamas. As I reentered the courtyard, Esteban scurried into the house and was hurriedly putting on his pants as I followed him inside.

Rufina had gotten her soup onto the fire.

"Thank you, dear! Oh, Señora, look at your cold red hands! Here, sit by the fire and we'll chew coca. I'd fix you coffee, but dear me, there's no sugar. Ay Señora! You should have brought some."

"Here," I answered resignedly, fishing a small bundle out of my pocket.

"Urpicháy!"[2] Rufina snatched the bag. "Oh good, oh good, we're going to have coffee! We still have the bag Father brought last month from Cuzco. Here, let's get some water boiling!"

The rest of the children descended from the bed and started to prance around and grab at the sugar bag, but Rufina shoved it firmly into a niche behind her. Luis forced his eyes open and hoisted himself onto one elbow, groping around for his coca bag. Inucha, the three year old, found it in the bedclothes.

"Good morning—and how are you Señora Catalina? We're wiped out here."

I owned that I was feeling a bit poorly myself, for I had stayed up drinking with them until midnight.

"Dear me," Luis continued. "That *trago* is nasty stuff. After you left we drank until three—or was it four?—in the morning. Then it ran out and we couldn't find anymore anywhere . . . Mother, give the Señora some coca, won't you?"

Rufina complied, indicating with a look that I could better afford to give it to her. Luis, sniffling and groaning, sent over a coca *k'intu* with Esteban, and I reciprocated, giving Rufina one as well. She paused to accept it as she stirred the soup, tended the fire, and sent out a constant stream of admonishment to the children, who ignored most of it. Felicha, the thirteen year old, sulkily washed out the family's cups.

"Catalina!" exclaimed Luis. "Did Julian invite you to his house again? Why do you go there? They just sweet-talk you and then only feed you *watias* [potatoes baked in the earth]. *Achakáw!* The misers! They should roast you a pig; they have more piglets than anybody. You're just wasting your time over there."

Coffee was ready. Rufina took it off the fire and dumped in the whole bag of sugar. "Here, take this to your father." She sent over a cup of coffee with Esteban.

51

Luis closed the coca bag and threw his coca quid under the bed.

"I'm tired," he said, hoisting himself on his elbow to sip the hot coffee.

After breakfast, Rufina went out to the corral and sent the herd off with Felicha, who trudged away looking reproachfully over her shoulder. Inucha and eleven-month-old Cirilucha hung around eagerly while their mother milked the cow. As I came outside, she commented in relief that no lambs had died of cold during the night. She fussed about Inucha, who was running a low fever, and asked whether I had more sugar to sweeten the medicinal herb tea. The children drank their fill of the milk before she returned to the house to hang the pail from a rafter for cheesemaking. Outside again, she stood looking over the low adobe wall toward the neighborhood of Qhalipampa, watching for her sister Gavina who was supposed to take the cow to pasture. She mumbled that she had to get to work at the unspun fleece and sew up Esteban's pants, which were nothing but rags. Again, she worried about Inucha and reviewed possible herbal remedies under her breath. Luis ambled out of the house and set off down the mountainside to look for firewood. Rufina turned away from the wall and settled down in the courtyard, carefully picking burrs out of the unspun fleece. So began their day of rest.

Doña Rufina was about five feet two inches, tall for an Andean woman, long-headed, with high cheekbones and craggy features. One of her upper front teeth was missing, and this made her self-conscious about smiling. She was said to have been a handsome girl. Now forty-five, her skin had weathered in the frost and sun to a copper brown; her hands and feet were black, gnarled and roughened like tree bark from a lifetime of agricultural labor and herding.

Rufina's shawls and skirt borders did not display her own handiwork, for she did not weave well. She spun the wool from her animals into thread that she gave to other women, along with gifts of coca leaves, to weave for her. Nevertheless, she was well respected in Sonqo as a strong woman who shared her husband's religious and civic responsibilities with both willingness and administrative perspicacity. During the final year of her life, suffering through her last difficult pregnancy, she supported Luis in both the community presidency and the last and most difficult of the religious *cargos* (offices), sponsorship of the annual pilgrimage to Qoyllur Rit'i.

I was not particularly close to Rufina. She was usually formal and reticent, and as her illness progressed she withdrew further. My interests did not strike a responsive chord in her: she did not care for stories (*"Manan hap'inichu"* ["I don't grasp them"], she would tell me); she did not know the names of textile motifs; what she knew about Sacred Places she did not care to tell me. Her interests and abilities were in animal husbandry. Too late I realized that on this subject she became open and expansive, and I could have learned much from her.

When I arrived from Cuzco after Rufina's death, I found her children sitting quietly in the house. They had swept and reswept the floor to keep them-

Rufina's youngest children, Cirilo (left) and Inocencia (right), play in a harvested potato field.

selves busy, but they had not tried to start the fire, and the adobe stove sat cold and empty. It was a *chiri wasi*, a cold house, an unnatural home without warmth, the kind schoolteachers and visiting students live in. A house should be warm and protective—"like a mother hen who keeps her chicks under her wings," Luis once told me, his face lighting up as he spoke.

Mornings were a great trial for Luis in the weeks following his wife's death. He woke up tired and stiff to find the house cold, the children hungry, and no one to get up, light the fire, bring water, and start the day for them. He would call crossly to Felicha, who slept like a log, and would finally get up and start breakfast himself, something he found rather shameful. As he dressed the children with great care and tenderness, he murmured disconsolately.

"*Karajo . . . Imayna kasun? Pin mihuchiwanchis? Pin hampichiwanchis? Pin p'achakuwanchis?*" ("Damn it all . . . What'll become of us? Who will feed us? Who will doctor us? Who will clothe us?").

At night Luis would sit with Rufina's sister, Valentina, and her husband, Serafeo—his *qatay-masi*, fellow son-in-law—talking brokenly about his herds.

53

If he and the children tried to care for the animals they'd kill them all, he insisted. Already a couple of lambs had died. Now, a woman knows how to keep track of animals. She can doctor their illnesses. She knows which have conceived and how many months along they are. She knows the approximate hour to expect the births and how to attend female animals in labor, for a woman understands pregnancy and birth. How can a man know about these things?

When I returned to Sonqo two years later, there was a new wife in Luis's house—tending the fire, feeding the family, clothing the children, doctoring their hurts, and keeping track of the animals.

Warmi-Qhari

Our phrase "man and wife" is expressed in Quechua by a single composite word, *warmi-qhari* (literally, woman-man). The household, as a functioning productive unit, is built around this fusion of two different but interdependent kinds of human beings, females and males, with their separate but complementary spheres of knowledge, interest, and ability.

The daily routine for Sonqo *Runakuna* takes shape around the tasks necessary for the household's maintenance and perpetuation. Most of these tasks are directly concerned with growing and processing food, making clothing, supporting the household's *cargos*, and fulfilling its obligations to neighbors and kinsmen in the traditional system of reciprocal aid. Every year money looms larger in the household economy, and each October sees more fields sown with oats and barley destined for sale.

Daily life is given shape by work—by the tasks themselves and by the means for accomplishing them. Work itself is informed by the way Sonqo *Runakuna* conceptualize these tasks—by how they think about what they do. They think about the world in a highly sexualized way—sexualized, not in an erotic sense, but in the sense that at any given moment, the object or activity at hand assumes a value associated with the sexes and with their interrelationship.

The sexualization of the cosmos is connected both as cause and effect to a strong sexual division of labor. Walking through Sonqo, you might see women working with their husbands in the fields; in one courtyard you might see a woman weaving fine textiles, and in the next you might see a male weaver working on a similar piece with similar designs. In the evening you might stop at a house where a man is preparing dinner while his wife stays out to guard a partially harvested field. But if you talk to *Runakuna* about what they are doing, you will find that in their minds these tasks are associated with either one sex or the other—and this affects how the job is done, its relationship to other jobs, and the attitude with which it is undertaken.

The woman's express task is to keep the home running. Unless she is seriously ill, the mother (or daughter-in-law, if there is one) rises first, starts the fire while the children sleep and her husband is just beginning to stir, and brings in the first water of the day. As she opens the door she crosses herself and greets *Inti*, the Sun. By the time her husband descends from the bed she has breakfast well underway. He too prays before the door, then turns and greets his wife formally—"*Bwenus dias, Mamáy*"—before he goes out. While she cooks, he does odd jobs: going for water, bringing in firewood, sometimes working in a nearby field.

In the complementary division of labor, the man works in the fields and transports produce from field to storeroom. Women look after the stores and prepare and serve food. They also look after the animals and do much of the herding. Women milk the cow, if they have one, and make cheese. Men usually look after the horses and the mules, which are used to transport produce. Women spin thread from wool, weave on the ground on a horizontal loom, and sew the family's clothes. Men knit their own caps, make fine woolen ropes for harnessing the animals, weave on an upright loom with foot pedals, and do some simple carpentry. Both men and women make *ch'uño*, the dehydrated potatoes that serve as a staple during December through February, when the fresh potatoes are gone; however, this task more often falls to the women as it is usually done close by the house. In general, tasks directly involving the home—except for building it—pertain to women. Men's tasks take them away from home; even the fields may be several steep kilometers away. Men also travel from the community to obtain money, working for a week or two in coca plantations or as porters in Cuzco, whereas most women seldom go farther than the local market in Colquepata.

Providing firewood for his wife's cooking is an important part of a man's duties. This job can easily take all day, for most of the houses in Sonqo are well above the creek bottom, and there are virtually no trees—only scrubby thorn bushes that are continually scrounged for dry branches by every passerby. Everyone also keeps an eye out for *q'awa*, dry cow droppings, which belong to the finder no matter on whose land or from whose cow.

A man who is seriously going for a few weeks' supply of firewood will have to climb down a long distance to some lower, more vegetated land of his own and tackle the large tangled bushes with his ax. When he has enough, he piles the wood on a horse or on his own back, or both, and slowly climbs home again. Finally he clambers into his courtyard looking like a walking woodpile, lets down his load with a sigh, unburdens his horse, and sinks down on the ground exclaiming "*Hananáw! Sayk'ukushani!*" ("Whew! I'm tired!"), sucking the thorns from his fingers and opening his coca bundle. While the children pull out sticks to play with, his wife stands around wondering where to store the firewood. If the weather is dry, she may end up leaving it where it lies; in wet weather she has to find space in the storeroom or house.

A woman is reluctant to let her low adobe stove cool off too much between one meal and the next. The ideal image of *Runa* woman has her seated on the ground next to her blazing *q'uncha*, a fine trail of smoke escaping from the smoke vent. Her pots, food, and small children are around her. She is ready to receive all visitors to the house with hot soup or boiled potatoes. She never lets the fire go out or the soup burn or boil over (this is still the image) while she nurses the baby and keeps the three year old out of the crockery.

The dishes she cooks are mostly potato and water soups with a few chunks of meat; yet Sonqo's women come up with a remarkable variety by using different herbs, different kinds of potatoes, different ways of cutting the potatoes or mashing the *ch'uño,* and by adding small amounts of precious vegetables or noodles. Soup is preceded by a course of *wayk'u,* boiled potatoes peeled with the fingers and eaten plain or with *uchu* (hot pepper). Morning and evening meals are the big ones; lunch may simply consist of *wayk'u,* though if her husband is doing agricultural work she may prepare him a full midday meal. "The women are helping us," say men laboring in a field with no women in sight. They mean that the women are home cooking for them.

A man sets off for his fields around eight or nine in the morning—sometimes earlier if the work is piling up—with the long *chakitaklla* (foot plow) or the smaller *rauqana* (harvesting hoe) over his shoulders, leading a horse or mules laden with seeds and manure in planting time. He heads up or down on steep trails for as much as an hour, for his fields can be found near the valley bottom or in the frigid *ruki papa* fields of the highest *puna.*[3]

Arriving at his field, he may meet neighbors whom he had called upon for *ayni,* the reciprocal sharing of help. Or he may sit down alone to chew his coca and think about the work to come. If he is host to a work party he passes out coca leaves, and before starting work the companions share coca *k'intus* with each other, invoking *Pacha Mama* and various Sacred Places. At a later date the host will return the *ayni* by spending a day in each of the others' fields, where he in turn will receive a hot meal and coca leaves.

If the work party has gathered to plow a field, the host organizes his companions into three-man teams. In each team two men, standing side-by-side, simultaneously drive the blades of their foot plows into the ground, working quickly and rhythmically with a strong and dancelike grace. Facing them, a third worker places the clods to each side, leaving a wide, pathlike furrow. Planting also requires teams of three—one man to work the foot plow, one to drop seeds in the furrow, and another to cover them with fertilizing manure. The teams vie to see which can work fastest, passing the day of hard labor in an atmosphere of friendly competition.

Harvest, in contrast, requires many hands but no teamwork, special strength, or skill. From May through July one may see children, women, and old people digging away in the dusty fields.

Around one o'clock, the host's wife arrives with lunch. She comes accompanied by the kinswomen she, too, has called upon for *ayni.*[4] Around three o'clock the workers break again to chew coca, and then work until five in the afternoon or later.

The man comes home tired; he may sit close to the fire, helping peel potatoes or *ch'uño,* or he may set to work grinding *ch'uño* or barley for the soup. His wife is usually pretty tired herself. If she was not home cooking for his work party, she was probably out with their herd and exhausted from climbing in search of pastureland and sitting out all day in the weather.

During the dry season many women move with their herds and smaller children to a *wichay wasi* (high house) near the high marshy pastures, while her husband and older children remain in the family's main house. Traditionally, herding was children's work, freeing women to stay home to cook and weave. Nowadays children spend more time in school or go to Cuzco to work as household servants, and their mothers spend more time with the animals.

Grown women find herding a lonely and stultifying task, taking them far from the house in all kinds of weather. As a result, closely related families usually pool their herds, freeing some women to stay home while others spend every day for weeks or months off with the animals. Since different kinds of animals have to be herded in different environments (the cows need to go to the valley bottom while the llamas must go to the high *puna*), these arrangements often involve several families at once. Seldom does a woman free herself entirely from herding responsibilities.

Animals provide the raw material for one of woman's most absorbing occupations—the spinning and weaving of cloth. A woman spins as she walks with her herds, a wooden drop-spindle whirling under the right hand and fleece wound around her left. A woman turns to her spindle when there is nothing else to do, stopping only to open her coca bundle and chew for a while with friends. In this way, with the help of her husband and older children, she produces the large balls of yarn that fill the niches of her house and hang from the rafters.

The coarser-spun threads she uses for the weft of her weaving; the finer ones she uses for the warp. If she is making a narrow piece—a belt or skirt border—her only equipment is string and a single small stick, stuck vertically into the ground. She attaches one end of the warp to her waistband and the other, at a distance of many yards (there are six or seven yards of material in a skirt), to the stick. Then she composes the string heddles with great concentration, for elaborate patterns require a large and complex set. Sometimes she traces part of the design in the dirt, thinking how to translate it into loops of string. That done, she takes up her little bundle of weft and sets to work, rolling the finished work up to her waist and moving closer to the stick as she progresses.

Dressing a horizontal or backstrap loom for a complex poncho or *lliklla* (woman's shawl) may take well over a day. A weaver will sit motionless before her half-dressed loom, forehead furrowed, chewing her coca. Then she starts up, her concentration broken, to retrieve a baby or look for some lost pigs. She sits down again and with a sigh searches for her lost thoughts. When she is ready to begin weaving, she takes out more coca, blowing on the leaves with an invocation to female Saints:

Awanaypaq	For my weaving
Mama Consihida,	Mama Consibida,
Mama Rosario,	Mama Rosario,

57

Using the horizontal loom suitable for female handicrafts, Gavina sits in her courtyard weaving a poncho for her husband.

Mama Sinakara.	Mama Sinakara.
Makiykiwan awasaq.	May I weave with your hands.

Finally she begins, hardened fingers picking up the threads for her design almost faster than the eye can follow, the shuttle passing through, then the weft beaten into place and all the threads smoothed and straightened out with painstaking care.

These women, whom a local schoolteacher described as *"casi selvaticas"* ("half-wild"), and who often refer to themselves as *ñawsa* (blind, meaning illiterate, uneducated), display great mastery of this difficult art, combining manual dexterity with highly abstract mental processes.

Few of the middle-aged women who are now weaving attended school, so their apprenticeship began by the time they were five or six years old. As with other daily tasks, there is no formal teaching. The children watch and play at being adults, setting up tiny looms or spinning thick, lumpy strings while their mothers turn out yards of fine, even thread.

Men weave on the upright loom with foot pedals, turning out coarser material than do women on their horizontal looms; and unlike women, men do not weave complex patterns into their handiwork. When I asked Erasmo the reason for this division of labor, he answered that the *pampa* (flat, horizontal ground) is the place for women, and this is why their looms are stretched out horizontally. Men should work in an upright position, standing or sitting on a seat, so weaving on an upright loom and knitting are suitable for them.

58

Hands and Feet: The Complementarity of the Sexes

A few years later, I put the same question to Don Luis as we sat in the sun spinning.

"Women know how to use their hands; men know how to use their feet," Luis answered. "Women wouldn't know how to use the foot pedals. That's why their looms are on the ground, and they weave designs into the cloth, which takes a lot of handwork."

"Then why aren't you spinning with your feet?" I teased him.

He got a good half hour of chuckles out of that one, but never answered the question. I recalled how, when I learned how to spin two years before, Basilia had exclaimed in delight, "Well, you're finally a woman!" Her husband, son, and *compadre* sat beside her, all of them spinning.

This incident illustrates my point that male and female activities are conceptually distinct but flexible in practice. Men do almost as much spinning as women, and I have seen men weave fine ponchos, belts, and coca bags with complex designs on horizontal looms.

"In February when there's no agricultural work," Don Luis told me, "I'll be a woman and go around knitting."

All handicrafts are *warmi ruway,* women's tasks, even those performed mainly by men. Similarly, while farming is man's work, certain agricultural tasks are suitable for women, such as placing the seeds in the furrows and turning over the clods during plowing, both of which are tasks using the hands. However, men say firmly that a woman would not "know how" to use the foot plow *(chakitaklla)* to break open the earth, and seemed to find the suggestion rather shocking.[5]

Of women's tasks, the one most unsuitable for men is ladling food from cooking pot to plate. While Rufina was staying up in the high house, Don Luis would have good soup waiting for us when we returned from a visit to Cuzco. He had cooked it himself, but asked me to serve it. At first this struck me as a manifestation of male dominance, but with time I realized that serving is a woman's prerogative, for it emphasizes her proprietorship of the food as well as the man's obligation to her. Men seldom fail to thank their wives for cooked food, even in the most casual setting.

The sexes may complement and desire each other, but they are seldom tender with each other. Both men and women shower their babies with affectionate attention, but keep a distance from each other. I never saw spouses or sweethearts hold hands, walk arm in arm, or kiss—that is the way of *Misti-kuna.* With *Runakuna* it is quite the contrary—an affectionate couple tease each other with mild insults and pelt each other with small sticks and stones. A teenage girl can actually become violent, hitting the object of her admiration in the arms and face, calling him an ugly dog. At Carnival, a boy dances up to his girl singing seductively, but their dance soon turns into a contest as they whip each other's legs in a growing frenzy.

I did not learn much about sexual relations. In retrospect I was probably too hesitant about inquiring into my friends' sex lives, and they did not volunteer much information. Married couples conduct their sex lives in the family bed with their sleeping children around them; my impression is that sexual relations take place quickly and quietly, but may be repeated. Judging from their conversation, women as well as men enjoy sex, although they dislike their frequent pregnancies.

Men try to make it clear in conversation that they are the authority in their homes, even though this may be patently false. The house is the woman's domain, whereas men are always coming and going between house and field, between Sonqo and *Misti* towns like Colquepata, P'isaq, and Cuzco. When men leave the community to work as laborers or to sell produce, they often meet with humiliating treatment and return home drunk, ashamed, and furious. They try to assert themselves at home, the one domain where they can presumably claim authority. And even there, the claim is precarious.

"What is your husband like? Is he a good man? Does he beat you?" were often among the first questions a woman asked me when our husbands were absent. Women seem to enjoy commiserating with each other about the real or supposed brutality of their husbands. I cannot say how frequently wife-beating occurs. Men, of course, deny beating their wives—although they may suspect their brothers-in-law of beating their sisters, and several times I saw a woman with bruises that gossip blamed on her husband. One man told me frankly that he had beaten his wife when he came home frustrated from market.

Basilia considered herself lucky that Gabriel did not try to push her around: "Some of these men tell their wives how much spinning to do in a day and get mad if they come home and it isn't done. My husband isn't like that. He knows I get done what I can, and if I rest one day I'll work the next. He respects me and I respect him."[6]

Although men talk with bravado, they avoid making commitments they have not cleared with their wives in private. The most respected men in the community have strong-minded, capable wives. *Runakuna*—male and female—state categorically that men cannot fulfill their civic and religious *cargos* without their wives' support. Moreover, they say this is as it should be. The interdependence of men and women is accepted as the natural state of things; single adults are considered not only unfortunate, but unnatural as well. When I asked Gabriel why some fiestas have two sponsors, although they represent no territorial or social division, he explained that the two sponsors are like a *warmi-qhari:* a pair is most suitable.

It is impressed upon children from an early age that women and men should pursue their activities independently of each other. Boys from the age of ten onward are chided, teasingly at first but more and more sternly if they persist, for staying home with the women; girls simply cannot prefer to go with the men. When Felicha expressed a preference for male activities, she was subject to crushing and universal disapproval.

Rufina's sister Valentina and her husband are the only couple I know in Sonqo who make a real attempt to coordinate their tasks in order to spend time together. Don Luis grumbles about this, remarking that it is not good for them to do everything together like that. Before his wife's death, he and Rufina pursued their activities separately—that is, properly. And truly, they did, for Rufina sometimes spent days in the high house without a visit from him. Nevertheless, he was heartbroken and genuinely lonely when she died.

The agricultural pursuits of men lead them to socialize with other men. Although female pursuits tend more toward solitary activity, neighboring women like to sit together to weave or spin, and a woman calls on a network of real and spiritual kinswomen to help her with her husband's *cargos*. Although only men take on public offices, women usually refer to their wives as "having the *cargo*."

This sexual segregation includes social activities as well as economic ones. The social worlds of women and men are separate; women visit women and men visit men. Once I returned to the house and remarked that I had been visiting Don Apolinar. Don Luis's very old godfather, who happened to be visiting, hooted as though I had said something obscene, and Luis looked embarrassed. Later, when the visitor had left, he seized an opportunity to say pointedly, "Tomorrow you will visit Doña Sista [Apolinar's wife], and Don Ricardo [Rick] will visit Apolinar."

General conversation follows these lines. A man refers to the herd of sheep as his; his wife refers to the same herd as hers. They speak similarly of their neighbors' sheep. The man says they are the neighbor man's sheep; the woman says they are the neighbor woman's. Although husband and wife pool their possessions (women inherit from both parents, the same as men), from the woman's point of view they are hers; from the man's point of view they are his. But despite this way of referring to property, the husband and wife know precisely who inherited what from whom.

The separateness of the female and male worlds is emphasized at every public gathering, where women sit in a crowd separately from the men, to the left of the *alcalde* (mayor) and other senior officials. The men sit at a central ceremonial table with the *alcalde*; or, if they are not public functionaries, they sit in a line to his right. Visitors in a home arrange themselves similarly. In bed, a woman sleeps to the left of her husband. At public functions, the two groups mingle only formally, as when the *alcalde* calls up the sponsor's wife to drink *chicha* or receive coca. If the women have brought food, they dish it into bowls to be carried over to the male contingent by young barefoot men, usually the sponsor's sons-in-law or other affinal kinsmen. These servers are the only men to interact directly with the women.[7]

The day we first set foot in Sonqo, there happened to be a *faena* (communal work project) for which women were serving lunch. When we were invited to join, I went over to the women while Rick stayed with the men; this turned out to be a decisive factor in our being more-or-less accepted by the community. If I had sat with the men it would have been all over.

The group of women sitting to the left at a public function consists only of the sponsor's wife and the women she has called upon to help her. Other women stay home. While the men's group is usually full of talk and activity, the women are quiet and talk little even among themselves. They try to appear inattentive, though all the time they are watching the men from under the fringes of their broad-brimmed hats. The women serve and the men eat; the men show off and the women watch (though of course the women are showing off in their own way—bringing the tastiest delicacies, displaying their best woven skirts and shawls, carrying heavy loads of plates and boiled potatoes, coyly ignoring the male antics and laughter).

My first impression of Sonqo's women was strongly colored by these public gatherings. It seemed to me that the women were dominated by the men to the point of having no voice of their own—forced to watch and go hungry while the men danced and ate, restricted to a tiny world that hardly reached beyond their houses, dressed alike in their black skirts so that I could hardly tell them apart. I thought irritably that they looked like a flock of morose crows as I sat with them in the rain and watched the men eating.

This impression mellowed with time, for I came to see women as dominating their households, where their work and opinions are valued and respected. That women serve the food, and that they sit on the ground while men sit on seats, has to be understood in the context of men and women's mutual obligations and the identification of women with *Pacha Mama*.

Nevertheless, it cannot be denied that women are subservient to men in the public sphere. Both sexes greet men before women, and women receive food, drinks, and coca only after the men have been served. During Carnival I had my most vivid experience of how women take second place to men. A small group of us stayed on at the sponsor's house after everyone else had left. It grew dark and began to drizzle, so the sponsor invited "us" into his house—which turned out to be so small that by the time all the men had squeezed in there was no room for the women. So we *warmikuna* sat outside in the cold rain while the men whooped it up inside. Every once in a while, one of the men guiltily crept out to serve us *chicha*, apologizing for the poor accommodations. Every time a man came tipsily outside to urinate, he would mumble something like, "Oh, you still here?" "Indeed we are," we would tell him. But he would disappear into the house again.

We sat that way, in the dark and the rain, for at least two hours. None of the women complained or called their husbands. Finally irritation got the better of my detachment, and I left. It was close to another hour before I heard the others careening homeward.

The Velasco government entertained an official policy of expanding the peasant woman's role in public life and proclaimed 1975 *"El Año de la Mujer"* ("The Year of the Woman") to awaken a heightened awareness of woman's potential role in political activities. Various women's regional congresses were organized. I did not see any *Runakuna* react favorably to this. The men grumbled that women were "ignorant" and should stay out of such affairs. It was revealing to see how much the thought angered them. But the women laughed openly, asking how a woman was supposed to lug her small children to a congress. The idea made no sense to them. When we suggested to Don Luis that women would profit from traveling more, he was dumbfounded: What a bad idea! What would the women *do* if they traveled?

Of course, Luis is familiar with women who travel, for he goes occasionally to Cuzco in a truck whose passengers invariably include some women from Colquepata, traveling between their home market and the great market in Cuzco. In 1975 only one woman in Sonqo had adopted this practice, purchasing candles, kerosene, and *trago* for a small store she had established; in 1980 her younger sister followed suit. As traffic on the new road increases, more of Sonqo's women may begin to travel. Few men will view this development with approval, and many women will agree with their displeasure.

Peruvian market women are well known for their strong and aggressive character.[8] In September of 1975, I accompanied Sonqo *Runakuna* on a pilgrimage to the sanctuary of the Señor de Huanca in San Salvador. This pilgrimage is the occasion of a major market, where I saw market women bully men from Sonqo and other rural communities into selling them *ch'uño* that they had intended for barter. They literally attacked the men, grabbing and squeezing their bundles with a thinly veiled sexuality. It was amazing to see how passively the men submitted, while little old Basilia successfully refused to accept a bad bargain. Probably these market women embody the threat that Sonqo's men feel at the suggestion that women travel and congregate.

As her family's *uywaq* (nurturer), the woman in each household is expected to conform to the qualities inherent in Mother Earth, the immobile source of inner warmth and sustenance. Men depend on their women to provide this support, and most of Sonqo's women seem content to stay home and accept the male show of superiority, which they enjoy manipulating and exploding in private. They recognize that a widower is truly at a loss to manage his household without a woman, whereas a widow can manage fairly well on her own, especially if she has grown children or other relatives to help with the agricultural work. Some women enjoy this independence and choose not to remarry. The long-widowed Doña Catalina, for example, ran a prosperous all-female household in which she and her three daughters did their own agricultural work and engaged in small commercial ventures on the side.

Such households are seldom popular, for they threaten the system of complementary values associated with male and female activities. As we have seen, women work with their hands in a horizontal orientation; men work with their feet in a vertical one. In public, women sit in a crowd to the host's left; men sit to the host's right in a straight line. Female relationships are primarily egalitarian and personal, whereas men participate in a hierarchy of civil offices.

Of course, each man or woman is a complete individual; each possesses and uses both hands and feet, has a left and right side, and can occupy hori-

zontal or vertical postures. In other words, every woman possesses male qualities and vice versa; the problem is not to exclude these attributes of the other
sex, but to express them in a suitable way. Thus, a man should express his female aspect in a properly masculine manner; a woman should express her
male aspect in a feminine manner. Recall, for example, that within the female
domain of handcrafts, knitting is performed in a vertical posture, which has a
male value. Tasks like knitting are the female aspect of a man's role.

These sets of complementary contrasts—flexible and context-dependent—
run through every aspect of life in Sonqo; they provide the framework within
which *Runakuna* think and act. It is difficult to translate them into English terminology without giving the impression of a set of absolute, static oppositions.
The relativity characteristic of Andean thinking—the continual enfolding of
male and female principles that both contain and exclude each other—may
best be conveyed by an illustration taken from Andean ritual.

When a *despacho* (burnt offering) is prepared for the welfare of a human
being, its central and most important element is a small bunch of coca leaves
called a *k'intu*. This *k'intu*, which is offered "for the *Runa*" ("*Runapaq*"), is composed in the following way: the eight leaves are divided into four *k'intus* of
two leaves each (see Figure 3). Each of the four pairs is *warmi-qhari*—a male
and female pair (A). Then the four pairs are combined into two *k'intus* of four
leaves, each of which is also a *warmi-qhari* (B). Together, this pair of four-
leaved *k'intus* forms yet another *warmi-qhari*. Finally, the two *k'intus* are combined into a single *k'intu* of eight leaves that is attached to white paper by a
pin driven through its center (C). This *k'intu* represents the person on whose
behalf the offering is made. The complete *despacho* is said to have a head and
feet like a human being and must be burned with its head, the *k'intu*'s tip, facing east, where the Sun will rise. The eight-leaved *k'intu* is offered to the
Tirakuna, who in return restore the patient's *allin kawsay* (well-being).

The eight-leaved *k'intu* illustrates a general principle: each individual is a
microcosm within which male and female qualities are combined. Each individual can, however, provide the male or female element of another pairing
to form another individual, a microcosm of a higher order. Thus, while each
man or woman is a complete individual with both male and female qualities,
the two unite to form another individual of a higher order: a *warmi-qhari*, nu-
cleus of the household.

The Webs of Dependence and Opposition

A married couple is *yanantin*, a matched pair.[9] Husband and wife depend upon
and complete each other. Their interdependence reaches beyond their household, for with their marriage the two kindreds *(phamilya)* are linked in a strong
and obligatory bond of mutual aid. As the couple grows old and each of their
children establishes households, the web of reciprocity expands. Each of
Sonqo's eighty-four households has a different network of kinsmen, and the

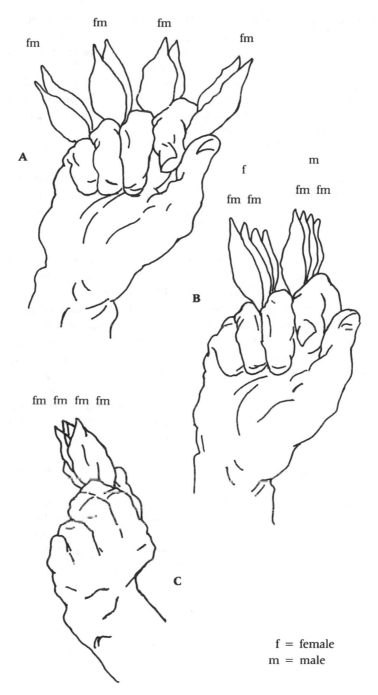

Figure 3. The preparation of the eight-leaved coca *k'intu* offered "for a human being." (Drawing by Robyn Johnson-Ross)

social fabric is formed by the intermeshing of these eighty-four webs of kin-ship and mutual aid.[10]

A set of *ermanus* (siblings) forms the core of each *phamilya*. The bond be-tween siblings—especially those close in age—is strong and intense.[11] As chil-dren, brothers and sisters sleep snuggled together in the family's bed; they eat and play together and share herding responsibilities in the *puna* pasturelands. Older children are expected to help care for their younger siblings, and the *kuraq/sullk'a* (elder/junior) distinction persists strongly throughout their adult lives, the younger *ermanus* looking to the elder ones (particularly the eldest) for advice and direction.

Siblings are connected not only by intense affective bonds, but also by the common inheritance they receive from their parents. Although each child (male or female) inherits individual use-rights to specific fields, siblings collaborate closely in agricultural activities and often use one another's land. For example, Josefa and her sister Inocencia decided together which fields in their ample in-heritance to work in a given year. Josefa's husband, Crisologo, a Chumbivil-cano who married into the community, pointed out fields that had been planted with his seeds and cultivated with his labor, whose produce he would consider his own; nevertheless, he clearly identified the fields as belonging to Inocencia. In other words, the final word on their use-rights belonged to Ino-cencia and her husband, and Inocencia would pass these use-rights on to her own children. Although I did not study land tenure systematically, I saw some evidence that this flexible cooperation within the sibling group may lead to conflicts in the next generation. Cousins, while calling one another by sibling terms, do not necessarily cohere as a close-knit group of *ermanus,* and they fre-quently quarrel over use-rights to their parents' land. Similar tensions may arise between uncles or aunts and their grown nephews or nieces.

For example, the year after his sister María died, Luis planted one of her potato fields. Although María had three grown children (Erasmo, Julian, and Sista), her husband, Francisco, seemed glad to delegate use-rights for the year to Luis, with whom he had a strong and affectionate relationship. Apparently the field, which adjoined Luis's, had completed its fallow period, and Don Francisco could not muster the resources to plant it. I suspect, however, that Luis hoped to maintain an implicit claim to the field, an interpretation sup-ported by his subsequent resentment when Julian attempted to claim his in-herited use-rights.

Running parallel, as it were, to each sibling group, is the labor pool formed by the siblings' marriages. A man spends a good part of his adult life work-ing, not only with his wife's brothers, but with the husbands of his wife's sis-ters, whom he calls *qataymasi* (fellow *qatay*). Similarly, a woman spends much time not only with her husband's sisters, but with the wives of her husband's brothers, whom she calls *qhachunmasi.*

Men look to men for help, and women to women. Thus it was up to Luis to mobilize his available male relatives and up to Rufina to mobilize the fe-males. Rufina, for example, had two younger sisters, Valentina and Gavina, and a younger brother, Domingo. Luis had two older sisters, María and Basilia, and one younger sister, Juana. Luis had no lack of *qatays* (sisters' husbands), nor of *qataymasi*s.[12] He did not collaborate equally with all these male in-laws, however. One of his closest collaborators was Serafeo Quispe, Valentina's husband.

Rufina and Valentina were very close. They lived less than a ten-minute walk from each other and helped each other with child care; animal tending, and cooking. Valentina wove some of Rufina's best clothing. A tie of *compadrazgo* cemented the close collaborative relationship of the two households when Luis and Rufina performed the first haircutting for one of Valentina and Serafeo's children, thus becoming the child's godparents. Luis's and Rufina's relationship with Gavina and her husband Julian—also their neighbors—was never as close, although Julian is Luis's nephew. Luis criticized Julian as a shiftless good-for-nothing who squandered his wife's ample inheritance, and he preferred to collaborate with Serafeo.

The affines' duties include not only labor obligations but ritual responsibilities as well. For example, as Rufina's eldest *qatay* (sister's husband), Serafeo should have assisted at her burial. The morning of Rufina's death, Luis heard that Serafeo was setting out for Cuzco to work as a street porter. Recognizing his wife's critical condition, he sent one of the children after his brother-in-law to ask him not to go. Serafeo dismissed the warning.

"I'm only going to Colquepata," he told the child evasively—and then went off to Cuzco. Why change his plans because Luis was scared? The two men irritated each other as much as they depended on each other, both practically and emotionally.

On his return from Cuzco, however, Serafeo had no choice but to pick up his abandoned responsibilities and follow through on them. Thus, as we sat in the cemetery chewing coca, Serafeo came skulking along the low stone wall, looking as though he wished he were invisible. Normally dressed in finely woven garments with complex patterns of red and black, he was now wearing a ragged brown poncho. His face, swollen with crying, was morosely defiant. It took some courage for him to come, for Luis was furious with him.

Luis jumped to his feet, glaring and clenching his fists, as his *qataymasi* entered the cemetery. I was alarmed, but Serafeo forestalled the attack by bursting into tears. The two embraced, Luis reproachful and Serafeo apologetic and full of excuses. Finally, Luis gave him some coca and Serafeo joined us as we left the graveyard without further ceremony and trudged up to the house.

Expanding the Web of Kinship

The mourners at the gravesite included Alcides and Idilio. Alcides, son of Luis's sister Basilia, was also Luis's godchild by marriage sponsorship. He was a frequent visitor in Luis's house, looking for company, advice, and support, and occasionally helped in the fields. His wife Luisa sometimes tended the animals.

Idilio was an old man linked to Rufina's father, and then to Luis by ties of patronage never formalized by *compadrazgo*. Idilio is poor, with little land and few animals, and his deceased wife was from a distant community in the province of Sicuani. Although both he and Luis are consistently vague about the nature of their relationship, it seems that he was attached to Rufina's wealthier father as a kind of tenant herdsman and continued in that capacity with Rufina and Luis. He was extremely fond of Rufina, and her children affectionately called him *"Machuláy"* ("Grandpa"). After Rufina's death, the closeness of the relationship gradually dissipated.

These mourners constituted only a part of Luis and Rufina's total network of mutual aid, a network whose formation had begun twenty-five years earlier when, as a relatively poor young man, Luis first came to live with Rufina. One night his mother and stepfather visited Rufina's parents, bringing gifts of coca and *trago*. Once the gift was accepted and the two sets of parents had chewed coca and drunk together, the new union was recognized as sealed, beginning the first stage of their married life.[13] After a few years, Luis and Rufina built their own house and established themselves as an independent household. Throughout their married lives, they entered together into relationships of *compadrazgo*, spiritual kinship, to strengthen existing ties and create new ones.

Ties of *compadrazgo* are formed on three specific ritual occasions, each of which marks a transition in the life of a child or a married couple. These are *bawtismo* (baptism), *rutuchikuy* (first haircropping), and *matrimonio* (Catholic and/or civil marriage). A couple's first *compadres* are acquired with the baptism of their first child. After consulting their own parents, they choose another couple—usually older and better established than themselves—to sponsor the baby's baptism. Sometimes they choose a *Misti* shopkeeper in Colquepata or a truck driver—someone whose influence and access to money may prove advantageous.

Besides holding the baby during the baptismal ritual, the sponsoring couple is expected to supply their new godchild *(ahijado)* with a suit of clothes and to buy drinks and other treats after the ceremony. Eight days later, the parents and the baby visit their new *compadres*, bringing with them a holiday dinner—plates of rice or noodles, roasted guinea pig, chunks of boiled lamb, the fine white *ch'uño* called *moraya*, and other delicacies depending on the season. With this meal the bond is sealed, and the two couples address each other as *"Compadre"* and *"Comadre."* Throughout his or her life, the child speaks of his godparents respectfully as *"marq'ay compadriy"* and *"marq'ay comadriy"*— "my *compadres* who carried me in their arms." This indissoluble lifetime relationship binds not only godparents and godchild, but the two married couples as well. Henceforth the two couples owe each other *ayni* (reciprocal help). The *marq'ay compadres* look after their godchild's welfare with gifts, hospitality, and moral support, and they in turn can call on the godchild's labor.

Compadrazgo is a Mediterranean institution brought to the Andes by the Spanish in the sixteenth century. That Andean people have adapted it to their own cultural forms is well illustrated by *rutuchikuy,* the ritual first haircutting, a practice of pre-Spanish origin.[14] The ritual takes place after a child has developed a full head of hair and, like baptism, marks his or her entry into the world as a social person. Unlike *bawtismo, rutuchikuy* is a private ritual. The new *compadres* are invited for dinner by the child's parents, after which they chew coca and drink together before cutting the child's hair. The new *compadres* are expected to present their godchild with a sheep, cow, or comparable sum of cash to form the core of the child's future inheritance. In return, the *compadres* theoretically receive the child's hair—intimately connected to his or her spiritual energy—to be burned eight days later as an offering to the Earth and the Sacred Places. In actual practice the parents often keep the hair and perform this final stage of the ritual themselves.

The bond formed by *rutuchikuy* is a strong one. Ideally the first ritual haircut is reinforced several months later by a second haircutting performed by the same *compadres;* many couples, however, choose different *compadres* to perform the second *rutuchikuy,* opting to form two sets of weaker bonds. A visitor to Sonqo may see children three or four years old with great mops of matted hair, waiting for the first compadres to return for the second cutting. (At the other extreme, Alcides and Luisa held the first *rutuchikuy* for one of their children at about four months, when the fuzz on his little head was hardly long enough to be cut.) *Rutuchikuy* is easily manipulated for the parents' benefit, especially with *compadres* from outside the community who may be fooled into believing they are participating in a first or second haircutting (or they may realize this and choose to share the fiction in order to form an advantageous relationship). According to local gossip, some couples have held this ritual three or four times for the same child.

When we came to Sonqo in 1975, Rufina's youngest child, round-faced eleven-month-old Cirilucha, was newly shorn. His new *compadre* was an itinerant merchant from Quillabamba, a center for coca production. He wore Westernized clothes, spoke fairly good Spanish, and had an uncle who was reputed to be an *altumisayuq,* the highest grade of shaman. For Luis and Rufina he would provide access to cash, coca, and shamanism; they, in turn, provided him with highland products—wool, potatoes, and textiles—to peddle in Cuzco and Quillabamba.

This *compadre* was expected to return in November along with his wife, who had been unable to attend the first haircutting ritual. By mid-December they had still not shown up, and Luis turned to us to perform the second haircutting. He had secretly been hoping for this opportunity—as he admitted in a little speech he delivered as the four of us were drinking *trago,* chewing coca, and embracing one another after the ceremony:

I'm glad we're *compadres* at last All year I worried, saying to myself, "We should be *compadres,* we should be *compadres.*" But there was no opportunity. Now no one can criticize me (as they have, you know) saying, "Why have you taken in these foreigners? Why are you feeding and helping them?" Now I can just say, "They're my *compadres*," and nobody can criticize me anymore.[15]

The Quillabamba *compadre* arrived, alone, three days later. I expected an unpleasant scene, but he accepted Luis's explanation and apology amiably enough. Apparently the relationship was too advantageous to endanger with angry words.

Normally a couple has several children before participating in religious or civil marriage ceremonies. In 1975 a priest visited the community for the first time in seven years, and there was a flurry of tension and excitement as several couples prepared for a group wedding ceremony. Like baptisms, weddings are usually performed in Colquepata on 15 August, when a priest presides over the festival of *Mama Asunta* (the Virgin of the Assumption), the town's patron saint. The couple to be married chooses two pairs of sponsors to serve as *hatun compadres* (senior sponsors) and *ara compadres* (assisting sponsors). After the ceremony, the three couples retreat to the newlyweds' house. There, they are received by the newlyweds' kinsmen, particularly their *qataykuna* (brothers-in-law) and *qhachunkuna* (sisters-in-law). They eat and drink far into the night. The next morning the new *compadres'* helpers—their own kinsmen and *compadres*—arrive with piles of food, bundles of coca, and bottles of *trago*, and the party continues into the next night.

Eight days later the newlyweds visit their new *compadres* with coca, *trago*, and food, and the ritual is complete, the new bonds established. The newlyweds are the sponsors' *ahijados*, and they address them as *padrino* and *madrina*. They owe their *padrino*s respect and labor, while the *padrino*s are expected to concern themselves with the marriage as counselors and conciliators.

Even among blood relatives, an active relationship of mutual aid is usually sealed through a bond of *compadrazgo*. Luis is *compadre* through marriage sponsorship to his sisters' sons Julian, Erasmo, and Alcides. Erasmo is *compadre* through baptism to his own brother Julian. Initially it surprised me that so many *Runakuna* had formed these apparently redundant bonds of *compadrazgo*, for it seemed more advantageous to extend the web of alliances as far as possible beyond the bonds already given through kinship. However, this practice of overlapping *compadrazgo* with kin ties does make sense. Choosing *compadres* is part of a delicate balancing act: a couple tries to fulfill their ritual responsibilities and assure themselves of adequate labor and moral support without overextending themselves or creating a situation in which their children will have to find mates in inconveniently distant communities. Sonqo is a small, essentially endogamous community, where eligible spouses are already in short supply due to a marriage rule decreeing first and second cousins unmarriageable. Moreover, sexual relations are considered incestuous not only among *compadres*, but also among the children of *compadres*. Thus, it can be advantageous to overlap the two webs of spiritual and biological kinship.

The bonds of *compadrazgo*, in combination with marriage alliances and consanguineal kinship, form constellations of mutual obligation and dependence that shift with time as new *compadrazgo* relationships are formed, young relatives come of age, and old bonds fall into disuse through death or quarreling. Like kin ties, bonds of *compadrazgo* can become as much a burden as an asset, and like kin ties they can be ignored or honored in the breach.

A little less than a year after Rufina's death, Luis took a widow from Colquepata to live with him, and they were married the following 15 August. They later moved from the neighborhood called Pillikunka to Towlakancha, a neighborhood closer to Colquepata, where Luis had been born and inherited use-rights to land. It was an isolated spot, and Luis enjoyed the quiet after his hectic and often unpleasant two years in the limelight as Sonqo's president.

In 1983 Julian and Gavina moved to Towlakancha and built a small house less than a hundred yards from Luis's house compound. Julian was Luis's nephew and his *ahijado* through marriage sponsorship as well as his *qataymasi*, or fellow brother-in-law (for Gavina is Rufina's sister). Nevertheless, Luis wanted nothing to do with him and was extremely irritated to have him in the vicinity. In July 1984 Julian set to work building a bigger house. Luis decided that he needed a new house too, nearer to Julian's. Normally, neighbors who build houses at the same time collaborate in the work, but Luis pointedly refused the suggestion and worked only with the help of his sons, and Julian called upon other *compadres* to help him. This was a mildly scandalous situation: "Aren't they doing *ayni* for each other?" *("Manachu ayninakushanku?")*, Doña Sista (Julian's half-sister and Luis's niece) asked in disbelief.

Luis complained that Julian was building the new house compound on top of his major footpath and next to the same irrigation canal that he uses. He made constant wisecracks to the effect that Julian was a shiftless, ill-tempered drunkard and hypochondriac. Julian told me at length how he had inherited access to the land from his mother (Luis's sister María) and had as much right to live in Towlakancha as Luis did. Gavina bemoaned the situation, insisting they should all be friends, while at the same time describing Luis's second wife, Balvina, as *"nishu-luku"* ("extremely crazy"). As the two expanding house compounds approached each other, the hostility of the two households increased.

Luis's remarriage strained his relationship with Serafeo and Valentina almost to the breaking point. The two families now live an hour's walk apart and rarely see each other, although they often criticize each other in conversation. When Valentina paid me a visit in Towlakancha, the coolly polite reception afforded her by Luis and Balvina contrasted touchingly with the children's excitement over their aunt's visit.

Luis remained on the same old footing with Alcides, who is his own sister's son and therefore no relation to Rufina. They bicker frequently and openly, sometimes avoid each other for months on end, then make up and work and visit together until the next spat occurs.

Reciprocity and the Flow of Life

The essence of social relations in Sonqo is to be found in the give-and-take of reciprocal relationships of mutual aid. Andean people are strongly conscious of reciprocity in its various manifestations, and the Quechua language contains a fairly elaborate vocabulary referring to modes of exchanging labor and goods.[16]

By far the most important modes are *ayni* and *mink'a*. *Ayni* refers to the sharing of work among kinsmen, *compadres,* and neighbors. In contrast to *yanapay* (help), a term that connotes aid freely given, usually among members of the same household, *ayni* connotes aid in which accounts are (at least implicitly) kept and should be repaid in kind. Similarly, injuries are also repaid in *ayni*. When angry word matches angry word, blow matches blow, rejection matches rejection—that is *ayni* of a negative kind. Life revolves around *ayni*. Nothing is done for free; in *ayni,* every action calls forth an equivalent response.

Mink'a contrasts with *ayni* by referring to an asymmetrical situation in which one party owes services to the other. Erasmo explained the difference with an illustration: "When I ask Don Luis to come help me in the field tomorrow, that is *mink'a;* when Don Luis comes to help, that is *ayni*."

In other words, to *mink'a* someone is to call home a debt or to exercise a right; to do *ayni* is to repay the debt and tip the balance in one's favor. *Ayni* has a double aspect: when Luis comes to Erasmo in *ayni,* he is both repaying and lending services. A day's work in Erasmo's field gives Luis the upper hand: now *he* can *mink'a* Erasmo. Then Erasmo will come to work for Luis in *ayni,* tipping back the balance in his (Erasmo's) favor.[17]

In some contexts the word *mink'a* is used as a noun. A *mink'a* is a large work party called by an individual to accomplish a major task like plowing a field or building a house. When Erasmo built a house for his young married son and called on a group of kinsmen and *compadres* to help him, that was his *mink'a*—his calling on those who owed him help. Some of them, like his brother Julian, can expect the same kind of help from Erasmo some day. Others, like his son's wife's brother, simply accepted the *mink'a*. They went home recompensed with the housewarming party and will not call on Erasmo for comparable services.

Asymmetrical relationships that involve status differences tend inherently toward *mink'a*. For example, a father-in-law can always *mink'a* his son-in-law but—unless the two are close in age or on particularly friendly terms—the son-in-law does not call back the debt. In recompense for his services, the son-in-law receives a hot meal, a large handful of coca leaves, and, usually, some fruits of his labor (potatoes at harvest time, for example). Similarly, Luis can *mink'a* Idilio, but I have never known Idilio to *mink'a* Luis. Their patron-client relationship keeps Idilio in a state of permanent obligation to the wealthier

Using the short-handled hoe *(rauqana)*, Rufina (center) harvests a potato field with the help of two *comadres*. Her companions' costume indicates that they originally came from the region of Sicuani.

Luis. In this context, *mink'a* is similar to wage labor, with payment in food and produce rather than in money.[18]

Thus, in asymmetrical relationships, the person of higher status always has the upper hand; the relationship is characterized by the presence of *mink'a* and the absence of *ayni*. Status equals, on the other hand, participate in a symmetrical relationship characterized by *ayni*. At any given moment one of these *ayni* partners is indebted to the other, but by continually reversing the obligation, they balance their relationship over the long run. *Mink'a* is inherent in *ayni*; in fact, one might describe *ayni* as "reversible *mink'a*."

Reciprocity is like a pump at the heart of Andean life. The constant give-and-take of *ayni* and *mink'a* maintains a flow of energy throughout the *ayllu*. This flow extends beyond the human community as well. The obligation extends to domesticated animals and plants, to *Pacha*, to the many animated places in the landscape itself, and even to the Saints. The earliest Quechua dictionary, published in 1608 by Gonzalez Holguín, includes the entry, *"Minccacuni santo cunata yanapahuaynispa"* ("I *mink'a* the Saints, saying 'Help me!'").[19]

Although I have not heard this phrase used in Sonqo, it is consistent with *Runakuna*'s attitudes. Just as Erasmo can call on Luis for the help he owes, so he can also call on the Saints, on his community's ancestors, and on its many and powerful Sacred Places. His relationship with deities is similar in kind to his relationship with other human beings; both are based on the play of obligation and counterobligation. Erasmo "feeds" the *Tirakuna;* they owe *allin kawsay* (well-being) to him and his household. The whole cosmos participates in the give-and-take of reciprocity.

Labor exchanges are only one manifestation of the general human responsibility to direct the flow of energy in a positive way. This is done in many contexts—in marriage alliances, in the discharging of community *cargos,* in private and communal rituals, even in how one offers speech and how one receives the speech of others. Bad or sinful behavior involves the denial of this participation through the wasting of energy or the participation in negative exchanges that direct the flow of life into destructive channels.

This responsibility is inherent in life; there is no getting out of it. As all things are alive and interconnected, our responsibility extends to the whole world.

Chapter Three
~~~~~~~~~~~~~~~~~~~~~~~~

"And Then in That Sun"
The *Ayllu*

Another Kind of People

Sonqueños enjoy questioning me about my country. They want to know what kinds of crops we grow here and what kinds of animals we raise. They find it strange that we have no llamas, do not eat guinea pigs, and cannot make *ch'uño.* Stranger yet that we have no coca. But I in turn was taken aback by some of their questions.

"Do you have the same sun in your country?"

"Of course we do," I would answer, puzzled.

With time I came to realize that they were, in effect, asking whether I was a human being. Did I belong in this world or was I, like the *Machukuna*, a visitor from another *timpu* existing in the light of a different sun? It was a question of the same order as their queries concerning our biology:

"Do women menstruate in your country?"

"Do they give birth?"

"In your country do people die?"

The social, moral, and biological order of this world came into existence with our Sun and will perish along with it, just as the world of the *Machukuna*—their big towns governed by lord mayors, their fine potato fields—perished when our Sun rose for the first time. The *Machukuna* cannot survive in the sunlit clarity of our world, for their proper Sun is our Moon. While they were dying the *Runakuna* came to life. The Sonqueños' mythic history recalls this original sunrise in which their ancestors emerged from the land itself and founded Sonqo *ayllu*, the community of *Runakuna* living in Sonqo. This chapter is about the *ayllu*: about the concept itself and about the *ayllu*'s functioning as a social entity, an organized collection of people.

I will now continue with Don Luis's version of Sonqo's mythic history (begun in Chapter 1), resuming with the creation of Sonqo's three original ancestors. Luis's narrative is short and rather cryptic. Like other *Runakuna*, he is not accustomed to telling this history as one long narrative, a style of speaking suitable to *kwintus*, the traditional tales about talking animals, *condenados* (souls of the damned), and the like. Accounts of Sonqo's past are told differently, simply cropping up in conversation every now and then. History for the *Runakuna* has a fragmentary quality, and Luis obviously found it strange to sit with the tape recorder and piece the fragments into one long narrative. And I have turned his narrative into fragments again, in order to insert information I learned from other Sonqueños and from Luis in other conversations.

Hinaspas chay Intipiqa huqñataq Runakuna karanku. Hinaspas huqñataq kasqa kay Sonqo llaqtapipas. "Intis lloqsimusqa," nispa wahanakusqaku Machu Runakuna.
    Chay phawamusqa Yutukallimanta Chura phawamusqa. Uhukanchamanta Yukra. Qolqekanchamanta Puma. Hina. Chaykunapi phawamusqa.
    Chayqa, chay timpupiqa, chay Machulaq timpun tukuqtin, chay Machu Runakuna, huq Runañataq qallarimusqataq. Phawamusqa, arí! Chaymanta Runakuna karanku.

And then, in that sun, there was yet another kind of People. Right here in this town of Sonqo there was, it seems, [while] the Old Ones were yelling to each other, "The Sun's coming up!"
    Out of Yutukalli sprang the Chura. The Yukra from Uhukancha. The Puma from Qolqekancha. That's how it was. They sprang up in those Places.
    And so, in that *timpu*, while the Old Ones' *timpu* was ending, yet another kind of People began to exist. Yes, they sprang up! And then there were *Runakuna*.

Sonqo's original ancestors—Puma, Chura, and Yukra—sprang up out of three Sacred Places in Sonqo. "Spring up" does not really catch the full sense of the verb *phaway*, which can mean fly out, like a partridge starting up out of some underbrush, or run out, like water escaping from a punctured container. Luis likened these three first *Runakuna* to toads that hop out of furrows in the fields as though generated spontaneously from the soil.
    A sixteenth-century Spanish chronicler-priest collected origin myths from Inca informants, who told him that the creator, Wiracocha, had sent out the first human beings from Lake Titiqaqa via underground waterways to emerge out of caves, springs, and lakes and populate the country.[1] In each locality these people founded an *ayllu* whose members have worshipped their local origin places, or *paqarinas*, through the generations. As in Inca myths, Sonqo's ancestors emerged from Sacred Places in Sonqo's territory and stayed there to found an *ayllu*. Puma and Chura are surnames still found among Sonqo's inhabitants, and the surname Yukra occurs in several neighboring communities.
    I interrupted Luis to ask whether all three original ancestors were male. He affirmed that they were. Neither he nor anyone else—male or female—has been able to tell me where the first women came from, and the *Runakuna* do not seem to find the issue problematic. They do mention, however, that the

76

Yukra family was lost to Sonqo *ayllu* when a Yukra maiden went over to the community of Kuyo Grande "lugging water" *("unu aysasqa")*. There the men "captured" her and she never returned to Sonqo. Ever since then there have been lots of Yukras in Kuyo Grande and none in Sonqo. (Of course, this does not make literal sense, for women pass on their surnames for a single generation only—but again, this inconsistency does not seem to bother the Sonqueños.)

Chaymanta, askha Runakuna kallantaq, Chayqa. chay Runakuna kasqaku llaqtayuq, hina. Ilaqtayuqpuniña karanku riki! Chaylla Runa karanku, chaymantaqa riki, askha Runa kapullarantaq. Huñukusqa, huñusqachá Runakuna askha karanku riki!

And so, there were a lot of People again. It seems they had a town—yes, they definitely had a town! First there were just those People and *then*—there were a whole lot of them again! They gathered together, and it sure must have been a big group of people!

Like the *Machukuna* before them, the *Runakuna* multiplied and lived in settled towns *(llaqtas)*. Other Sonqueños mentioned that the *Machukuna*, too, had had three main authorities, named Alfonso, Lucas, and Dio (Diego). Also like the *Machukuna*, the original community of *Runakuna* was destroyed:

Chaymanta, chay Runakuna tukukapullarantaqchá! Pisti Timpu karan. Pistiñataq kasqa. Hina. Chay pachata phukuspa hamusqa Pisti kanampaq q'episapa Runacha.[2] Q'ellu Unutas wasapayamusqa. Wankaranitas wasapayamusqa. Hina.
    Chaymanta Pisti qallaripusqa. Q'ALA Runakuna kapusqa![3] Wawakunallaña kidasqa. Wasipis qowi tukuyun Runakunata. Khuyaysiyá chay timpu kallasqakutaq, qollaypullasqakutaq! Manas kasqachu. Chay timpu—anchay Pisti Timpu kasqa.

But then, those People got finished off too! It was the *Pisti Timpu* [Era of Plague]. There was a plague. So it was. At that very moment a little man came to make the plague, laden down with a pack and blowing a conch shell. It seems he crossed Q'ellu unu, it seems he crossed Wankarani. So it was.
    And so the plague began. The People were WIPED OUT! Only a few children remained. They say that in the houses the guinea pigs devoured the People. Oh how they suffered in that *timpu* [when] they were killed off! Nothing was left, it seems. That *timpu*—they say that's what the *Pisti Timpu* was like.

Again, Luis's narrative bears similarities to a colonial chronicle: Martín de Murúa tells us that during the reign of the ninth Inca King, a man dressed in red and carrying a trumpet appeared on a mountain pass north of Cuzco.[4] He intended to blow his trumpet to bring on an *unu pachakuti* (apocalypse by water). But the king persuaded him to desist, therefore earning the name Pachakuti for himself. In Sonqo's mythic history, too, disaster is brought by a man with a trumpet—but no one stops him, and the catastrophe does take place.
    Sonqo *Runakuna* recall the *Pisti Timpu* in gruesome detail. They say parents dug up the graves of their own children to eat them, and infants were left trying to nurse from their dead mothers' breasts. The *Pisti Timpu* is described as a

time of reversals, when domestic animals ate their human masters and parents withheld nourishment from their children, whose bodies they consumed.

"It was like that when the *Machukuna* were finished off," remarked Basilia, as we talked about the *Pisti Timpu*.

She launched into a vivid description of the *Machukuna* being scorched to death as they tried desperately to hide. To her, the order of episodes in the mythic history seemed unimportant.

Luis's narrative continues:

Chay timpuqa manas qolqetas tarisqachu. Qanchi miyu kasqa despues kanchi miyuta pagasqaku! Original mañay, visitante mañay. Anchay chay timpu Runakuna kasqa. Runakuna! Qhepa timpuñayá chay. Antiskunaqa, Machulakunaq timpunqa huqyá!

During that *timpu* there was no money to be found. If you had thirty-five centavos, it seems you had to pay out thirty-five centavos! There was *original mañay* and *visitante mañay*. That's how the People were in that *timpu*. The People!

[But] that *timpu* came afterward. The Earlier Ones, the *Machula's timpu* was a different one!

Luis is talking about taxes in this cryptic passage. During the colonial and early republican eras, *original mañay* was the tax owed by *originales,* or natives to the community, whereas *vistantes,* outsiders who had settled in the community, paid *visitante mañay,* a lower tax. What an odd and telling juxtaposition—that Luis suddenly turns to taxes while describing an epidemic! This apparent non sequitur makes more sense in light of the fact that money became a kind of scourge following the Spanish Conquest. Indigenous communities were expected to pay taxes in kind or in cash—although they had formerly paid taxes to the Inca in labor, and their local economies were based on subsistence agriculture, barter, and labor exchange.[5] To acquire money, many individuals entered into abusive wage labor contracts, sold their lands, or simply fled from their communities in order to avoid the higher tax owed by *originales.* By mentioning taxes within the context of the *Pisti Timpu,* Luis implicitly compares this economic scourge to the epidemics of disease that periodically swept the countryside for almost two hundred years following the conquest, and which have continued in a milder form up to the present. Disease and taxes destroyed the *ayllu;* conceptually they belong together in the same *timpu.*

Pisti Timpu tukuqtinña, chayqa huq Runakuna karanku. Chay phurmallataq karan: Anton Qespikuna KINSA! Ayapata Anton Qespi. Pillikunka Anton Qespi. Pakupuhru Anton Qespi. Hina Machu Runakuna kallantaq. Chaymanta qhepamanña chay kallantaq.

When the Pisti Timpu ended, then again there was another kind of People. And it took that [same] form: THREE Anton Quispes! Ayapata Anton Quispe. Pillikunka Anton Quispe. Pakupuhru Anton Quispe. And so they were like the Old Ones. And that was later yet.

The tripartite structure persists, for when a third manifestation of Sonqo *ayllu* takes shape after the Pisti, it is led by a trio of community leaders *(kamachikuqkuna)*, the Three Anton Quispes. As these three shared the same name, they were differentiated through the Places where they lived: the neighborhoods of Ayapata, Pillikunka, and Pakupuhru. Sonqueños explain that the Quispe family were among the *hawamanta Runakuna* (outsiders) who repopulated Sonqo *ayllu* after its decimation by the plague. The three Anton Quispes emerged as leaders.

Pillikunka Anton Quispe was senior of the three. He is said to have been Rufina's paternal grandfather. He was a tall, imposing man, with long, thick braids and a *montera* (flat fringed hat), a style appropriate to men as well as women until the early twentieth century. Pakupuhru Anton Quispe was sometimes nicknamed Sompicha Anton Quispe after his *sompicha,* or Western-style felt hat. And Ayapata Anton Quispe was not originally Anton Quispe at all. He came from another community—just where is now forgotten—and married Juana, sister of Pillikunka Anton Quispe. Since he went around with the other Anton Quispes, the *Runakuna* called him Anton Quispe, too. Together, the three used to walk around the *ayllu* with whips, ready to beat the idle and lazy. *Runakuna* would exclaim, "The Three Anton Quispes are coming!" and take off their hats.

This behavior is more typical of *hacendados,* owners of landed estates where Indians lived and worked virtually as serfs, than it is of authorities in indigenous communities. Apparently the Three Anton Quispes headed a faction that dominated the political and economic life of the community, solidifying their position by symbolically taking over the ancestral role originally pertaining to the Puma, Chura, and Yukra. Doña Josefa, who is not descended from Quispes on either side of her family, remarked irritably that "it's because of those Three Anton Quispes that now there are so many Quispes in Sonqo."

Indeed, when I reviewed the local school's register in 1980, I found that over half of Sonqo's children have Quispe as their paternal or maternal surname. In contrast, there are few Churas, and the Pumas are on the verge of extinction. The three original *Runakuna*—Puma, Chura, and Yukra—can no longer serve as ancestors for the majority of Sonqo's current population.

After Quispe, the second most common name is Hualla. And Erasmo Hualla tells me that there were three original Huallas, too! They came together from Hurin Qosqo as *qataykuna* (sons-in-law) who married into Sonqo.

Luis's narrative ends bitterly:

Hina chaykuna kanyá! Chaytan paganku qanchi miyuta kusinera mañay. Hina chaykunamanta allpaykuqa huchuy huchuylla. Wakimpaq manan kanchu.

That's the way they were.[6] To them they paid thirty-five centavos in kitchen service.[7] And it's because of them [the Anton Quispes] [that] our landholdings are very tiny. For some there's none at all.

I interrupted here:

Ha! Manachu?

What! There isn't?

Luis replied:

Manan wakimpaq kanchu. Hinallatapis.

Not for some of us there isn't. You're welcome.

When Peru achieved independence from Spain in 1821, communal land-holding was legally abolished in favor of private ownership, which allowed individuals to sell their parcels of land without interference from their communities. This policy sounds very fair and democratic to us, but in the context of a stratified and ethnically fragmented nation, it had exactly the opposite effect. Indigenous communities were no longer able to act as effectively as corporate bodies to defend encroachments on their lands, and poor or otherwise vulnerable individuals were easily coerced into selling their property or forfeiting it in payment of debts. Communities like Sonqo saw their land base eroded and found themselves internally divided. In 1925, more than a century after independence, indigenous communities finally won legal recognition as corporate bodies holding lands in common. Indians were granted citizenship shortly afterward, and legislation was enacted that recognized the inalienability of indigenous community lands.[8]

Legally, then, Sonqo's lands are corporately owned. The *ayllu* as a body reserves the right to redistribute land, but in practice land is held individually, inherited from parents by children, and is often the subject of passionate disputes. Occasionally the *alcalde* (mayor) redistributes land in a February ceremony called *Chakra Mañay* to settle particularly bitter disputes or to distribute lands that have reverted to the *ayllu* due to death or to permanent migration.

Apparently the Three Anton Quispes aggrandized themselves at the expense of their *ayllu*-mates by buying up land from poor or vulnerable individuals, producing an unequal distribution of land that persists to the present day and inspired Luis's concluding comments.[9] When I pressed him for details, he became uncomfortable and ended the recording—his "You're welcome" signaling that I should thank him and shut up.

Oral traditions seldom present us with the linear succession of factual events that we expect of our own written histories. They make sense of events by structuring them in patterns that follow cultural logic.[10] Sonqo's mythic history expresses a sense of time passing discontinuously in parallel episodes that share the same pattern. The three *Machukuna* are replaced by the three first *Runakuna,* who are in turn replaced by the three Anton Quispes. After each apocalypse, the *ayllu* is reestablished on the tripartite pattern, first by the Puma/Chura/Yukra, and then by the Three Anton Quispes.

80

Each of the parallel episodes represents Sonqo's population as strongly bonded to Sonqo's places. The *Machukuna,* who appear in the first episode, are associated with the locality, and their ruined "houses" are part of Sonqo's familiar landscape. They cluster on Antaqaqa, Sonqo's most powerful and venerable Sacred Place. The obligatory invocations that begin every coca chewing session almost inevitably include Antaqaqa, the *Machukuna,* or the *chullpakuna* (the *Machukuna*'s houses).

In the next parallel episode, the Puma, Chura, and Yukra spring out of three Places. Generated by the land itself, they connect their descendants with the locality from which they sprang. This connection is ruptured during the *Pisti Timpu,* when the *ayllu* descended from these original three is destroyed and replaced by a population of outsiders with no intrinsic connection to the land on which they live. The final episode of the Anton Quispes reestablishes this connection, so necessary to the *ayllu*'s existence. The Anton Quispe incorporate place names into their own names; likewise, the three Places—Ayapata, Pillikunka, and Pakupuhru—become known as the Anton Quispe *ayllu*s.

In the *Pisti Timpu* episode, oral tradition apparently preserves the memory of the social and demographic holocaust that decimated the Andes' indigenous population in the wake of the Spanish Conquest. In the 1720s yet another major epidemic swept the Cuzco area and decimated the district of Colquepata.[11] With the efficiency characteristic of oral history, several epidemics seem to have been telescoped into one catastrophic *pachakuti* that was, furthermore, exacerbated by crippling taxation.

Historical documents agree with the oral tradition in telling us that during the 1590s the *ayllu,* as it then existed, met a violent end as the decimated population was uprooted and relocated in the district capital. During this period many people throughout the Andes fled their communities to escape from tax collectors, missionaries, and overseers, or to go in search of wage labor. Some died in tropical *haciendas* of unaccustomed disease and heat; others were worked to death in mines and textile sweatshops called *obrajes.*

"Oh, how they suffered in that *timpu* [when] they were killed off!"

That was the end of the world as it had been, and the oral tradition reinforces this point by presenting it in mythic terms as a *pachakuti,* brought by a man with a backpack and trumpet, who inexorably crosses the ridges of Q'ellu Unu and Wankarani between Colquepata and Sonqo.

After the epidemic of the 1720s, Sonqo's population began to recover in numbers and absorbed many *forasteros,* uprooted individuals who for one reason or another had become separated from their landbase. How to accommodate these outsiders became a chronic and vexing problem in Sonqo, as it did in many communities throughout the central Andes. The late eighteenth and early nineteenth centuries saw yet another influx of *forasteros* during the unsuccessful rebellion of Thupa Amaru and the War of Independence against Spain.[12] Oral tradition economizes by telescoping the memory of these two similar historical periods into a single episode, in which a new population of outsiders reconstitutes the *ayllu* according to the old tripartite pattern. The new

81

trio of authorities/ancestors is intimately connected with local Places, for only through their neighborhoods—Pillikunka, Pakupuhru, and Ayapata—are the three Anton Quispes distinguished from one another. This connection with the land validates the new group of settlers as an *ayllu*.

People, Sacred Places, and Community

It is hard to pin down the meaning of *ayllu*, because it varies according to region and time period. For the Incas, *ayllu* was a group of people descended from a founding male ancestor. A person's position in the social hierarchy, as well as eligible marriage partners, were determined in complex ways by his or her relationship to the founding ancestor.[13] There were also *ayllu*s whose membership was based on shared occupation, like Cuzco's *Tarpuntay* priesthood and groups of North Coast fishermen.[14]

In many contemporary Andean communities, the word *ayllu* refers to a bilateral kindred, the group of people a given individual recognizes as kinsmen on both parents' sides of the family.[15] Sometimes the word *ayllu* refers to moieties, or two halves, of a community,[16] whereas in other contexts it refers to work groups temporarily mobilized to accomplish a specific task.[17] Moreover, different usages can co-occur in a single community, and any given use of the word seems to make sense only within a limited context.

Let us begin with the *ayllu* as we find it in Sonqo. It was while explaining the word *ayllu* that Don Luis began to talk to me about Sonqo's mythic history, for he tended to lapse into myth to communicate aspects of the concept not accessible to direct explanation. In Sonqo the word *ayllu* usually is used in reference to the community as a whole. *Ayllu Runakuna* are the people of the community, and decisions made in the communal assembly are said to be the *ayllu*'s decisions.

However, the word *ayllu* can also refer to neighborhoods within the community. I learned about these neighborhood-level *ayllu*s while sharing *trago* with Luis one evening. He had been in an expansive mood all day and made an elaborate invocation over the libation, including the word *Pillikunka*. I asked what *Pillikunka* meant, and he replied, *"Kay wasi, kay ayllu"* ("This house, this *ayllu*").

Luis explained that Pillikunka was the small ridge where his house was located. His house, along with two other house compounds located on the same ridge, constituted Pillikunka *ayllu*. He pointed out Qhalipampa *ayllu*, a flat expanse with four house compounds, slightly lower and to the west. Basilia, he continued, lived in Qoyapuhru *ayllu*, along with her son Alcides and the families of two female second cousins (Basilia's father's brother's daughter's daughters).

As I followed up on this information with other Sonqueños, I realized that for them locality is the main criterion used in defining the *ayllu*. A named place big enough to have houses built on it is a potential *ayllu;* but it is not actually an *ayllu* until *Runakuna* establish houses on it. And it must be *Runakuna* who live there. When I asked Luis the name of the school's *ayllu* he replied vehemently, "There used to be an *ayllu* there before the school was built, but now the school is just the school and the teachers are just teachers."

Wasi (house) and *tiyana* (seat, or living place) are synonyms for the neighborhood-level *ayllu*. Fellow members of a neighborhood *ayllu* need not be related through blood or marriage; they are *ayllu-masi* (*ayllu*-mates) by virtue of common residence. In practice, *ayllu*-mates are usually kinsmen, since use-rights to land are inherited from both parents by children of both sexes.

Siblings often live in different *ayllu*s with *ayllu*-mates who are more distantly related, like Basilia and her second cousins. The word *ayllu* is not, as far as I know, applied to the *ermanus*, groups of siblings and their spouses who work land together, closely bound by ties of mutual reciprocity.

When a man builds a house on land inherited by his wife, they both consider themselves members of that *ayllu*, and there is no stigma attached to this. People build their houses where it is convenient, and spouses refer to each other's land as their own. Families frequently move to new locations, for in different years they use fields and pastures in different parts of the community. When they move they cease to be members of their former neighborhood *ayllu*.

It would be difficult to compile a complete list of Sonqo's neighborhood *ayllu*s, accounting for all eighty-four households. For one thing, *Runakuna* sometimes disagree over place names. Luis gave Isabel Quispe's *ayllu* as Intikancha, whereas she gave the name as Ichhupata and located Intikancha down the hill from her house. Also, families may maintain more than one house. In 1975, for example, Alcides and Luisa lived in Waskhawaylla, Ichhupata, and Qoyapuqru.

Ayllu membership fluctuates with the years. In 1975 Qhalipampa *ayllu* was comprised of a single extended family of four households. María and Francisco lived in a house adjoining that of their daughter Sista and her husband, Apolinar. María's two sons from a previous marriage, Julian and Erasmo, lived nearby with their respective families. When I returned to Sonqo in 1984, I found that María had died and Francisco had built a house on Pillikunka with his new wife and their baby daughter. Julian and Gavina had moved to Towlakancha, and Sista and Apolinar also had built a new house in another neighborhood. Of the former members of Qhalipampa *ayllu*, only Erasmo and Cipriana remained—but they had been joined by a new household, for their eldest son, Hipolito, brought home a wife in 1979.

The number of neighborhood *ayllu*s in Sonqo has no inherent limits but is determined by geographic and demographic factors: the number of named places where houses can be built, the number of households in the community at any given time, and the distribution of inherited rights to build on given places.

The demography is affected by many factors. The years between 1975 and 1984 saw a marked shift in population to the southeast and to the higher, colder parts of the community's territory. This is a striking reversal of the traditional tendency to locate the main house *(hatun wasi)* at lower, warmer altitudes, with subsidiary houses located higher up in the *puna*. The change came about partly in response to the traditional system of crop rotation, as the southeastern potato fields were completing their seven-year fallow period. At that time Sonqo's territory was still divided into eight sections called *surt'i*s (from Spanish *suerte*). Each year the *Runakuna* concentrated their fields in a given *surt'i* and moved on the following year to the next *surt'i*, a practice that produced a seven-year fallow period for any given field. As Sonqo's territory is large, families sometimes changed their residence in order to live nearer to fields currently in use.[18]

But new factors also contributed to the demographic shift: the recently constructed road dirtied the water supply for households living below it, and several families decided to move to higher land with better water. Also, with their growing involvement in the cash economy, many Sonqueños planted their lower fields in oats and barley, disregarding the traditional *surt'i* system. Oats and barley are easily damaged by stray animals, so the herds now have to be pastured at higher altitudes to protect the fields. This led many families to establish their main houses high in the *puna;* they found it easier to walk to their lower fields than to herd the flocks long distances every day.

The church was relocated in 1983 to separate it from the graveyard, a move encouraged by Colquepata's new priest, who argued that the shallow graves produced an unhealthy atmosphere. Thus, the church's new location is higher and to the southeast, closer to the actual center of the community's population and reflecting the general demographic shift.

Sonqo's demography changed so dramatically that when I returned in 1984 after a four-year absence, I felt almost as though I had come to a new community. Back in 1975, for example, Towlakancha had stood deserted. It was not an active *ayllu,* for it had no inhabitants. By 1984 three families were living there: Luis and Balvina, Julian and Gavina, and Luis's daughter Felicitas and her husband, Saturnino. Towlakancha had been reactivated as an *ayllu,* for again a group of *Runakuna* was living there.

Uninhabited places are not *ayllu*s. But neither is a group of coresidential people. An *ayllu* exists through the personal and intimate relationship that bonds the people and the place into a single unit. Only when *Runakuna* establish a relationship with a place by building houses out of its soil, by living there, and by giving it offerings of coca and alcohol is an *ayllu* established. The relationship is reciprocal, for the *Runakuna*'s indications of care and respect are returned by the place's guardianship. Mestizo schoolteachers do not make offerings of coca and alcohol, nor do they experience a personal bond with the place; therefore, the school cannot be an *ayllu*. That place has been destroyed as an *ayllu,* unless with the passing of time the school is deserted and *Runakuna* build houses there again.

Although *ayllu*-mates share this relationship membership by virtue of coresidence, coresidence by itself is not enough to create an *ayllu*. To describe Sonqo's *ayllu*s simply as residential groups would not only miss their essence but would obscure their underlying commonality with the *ayllu*'s manifestations in other parts of the Andes. Sonqo's *ayllu*s are strongly localized, but Sonqueños experience localization in terms of their personal relationship with the place—the place who, in their terms, is *"uywaqninchis"* ("our nurturer"). *Ayllu*-mates derive their well-being from the same locality, and through this shared relationship they are set apart as a distinct social unit.

What relationship do these neighborhood-level *ayllu*s bear to Sonqo *ayllu*, the community as a whole? Sonqueños conceptualize the *ayllu* in an expansive and hierarchical manner, with lower-order *ayllu*s nested within *ayllu*s of a higher order. Luis explained that together the neighborhood *ayllu*s make up Sonqo *ayllu*. Similarly, Sonqo is grouped with other community-level *ayllu*s to make up Colquepata *ayllu*, the district; which in turn is part of Paucartambo *ayllu*, the province; which in turn is part of Cuzco *ayllu*, the department, and so forth.[19]

At each level, the *ayllu* is a topographically distinct place. From the high *puna* no-man's-land, one has a view of Sonqo itself as a single place, a many-armed ridge stretching like a huge animal from the high pass of Panapunku down to the river valley. From this height, the adjoining community-*ayllu*s are also revealed to be geographically defined by valleys on either side of this ridge.

Runakuna say that from Wañakawri the whole district of Colquepata is revealed as a distinct place, a river valley encompassing the ridges and creek valleys of its component *ayllu*s. As places are nested within places of greater magnitude, so *ayllu*s are nested within *ayllu*s. And as places are distinct from one another at one level while merging together at another, so too are groups of *Runakuna* differentiated as members of distinct *ayllu*s at one level while remaining united in a single *ayllu* of a higher order. Each of these extensions draws the individual into a larger group of people, beginning with the immediate family, extending to the neighborhood, and then to the community, the district, and the province.

In spite of the interminable bickering characteristic of community life, the *ayllu* is a major emotional focus for Sonqo *Runakuna* as well as a great source of security and moral support. Each Sonqo *Runa* looks to Antaqaqa and the other Sonqo *Tirakuna* for parental-like protection; it is this common relationship—like being children of the same parents—that creates a sense of intrinsic and indissoluble community among the members of Sonqo *ayllu*. Shared residence is experienced as shared descent.

The hierarchy of *ayllu*s (neighborhood → community → district → province) follows the hierarchy of *Tirakuna*. The high snow-covered peaks, which can be seen over a large region, provide common foci for a greater geographical area than do local landmarks like Antaqaqa. Local *Tirakuna* are the focus of local festivals held in community level *ayllu*s, whereas a festival associated with a major *Apu* draws pilgrims from an entire region of province-level *ayllu*s. During Corpus Christi, the great snowy peaks of the Qoyllur Rit'i range draw together approximately ten thousand people from hundreds of communities. High in the glacial sanctuary, pilgrims from Sonqo join pilgrims from other *ayllu*s of Paucartambo, all characterized by the same style of dress, ritual dances, and music. There they encounter *ayllu*s from the neighboring province of Quispikanchis. Each community places a small image of Christ at the foot of a larger and reputedly miraculous image. Symbolically recapitulating the union of *ayllu*s, the small Christs form a cluster around their common focus, a boulder imprinted with an image of the Christ Child. Thus, spatial (or geographical) hierarchy coincides with the religious hierarchy of *Tirakuna*, which is also the hierarchy of social organization.[20]

In short, the *ayllu* as it is manifested in Sonqo is a group of people brought together as a unit through their common connection with the Sacred Places. Moreover, this connection exists through time, for *ayllu* members include not only living *Runakuna*, but their ancestors as well. As generations of *Runakuna* pass into the territory of Sonqo, they remain there as ancestral *Machula Aulanchis*, repositories of vitality and well-being.

This manifestation of *ayllu* is widespread in the Andes and has its origins in preconquest times. For example, a colonial chronicler and evangelist reported from a valley in the central highlands that

ayllu refers to a number of people with a common origin, as we would say "Mendozas" or "Toledos." And this usually is a rock outcrop or a mountain peak which has its special priest, usually is the site of the cemetery, and which every year is the object of a festival.[21]

But what does this localized *ayllu* have to do with the *ayllu*'s other manifestations? Why does the word refer in one place to a localized group, in another to a lineage, and elsewhere to a kindred, a moiety, a group of specialists, or a work party?

In answering this question, it is important to bear in mind that Andean people tend to focus on processes, or modes of relatedness, rather than on categories of similar things: "*ayllu* is the name of a mode of relatedness and not an entity with specific dimensions" (Salomon 1991:22). To ferret out the common denominator of *ayllu*'s various meanings, we have to examine the contexts in which the word is used and ask what is happening in each one. What we find is that in each case people are being sorted out into groups.

In his 1608 dictionary, Gonzalez Holguín defined *ayllu* as *"el genero o especie en las cosas"* ("kinds or species of things"). He translated the phrase *"ayllu pura, o aillo ayllucama huancuni"* ("within an *ayllu* or gathered into *ayllu*s") as *"iuntarse los de un linage, o cosas deun genero"* ("to gather together the members of a lineage, or things of a kind").

Later definitions are equally general:

"Any social or political group with a boundary separating it from the outside"
  (Zuidema)
". . . any group with a head" (Isbell)
"An *ayllu* is basically a faction. . . . As in all factions, its unity depends on a leader"
  (Skar)[22]

In my interpretation, *ayllu* refers to the collection of several individuals into a group that is distinct from (and thus potentially opposed to) other groups that might be formed in the same context. *Ayllu*-mates are united by a common focus—and this focus may be an ancestor, a Sacred Place claiming their common allegiance, an individual claiming them as kinsmen, a common specialization, or even a shared task. In different contexts an individual may belong to different kinds of *ayllu*s with different memberships.

The common focus, whatever it is, directs and provides for the sharing, storage, and transfer of energy. In Sonqo, where Sacred Places provide this common focus, *ayllu*-mates send their *samincha* offerings to a Place who controls their health, luck, and vitality. In a work party the laborers, recompensed by the host's food, coca, and alcohol, focus on a common task that absorbs their energy. Lineage-mates owe their existence to their common ancestor's procreative energy, which they store and transfer to the next generation.

Factors dominating the formation of groups may vary in different historical, ecological, and social circumstances. Descent is more important to group membership for members of a ruling class, like the Inca nobility, than it is for rural peasants, who define their group membership primarily in terms of locality and shared activities. In regions where reciprocal trade between the potato-growing highlands and the maize-growing valley assumes an overriding importance, an *ayllu* may form that is composed of two sections—one producing maize and the other potatoes. Each of these sections is called an *ayllu*, and together they form an *ayllu* of a higher order.

Factors underlying *ayllu*-formation may overlap. Although Sonqueños emphasize their relationship to the locality, the mythic history tells us that descent is also a factor in the formation of the *ayllu*. In fact, the principles of locality and descent are merged, as Sonqo *Runakuna* trace their origin back to the Puma, Chura, and Yukra who sprang from the territory itself. After the *pisti* (plague), newcomers had to claim this connection with the territory as their own in order to validate themselves as *ayllu* members.

Political factions also express themselves in the mythic history: after the plague, the domineering Quispes "hogged up" (as it were) all three ancestors in a covert statement that Sonqo *ayllu* is a Quispe *ayllu*. No wonder non-Quispes find the story so irritating! (And one has to wonder whether those three Huallas weren't waiting in the wings to replace the Three Anton Quispes with the Three Huallas.)

Locality, descent, and political factionalism all play a role in defining Sonqo *ayllu*; each provides an idiom to express group membership that can in some sense be translated into the other idioms. For example, at first glance the Quispes seem to be related through common descent. But are they? That third Anton Quispe was originally somebody else: he *became* a Quispe by allying himself with them in marriage and through behaving like one of them, *using the idiom of common descent* to effectively erase his previous identify. Then he proceeded to identify himself, as a Quispe, with one of Sonqo's Places, thenceforth known as an Anton Quispe *ayllu*.

The oral tradition shows us how the *ayllu*'s inherent flexibility allows it to reformulate itself through time. In practice this flexibility seems to have been diminished after the Spanish Conquest, as colonial administration defined communities in terms of rigid boundaries supposedly fixed in perpetuity. The defense of these boundaries took on paramount importance in the continual struggle to maintain independence from the *hacienda* system, leading to a more rigid and static definition of the *ayllu*—in terms of a permanent bounded territory—than might have otherwise been the case.[23]

The *Ayllu* in Practice

One of the great divides in the Sonqueños' social universe is the opposition between *Runa* and *Misti*. Only *Runakuna* live in *ayllu*s, for only they maintain the relationship of personal reciprocity with the land through which the *ayllu* is actualized. Nevertheless, the *Runakuna* in their *ayllu*s are not an entity unto themselves. In explaining the defeat of their Inca ancestors, *Runakuna* say that *Taytanchis* (Our Father) arrived one day *"dokumentuyuq"* ("with documents") and dispossessed the Incas of their land. Confronted by the official papers, there was nothing for the Incas to do but leave. *Runakuna*, the Incas' cultural descendants, cling to what poor land they have and wonder rather skeptically whether the *pachakuti* (apocalypse) will ever arrive to revalidate their ancestors' prior and unwritten claims. The tradition expresses very well their attitude toward the official Hispanic bureaucracy as an intrusive and hostile, but powerful and unavoidable, force in their lives. The apparently arbitrary but legally sanctioned claims of the *Mistikuna* were often, in their experience and in that of their forefathers, backed by the physical force of the police and the military. The new police station in Colquepata and the *guardia civil*'s regular patrols through the countryside leave the *Runakuna* tense and uneasy, for they all know of family or friends who have been arrested, and some have been hauled off to jail themselves for minor or nonexistent offenses. In the *Runakuna*'s eyes, the agents of the law exercise power arbitrarily, like the mythic *Taytanchis* with his documents.

The effect of outside influences is reflected negatively in the *ayllu*'s mythic history, which represents taxation as a plague belonging in the *Pisti Timpu*. The Anton Quispes, too, were apparently able to aggrandize themselves by ignoring the communal nature of Sonqo's landbase and by using the national legal system, which recognized private ownership, to their own advantage.

Outsiders are also negatively represented in the demonic creatures of local folklore. The *ñak'aq*s (slaughterers), for example, are supernaturally evil Mestizos who fall on nighttime travelers and kill them with their knives. They may mesmerize the victim with their flaming eyes and extract their body fat. All outsiders, particularly men, are considered potential *ñak'aq*s.

*Saqra*s are demonic cannibals with a second mouth on the back of their necks for eating people. They inhabit isolated huts or remote villages high in the *puna* where they receive unwary visitors with every show of hospitality—

and then dupe their guests into eating meals of human flesh before they, too, are killed and added to the cooking pot.[24] As Sonqo becomes increasingly incorporated into the money economy—and as Sonqueños raise more cash crops and state that life without money is impossible—conversation turns less to the *saqra llaqta* (demonic town) and more to the *saqra tinda* (demonic store). Nocturnal travelers, they say, hear voices and singing as the hillside opens beside their path to reveal a rich Mestizo store full of manufactured goods, bright lights, laughter, and music. The urge to enter is nearly unmasterable, but the fool who does so finds that the store soon vanishes, leaving him back on the path and deathly ill.[25]

Prior to the agrarian reform of the 1970s, Sonqo *Runakuna* bitterly resented the neighboring *haciendas* that nibbled away at their territory. To protect themselves from the hostile and exploitative social environment, they tended to withdraw from relations with Mestizos and to avoid participation in the national money economy, thus reinforcing the *ayllu* as a major emotional focus and a source of self-identification.

But the tendency toward withdrawal was never—and never could have been—completely realized in practice. In spite of their legal status as members of an independent community, Sonqo *Runakuna* are closely bound to the *Mistikuna* of Colquepata by a web of social and economic relationships—some created by patron-client bonds, others by the *Mistikuna's* control of the district's political apparatus. Before the agrarian reform, *Runakuna* sometimes worked as wage laborers in neighboring *haciendas,* where they were related to the peons by bonds of marriage and *compadrazgo.* In the 1950s a primary school was built in Sonqo, and Mestizo schoolteachers came to live there—not only to teach the children Spanish and prepare them to participate in the national society, but also to serve as advisors and intermediaries between the community and the national bureaucracy. With the agrarian reform, a new set of officials appeared on the scene implementing a new set of programs formulated by a new set of government agencies.

Foremost among these officials was the *promotor* for SINAMOS *(Sindicato Agrario de Movilización Social),* an agency created by the Velasco government to implement its programs for social reform. The *promotor* spent much time and energy quarreling with the schoolteachers, whose national union was generally opposed to the government's programs. Sonqo *Runakuna* found themselves sitting in long assemblies, fidgeting and exchanging glances as the schoolteachers and the *promotor* bickered over how to run the proceedings.

The Eustaquio Incident

During one assembly, in September of 1975, the *promotor* seized upon the teachers' absence to preside over the election of the *ayllu's* ritual representative, the *alcalde.*

Ostensibly, the assembly concerned the school, although the school-teachers were away at the time. It was late in the day before the *promotor* turned to new and previously unannounced business: election of the *alcalde* (mayor) for 1976. The *Ayllu Runakuna* were nonplussed by the new item and offered some resistance, complaining that since Sonqo's president (Don Luis) was absent on personal business they should put off the vote until a later date. This, however, was all to the good as far as the *promotor* was concerned, for Luis had proved far too independent and astute for his taste. He kept insisting and pushed the matter to a vote.

The government's policy at that time was to phase out the preexisting political organization in indigenous communities and replace it with two governing councils, the *Consejo de Administración* and the *Consejo de Vigilancia*. The old system of *varayuqkuna* (holders of the staffs of office) and the religious *cargos* (sponsorships) had not been explicitly prohibited, in hopes that they would die out by themselves as *Runakuna* (now officially called *campesinos*, peasants, rather than *indígenas*, natives) turned their interest to other forms of community leadership. Although the *alcalde*ship belonged to this category, government administrators continued to take an interest in the selection of this still influential official, requiring that the *ayllu*'s choice be approved by the provincial government in Paucartambo.

It was clear that nobody was eager for the job. The *promotor* explained that the *alcalde* should only serve as leader at communal work parties; his other more burdensome duties were to be discontinued. When there was no response, he gave the *Runakuna* a little lecture on the value of continuing their traditions. Don Justino, the current *alcalde*, stood up and said that the candidate should have some access to cash income, as the job was impossible without it. Finally three men were nominated—Don Eustaquio C., Don Adriano Q., and Don Victor H.—all three adamantly insisting that they could not afford to undertake the *cargo*.

Adriano and Eustaquio were both young men in their late twenties, married and the fathers of small children. Both were generally well-liked, participated as dancers in community festivals, and had passed the prerequisite offices of *regidor* and *segundo*.

Don Victor, the third candidate, filled the suggestion that the new *alcalde* have access to cash income. He was a much older man, whose grown children had moved away permanently from the community. Although he involved himself in small commercial enterprises and had adopted Mestizo dress, Victor was active in civic affairs, having served as president of administration in 1973–74, and *carguyuq mayor* (senior sponsor) for the feast of Santa Cruz in 1975. Nevertheless, when the votes were counted Victor received only two. In 1977 he died suddenly in his potato field without ever having served as *alcalde*.

Eustaquio won with thirty-eight votes, followed by Adriano with twenty. Eustaquio was well liked, and the assembly clearly voted as though it were conferring an honor.

But Eustaquio was furious to the point of tears. He jumped to his feet, complaining that it was unfair to choose him while there were older men who were eligible and had not served. Don Justino quietly tried to present him with the *alcalde's vara* (staff of office). Eustaquio refused, and the two struggled for a while as the *alcalde* tried to pass on his office, Eustaquio in tears would not take it, and the staff itself came close to falling on the ground. Finally Justino gave up and retreated, still holding the *vara*. The *promotor,* eager to finish up and begin his hike home to Colquepata, repeated his speech about how the *alcalde* was now only a leader of work parties, and the assembly ended.

Throughout October and November, gossip had it that Eustaquio was holding firm and refusing to accept the *cargo,* much less plan for it—but the *Runakuna* assured me that he would eventually come around. It is not unusual for the *alcalde*-elect to complain about his *cargo.* Then on 7 December, when time was already running out, Luis came to our room with an official letter and asked us to read it for him. Eustaquio had gone for support to the provincial offices of the *Liga Agraria,* a government-sponsored peasants' union; he really was serious about refusing his *cargo.* The letter declared (in Spanish) that Eustaquio did not have to serve, that the *cargos* were not *"obligatorio,"* and that the whole *cargo* system "ought to disappear" *("debe desaparecer")* because it only reduced people to poverty. So the *ayllu* was confronted with a crisis: 1975 was fast drawing to a close, with no *alcalde* for 1976.

But nothing was done about it—not overtly, that is. Don Luis said that perhaps he, as president, should sponsor Carnival, the *alcalde's* most difficult and expensive duty. The thought seemed to leave him feeling martyred and virtuous; he described at length what a fine Carnival he had sponsored years before during his own term as *alcalde.* I asked what would happen to the other offices—would there be *regidores* with their conch-shell trumpets?

"Kanqa," Luis answered. *"Noqayku kashaykun!"* ("There will be. We exist!")

I began to overhear rumors that the elders were going to ask Alcides to step in. Although slightly younger than Eustaquio, Alcides was also eligible for the post and, always active in traditional celebrations, he was unlikely to refuse.

Basilia fussed and fretted at the thought that her son might be selected as a replacement. One day while I was visiting them, the *alcalde* arrived asking for Alcides, and the two held a long conversation in subdued undertones. On my way home that day, I was stopped several times by people who wanted to ask one question: Had the *alcalde* presented Alcides with a bundle of coca, and had he accepted? He had not, to my knowledge.

Meanwhile, a decisive event occurred on 8 December during celebrations for *Mama Consibida* (the Virgin of the Immaculate Conception), when the *Ayllu Runakuna* were gathered in front of the church, the women sitting in a little group off to the side and the men seated in a row behind the ceremonial table. Eustaquio was playing the flute with a group of musicians.

After the food had been eaten and *trago* and *chicha* were being served, Eustaquio's mother spoke up from among the women. She was a respectable middle-aged *Mama,* characterized as *wira* (fat), a respectful term with connotations of prosperity and substantial character. She spoke out without standing up, without even looking at her son or at any of the men.

"Iman kanki? Runachu kanki?" ("What are you? Are you a *Runa*?"), she yelled at him.

She continued with a long stream of condemnation and reproach. Although most of the men disapproved of Eustaquio's refusal to serve, they eventually began to argue with her in a subdued and horrified undertone, asking her to be quiet and not humiliate a man in public. The rest of the women sat silent and expressionless, apart from a few gleams of self-righteous satisfaction. Eustaquio stared straight ahead and said nothing.

The whole scene had a quality of blatant indirection. The woman was screaming at her son; the son was ignoring his mother; the men were trying to shut up the woman; and no one looked anybody straight in the face.

Before the end of December, Eustaquio agreed to serve as *alcalde,* and at the Carnival celebrations his mother was the dominant hostess.

Although the *Runakuna* let the *promotor* have his way and went ahead with the vote, they elected their own candidate. Apparently their internal decision-making process had already gotten underway, for there was no need to work through all the eligible candidates during the assembly. Probably Don Victor's nomination was a spur-of-the-moment addition following the suggestion that the candidate have a cash income. As a man with Mestizo contacts and some command of Spanish, he would have met with the *promotor*'s approval as well. Nevertheless, he met with scant approval from the *Runakuna*. Although the assembly was taken by surprise, the list of possible candidates apparently had already been pared down to Eustaquio and Adriano. Eustaquio's time had come, and left to themselves the *Ayllu Runakuna* probably could have resolved the problem of his refusal before the formal election. In the end, the prevailing influence was not that of SINAMOS, nor that of the *Liga Agraria,* nor even that of Sonqo's elders: the *ayllu*'s will was imposed by Eustaquio's mother.

The Burdens of *Ayllu* Membership

Quechua has adopted the Spanish word *cargo* for community offices and other responsibilities that the *ayllu* requires of its members. And a suitable word it is, for the offices are treated as onerous burdens. The *carguyuq*'s (officeholder's) family may enjoy the excitement as well as the prestige that accrues to their household, but they also find their duties time-consuming and expensive. They feel the strain of being in the limelight, subject to public scrutiny.

Nor do the *cargos* carry much real power with them, for the *ayllu* guards its prerogatives jealously and distrusts its own officials. Luis was nearly impeached as president for accepting a government loan to plant eucalyptus trees without first calling a community assembly, although the agent arrived un-expectedly with the offer and refused to stay in Sonqo long enough for an as-sembly to take place.

The Councils of Administration and Vigilance, instituted in 1970 as part of the Velasco regime's reorganization of community government, were de-signed to give peasants a stronger local apparatus with which to participate in the affairs of the nation. Members of the administrative council—president, vice president, treasurer, and one or more *vocales* (committee members)—have the difficult and often complex duty of implementing governmental programs and acting as the *ayllu's* liaison with government agencies and the school. The vigilance council, consisting of a president and a councilman *(vocal),* arbitrates disputes and concerns itself with internal peacekeeping.

The presidents are expected to preside over communal assemblies where problems are openly discussed and decisions voted upon through a show of hands. The assembly is the *ayllu's* voice; its decisions are the *ayllu's* decisions. Each household sends a representative, normally the senior male, although older men sometimes send an unmarried teenage son in their stead. Women attend only as widows or when their husbands are absent and seldom partici-pate in the discussions. Usually a schoolteacher helps the officers to read and interpret Spanish documents and draw up decrees and requests.

The councils coexist with the old system of *varayuqkuna* (staff bearers), a four-step hierarchy through which young men prove themselves as respon-sible members of the community. A young man usually starts up the ladder in his early teens, first serving as *regidor alguacil* (assistant town crier). A few years later he serves as *regidor mayor* (senior town crier). Later, when he is already married and in his twenties, he and his wife undertake to assist the *alcalde* as *segundo* ("second," i.e., assistant *alcalde*). Finally, in his late twenties, thirties, or even forties, he and his wife take on the *alcalde*ship. Sonqueños compare this hierarchy of staff bearers to the grades in school and consider participa-tion to be part of a man's education.

When an announcement is to be made, the four town criers—two assis-tants and two seniors—set out at dawn or sunset on a roughly oval path through the community. Each goes to one of four promontories (Harrawani, Hatun Harrawani, Aseroqkancha, or Yanqay) to blow their conch-shell trum-pets—the assistants beginning with their lower-pitched *pututus*, followed by the seniors' higher-pitched ones. They blow three sustained notes and then yell their announcement three times at the top of their lungs. Then they re-peat the whole procedure twice more (for a total of three times).

The *pututus'* hollow and penetrating sound reaches Sonqo's farthest cor-ners. *Runakuna* pause in their cooking, herding, or agricultural work and strain to hear the announcement. Often they need not be told, or a word or two is sufficient to convey the whole message, for the news has already passed through the grapevine.

The town criers blow their *pututus* at prescribed intervals during work par-ties and Saints' Day celebrations. They contribute *trago* to work parties and serve food and drink to the laborers. Each of them carries a plain wooden staff, the assistants' staff shorter than the seniors'.

The segundo does not carry a *vara*, although he shares the *alcalde*'s burdens and prestige. The *alcalde*-elect selects him from a pool of eligible and willing men. Occasionally two men serve together as *segundo* to further share the burden.

Gabriel complained that properly the titles Don and Doña should be reserved for couples who have served as *alcalde* and objected to current usage, which applies the titles to any married person. Gabriel told me that when *he* was young, a couple who had not passed the *alcalde*'s cargo were simply called by their first names "like children" and were not considered full adult members of the *ayllu*. During Carnival celebrations, community elders criticized the sponsoring couple mercilessly, treating them like *chakimakis* (servants). Wealthy parents vied with one another to push their children through the four steps of the hierarchy at an early age, sometimes before the age of twenty.

The *alcalde* presides over public rituals that affirm and renew the *ayllu*'s existence. He heads communal work parties and initiates the dancing at Saints' Day feasts. He sponsors *Musuq Wata* (New Year) and Carnival, major celebrations attended by the whole community. On New Year's Day he is invested in the district capital by the Mestizo *alcalde* of Colquepata. Then, with his fellow staff bearers, the *alcalde* leads his *ayllu*-mates running back to Sonqo, where he serves them food and drink and entertains them with music and dancing.[26] About two months later he hosts Carnival, again receiving the *ayllu* at his house. Similar duties continue throughout the year: he is expected to serve food and *chicha* at the four annual work parties—*Yapuy* (Plowing of Communal Lands), *Allay* (Potato Harvest), *Tarpuy* (Planting), and *Mamachaq Wasin Allichay* ("Repairing the Little Mother's House," i.e., the church). On top of these responsibilities, the other staff bearers visit him before every Saints' Day, along with musicians and dancers, expecting to be generously served.

During his year of tenure, the *alcalde* and his wife invest their time and household economy in public functions that express and help perpetuate the community. Although he is not a major decision-maker, council members and elders consult with the *alcalde* about community affairs. With the help of his parents and elders, the *alcalde* chooses his *segundo* and *regidores*; he, in turn, helps the sponsors of religious fiestas choose their successors. He proposes dates for the annual work parties, and his command sends the town criers out with their *pututu*s. New marriages and domestic troubles are his concern, and he visits families with problems and those who are mourning a death. All this is part of the education process, rendering him a responsible adult man, knowledgeable in the ways of Sonqo *ayllu*—a man, moreover, who has "paid his dues" and can count on his community's practical and moral support.

The *alcalde*'s presence, with his silver-studded staff and official *montera* (flat fringed hat), validates public functions in which the *Runakuna* act as a collective body and are actualized as an *ayllu*. It is in this sense that the *alcalde* is *kamachikuq*, an authority, or more literally, an actualizer. His authority does not lie in political coercive power, which is minimal; rather, it lies in his capacity to serve as a focus around which the *ayllu* coheres. For his tenure in office, the *alcalde* submerges his individual interests within those of the *ayllu* to emerge as the human symbol who expresses its collective existence and will.

How *do* things get done in Sonqo? Although I lived in the president's house compound in 1975 and attended the assemblies, I often had the feeling that the way things were "really" getting done was eluding me—for much of Sonqo's political life is informal in nature and has a sub rosa quality to it. Most decision-making goes on outside the formal assemblies—away from the watchful eyes of teachers and government agents. It is carried out by influential members of the community, who call on one another in the evening or before breakfast to chat and chew coca and confer soberly during work parties while the young men labor noisily at the heavier tasks.

These older men of high prestige and influence are the *kuraq taytakuna*, the elder fathers. They do not emerge in public as a decision-making group, but through their informal conferences a consensus elusively and almost imperceptibly develops—finally to find expression in the assembly and to be articulated and validated by the *alcalde* and council members. It is difficult to identify the real centers of authority in such a community; keeping its decision-making processes invisible helps the *ayllu* retain its independence.

How does one achieve the status of *kuraq tayta*? Passing through the hierarchy of staffs confers adult status on a married couple but does not guarantee them elder status when they reach old age. Luis, for example, once remarked that Marcelino Mamani, nicknamed Machu Mamani (Old Mamani) was "old but not elder" (*"machu, manan kuraqchu"*) because he had fulfilled only a few minor religious offices and, what's more, he was living as man-and-wife with his own goddaughter.

An elder is supposed to be morally upstanding, levelheaded, moderate, and well-spoken. Again, possessing these characteristics is not enough, for after the hierarchy of staffs another set of *cargos* comes into play. Elders should have sponsored religious celebrations like Saints' Days, Holy Week, and Corpus Christi—observances that pay the *ayllu's* debts to saints and Sacred Places both inside and outside Sonqo. The expensive celebrations, which include costumed dancers, musicians, and quantities of food, *chicha*, and coca, are not simply displays of wealth and generosity, but are acts of devotion as well—for the sponsor shoulders the *ayllu's* spiritual burden along with his heavy economic responsibilities. Whatever else a man may do, he cannot achieve elder status without "passing the *cargos*."

There is no clear hierarchy of religious *cargos*. I do not know of anyone who has actually sponsored all of the Saints' Days and pilgrimages celebrated in Sonqo, nor do I know two people who passed their religious *cargos* in the same order. The Corpus Christi *cargo* is generally (but not always) passed last, when a man is around fifty. Saints' Day celebrations have two sponsors, senior and junior, whom Gabriel likened to a *warmi-qhari* (man and wife). The junior *cargo* is generally a prerequisite for the senior one.

95

Pilgrimages wax and wane in prominence, with the exception of Qoyllur Rit'i, whose overwhelming importance seems unshakable. It is said that formerly the pilgrimage to nearby T'oqra was a grand affair, but currently only a few individuals attend, and Sonqo sends no official delegation. The Oqruro pilgrimage was observed in 1975, but since then the Sonqueños have neglected it. In 1975 no one from Sonqo went to Accha, but in 1984 Accha was on the ascendant again. In 1975 Sonqueños were talking about a new pilgrimage to Saqaqa and considered getting together a delegation of costumed dancers. They never got around to going, but it seems possible that the Saqaqa pilgrimage could materialize another year.

Similarly, each year a different set of Saints' Days is actually realized. In 1975, for example, the pair of sponsors for San Geronimo proved unable to fulfill their responsibility, and the celebration fell through. The failed sponsors suffered a loss of face that they will have to recoup some other year.

The system's fluidity has advantages, for it presents a couple with a variety of options. Their passage through the shifting maze of religious sponsorships has creative aspects as an act of self-expression that no two households fulfills identically. Luis and Rufina, for example, sponsored Corpus Christi the same year Luis served as president of administration, a coup that capped off his career.

By the same token, no one can pass through the system "perfectly," for the number and order of *cargos* is too vaguely defined. Ideally, a man "finishes" sometime in his fifties by "having done everything." But the definition of "everything" is never clear. Luis liked to refer to himself as "finished," but when I asked him whether he were *kuraq* (elder), he hesitatingly confessed that he had never led the pilgrimage to Accha. Although I have not heard anyone else hold this against him, he seems to feel that the omission could be thrown in his face if he ever needs bringing down to size. The system's flexibility thus provides a leveling mechanism, a potential Achilles' heel for any *kuraq tayta*. Eldership rests on an informal consensus that a man has led a good life but after all, nobody is perfect.

Women and the Political Process

I made it a regular practice to sit with the women while attending community assemblies. Although this helped make my presence acceptable to the *Runakuna*, I found it immensely frustrating. Not only did I have to try to follow rapid and passionate arguments in Quechua, but the women regularly sat too far away from the men to hear well, much less participate in the proceedings. My suggestions that we sit closer were met with refusals—the sun was too hot over there, or, quite bluntly, they were scared. Women seldom spoke unless the discussion concerned them directly, and then there was an uncomfortable scene. Men did not like having women enter the public forum, and the women did not like entering it.

If my experience in Sonqo had been limited to these formal public occasions, I would have thought that women had no voice at all in the running of the *ayllu*. The assembly creates the impression that decision-making is the province of vigorous males, with women and old men excluded from the political process. But like a stage play, this public drama fixes our attention on the actors alone, obscuring the fact that the action is produced and directed behind the scenes. Women and old men are Sonqo's invisible production crew. At least half the action happens offstage, and the anthropologist, government agent, or schoolteacher who watches only the public drama will inevitably fail to understand how the community functions.

This is not to imply that the assemblies, with their debating and voting, are a mere facade. On the contrary, previously subterranean currents of consensus and dissent surface in the assembly. The assembly articulates issues as a matter of public record and resolves them democratically. Obviously this gives men in their prime an edge in control of community affairs—but only an edge, for when the assembly ends, they go home to face their wives and aged parents.

The Eustaquio affair is a good illustration. Although the *ayllu* was pushed into a premature election, the decision was already essentially made. In a less formal situation, Eustaquio's parents and various elders could have exerted their pressure on him—and he could have expressed his reluctance—privately and more subtly, giving both sides more room to capitulate.

In the long run it fell upon his mother to bring him around by bawling him out in public, coercing her son to undergo the final rite of passage into adulthood by treating him like a baby. As a woman she succeeded where the men had failed—not through arguments in the assembly, but by exposing her domestic role in public.

But there are situations in which a woman *has* to enter the public arena, and obviously a woman with no husband, or one who is at odds with her husband, is at a serious disadvantage. Men represent their households in the assembly, and a woman who tries to represent her own interests is not likely to meet with much success.

For example, at one assembly a widow from Sipaskancha showed up with a request. She had been married to a Sonqueño but returned to Sipaskancha after her husband's death; now she was demanding her widow's rights of seed and labor from the Sonqueños. The assembly rejected her demand without hesitation, and the president returned her gift of *trago* unopened.

Abandoning the attempt to press her case as a single woman in a male forum, the widow changed her tactics and turned to the task of mobilizing sympathy among other women who had married into Sonqo. At the next work party, these women appeared among the kinswomen of the hosting officials, bringing food and *chicha* for the menfolk. When the work was finished, the gathering separated to chat and chew coca in the usual male and female groupings—men in a line, women in a crowd seated firmly in their many skirts. Only then did the widow reappear to be lavishly welcomed by the cohort of sympathetic women. *Runakuna* consider it unpardonably rude to turn away a guest who has already been welcomed—so there she stayed, although most of the men and many of the women were quietly displeased.

After a while she presented Don Luis, the president, with two bottles of *trago*. He accepted them and had them served to the gathering. Then Erasmo, whose wife is also married-in, rose to argue the widow's case. Even before he began it was clear that the widow had won. The debate centered not on whether she would be helped, but on how much help she would receive.

Later I asked Luis why he had accepted the *trago* on behalf of the *ayllu*, when it committed the assembly to an obligation it had already refused.

"The *mamakuna* accepted her," he answered, "so we had to accept her too."

The widow achieved her goal by confronting the men, not on their own terms, but on a woman's terms. She mobilized a base of collective female support at a public function properly attended by both sexes and did not arrive until the women had established themselves there as a group. With these female supporters she maneuvered the men into risking a serious breach of etiquette. Finally, when there was no denying her, she used a male representative to articulate her cause to the male assembly.

In this way the *wira warmi*, "substantial woman," is far from passive. She has a female way of asserting herself. Women support and anchor the life of the community, and it is in this that their power lies.[27] While men assert themselves as individuals (or as representatives of individual households) variously placed in the *ayllu*'s fluid hierarchy of statuses, female power is exerted collectively and consists primarily of the powers of veto and commentary. Only in extreme cases do women go public, and then they cause a kind of social earthquake, an upheaval of the private substratum of community life.

Now this may seem to us like female subordination, but it is something more subtle and complex. The powers and limitations of Sonqo's *mamakuna* are inherent in the sociocultural system in which they operate. That female power is invisible, elusive, and holds a great potential for violence has contributed greatly to the stubborn resilience of native Andean culture. In the centuries following the Spanish Conquest, women of the high *puna*—less accessible than men to tax collectors and missionaries—were instrumental in preserving indigenous religion and culture.[28] Women have also played a prominent role in the Andes' long history of peasant rebellions.[29]

"The *Mistikuna* like to lord it over us," remarked Basilia as we ambled along behind her sheep late one afternoon. "But in their hearts they're afraid of us."

She fitted a stone to her finely woven sling and sent it flying in the direction of Colquepata.

"We women standing so innocently with our herds—they know that— brrr! brrr! chhaaq! chhaaq!—we could go after them with our pretty slings. We're not afraid."

Another stone went whizzing off in the direction of Colquepata.

Land, Life, and Death: Return to the *Ayllu*

Sonqo's political process turns on the interaction of private (female and aged) and public (young and male) spheres. This brings us back to a familiar theme—for cosmos, household, and *ayllu* function according to analogous principles. Events in this world happen at the interface of the interior and the exterior, the subterranean and the celestial, the female and the male, the old and the young, the living and the dead. This is where exchange, transformation, and actualization take place.

The female and the male—the quintessential opposition in this sexualized worldview—form different kinds of relationships with the world. Males form hierarchical relationships, participating as individuals within a public arena; women relate to one another laterally—that is, in a collective, private, and egalitarian mode. Within the male context, mature men move as individuals up the vertical ladder of *cargos*, whereas old men reenter the lateral substratum and speak as elders with a private and collective voice. In the general context of *Runakuna*, individuals pass through their separate lives only to lose their physical identities in the cemetery's collective heap of bones, and to merge their social identities in the collective ancestral category of *Machula Aulanchis*.

The *ayllu's kamachikuqkuna*, its authorities or actualizers, depend on the collective base of elders and women. The Senior Fathers have worked their way through the hierarchy of staffs and the maze of religious sponsorships to merge finally into a collective category of elders. As their public individual voices weaken, their role in the formation of informal consensus increases. Obviously men do not cease to be individuals in old age any more than women lack individual personalities; however, their individual voices mingle to emerge as a collective opinion: the voice of the *ayllu*.

Elderly men are often affectionately called *"Machula"* ("Grandpa"), the term also applied to the collective ancestors who reside in the ruined towers of Antaqaqa. Elders will enter the category of *Machula Aulanchis* fairly soon, and as such they are the male aspect of the *ayllu's* collective substratum. The hierarchical apparatus of public life depends on a communal and nonindividualized base: as *Pacha Mama* provides a generalized base for the hierarchy of plural individual *Tirakuna*, and as the ancestral *Machulakuna* on Antaqaqa support and yet contrast with the community of living *Runakuna*.

Ultimately, *Machulakuna* merge with the territory itself. Throughout their maturity, the men and women of Sonqo's households maintain their *ayllu* by bearing its spiritual and material obligation to the Sacred Places. The territory is like a guardian or a parent who gives birth to them, sustains them, and absorbs them in death. Living *Runakuna*, as *Machulakuna* of the future, have their eternal existence assured in the existence of their *ayllu*. They return to the ultimate ancestor, the territory from which the first *Runakuna* "sprang out like toads." From within Sonqo's soil they will sustain their descendants.

Basilia died in Colquepata one February market day in 1979.

When I came back to Sonqo in May of 1980, I found her *ayllu*-mates still dazed by the death. *Runakuna* are accustomed to death as a presence in life; normally they send off the soul in order to get on with living as quickly as possible, but this was harder to do in Basilia's case.

Alcides was serving as *alcalde* that year, and Basilia must have been in a frenetic state. Josefa described her setting off for the last Colquepata market before Carnival, "laughing, with a big bundle on her back." A few hours later a man rushed up from Colquepata with a message that Gabriel should come quickly, for his wife was gravely ill.

Gabriel rushed to the house of the *Runa compadres* where Basilia and Alcides had stopped to visit on their way to market. There she had accepted a shot of *trago* and then keeled over and died with the glass still in her hand. Gabriel found Alcides standing by his mother's body immobilized by bewilderment and surrounded by a market-day crowd that had surged into the courtyard as soon as the sensational news spread through town. The *sanitario* (medical official) and the district officers rushed in to investigate, excitedly exercising their duty and prerogative.

"And then," Gabriel was to tell me brokenly, "the *Mistikuna* took her away for an operation."

But his *ayllu*-mates expressed themselves more bluntly. "The *Mistikuna* took her away," they said, "to be butchered."

Colquepata's Mestizo officials invoked a law requiring autopsies in all cases of unexplained death. Chances are that if Basilia had died in Sonqo no one would have bothered to pursue the law, especially as she showed no sign of contagious disease. For those who knew her intense and rather choleric personality, and her tendency to exhaust herself with overexcitement, a heart attack or stroke seemed the most likely causes of her death. But since she had the bad luck to die in town on market day, she provided the authorities with an opportunity to show their devotion to duty by carting the body off to the provincial capital.

"It was all unnecessary," Erasmo was to comment, still pondering the events in 1984. "Alcides should have smiled nicely at the officials and bought them all drinks. He could have sweet-talked them into giving the body back." Hard judgment to pass on a man whose mother had just dropped dead in front of him, but probably accurate.[30]

Her family walked numbly along to Paucartambo and waited until the body was returned to them a few days later. They buried her right there, for who could walk all day back to Sonqo carrying a mutilated corpse? Eight days later they returned to Paucartambo for her wake to send the soul away.

Runakuna have absolutely no doubt what it means when *Mistikuna* take a cadaver away for mysterious operations. They extract the body grease—to be sold to nuns to make candles for convents, or to grease the motors of cars and airplanes, or to provide gelatinous capsules for strange gringo medicines.

I found Gabriel changed into an old man, sitting in the corner crying for his wife.

"I was already old and she was still like a girl. I was a sober man but she'd run around laughing like a kid. I had to rest a lot, but she never got tired."

The *Runakuna* echoed his laments. Basilia had been vigorous and seemingly healthy. She should have died old and frail, and in her own *ayllu*. Her death was not a good death. In house after house I heard the refrain:

Sipas kaqti wañupun.	She died young.
Qhali kaqti wañupun.	She died healthy.
Manan kaypichu,	And not here,
Manan Sonqopichu.	Not in Sonqo.
Manan kaypichu,	Not here,
Manan Sonqopichu.	Not in Sonqo.

Chapter Four

Coca Knows

"Pacha Mama, Tirakuna, Sonqo"

At five A.M. one March morning in 1976, I left Sonqo to return to the United States. Don Luis was accompanying me to Cuzco, but he sent me on ahead of him. He walked faster than I and would easily overtake me on the muddy paths, which were drenched after three months of heavy rain. The sun had not yet fully risen, and a heavy fog was rising out of the valley. As I walked over the now familiar footpath, wondering when and if I would return there again, I felt as though I were saying goodbye to the *Tirakuna*, whose names I had come to know and who had tolerated my intrusion.

But in the fog the *Tirakuna* had changed entirely, or so it seemed to me. I could hardly see my feet in front of me and slipped off the path several times. The hills and ridges loomed and dipped around me strangely, and for a while I got completely lost. As the fog lifted I found myself on a path below the one I had intended to follow and had to scramble up a long way to get onto the muddy highway where I was to meet Luis. (Actually, "highway" is a mis-nomer, for the road was completely impassable to motor vehicles, scored as it was with ruts and washouts.)

Luis caught up with me, marveling at my slow progress, and I commented in relief how good it was to be walking on the road. He looked at me with his characteristic deadpan irony.

During the Feast of St. John, Serafeo (center left) and Valentina (center right) share coca *k'intu*s and *trago* with their grown son, Santos (left). Their young daughters look on, sucking on hard candies.

"It's a wonderful road," he replied. "Just wonderful. Especially now."

We were clambering through a rut so deep we had to climb in and out of it while the mud came almost to our knees.

It was hardly a propitious leave-taking. Later in Cuzco, I asked Don Luis why the fog had come up and confused me like that. Were the *Tirakuna* displeased with me?

"You still don't blow your coca *k'intu*s properly," Luis answered. And again, he showed me how to do a proper *phukuy* (ritual blowing). Let me pass on what I learned from him.

To make the *k'intu* you choose three or more of the best leaves from your coca bundle. If your leaves are broken and ragged, you make do with them the best you can, but if they are moldy you throw them out. You place the leaves, shiny side up, one on top of the other and hold the little bundle between your thumb and forefinger. If you offer the *k'intu* to a companion, you present the shiny side. If you consume it yourself, you hold the shiny side toward yourself.

You wave the *k'intu* a few inches from your mouth and blow on it softly. This is *phukuy*, ritual blowing. As you blow, you make your invocation. Actually, "invocation" is not quite accurate; your words are more like the address on a letter, for they identify the recipients of the coca's fortifying essence.

Your *phukuy* should always include the Earth (*Pacha, Pacha Mama, Santa Tira, Pacha Tira,* etc.); the Sacred Places (*Tirakuna, Apukuna,* etc., or aspecific named Place like Antaqaqa); and your *ayllu,* either the neighborhood or the community. The *Machula Aulanchis* and *chullpas* can stand in for the *ayllu* to fulfill the last rule.

"*Pacha Mama, Tirakuna, Sonqo*" is a good basic *phukuy.*

You can add a request as you direct the *samincha* to its powerful recipients: "Let me have a good trip," or "Please make it stop raining." I long failed to realize how much concentration is needed when an important request is at hand, for you must focus single-mindedly on what is being asked while directing the request via the coca's *sami.* Erasmo prided himself on the effectiveness of his *phukuy* and pointed out instances when his request was quickly granted. Before I left Cuzco in 1984, he offered to do *phukuy* for my trip and asked me for the exact time my plane was scheduled to leave.

"*Noqaqa yachani allinta*" ("I know how to do it very well"), he said with the pleased air of one who can offer a significant favor.

Luis instructed me that in Cuzco I should blow to the local *Tirakuna:* to the ancient fortress of Sacsahuaman and to Calle Sapphi, the street where my room was located. "*Santa Tira, Apu Sacsahuaman, Calle Sapphi*" was a respectable Cuzco *phukuy* and would ensure that my immediate environment would feel kindly toward me.

"We do this for our well-being" ("*Hina ruwanchis allin kawsayninchispaq*"), Luis commented as he blew on his coca *k'intu.*

The Etiquette of Coca Chewing

Hallpay provides a frame within which peaceful and constructive social interaction takes place. An invitation to chew coca is an invitation to social intercourse. Friends who meet on the road pause to chat and to chew coca; men gathering to work in a field settle down to chew coca beforehand. When serious or troubling problems are at hand, *hallpakuy,* or the shared chewing of coca leaves, expresses the participants' commitment to rational and peaceful discourse. For the solitary individual, the brief *hallpay* break provides a meditative interlude in which to gather stray thoughts and prepare mentally for the task ahead.

Coca's uses are hedged about with ceremony. The exact etiquette for chewing coca varies from region to region, but whatever the specific social forms, coca is always shared. Among the Quechua-speaking Qollahuaya of northern Bolivia, for example, men exchange coca bags with one another while women chew from a common pile.[1] In the Cuzco region, both men and women exchange coca *k'intus* with prescribed phrases of invitation and thanks.

For example, let's say that you and I sit down to chew coca. We first each make a *k'intu* and perform the ritual blowing *(phukuy)* before chewing it. Then we make *k'intus* for each other. I offer my *k'intu* to you by saying, *"Hallpakusunchis"* ("Let's chew coca together"). You receive the *k'intu* with thanks and do *phukuy* again with this *k'intu* before chewing it. While chewing, you prepare a *k'intu* for me. Ideally, all *k'intus* are reciprocated.

We both gradually add leaves to the wads in our cheeks, and after awhile we add a tiny bit of *llipt'a,* hard compressed ash resembling a charcoal briquette, to activate the coca's stimulating alkaloids.[2] After twenty to thirty minutes a good-sized wad has been built up, and if there is work to be done, we thank each other and get on with the job. The wads stay in our mouths for about forty-five minutes, after which we carefully remove them and gently throw them away on the ground. One never spits coca; *Runakuna* find this unthinkable. Neither should coca be swallowed. For me this is the hard part. Julian liked to tease me by demanding that I display my coca wad and then scolding me for having inadvertently swallowed most of it—like an adolescent not yet *santuyuq* (possessing skill) in coca chewing.

Hallpay is performed approximately five times daily as part of the normal routine. *Runakuna* chew coca after their three daily meals and pause for a coca break in midmorning and midafternoon. Although these coca breaks function much like our coffee breaks, the ceremony surrounding them has social and religious dimensions that the coffee break lacks. If we said grace over our coffee and exchanged cups the similarity would be stronger. Coca chewers share *k'intus* with each other in a tangible expression of their social and moral relationship, while simultaneously sharing the leaf's *sami* with the Earth and the Sacred Places.

The social group is defined and organized by the *k'intu* exchanges, for social ranking is implied by the order in which *k'intus* are offered. High status individuals should receive *k'intus* before those of lower status. In practice, the relative status of participants is seldom clear-cut. Men rank higher than women, but age ranks higher than youth. A respected old lady may receive *k'intus* before a callow young man (who may or may not feel slighted by the action). Guests rank higher than coresidents, and the passing of many *cargos* ranks higher than marginal participation in the *cargo* system. Wealth itself confers high status only indirectly, by facilitating the passage of many *cargos*. The size of the gathering and the distance the participants are seated from one another are complicating factors. One should rise and carry *k'intus* to a very high status person, whereas companions of equal status who sit at a distance may be politely bypassed.

Any actual coca chewing session calls for a complicated spur-of-the-moment combination of various criteria, forcing each participant to organize the situation in hierarchical terms. Conversely, each person is put in his place by his companions. *K'intu* exchanges therefore define a gathering of individuals as a social group; they commit each individual—for the duration of the *hall-*

pay, at least—to group membership, and they situate him or her relative to other participants.

In Sonqo a respected *kuraq tayta* (community elder) like Don Inocencio Quispe can expect to join a gathering and receive *k'intus* from all of the coca chewing adults, even when they have to rise to bring the *k'intu* to him. Inocencio has long passed the essential *cargos,* including those of *alcalde* and Corpus Christi sponsor. He is a hardworking, vigorous man in late middle age, strong-minded, pious, and well-to-do. He is reputed to have seen the cathedral submerged in Lake Q'eskay, a sight vouchsafed only to the virtuous. His attendance at the ceremonial table at all public occasions is taken for granted.

If more than one elder is present, one tries to prepare their *k'intus* at the same time and present the first to the elder sitting nearest. These elders may precede community officials with the exception of the *alcalde* who, when he is present in his official capacity, always takes precedence.

I found that I was ranked in various ways: as the person of highest status in the group; as the woman of highest status (that is, on the border between men and women); or occasionally as the person of lowest status. The older, more traditionally minded men consistently ranked me with the women even when, as a trouser-clad guest, I was seated with the men. Don Francisco Quispe used to pass me by with a significant glance, and once when I got up and sat on the ground next to his daughter he muttered his audible approval. Women often preferred to treat me as the highest ranking woman rather than as a man. *Runakuna* who did not like my being there shared their *k'intus* with me last, usually only in response to my offering one first. A *k'intu* does not go unreciprocated, even from persons one dislikes.

All this changed when I switched from blue jeans to the traditional black *pollera* (skirt). Suddenly everyone ranked me as a woman—usually as a young, low-ranking woman. By putting aside my Westernized man's clothing I lost my senior status, a move that was met with universal approval (among *Runakuna,* that is; the schoolteachers were horrified). The lower status was, in its way, a compliment and a mark of acceptance.

Since it is important that a coca chewing session be respectful, relaxed, amicable, and meditative, *Runakuna* rarely use coca chewing etiquette to harass one another. Occasionally it seemed to me that one individual, with malice of forethought, presented a companion with *k'intu* after *k'intu,* forcing the recipient to spend the whole session composing and offering *k'intus* in return. Such villainy is easily thwarted when the teaser is of lower status, as the victim can simply stop reciprocating. Sometimes I felt put upon when a group of three or four chewers showered *k'intus* upon me at the same time, forcing me: (1) to decide from whom to accept the first *k'intu*; (2) to receive the *k'intus,* complete with *phukuy,* in rapid succession; not to mention (3) to set to work composing and offering *k'intus* as fast as possible, surely a comical sight. Nevertheless, I am not sure my companions intended to torment me. I have seen elders join a group and receive the same treatment, simply by virtue of their late arrival.

Orientation in Space and Time

K'intu sharing cements a relationship with the fellow members of one's group, whereas *phukuy* draws the human actor into a relationship with the Earth and the Sacred Places. The invocation of animated geography provides a particular kind of orientation in space. The "grammar" of *phukuy* requires that one call upon the vast, generalized Earth, upon local Places, and upon more distant regional Places. *Runakuna* orient themselves within a nested, hierarchical sense of space as they direct their attention to local Places who punctuate their landscape, as well as to the high *Apus* who overlook a larger region.

When *Runakuna* travel they approach unfamiliar *Tirakuna* in other localities with a mixture of interest and apprehension. They know these Places are likely to look upon outsiders with hostility, or at best with indifference. They assiduously blow their *k'intus* to the new locality by way of introducing themselves. Basilia was doing me a favor when she instructed me to blow my coca to Antaqaqa as I first entered Sonqo. On another occasion, I upset my companions by wandering off while they were doing *phukuy* in the high *puna* before crossing a bad-tempered mountain pass named Panapunku. My disregard for the placation of important and hostile powers could have gotten us all in trouble.

In contrast, when *Runakuna* chew coca during their routine activities, with familiar *Tirakuna* around them, their *phukuys* are brief and pro forma. A chewer simply whispers under his breath while blowing the leaves, without calling attention to the words. A loud, elaborate *phukuy* is likely to be directed as much to one's companions as to the *Tirakuna*. The invocation provides a way to confide anxieties without having to admit them directly. For example, the night before he was to travel to Cuzco for a confrontation with a Mestizo official, Don Luis blew over his *k'intu* asking that he might have a good trip. This expressed his nervousness and opened the way for supportive behavior on our part without his having to come out and say, "I'm scared." In other contexts, one may find a whole group of chewers passionately, if quietly, asking the *Tirakuna* to make it stop raining, to help them find their lost animal, and so forth. In this way, they commiserate over their troubles, create an atmosphere of mutual support, and assure each other of their good will.

Phukuy provides a good opportunity to show off rhetorical prowess (Rufina used to giggle appreciatively when Luis launched into a long-winded *phukuy*). The best invocations, however, use verbal artistry to impress one's companions while, at a deeper level, communicating precise information to the *Tirakuna*. The following poetic invocation by Erasmo reveals a dense semantic structure:

Pacha Tira Mama, Machula Aulanchis, Aukikuna. Manan para paramanchu tarpunaypaq.

(*Pacha Tira Mama, Machula Aulanchis, Aukikuna.* Don't let it rain on my potato planting.)

107

Every word of this invocation expresses Erasmo's preoccupation with planting. The word order is significant as well. *"Pacha Tira"* shows his awareness that the Earth may be dangerous during planting time, and he placates her with the addition of *"Mama."* He then calls on *Machula Aulanchis,* who as fertilizing ancestors concerned with the potato crop are particularly important to Erasmo at the moment. He calls on the Sacred Places last, using a generic title, *Aukikuna,* which is occasionally applied to the ancestors as well as to the local Places. The invocation orients Erasmo to his current activities by communicating his intentions and needs to the categories of deities most important to him at that moment.

The *Runakuna* orient themselves similarly each time they chew coca before beginning work. Coca chewing focuses their minds on the task and helps them articulate its nature. Coca chewing also marks off the passage of time. The length of a chew, about forty-five minutes, can be used as a temporal unit. The sequence of coca chewing sessions—after breakfast, in midmorning, after the midday meal, in midafternoon, and at night after dinner—divides the day into longer intervals.

On a more distant, or greater, dimension of time, the invocation of the *ayllu* directs the chewer to ancestral and parental-like figures such as *Machula Aulanchis* and Antaqaqa. Moreover, the act of chewing coca declares the chewer's cultural loyalty to and identification with traditions handed down from the Incas, beings of the past and future, who are hidden from the present.

In *phukuy, Runakuna* orient themselves to local and distant geography by entering into a personal relationship with Sacred Places. Since space and time are isomorphic for them, *Runakuna* orient themselves in local (or immediate) time and in distant time as well. Through these actions they are also oriented relative to their fellows.

The Social Contract

The *ayllu,* in its most general definition, is a group of individuals cohering as a social body around a place, ancestor, or task that provides a unifying focus. The ceremony of *hallpay,* in which participants exchange *k'intus* and share the coca's *sami* with Sacred Places, provides the framework within which this social cohering takes place.

All reciprocity has a symbolic aspect; an exchange of any kind expresses a relationship between the people involved. *K'intu* exchanges carry a particularly heavy symbolic load. In economic terms the value of the exchanged leaves is negligible. But while the economic aspect of the exchange is minimized, the symbolic aspect is maximized, for the exchange seals a social contract.

A request to do *ayni* is accompanied by a handful of coca, and once the coca is accepted, refusing the job is unthinkable. Similarly, a man chosen for a *cargo* signifies his agreement to serve when he accepts the coca bundle offered by the *alcalde*. A marriage contract is sealed when the groom's parents visit the bride's with presents of coca and alcohol.

In these contexts, refusal of the proffered coca signifies refusal of the contract. When Alcides refused the *alcalde*'s coca bundle during the Eustaquio crisis, his *ayllu*-mates understood that he wanted to withhold acceptance of the *cargo* until he was sure Eustaquio would not take on the *alcalde*ship. But to refuse coca in routine *hallpay* is to deny human intercourse—or at least to reject interaction with the other on an equal and amicable footing as comembers of a group.

When Luis vehemently insisted that the school was no longer an *ayllu* because Mestizo schoolteachers lived there, I asked him about myself and Rick. Did we belong to an *ayllu*? Luis replied that we were members of Pillikunka *ayllu* because we lived like *Runakuna* and chewed coca.

Three characteristics—to live as a *Runa*, to belong to an *ayllu*, and to chew coca—are intrinsically connected, for it is through coca that the relationship between people and their locality is maintained. It is understandable, therefore, that Sonqo *Runakuna* find the increasing shortage and high price of coca a great hardship. To be without coca is, for them, inconceivable.[3]

Among *Runakuna* the social contract is continually resealed, since adults chew coca several times a day in various contexts. *Hallpay* is a deeper contract than that expressed by the greetings, farewells, thank-yous, and expressions of esteem that frame virtually every encounter. It is deeper because coca itself is a sacred substance with a powerful *sami*, whose consumption creates communion among human beings and between humans and deities. Sonqueños explicitly point out this aspect of coca chewing. Coca is the quintessential Andean sacrament; they call it *hostia*, the host, in an explicit analogy with the Catholic communion service.

"Sacraments are not only signs, but essentially different from other signs, being instruments."[4] Mary Douglas's statement certainly holds true for the coca leaf as well as for the wine and the wafer of Christianity. From the perspective of the participants in *hallpay*, coca plays both symbolic and instrumental functions. Coca chewing is not only a sign of orderly social relations; it is also an instrument through which these relations are defined, created, and maintained. Through coca, the Earth, the Places, and the Ancestors are integrated with human society.

As a channel for communication with the powers that be, coca has far-reaching pragmatic effects on existence. *Runakuna* monitor their relationship with the Sacred Places through the vicissitudes of fortune: tripping, losing a sheep, getting caught in the rain, getting lost in the fog—all are signs of something amiss in the relationship. To avoid such an unbalance, *Runakuna* blow on their *k'intus*. It is not surprising that my first and longest stay in Sonqo began and ended with lessons in *phukuy*.

Coca, the Transmitter

Pacha and the *Tirakuna* communicate with human beings via coca, but not everyone knows how to interpret the messages encoded in the leaves. *Coca qhaway* ("looking at coca," the art of coca divination) takes years of study and practice, as well as a lot of inspiration.

Most Sonqueños know the rudiments of coca divination, but in serious matters—like severe illness or plotting the course of an important action—they turn to a specialist. Unlike *hallpay,* a ceremony carried out by all adults as part of their routine, *coca qhaway* is an extremely serious act that is performed in secret. In 1984, nine years after I first came to Sonqo, Erasmo offered to teach me about coca divination with the admonishment that knowing a little about *coca qhaway* is worse than knowing nothing at all. Some people, he remarked, think they know more than they really do and divine badly. They take advantage of people and pronounce falsehoods.

I asked Erasmo whether he objected to my writing down what I learned from him. To the contrary, he rather liked having his instruction written down—as long as I wrote it in English and published it in my country, where Sonqo *Runakuna* would not know about it. My fellow gringos could not misuse it, Erasmo said, since they don't have coca anyway.

Erasmo showed me two kinds of *coca qhaway:* one to determine the cause of illness and the other to determine the nature of events distant in space and time. This second type of *qhaway* predicts how one's luck will hold, reveals the causes of past events (the identities of thieves, for example), and tells how distant loved ones are doing.

Both types of *qhaway* are preceded by an invocation. The *paqo* (diviner) calls on *Pacha Mama* and on the *hatun Rurgrarkuna* (the great Places) of his client's locality. Erasmo insisted that I tell him the names of Places where I lived in the United States, explaining that without them the coca would not "know" the answers to his questions. He explained that the *qhaway* process was the reverse of *phukuy:* in *phukuy,* human beings send messages to the Places via coca's *sami;* in *qhaway,* the Places send messages to humans via configurations of coca leaves.

The opening invocation may be long and poetic, praising the Earth and the Places, explaining the client's problem, and asking for their advice. The invocation invariably ends with the cry *"Sut'ita willaway!"* ("Tell me clearly!") as the diviner dramatically throws down his coca bundle or handful of coca, depending on the type of divination.

In both types of *qhaway,* the coca-carrying cloth *(unkhuña)* serves as a field against which the diviner interprets configurations of leaves. To divine distant events, he spreads the cloth before he begins and places a coin in its center. This is the *ñawin* (eye). Taking a handful of leaves with his right hand, the diviner lets the coca run through his fingers onto the coin. Then he studies the configurations carefully to understand their meaning. Leaves landing right side up or pointing to the right are good signs; those falling upside down or point-ing to the left are bad. The diviner picks out certain leaves as significant, as standing for particular individuals or objects. A large leaf with a small leaf on top of it, for example, was me with my "cargo" of stories to carry back to the States.

The *paqo* divining *unqoqpaq* (for a sick person) invokes the deities while holding the filled coca-carrying cloth folded first in half and then in thirds. As he cries *"Sut'ita willaway!"* he pulls forcefully on the ends three times, with a cracking noise and a puff of dust. Then he throws down the bundle and opens it to reveal a configuration of leaves explaining the nature of the ill-ness and its prognosis. Again, leaves shiny side up and pointing to the right are good signs, whereas those upside down and pointing leftward are bad. A large leaf sitting apart from the others can indicate the patient. If it points away from the diviner the patient "is going away" *("ripushan")* and will die; if it points toward the diviner the patient "is turning back" *("kutimushan")* and will recover. A leaf folded over at both ends shows that the patient is *"Tira hap'isqan"* ("seized by the Earth") and should make a *despacho* (burnt offer-ing). Leaves falling perpendicularly in a cross are very good signs. Irregularly folded leaves indicate great sickness, whereas leaves folded neatly along the middle indicate health.

There are other signs I have not learned, some of which concern sorcery, but in general the code is fairly limited in terms of its repertoire of signs. The difficulty of *qhaway* lies in learning how to interpret the configurations of leaf signs *within the context of the given situation*. This is where the diviner's inspira-tion and experience come into play, and why it is easy to read coca badly (for the basic vocabulary of signs is easily learned) and extremely hard to read coca well. Since coca reading is context-dependent, the meaning of any given con-figuration will vary according to the person for whom it is read and his or her situation. The *paqo* must astutely apply all his knowledge and insight con-cerning his client if he is to successfully interpret what the coca has to tell him.

Obviously, coca reading provides great opportunities for quackery; but a quack *paqo*—who simply takes his clients' money to tell them what they want to hear—will eventually fall into disrepute as his diagnoses are recognized as mistaken or unhelpful. A diviner can encourage his client in the course of a reading, but he may also force the recognition of unpleasant truths and pre-scribe difficult changes in behavior. A good diviner studies a situation before he agrees to even go ahead with a reading.

In 1984 a Mestizo official from Colquepata sought out Erasmo's services. The official's wife was refusing to cook for him, and he believed her to be *layqasqa* (bewitched). He wanted Erasmo to divine the source of the spell. Erasmo talked to the official for a long time and finally refused to do the read-ing, explaining that he did not think sorcery was involved and suggesting that the official try treating his wife better. The man went off annoyed to find an-other *paqo*. In the short run Erasmo's response resulted in the official's an-tipathy, but in the long run it may be recognized as the more helpful insight.

The fact that the *paqo* draws on his own knowledge of the client and his problem to interpret the coca leaves does not mean that he or she cynically uses the *qhaway* as a kind of mumbo-jumbo to validate his own guesses. As far as a diviner and his client are concerned, coca always knows the answers. In other words, the configurations of leaves are always meaningful; the *paqo*'s problem is to focus all his knowledge and insight in order to perceive what the meaning is.

Learning to be a *Runa*

All adult skills are said to have been invented by specific Saints (see Chapter 1). *Hallpay,* one of the most significant of these skills, was invented by one of the greatest Saints, Mamacha Santisima María (Holy Mother Mary; see Introduction). The person who is *santuyuq* (skillful, possessed of the Saint) in coca chewing has established contact with the *mamacha*'s creative virtue and her consoling power. Properly chewed, the leaves absorb grief and pain and comfort the chewer like a mother.[5]

As with other skills, one becomes *santuyuq* in coca chewing by reinventing the activity through a long if playful process of trial and error. Although children are excluded from routine *hallpay* until well into their teens, they display great interest in coca chewing. They enjoy helping their parents share *k'intu*s by carrying the leaves proudly and carefully from one adult to the other. Sometimes children sit next to an open coca bundle, trying with great concentration to put the leaves together into a respectable *k'intu*. Parents criticize their children's handiwork and usually reject the *k'intu*s, showing them leaves they have placed wrong side up or pointing out that they have used brown and broken leaves while better ones were left in the bundle.

Children are often included in the preparation of the ritual offering bundles burned on the eve of certain festivals. Brimming with excitement, they gingerly chew the leaves and prepare *k'intu*s to be offered to Pacha and the *Tirakuna*. Thus, their first full participation in coca chewing begins, not with routine *hallpay,* but in the intensified context of family ritual. Later, as adolescents, they will be included in routine *hallpay* as they begin working with adults on grown-up tasks. Boys are invited to chew as they participate in work parties on an equal footing with men; likewise, girls are offered *k'intu*s as they take on adult responsibilities among women cooking for a festival or a work party.

Hallpay and *hallpay* manners suffuse the atmosphere in which *Runakuna* grow up and in which they absorb their culture. *Hallpay*'s dense symbolism unifies diverse dimensions of a *Runa*'s physical, mental and emotional experience. Since the symbols are actions, an individual is put in the position of "acting out" basic cultural principles, of entering several times a day into a contract to participate in *Runa* tradition. As Goffman says,"when an individual becomes involved in the maintenance of a rule, he tends also to become committed to a particular image of self."[6] Coca chewing etiquette, a set of collectively held rules of conduct, reveals a process of self-definition on the part of *Runakuna*.

"How can we know the dancer from the dance?" The *Runa* self is formulated in and through the "dance" of *hallpay*. When a *Runa* decides to become a *Misti*, he turns from coca chewing to new cultural dance and a different definition of self.[7]

Chapter Five

Drinking Together

Three Examples

In August the parched Earth cracks open to drink the first rains, which slowly return after the sunny, dusty months of June and July. In September planting begins, and in October and November the potatoes, beans, *tarwi* (small beans resembling chickpeas), barley, and oats sprout and begin to decorate the brown hills with patches of green. December, January, and February are the wettest and leanest months. There is almost no fresh food; the crops are still in the ground, and Sonqo *Runakuna* live on *ch'uño*. On 30 November each family eats a big dinner called *wiksa wisq'ay* (closing the stomach). Adults and children alike stuff themselves in what may be their last chance to eat well until Carnival week in February or early March. By that time the first potatoes and *ullucus* are in; *tarwi*, the Carnival season staple, is soaking in little pools; and corn is available in the valley for making *aha* (corn beer), which Spanish speakers call *chicha*.

Sitting behind a ceremonial table, the *alcalde* receives his *ayllu*-mates during Carnival. On the table are two wooden goblets called *qeros*, a low clay bowl called a *puchuela*, a bundle of coca, and a three-pronged whip. The *alcalde*'s silver-studded staff is thrust into the ground at the table's right. His wife and mother sit on the ground to his left with pitchers of *chicha*, a big bundle of coca, and pots of food. In front of the table is another *chicha* jar; two barefoot youths sit next to it, facing the *alcalde*.

The *alcalde* rises to serve *chicha*. The youths fill the goblets and place them on the table. He surveys the gathering, particularly a group of new arrivals, and summons the oldest male among them.

"Taytay Inocencio, hamuy aha ukyaq" ("Father Inocencio, come drink some *chicha*"). Inocencio approaches, hat in hand.

The *alcalde* holds out a *qero,* saying *"Ukyayukuy, Taytáy"* ("Please drink, Father").

Inocencio accepts with thanks: *"Yusulpayki, diospagarasunki Taytay Alcalde"* ("Thank you, may God repay you, Father *Alcalde*").

He dribbles some *chicha* onto the corners of the table. Then he pours some onto the ground for *Pacha* and flicks some into the air for the *Tirakuna*.

Then he offers the wooden goblet back to the *alcalde,* saying, *"Ukyakusun-chis"* ("Let's drink together").

The *alcalde* takes a sip and returns the goblet with thanks. Inocencio may go on to offer sips to other people before he drinks down the remaining *chicha* in a single gulp and returns the qero to the *alcalde,* thanking him profusely.

But the *alcalde* presents him with another *qero of chicha,* and after that with the low clay bowl, the *puchuela*. Only after having downed the third drink does Inocencio return to his place. He sits down, claps his hat back on his head, and the ritual is repeated with another visitor.

Meanwhile, the *alcalde's* wife has been calling over the visiting women and presenting them with *chicha* in the same manner. After the *alcalde* has served all of the men he calls over a few of the women. The women, however, never call over men.

When all the newcomers have received *chicha,* the *alcalde* and his wife begin distributing handfuls of coca leaves, following much the same procedure used in offering *chicha,* except that recipients of coca do not chew their leaves while standing before the ceremonial table. Each accepts with thanks, gathers the leaves in the folds of poncho or skirt, and carries the leaves back to his or her place.

Then they each chew coca quietly and privately. When the *alcalde* has finished the distribution, they begin to exchange coca *k'intus,* first sharing with the *alcalde* and then with each other, quietly blowing each *k'intu* with invocations.

After about half an hour the women break out the food, and the coca wads are discreetly discarded. The young men carry dinner plates to the guests, and when this meal has been eaten, another round is served.

After two rounds of food the drinking continues. The *alcalde* turns the distribution of *chicha* over to his two assistants, who also produce *trago.* Some of the older men begin to play long, deep-voiced flutes, snare drums, and the *bombo* (base drum). One couple begins to dance, then another and another. When the musicians tire, the *alcalde* turns on his battery-run record player that is attached to a loudspeaker (also battery-run) perched on the thatched roof of his adobe house. The sky clouds over, the rain pours down, and the people continue drinking and dancing.

115

Drinking and dancing and chewing coca.

Hours later, exhausted and flecked with mud, the people gradually disperse. In couples or small groups, the intoxicated dancers reel homeward.

A small group of *Runakuna* on the way home from Sunday market stops to rest a few kilometers from Colquepata, pulling out their coca bundles and chatting quietly as they share *k'intus*. Eventually someone rummages in his bundle of purchases and produces a shot glass *(copita)* and a bottle of *trago* stoppered with an old corn husk.

"*Machakusunchisyá!*" ("Let's really get drunk!"), he exclaims, raising the shot glass with a grin.

"*Amayá! Huq copitalla!*" ("Don't say that! Just one round!"), his companions reply.

One woman hurriedly gathers her things and scurries off, calling goodbyes and excuses over her shoulder. The others yell after her teasingly, but let her go.

The owner of the *trago* pours a shot, dribbles some onto the ground, flicks a few drops into the air, and downs the drink. Then he pours another and offers it to the most senior person present.

"*Tomakuy Taytáy*" ("Please drink, Father"), he says.

"*Gras urpíy*" ("Thanks, my friend"; literally, "my dove"), his companion answers. He performs the libation and salutes the company.

"*Salud, tomanki!*" ("Cheers, you drink!").

"*Tomakuy*" ("Please drink"), they reply.

He gulps down the shot, and the round continues. Again and again, the donor of the *trago* pours the shot, proffers the shot glass, and receives the glass back again.

After a few rounds the bottle is empty. Another person produces a bottle, asks to borrow the shot glass, and serves out the *trago*. By that time, pleasantly tipsy, they are eager to continue drinking, but no one else is forthcoming with *trago*. Serafeo has some in his bundle, but he keeps this information to himself, hoping no one will hear the bottles clinking as he picks up his load and sets off. The *trago* is for his son's haircutting ritual, and he has no intention of emptying the bottle on an idle afternoon.

Basilia is sitting in front of her house sorting seed potatoes and fussing. Gabriel went off to P'isaq two days ago and has not yet returned. She fears the worst. Surely he got drunk and was beaten up and robbed. And then the *guardia* put him in jail. Or maybe a labor recruiter got him drunk enough to sign up for work on a lowland plantation. If that happened he may not get home for a year. These men, these men, they always drink when they go to town. He shouldn't have gone alone.

"*Ay, Runay Runay!*" she whispers. "*Lakikushani anchata!*" ("Oh my *Runa*, my *Runa!* I'm so worried!").

But Gabriel comes bursting into the courtyard. On his back is a large, heavy tin of *trago* I hardly would have thought two men could carry up the steep ascent from P'isaq. For his expedition he had put aside his *Runa p'acha* (*Runa* clothing) and donned a dirty gray suit about three sizes too big.

He is roaring drunk. Weeping drunk. Stamping and screaming drunk. With the *trago* still on his back he dances around the courtyard in circles.

"They called me an Indian dog! An Indian dog!" Tears are streaking his dusty cheeks. "'Where did you get this money?' they asked me. 'Whose clothes are those you've stolen?' they asked me. Their children threw stones at me. They called me a dog! Called me a dog!"

The circles diminish in size and velocity, and Gabriel finally sets down the *trago*. Still crying, he staggers into the house and collapses onto the bed.

Radiant with relief, Basilia follows him inside and lights the fire in her *q'uncha*.

How to Drink in Sonqo

Alcohol consumption in the Andes varies considerably according to a community's altitude, prosperity, and its incorporation into the money economy.[1] In Sonqo, three types of alcoholic beverage are consumed:

Chicha (*aha* in Quechua) is made only for special occasions. In this respect Sonqo differs from maize-producing communities in the valleys, where drinking *chicha* is part of the daily routine. In Sonqo, *chicha* is a luxury drink served at public celebrations of the *ayllu*, like Carnival, and often at household celebrations as well. Sonqo *Runakuna* get maize for their *chicha* from relatives or *compadres* in lower-altitude communities, who trade their maize for potatoes or *ch'uño*, or sell it for cash. Occasionally Sonqueños buy maize for their *chicha* in the markets of Cuzco, Colquepata, or P'isaq.

After it is carried back to Sonqo, the maize is left to sprout in large ceramic pots, and the sprouted kernels are then ground and boiled with water over a very hot fire. A little sugar is added, and the brew is left to ferment for a few days. Although the *chicha* produced in Sonqo's cold climate is far inferior to the rich drink of the valley communities, Sonqueños set great store by their *chicha*—thin, sour, and weak though it may be.

Trago (cane alcohol diluted to about 70 proof), on the other hand, is easily obtained in the small stores of Colquepata, P'isaq, and Cuzco. As a drink, *trago* is foul tasting, but it intoxicates rapidly and requires no preparation. Occasionally, individuals buy large tins to carry back laboriously to Sonqo to sell at a profit and to bask in temporary prestige as the local liquor supply. Where

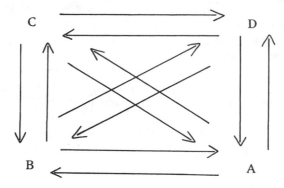

Figure 4. Symmetry of coca chewing etiquette.

trago is concerned, Sonqo fluctuates between feast and famine. July is the month of heaviest drinking, for the harvest is finally finished, the roads are dry and easily traveled, and *Runakuna* have both leisure time and cash gained from selling their produce.

Sonqueños also drink beer, which they consider prestigious but inefficient as an intoxicant and difficult to transport. Beer's uses are similar to those of *trago*, although beer is seldom used for ritual purposes.

Finally, most Sonqo *Runakuna* keep a small bottle of *vinu*, red wine or vermouth, hidden in the niches of their storerooms. *Vinu* is reserved for ritual offerings; I have never known *Runakuna* to drink it socially.

It is difficult, if not impossible, to live in an Andean community without drinking. As with coca, a willingness to drink and to share alcohol indicates a sociable attitude, and as with coca, it is important to drink according to prescribed ceremonial rules. Good drinking manners resemble coca chewing etiquette: both involve prescribed phrases of invitation and thanks; both require an offering to the Earth and the Sacred Places; and both begin in an unhurried, respectful atmosphere (though drinking quickly becomes more exuberant for obvious reasons). In drinking as well as in coca chewing, the act of sharing takes on central importance. Both also involve hierarchical ranking among members of the group.

There is an important difference between drinking and *hallpay*, however. In an *hallpay* session, all the participants exchange *k'intu*s with one another, whereas in a drinking session, alcohol is doled out by a single individual to the members of the group. Moreover, each person drinks individually and does not return the favor immediately. Reciprocity in drinking is asymmetrical; the donor is clearly distinguished from the recipients.

In coca chewing, on the other hand, the reciprocity is symmetrical among the participants (see Figure 4). The arrows indicate *k'intu*s. Each participant pairs up with each of the others to create a web of dyadic relationships. Each person chews from his or her own supply as well as from the others'.

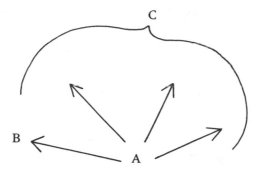

Figure 5. Asymmetry of drinking etiquette.

In drinking alcohol *(tomay* or *ukyay)*, a single host (A) doles out drinks to each guest (B, etc.) in succession; there is no immediate reciprocity except for thanks (see Figure 5). The arrows indicate drinks.

In any drinking interaction there are three participants: (A) the person who serves the drink; (B) the person who receives the drink; and (C) the other members of the group, who form an audience. The audience is an important element of the interaction; for example, B always salutes the audience (C), and they respond by urging him to drink. Moreover, B may offer sips of his drink to members of the audience to do them honor and sometimes to avoid drinking himself. In its most elaborate manifestation, the serving and consumption of a single shot of *trago* may involve the following ten steps:

Juan is the server, with a bottle of *trago* and a shot glass; Mario is the recipient; Valentino is a member of the audience.

(1) Juan to Mario: *"Tomakuy"* (Please drink"). Offers the shot glass to Mario.
(2) Mario to Juan: *"Yusulpayki"* ("Thank you"). Accepts the shot glass with thanks.
(3) Mario to Valentino: *"Tomakusunchis"* ("Let's drink together"). Offers the shot glass to Valentino.
(4) Valentino to Mario: Accepts with thanks; sips; returns the shot glass to Mario.

Steps 3 and 4 may be repeated with other members of the audience within practical limits.

(5) Mario makes a libation to *Pacha* and the *Tirakuna*.
(6) Mario to the Audience: *"Tomanki"* ("You drink").
(7) Audience to Mario: *"Tomakuy"* ("Please drink").
(8) Mario drinks.
(9) Mario to Juan: Returns shot glass with thanks.
(10) Juan to Mario: *"Hinallatapis"* ("You're welcome").

The apparently similar phrases *"Tomakuy"* ("Please drink"), *"Tomakusunchis"* ("Let's drink together"), and *"Tomanki"* ("You drink") are not interchangeable (as I learned through many blunders).

"Tomakuy," or *"Ukyakuy,"* is a polite imperative (the root is *toma-*, *-ku* is a suffix indicating reflexivity and politeness; *-y* indicates the imperative). The use of this imperative is the prerogative of the person dispensing the drink, who may be the donor of the *trago* or a junior person doing the honors in the donor's stead. When, on occasion, a person dares to refuse a drink, he or she hands it back to the server saying *"Tomakuy."* Then the server must either keep pressing it on the refuser or must accept it himself by following the normal routine for accepting a drink.

If the first recipient (B) gives his drink to a companion (D) with the word *"Tomakuy"* (rather than *"Tomakusunchis"*), D is supposed to consider himself served the whole shot; he does the libation, drinks, and returns the shot glass to B, who then returns it to A (the original server). If B proffers it with the word *"Tomakusunchis,"* on the other hand, D should take only a tiny sip before handing it back to B. *"Tomakusunchis"* ("You and I will drink this together"), draws another person (D) into the interaction. (The suffix *-sunchis* is first person plural inclusive with the future sense.) Usually, only high status individuals are recipients of *"Tomakusunchis."*

When B salutes the audience (C) with the word *"Tomanki"* ("You drink"), he implies, "I am drinking for you; you drink when I drink." B expresses an identification with the audience; thus, although only one person drinks at a time, everyone drinks all the time in spirit.

Although each individual drinks in succession, the drinking is very much a communal process. The recipient may draw in other individuals and should not drink without saluting the company. *"Tomakusunchis"* and *"Tomanki"* stress the communal aspect of the drinking. Everyone, moreover, drinks from the same shot glass.

The person dispensing the drinks has the authority to give or to withhold, as well as to express, the hierarchical relations of those present by determining the order in which drinks are served. The server's use of the polite imperative emphasizes his control of the situation. At any one time there is a single donor and many recipients. The recipients are integrated into a group and related hierarchically to each other by the donor, to whom (or to whose substitute) the shot glass continually returns.

In routine *hallpay* etiquette, on the other hand, each individual is both donor and recipient of coca *k'intus*. Each person expresses his or her own version of the group's hierarchy, and in turn sees himself or herself placed hierarchically by each of the other participants. In drinking parties, by contrast, a single person determines the hierarchy. The Carnival example shows how this becomes important in public celebrations of the *ayllu*, when the *alcalde* distributes *chicha* to the community.

Hallpay is thus reminiscent of *ayni*, with its egalitarian emphasis and symmetrical reciprocity, whereas the drinking party is similar to *mink'a*. The recipient of alcohol cannot return the favor immediately, unlike the recipient of coca, who gives back *k'intu*s from his or her own coca supply. In the work parties called *mink'a*, a group of people works for a single host, who in this context is hierarchically superior to them all. He recompenses the workers for their labor in food and drink. In drinking parties the host presents the shot glass with the imperative *"Tomakuy."* The recipient obeys, going through a routine that binds the group into a community with spiritual beings who share the libation. This the host could not do alone. The drinking party is an inevitable aspect of the work party, and the drinking ceremony quite accurately expresses the *mink'a* aspect: the patron/host serving, the worker/guest receiving.

Like *hallpay*, the presentation of alcohol is an important way to seal new contracts. To accept a gift of alcohol is to know oneself compromised, and *Runakuna* seldom accept such gifts until they find out what it is they are agreeing to.

I had to learn this the hard way. One evening Don Apolinar invited me and Rick for dinner, and we happily agreed. Luis mumbled that we should find out what Apolinar wanted, but we assumed it was simply a friendly gesture. After serving us a fine dinner and plying us with *trago*, Apolinar asked us to cut his little daughter's hair, a request that could not be refused with good grace. This situation is typical, although a *Runa* would have been less easily duped. If both parties understand in advance what the request is to be, acceptance or rejection of the *trago* resolves the issue without the request's ever being mentioned.

The hierarchical and asymmetrical nature of drinking etiquette makes *trago* especially suited for purposes of requesting a favor. The solicitor, as the one who asks the favor, compensates for his subordinate position through his superior position in the drinking ceremony. The person solicited, as recipient of the *trago*, can only reciprocate by accepting the request. As in coca chewing, the invocation of sacred powers gives the debt a strongly moral character. By accepting a sanctified communion, the recipient agrees to shoulder moral responsibilities.

The Sipaskancha widow (in Chapter 3) got her way by cleverly manipulating the etiquette for receiving guests and accepting gifts of *trago*. The president could not reject her gift without rebuffing the women who had accepted and welcomed her into their gathering. But as it turned out, the women themselves were divided in their stand concerning the widow. Those who were against her could not throw her out once she had been welcomed, anymore than the men could; nor could they jump to their feet and object when the president accepted the *trago*.

It was with the dissenting women that the widow overstepped herself. After the men had finished drinking and agreed to help her, the widow produced another bottle of *trago* "for the *mamakuna*." She presented it to the *alcalde*'s wife, who was unsympathetic to her and refused the offer by staring stonily ahead. The widow persisted, but she finally had to give up and serve the *trago* herself. The *alcalde*'s wife sourly accepted the shot glass. Then the widow made the rounds of the women, presenting each with a shot of *trago*. Each woman's response expressed her opinion of the situation. Some accepted with smiles and thanks, others with poor grace. Rufina made a face and said the *trago* was terrible. Basilia and the widow entered into a long, ever-so-polite banter about who had better manners.

"Oh, little dove, *we* stay home where we belong."

"But, dear heart, *we* know how to receive our guests!"

It was clear that the majority of women were not in sympathy with the widow's request, but she won the day armed with *trago* and helped by a few strategically placed allies.

While *trago* is usually used to seal contracts between individuals or individual families (like the creation of marriage alliances or ties of *compadrazgo*), *chicha* is used in community celebrations. These celebrations seal a double contract: between the members of Sonqo *Ayllu* on one hand, and between the *ayllu* as a whole and its Sacred Places on the other.

At public rituals, libations of *chicha* provide a collective offering to *Pacha* and the *Tirakuna*. The sponsor provides *chicha*, which he presents to the *ayllu* in the person of the *alcalde*. As the *ayllu*'s representative, the *alcalde* distributes the *chicha* among the individual participants. Each drink is accompanied by a libation, and through many libations the *ayllu* shares the *samiincha* with its Sacred Places. The *alcalde*'s function is to distribute the *chicha*, rather than to offer the *chicha* himself on behalf of the *ayllu*. This distribution organizes and unifies the individual members of the *ayllu*, who offer the *chicha* themselves to *Pacha* and the *Tirakuna*.

Attitudes toward Intoxication

Coca chewing is felt to improve rather than impair one's ability to work. *Chicha* is an intoxicant (though a far less quick and effective one than *trago*), but in Sonqo this intoxication takes place within the contexts of religious celebrations and fulfills a religious function. Attitudes toward drinking *trago* are more complex, reflecting the wider range of behavior that results from getting drunk on *trago*.

It is striking how few channels there are in Quechua culture for the direct expression of negative emotions. Even the briefest interactions among *Runakuna* are framed by lavish (and to many Western sensibilities, syrupy and obsequious) expressions of mutual esteem. Greetings, farewells, and thank-yous are long, elaborate, and obligatory. During a conversation, the speakers constantly address each other as *"Taytáy," "Mamáy,"* or *"Urpíy,"* expressions of respect and endearment. Phrases like "Yes indeed, you're right," are generously sprinkled throughout conversation. This social obligation to shower others with constant endearment and reassurance creates an atmosphere in which it is virtually impossible to express negative feelings directly. As a result, the opportunities to express negative feelings indirectly, by manipulating the etiquette itself, assume great importance. The ceremony of drinking provides a particularly good opportunity to invert the outward display of esteem and drive home the knife with courtesy.

We have already seen how *trago* is used to pressure adversaries into unwelcome contracts, which is possible partly through the hierarchical superiority of the server to the recipient. But *trago* also tastes terrible and intoxicates rapidly, giving the server still another source of power: in the guise of honoring the recipient, the server can torment him and put him very much on the spot. The recipient knows that he is in danger of acting like a fool and being taken advantage of, yet he is hard put to avoid the shot glasses being thrust upon him.

All is not lost for the poor recipient, however, for *trago* is the one substance that can be refused with honor. To refuse coca is a veritable act of hostility; *chicha* may be poured into bottles and taken home, but cannot be refused. The recipient of unwanted *trago*, however, has avenues of escape if he knows how to use them. But he needs the cooperation of companions who will accept the drink for him, or—if he has the strength of character—he may press the shot back on the server (again under the guise of doing him honor). A drinking session thus develops into a deep game of oneupmanship.

Another form of oneupmanship is to challenge a companion's generosity. This often happens when a group is gathered in a place where *trago* is sold, or when people carrying *trago* meet and rest on the road together. Once one person offers a round of drinks or buys a bottle, the others are under pressure to do the same; not to do so leaves the first buyer in a superior position. A member of the group who should have contributed *trago* but did not is sarcastically reminded of the fact for days to come. I remember suffering through the lavish thanks of a young man when I served him half a bottle of *trago* that I had expressly saved and intended for other purposes. It went something like this:

Thank you, my dear, my mother, my lady. God will pay you, my dove. You give me half a bottle. Thank you, thank you. I don't mind if you don't give me the whole bottle, my dove, my little heart. I know you have plenty, but I don't mind. I'm content with only half, my little dove. I won't remember the other half, or tell anyone else that you didn't give it to me. I only thank you, my dove, my dear. God will pay you.[2]

Intoxication leads to various kinds of vulnerability. The most extreme situations of vulnerability occur when *Runakuna* drink among *Mistikuna*. In the context of the Mestizo town, the traditional functions of drinking within the *ayllu* are broken down. Basilia was not alone in complaining about her husband's market-day drinking. (Of course, she was not adverse to drinking on market day herself; but women in general confine their drinking to less exposed situations.) Men speak disapprovingly of their Sunday bashes, yet admit that they look forward to the break in the routine and the availability of liquor. The general assumption among *Runakuna* is that men, in particular, will drink whenever they get the chance. It is not the drinking itself that warrants dis-approval, but indiscretion about situations in which drinking takes place.

During his term as president, Don Luis once stayed in Colquepata for three days on a drinking binge. On his return he resumed his normal activities, sub-ject to no disapproval from his fellows beyond a relieved scolding from his wife. But he consumed no more alcohol for several weeks.

While men drink heavily when they drink at all, they are generally able to return to their appointed tasks without the interruption of a serious hang-over. I would not call more than a few Sonqueños chronic drinkers; rather, they are opportunistic drinkers. When alcohol is available they like to drink it, and they often continue drinking for as long as the supply lasts. In ritual, intoxication serves important religious purposes; but in many other situations, getting drunk is simply a temporary escape from life's hard work and sorrows and an excuse to release pent-up feelings. As long as opportunities to drink are limited, the situation contains its own check; when the booze runs out everything returns to normal. But as the availability of *trago* increases with im-proved transportation and access to cash, opportunistic drinking easily turns into chronic drinking. Alcoholism is not now a serious problem in Sonqo, but the potential is there. (See Afterword to the Second Edition.)

Alcides found Don Luis sound asleep on the road at night after his three-day binge in Colquepata. This is what particularly upset Rufina, for Luis could have frozen to death or been attacked by *sirenas* or *ñak'aqs*. One old venerable man of Colquepata, reputedly nearly a hundred years old, did meet his end this way after a drinking party.

Alcohol is expected to release expressions of grief or joy. One is expected to sing, dance, and weep while intoxicated. Crying while drunk is not only an emotional release; it is an expression of confidence in one's drinking com-panions. Often, too, festering hostilities, submerged under layers of praise and endearment, break out while *Runakuna* are drunk. While this is hardly sur-prising, it is noteworthy that drinking provides one of the few contexts in which displays of grief and anger are even tolerable. Moreover, tensions are exacerbated by the drinking etiquette itself, in which one person assumes a position of power vis-à-vis the rest of the group.

There is one context in which the act of drinking—as opposed to drunken behavior—is condemned. Solitary drinking is seen not only as a sign of self-indulgence and unsociability, but as strange, sorcererlike behavior. Drinking, like *hallpay*, is fundamentally an act that expresses social bonds, and when no other humans are present the drinking companions must be, by implication, spiritual beings.

Drinking with the *Tirakuna*

As a general rule, Andean people feel that anything that is consumed should also be shared, if not with one's fellow human beings, then with *Pacha* and the

Tirakuna. Even the *samincha* of cooked food rises in its smoke, and *Runakuna* often do a ritual blowing over a plate of food before consuming it. With coca, of course, they share the *samincha* by blowing across the leaves. Alcohol, too, has a strong *sami* that must be shared with others, including the Earth and the Sacred Places.

Gregorio Condori, a Cuzco street porter whose life history was recorded by two Peruvian anthropologists, tells us how a *Runa* married Apu Ausangate's daughter. He offered her a glass of *chicha* as though she were a normal woman.

> But the wife didn't want to drink; she would have been more receptive if he had made her an offering of *samincha.* Because, before you eat or drink anything, you have to blow its scent to the Earth and *Machu Awkikuna,* who are nourished on fragrant offerings of *samincha.* As she was an *apu*'s daughter, she wanted him to make her an offering of *samincha* so that she could savor the *chicha* that we drink. But the stupid man didn't understand that.[3]

And so the *Runa* lost his wife, along with his luck and his prosperity.

Runakuna sometimes blow across the top of their drink, but more often they offer the *samincha* through libations. To *Pacha,* they pour a few drops directly on the ground; this is called *ch'allay.* To the *Tirakuna,* they flick drops into the air; this is called *t'inka.* Another type of libation, reserved for animals during their fiestas, is *ch'uyay* (purification), the flinging of *chicha* onto the herds.

Erasmo insisted that he could tell stories well only at night, with the aid of coca and *trago.* After blowing over his coca leaves, he would spill out some *trago* to *Pacha Mama,* asking that he might speak well. Then he would flick some drops into the air, calling aloud on the *Apus,* asking them, too, to help him speak. Once shared, the *sami* would return to him, inspiring his memory and performance. Weavers, as well, offer the *samincha* of coca and alcohol before they begin a new piece, calling not only on the Earth and the Places, but on the *awaq mamachas* (female weaver saints). *"Makiykiwan awasaq"* ("Let me weave with your hands"), they say.

But the sharing goes further. It is not only *Pacha* and the *Tirakuna* who want to drink. The whole world is thirsty for alcohol's *sami.* Newly manufactured objects also receive libations. When she had finished building a stove in her new house, Basilia gave it a *ch'allay,* saying:

Purisima Mamacháy,	Purest Little Mother,
Allinta mihuchinki,	You will feed
wayk'unki.	and cook well.
Noqata mihuchinki	You'll feed me,
ichaqa!	won't you!

When an honored guest has a table set for him, he does *ch'allay* to the four corners of the table, and when *Runakuna* drink at the ceremonial table during Carnival, they offer it a libation as well. The door of a new house receives libations from the participants at a houseraising. Newly woven textiles, or even cloth still on the loom, can receive libations.

Even machines, those curiously self-animated objects, receive libations. When Erasmo bought a radio in Cuzco, he was terribly eager to get it home and perform its *t'inka*. Carefully, he unwrapped the new purchase and poured *trago* on its four corners, calling on Sonqo and his neighborhood *ayllu* of Qhali-pampa, as well as on Sacsahuaman, Calle Sapphi, and the store where the radio was purchased.

"Kuska wiñasun" ("Let's grow together"), he exhorted. *"Ama malogra-punki"* ("Don't break down").

Any manufactured object has gone through a transformation from raw material to finished product, during which its maker—the *kamayuq*, the one who possesses creativity—imbues it with a selfhood that must be treated with respect. We know that the house is thought to be alive, "like a mother hen"; she is made from the Earth, but given an independent selfhood by the people who built her and are sheltered within her. Similarly, Basilia addressed her stove as "Little Mother." Textiles, too, take on a selfhood imparted them by the saints who guide the weaver's hand and inspire her artistic imagination.

The idea that an object's creator imbues it with the life-force is an old one in the Andes. Certain Moche ceramics, made around A.D. 600, carry scenes in which utensils are depicted as in rebellion against their owners. Basilia's plea to her new stove, "Cook well," and Erasmo's admonishment to the radio, "Don't break down," imply their sense of similar possibilities.[4]

At certain times during the year, each household renews the vitality of the animals and the objects on which the family depends. The family members offer the *samincha* not only to the Earth and the Sacred Places, but to their animals and fields, to their dead, to their *ch'uño*, and to the house itself. The *enqas* and *istrilla*s emerge from hiding to chew coca and drink with the family members. The *Tirakuna* are "fed" a special meal, the *despacho*. In this context the meaning of the intoxication and satiation so characteristic of Andean ritual becomes clearer. In these household rituals, *Runakuna* eat and drink not only for themselves, but for their households, for their *ayllu*, and for their animated cosmos.

Chapter Six

Rites of the Household

Puchusayki: Four Examples

The first time I set out for Sonqo I worried about getting enough to eat. I could only pack so many chocolate bars, oranges, and cans of tuna fish. But as it turned out, my problem was exactly the opposite: how to avoid the quantities of food that *Runakuna* force on their visitors. The food itself is not the problem. I like the soups of lamb broth and boiled potatoes, the heavy stews of minced *ullucu*s with hot pepper, the inevitable first course of small variegated potatoes boiled in their skins, the occasional treats of pork morsels or roast guinea pig. I can even tolerate *ch'uño*. But the quantities! How many times have I worked my way through a huge bowl of boiled potatoes, only to have it refilled again and again! Guests—as I learned most unforgettably—have not eaten enough until they have eaten too much.

"*Puchusayki,*" my hosts would say when I tried to avert the third and fourth helpings I saw headed my way. This is not quite translatable into English: "I'll too-much you." "I'll satiate you." "I'll give you more than enough."

When I stayed with a family for several days or weeks, the quantity of food diminished to reasonable amounts, but as an honored short-term guest I had to suffer. Erasmo was especially cruel. He even recorded himself and his family feeding me. They can be heard on tape describing the food and exhorting me to eat while the sound of my hapless chewing provides a background.

In early August the llamas have their special day. Their human masters sit in the corral to keep them company—drinking, chewing coca, and singing all the while. The llamas are decorated with tassels—a painful business, for the threads are sewn into their ears with needles. Then they get to drink a special alcoholic brew composed of *chicha, trago,* soup broth, barley mash, and several medicinal herbs. It takes at least two men to control the large, lurching animals as bottle after bottle of his *hampi* (medicine) is forced down their throats. Finally, thoroughly drunk, the llamas stagger out of the corral; following them is their retinue of tipsy humans, playing flutes and singing.

On All Souls' Day the dead visit their families and are served up a huge holiday meal of special foods. Delivering this meal to dead guests poses a problem, for they cannot be served directly—nor can they be held down, like the llamas, and forced to consume the food. The dead eat their meal through the agency of a *mihuq* (eater), a ritual specialist who knows the Catholic prayers for the dead. He gobbles down the dinner while intoning prayers that direct the food to its dead recipients. The *mihuq* is a conduit through which the food passes to the souls.

n 1978 I returned to Sonqo by myself. Luis's teenage daughter Felicha met me at the truckstop and led me to the new house in Towlakancha where Balvina—whom I had not previously met—greeted me warmly and served me up a fine huge dinner. I ate and ate, and eventually—feeling about to collapse on the floor—I tried to explain that I could not manage another helping. Felicha refilled my plate with merciless good humor.

"*Ricardoq wiqsanman wiqsaykimanta churanki,*" she instructed. "Put it from your stomach to Rick's stomach."

Puchullaña! ("Enough already!"). These examples provide ample illustration that something more is going on here than the lavish hospitality of very poor people. Consumption and overconsumption of edibles plays a key role in every ritual I have witnessed in Sonqo. For *Runakuna,* force-feeding is a ritual technique for effecting communication among different categories of being. Household rituals include eating, drinking, chewing coca, and making music to excess in order to bring different aspects of the animated cosmos into contact with one another and thus maintain the flow of life. Ritual force-feeding expresses Andean assumptions about the inseparability of matter and spirit. *Runakuna* feed the objects of their ritual attention while they themselves are eating and drinking to excess. Sometimes the eating is itself a way of feeding, as when the *mihuq* eats in order to feed the dead. The *mihuq*'s act is not a symbolic feeding, a feeding by proxy; as far as *Runakuna* are concerned, it is the real thing.[1]

Feeding the *Tirakuna*

The Earth and the Sacred Places have voracious appetites and must be continually nourished with small offerings of coca, alcohol, and food. At least three times a year they require a special meal in the form of a burnt offering, the *despacho*. Each household head prepares the offering privately, at night, in the company of his family.

Despachos are offered on the eve of animal fertility rituals: *Uwiha Ch'uyay*, for the sheep, held on the feast of San Juan (Saint John); and *Llama Ch'uyay*, for the llamas, held during the first two weeks of August for herds with a dominant male stud. Every family, whether or not they perform *Llama Ch'uyay*, offers a *despacho* in early August, preferably on the eve of August First, simply called *Agustu*, the day the Earth is at her liveliest and most sensitive.

Families who neglect their *despachos* and other offerings, or who prepare them improperly, leave themselves dangerously vulnerable to bewitchment. A *layqa* (sorcerer) who wishes to harm them may enlist the offended deities' assistance by offering a *despacho* wrapped in black paper, whose ingredients identify the intended victim and the desired injury. Families or individuals who encounter chronic bad luck or illness often suspect sorcery as the cause and offer extra *despachos* to placate *Pacha* and the *Tirakuna*, thus "turning aside" the *layqa*'s offerings.

Individuals who are about to undertake important or dangerous tasks also offer special *despachos*. In 1984, for example, Erasmo prepared a special *despacho* to ensure me a safe trip home.

Coca *k'intu*s constitute the foundation of the offering. A *k'intu* is offered for each member of the family, as well as for *Pacha*, *Wasitira*, and each of the local and distant *Apu*s. As far as I could tell, no fixed list of *Apu*s is invoked; the household head tries to include as many as he can recall, usually with his wife's help. The total number of *k'intu*s varies from between twenty and thirty.

The *k'intu*s are supplemented by other ingredients said to appeal to the powers that be. "The *Tirakuna* like everything that we like," they say—and so bread and candy often find their way into *despachos*. The bundle also includes substances we would never eat but which the *Tirakuna* find appetizing owing to their special properties or associations: tropical seeds, coca seeds, unspun wool, gilt paper, incense, fool's gold, shells, and starfish. In Cuzco's *hampi qhatu* (medicine market), one can buy prepared *despacho* bundles containing all these ingredients and more. From this array of potential offerings the household head selects only those suitable to the occasion. *Runakuna* call the selection process *hampi akllay* (choosing medicine). From the *despacho*'s contents, *Pacha* and the *Tirakuna* understand what is requested of them. There is no set recipe of ingredients, for each offering serves as an individual "message" specially composed to reflect the situation at hand.[2]

The minimal offering is very small, consisting only of coca *k'intus*, animal fat, and a pile of tiny black seeds of the *canihua* plant. Luis was terribly disturbed when he discovered that he had no *canihua* for his San Juan *despacho* and made a lengthy search of the house and storeroom, declaring the offering incomplete without it. As for the rest, "Well, if you don't have a lot of ingredients you don't do a big *despacho*." In ritual, as in other aspects of their lives, Sonqo *Runakuna* make do with what they have.

Libations of alcohol accompany the offering. Ideally a trio of beverages—*chicha, trago,* and *vinu*—should be included, but usually only *trago* is available. Libations are made outside the house (to *Pacha*), on the floor (to *Wasitira*), and on the spot where the offering is to be burned. If the offering is prepared in conjunction with fertility rituals for sheep or llamas, the family opens its bundle of *enqas* and places them next to the offering as it is being prepared. As *khuyaqkuna* (caring protectors), the *enqas*, too, must be nourished with coca *k'intus* and libations of alcohol.

Although the *despacho* has serious consequences for the family's well-being, its preparation takes place in a relaxed holiday atmosphere. When I think back to the awed and perhaps oppressive solemnity with which I approached my first *despacho,* I realize how strange and surprising this must have seemed to Luis, for the usual feeling is more like our Christmas morning than like a church service. Younger children give out *oohs* and *ahs* of excitement as the bundle of *enqas* is opened, and they scramble eagerly to examine and handle the little animals, squealing, *"Michisunchis, michisunchis!"* ("We're going herding, we're going herding!"). Don Luis placed a radio blaring loud popular songs beside the *enqas* and the ritual ingredients. Andean ritual requires a festive atmosphere: why should the *Tirakuna* feel attracted to a bunch of gloomy-faced wet blankets?

Nevertheless, the *despacho* is undertaken in dire earnestness. The holiday atmosphere is mandatory, for the family wants the *Tirakuna* to leave feeling well-disposed toward them. The barking of dogs, flickering of candle flames, and unusual noises are taken to signal the presence of unwanted and angry guests, for malignant as well as benevolent beings may be attracted by the offering's aroma. Francisco and his family stiffened in alarm when a dog barked outside during their *despacho* preparations and were relieved when the unexpected visitor turned out to be Alcides rather than a *kukuchi*. Somewhat embarrassed, Alcides came in and made animated small talk throughout the proceedings as if to demonstrate his innocent intentions.

Hampi akllay (preparation of the *despacho*) follows a fairly set procedure. The family gathers around an empty woven sack *(costal)* placed on the floor.[3] A good coca-carrying cloth *(unkhuña)* filled with coca leaves is placed on the sack, along with a clean white piece of paper destined to enfold the offering. The father orients the square piece of paper so that one corner points toward him, and the opposite corner points away from him. For a while the family chews coca from the *unkhuña*, offering one another carefully prepared *k'intu*s.

Suddenly everyone starts grabbing small handfuls of leaves and cramming them furiously into each other's mouths. *"Hallpanki!"* ("You chew!"), they exclaim, rather than the usual *"Hallpakusunchis"* ("Let's chew together"). This is *hallpachikuy,* forced coca chewing; it means literally to make each other chew coca. Finally everybody ends up with impossibly big mouthfuls of coca, and they sit around grunting and groaning and giggling at each other until the wads are chewed down to a manageable size. Then the chewed wads *(hachu)* are placed inside the woven sack.

When calm returns, the father turns to the bundle of *enqa*s, placing three-leaved coca *k'intu*s under and over them. This coca is wrapped up with the little animals to nourish them until the next *despacho.* The family continues to chew coca from the carrying cloth, exchanging *k'intu*s according to normal coca chewing etiquette. These chewed wads, too, are placed in the sack.

The father then turns to preparation of the *despacho,* carefully choosing the best leaves for his *k'intu*s. The whole family joins in, and the children are scolded when they choose ragged or discolored leaves. While his family laughs and talks, the father focuses his attention on the *despacho.* He blows each *k'intu* with great intensity, adding an invocation under his breath. Then he places the *k'intu* on the piece of white paper.[4] It is a tiring process, and he may have to stop and rest. Once the *k'intu*s are completed, he chooses the other ingredients and places them on top of the *k'intu*s. All the while his family continues to chew coca, and the adults share a few shots of *trago* while quietly discussing the *despacho* ingredients. Occasionally his wife points out ingredients she thinks should be used.

The father then opens a bottle of *trago* and pours a shot, which he carries outside the house to do a libation "for the Earth." He also does a libation on the floor of the house, on the four corners of the sack, and on the *enqa*s before drinking a shot himself. As each person is served, he or she makes a libation on both the floor and the *enqa*s. Serafeo and Valentina used a carnation to sprinkle the *enqa*s, dipping the flower into two small clay bowls of *trago* held together in the left hand and then shaking it over the *enqa*s.

All that remains is to burn the offering. This is the tensest and trickiest part of the evening. While the mother places some incense and hot glowing coals in a pot, the father folds the piece of paper to form an envelope around the offering. Accompanied by a son or other male relative, he carries the *despacho* outside away from the house. In a sheltered spot—beside a wall or at the base of a rock—the father pours out the coals and kneels to pray. Then he places the offering on the coals and hurries back to the house. It should be burned with its head *(uma)* pointing east—*"Inti lloqsiyman"* ("to the rising Sun"). Otherwise, the offering would be upside down or sideways and pass "all confused" to the *Tirakuna.*

131

"How would *you* like to stand with your head tipped sideways?" retorted Luis when I questioned him on this point.

Seeing that I did not understand, he seemed to grope for a more accessible example and compared the *despacho* to a compass, whose needle always points north no matter how it's twisted and turned. Just as human beings are naturally oriented in space with their heads pointing upward and their feet downward and the compass needle's head points to the north and its base to the south, so too does the *despacho*'s head naturally point to the sunrise and its feet to the sunset.

While the *despacho*'s ingredients are placed one-by-one on the piece of white paper, the paper itself becomes a representation of the human body with an orientation reflecting that of its maker. Its head is the corner pointing away from the preparer, and the closer corner is its feet. The *k'intu*s must be placed on the paper with their tips pointing outward toward the paper's head and their stems pointing inward toward the paper's feet. As the paper is wrapped around the *k'intu*s and other ingredients to form an envelope, it undergoes a typically Andean transformation: the preparer folds the corner opposite himself (that is, the head) toward himself; then he folds the closer corner (the feet) away from himself. Therefore, Erasmo explained, the original head becomes the feet, and the feet become the head. However, the *k'intu*s inside this envelope maintain their original orientation.

After Erasmo explained this to me, he picked up his *unkhuña* (coca-carrying cloth) and showed me how it, too, undergoes this transformation every time it is folded (see Figure 6). Holding the cloth (A), he carefully instructed me, first, to fold the farther corner toward myself (B), and then to fold the closer corner away from me (C). This second fold indicates the new head. Next, he told me to tie the two side corners to close the bundle so that one corner joins the outward head fold, and the other points toward the base to form the new foot (D). "Look! This gives the *unkhuña* two heads and one foot," Erasmo commented with an air of revelation.[5]

Before they had access to paper, *Runakuna* must have wrapped the *despacho* ingredients in a piece of cloth and burned it along with the offering. Erasmo's comparison of the *despacho* paper and the *unkhuña* illustrates how the daily routine is imbued with ritual significance (for *Runakuna* carry around *unkhuña*s the way we carry purses and briefcases).

I did not witness the burning of a *despacho* until 1984, for it is normally a male task. However, when Erasmo prepared the *despacho* for my trip home, he instructed me to burn it myself the night before I left Sonqo, with Luis's help. Luis took me east of his house to a huge boulder near the base of Ixchhinu. He was very nervous and hurried. We both knelt as he poured the burning coals into a crevice at the base of the rock. The coals were strikingly red in the dark night, and the glow illuminated our faces as Luis prayed briefly for my safe trip. Then, all a-tremble, he urgently indicated the proper orientation for the offering (head to the east) and told me to put the *despacho* into the fire with my own hand, without looking at it. As I did so, he exclaimed *"Haku!"*

132

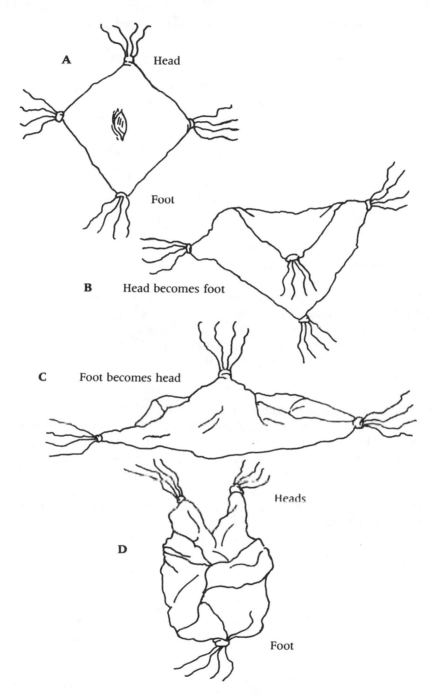

A   Head

Foot

B   Head becomes foot

C   Foot becomes head

Heads

D

Foot

Figure 6. Folding the coca-carrying cloth *(unkhuña)*. (Drawing by Robyn Johnson-Ross)

("Let's go!") and, whispering not to look behind us, he led me running back to the house.

Once inside, Luis relaxed, remarking that all had gone well—the offering had caught fire right away, it hadn't smoked, and no dogs had barked. We should not go near the spot that night: *"Mihushanku"* ("They're eating").

The next day we checked the rock to find that the offering had burned away to ashes, and Luis told me contentedly that I should have a safe trip.

In 1976 Luis's Carnival *despacho* did not go so well. He was in a poor state of mind, for he had lost two sisters the previous year—Juana in July and María in December—and then Rufina died in January. Luis approached the offering halfheartedly, with an air of emotional numbness. His son Bernardo, home from his job as a domestic servant in Cuzco, did not help matters.

"Watch this!" shouted Luis as he opened the *enqa*s. "If I should die who would know how to do it?"

"Watch what?" retorted Bernardo, curled up on the bed with his face to the wall. At sixteen he felt himself too sophisticated and progressive to indulge in such primitive practices.

Luis prepared some *k'intu*s and added fat and *canihua* seeds to them before folding the *despacho*. I asked him whether this offering was less important than the one offered at San Juan, and he replied, *"Manan, aswan más!"* ("No, it's more important!"). Then he paused—apparently realizing that his San Juan *despacho* had been more elaborate (including white wool, incense, and marigold seeds)—and added, "Well, if you don't have the ingredients you don't do a big *despacho*."

Actually, Luis had plenty of ingredients; I believe that in his demoralized state he just did not bother to add them. He also neglected to make a libation of *trago* outside, exclaiming later that he had "forgotten *Pacha*." Although he had *trago*, Luis did not remedy his oversight. Dispirited and sensing that his relationship with the *Tirakuna* was somehow out of joint, he seemed to have lost interest in maintaining good relations, going halfheartedly through the motions of preparing and burning the offering. Nevertheless, he did not consider it "ruined" until a dog barked.

Felicha had been tending the fire while her father was preparing the bundle. She placed the coals in the pot, exclaiming anxiously that Luis should not go out alone to burn it. He went over to the bed and gave one last, heartrending appeal to Bernardo, who pretended to be asleep. Finally, seven-year-old Esteban went out with his father, full of pride and responsibility.

After they had left, Felicha and little Inucha ran out to urinate, peering curiously after their menfolks as they squatted in the courtyard.

They all came back in, closed the door, and sat down again. Luis and I continued drinking *trago*. Then a dog barked outside.

Luis visibly crumbled. *"Achakáw! Malograpun!"* ("How horrible! It's ruined!"). He yelled at Felicha for not looking after the dogs.

I asked why barking spoiled the *despacho*. *"Qatisqa pasapun"* ("It's driven away"), he answered.

134

Felicha went out again and came scurrying back, squealing that there was a black dog standing on the ridge above the house. Luis peered out the door and turned away wordlessly, his round face sagging in horror.

"Oh nonsense," I thought. But when I looked out, there was indeed a black dog I had never seen before.

Black dogs are guides to the afterlife, and they have the ability to move between the worlds of the dead and the living. Here, only a few weeks after Rufina's death, there was a black dog—appearing apparently from nowhere and driving away Luis's *despacho*. The vicious circle of bad luck, demoralization, ritual failure, and more demoralization continued.

Eight days after the *despacho* is burned, the family brings out the *enqa*s again, along with the sack containing the wads of coca *(hachu)* that were chewed while the *despacho* was being prepared. The family chews new coca from a common bundle and adds this new *hachu* to the sack. Then the father empties the *hachu* into a small hole he has prepared in the corral and covers it with dirt and manure. Thus, the *enqa*'s "excrement" lies under the feet of animals that fill the corral with fertilizing manure. With this last step the ritual offering is complete. If all has gone well, the family looks forward to a healthy and prosperous year.

A Specialist's *Despacho*

As the year progresses and problems arise or life-threatening tasks are at hand, individuals may feel the need to supplement their regular *despachos* with special ones. A diviner may do *coca qhaway* and discover that *Pacha* and the *Tirakuna* are yet unsatisfied and require additional feeding. Then a slightly different *despacho* is prepared, one "or the person" *("Runapaq")*.

Erasmo washed his hands very carefully before preparing the *despacho* for my trip home, and then he passed a sheet of white paper over a burning piece of amber-colored incense. He fastened the paper to a coca-carrying cloth with a large pin driven vertically into its center. Then he prepared the four *k'intu*s I described in Chapter 2. They each had two leaves because two-leaved *k'intu*s are for human beings while three-leaved *k'intu*s are for domestic animals. Each *k'intu*, held between the fingers of his right hand, was a *warmi-qhari* (female-male pair); then he combined the four into two, also a *warmi-qhari*, and the two into one. Erasmo did the ritual blowing over this single *k'intu* of eight leaves; no more coca went into the *despacho*.

The invocation was long and lovely, but I cannot reproduce it here because Erasmo does not like me to write down his *phukuy*s. He called on Qolqe Puxyu (Silver Spring, my home in the U.S.), the Estados Unidos (the United States), and the *Apu*s Pachatusan and Hatun Antaqaqa, as well as his own neighborhood *ayllu* of Qhalipampa, calling on these Places to ensure that I would travel *"sumaqllata"* ("splendidly") to my country.

Putting the *k'intu* on the paper, Erasmo made the sign of the crossover the bundle. Then he sprinkled tiny black *canihua* seeds over the paper before raising the pin in order to attach the *k'intu* to the very center of the paper, its tip pointing toward the top.

Choosing from a bundle of ingredients I had purchased in the Cuzco medicine market *(hampi qhatu)*, Erasmo placed these items on the *k'intu* in the following order:

(1) *wiraq'oyas* (gray furry sticks), two[6]
(2) *llama untu* (llama fat)
(3) *coca ruros* (coca seeds), three pairs
(4) *misa galleta* (communion wafer; in this case a sweet cracker)
(5) *pallar* (large pale bean), one
(6) *chuwi* (small bean), one
(7) *condor phuru* (condor feathers), a sprinkling; to carry the *despacho* to my country
(8) *inchis* (peanuts), two
(9) *qori vara* and *qolqe vara* (golden staff and silver staff; also called *qori pinkullu* and *qolqe pinkullu*, golden flute and silver flute), a pair of gold foil sticks and a pair of silver ones
(10) *wayruros* (tropical seeds), two; these often have black spots, but Erasmo emphasized that for this *despacho* only pure red ones would do
(11) *istrillakuti* (star fish), two pieces
(12) *saqsakuti* (a big, black wrinkled seed), two pieces
(13) *garbanzos* (chickpeas), three pairs
(14) *arroz* (rice), a sprinkling
(15) *mani* (popcorn), two pieces
(16) *azucar* (sugar), a sprinkling (Erasmo was sorry that I had only brown sugar; white sugar is preferable)
(17) *sara paraqay* (large white corn), two kernels
(18) *gravils* (carnations), two; one *yana puka* (maroon), one *rosadu* (pink)
(19) *qhaqha chhunta* (micaceous sand), a sprinkling; Erasmo said this is gathered in places lightning has struck
(20) *kubyertus* (small lead figures), five
(21) *t'anta anise* ("bread anise"; anise seeds), a sprinkling
(22) *qori libru* and *qolqe libru* (gold book and silver book), two folded pieces of gold and silver paper
(23) *alfroka* (colored sprinkles, the kind we put on cupcakes), a sprinkling
(24) *insensyu* (incense), a sprinkling

The final sprinkling of incense was important. Erasmo mislaid the packet and spent a long time looking for it before it materialized under a poncho. Then he took a twist of colored threads and neatly pulled out a single white strand, leaving the rest in a tangle. He folded the paper around the ingredients, tied it with the thread, and had me mark the bundle's "head" with my pen. The single *k'intu* incorporating male and female aspects and surrounded by delicacies was wrapped in a representation of the human body that folded in on itself.

The tiny lead figures *(kubyertus)* represented a condor to carry the *despacho;* a person waving goodbye to indicate my departure; an *istrilla* (small star) and *ch'aska* (large star) to ensure my well-being; and an alpaca to stand for my *uywa* (herds). When I objected that I had no herds; Erasmo replied that the alpaca figure was good for whatever I raised or cared for.

Erasmo rejected several *kubyertus* as inappropriate for my offering bundle. A deer, for example, is used to turn away a jealous person; a goat hitting its kids is offered when a child refuses to be weaned; a man and woman holding hands attracts a lover; a single person ensures that the victim will go through life alone; a stretcher is used to cause an enemy's death; a lock is offered to keep someone from leaving.

Erasmo also rejected a piece of many-colored wool as suitable only for skin problems caused by exposure to *K'uychi* (the Rainbow). He set aside a snail shell as an inappropriate offering for the Earth, explaining that it could be used to cure a person suffering from extreme fright. *Fixyus* (*fideos*, macaroni) he rejected with great disgust, exclaiming that they never should have been included among the medicinal ingredients. When I asked why, he explained that *fixyu* sounds too much like *feo*, Spanish for ugly. How could we put "uglies" in a meal destined for the deities![7]

Erasmo prepared this splendid *despacho* for me after I became his *comadre* by cutting his only grandchild's hair, as if to demonstrate his good will and to cement the tie of *compadrazgo*. The *despacho* was a special gift on his part, comparable to the beautiful piece of weaving that Luisa and Alcides gave me a few weeks after I had baptized their infant son, Bonifacio. Erasmo and I chewed coca and drank *trago* as he prepared the *despacho*, his son Hipolito acting as assistant and observing the preparation as carefully as I was.

An Experimental Attempt

In 1984 Corpus Christi fell very late, so late that the final round of festivities interfered with the celebration of San Juan on 24 June. On San Juan Eve, Luis and Balvina were off in Chocopia helping a *compadre* with his Corpus *cargo*, and their children wondered what to do about the *enqa*s and the *despacho*.

Esteban, fifteen by this time, was anxious to observe the ritual, but he encountered the objections of Bernardo, who was visiting Sonqo again. At age twenty-four Bernardo was still unable to find a foothold in Lima or Cuzco and vacillated between Sonqo and his brother José who was working as a taxi driver in Cuzco. Bernardo advised Esteban to wait for the *Octavo* (eighth day after a festival), which, he declared, was perfectly good for celebrating San Juan. But thirteen-year-old Inucha agreed with Esteban. They considered asking Don Julian to come over and prepare the *despacho* for them, but decided he was probably too drunk. Julian had started celebrating San Juan early.

Bernardo went off to visit their sister Felicitas, who lived nearby. Long-faced, good-natured Toribio, Julian's sixteen-year-old, dropped in and confirmed that—yes—his father was pretty drunk already. I hung around to see what they would do.

Esteban purposefully led us into the house. Carefully, he got out the bundle of *enqa*s and opened them on the table. Inucha scolded him for opening it wrong. The *enqa*s were supposed to face the door, where the Sun enters the house.

The two teenagers began scouting around for their parents' coca and discussing what to do next. Ten-year-old Cirilucha watched wide-eyed but said little. Fondly, Esteban and Inucha caressed the *enqa*s and identified them for Toribio and me. The *enqa*s consisted of a male sheep, carved of white stone; two llamas, carved of gray stone; a dark, rounded uncarved stone with two holes stuffed with fat, identified as a male alpaca; and a flat gray uncarved stone with many irregular angles, identified as a *michiq warmi* (herder woman). There were several smooth brown and gray pebbles, which the children insisted were sheep, though in 1976 Luis had identified them for me as potatoes. A white stone tablet was carved to represent a house, six sheep, and a storehouse. A row of four sheep was also carved from white stone, along with a pair of cows that were tinted red. The cows were Balvina's contribution to the household. The white stone had originally been part of a larger tablet that was divided for inheritance purposes. Finally, there was a small, crude *chicha* jar.

Esteban sprinkled coca over these *enqa*s, explaining happily that they wanted to graze.

Next, Esteban and Inucha took a bag of *despacho* ingredients down from a peg on the wall, Inucha giggling a little but Esteban serious and resolute. They spread the bag's contents out on the table and looked bewildered. They were not so familiar with this part. They argued about this and that ingredient:

"Do we need *canihua*?"

"Naw, *canihua*'s not important."

Finally the teenagers gave up and put back the bundle. The burnt offering would have to wait. They turned back to the *enqa*s.

Bernardo came in and Esteban confronted him, nervous but determined. Mildly annoyed, Bernardo reiterated his opinion that they should wait for the *Octavo*.

"*Uywayki asindaman hayk'unqa!*" ("Your herds are going to get caught in an *hacienda!*"), retorted Esteban.

At this Bernardo sat down and carefully began placing *k'intu*s under each of the *enqa*s. The others were delighted and followed suit, urging me to help them.

I asked where *enqa*s are made, and Esteban replied that they simply come out of the ground and people find them. On August First they are especially likely to come out "to graze." Later that month, Esteban's father would point out a marshy spot that he described as "*enqaychuyuq*" ("possessed of *enqa*s"): "If you're fortunate you can find them—but if they don't want to be found they disappear into the ground or just look like regular stones so you don't recognize them."

Esteban began blowing *k'intu*s to the *Tirakuna*—to Towlakancha, Ixchhinu, Chulani, and Ch'aska Qaqa, Places located fairly nearby.

"T'ika Pallana, T'ika Pallana!" coached Inucha. The Flower Picking Spot was her favorite place.

"These *enqa*s are their *uywa* (flocks)," explained Esteban when he had finished.

It was raining—unusual for June and most unpropitious for San Juan. The night was cold, pitch dark, and their parents had not come home. Some holiday! But the *enqa*s had grazed.

Esteban gathered our chewed coca wads in the woven sack before we went to bed.

"It's the *enqa*s' manure," he said.

Kawsasqanchis: Feeding the Dead

November First, the day souls of dead *Runakuna* return to visit their relatives, is called *Kawsasqanchis* (Our Living; the word groups the dead with the living through the inclusive suffix *-nchis*). On the following day, *Kachaypari* (Send Off), the souls are sent on their way by the pounding feet of many dancers, as *Runakuna* dance intermittently in and around their houses. All the dead come—the good souls from *Taytanchis Lado* (Our Father's Side) and the *kukuchis* from the Snowy Mountains. Rufina described to Felicha how "pretty and green" the souls were as they hovered around the rafters. Later she was to tell me that her fatal illness began on All Soul's Day.

Kawsasqanchis is spent preparing and consuming holiday food in a cheerful mood resembling our Thanksgiving. Each family stays home to cook and eat in its own house, for if a soul were to find its relatives not at home it would go off *"renegaspa"* ("complaining") to another house. A special table (or a corner of the bed if a table is lacking) is set up for the souls' meal, and large portions of food are placed there before the family helps themselves to any. The same table is set up during the funeral wake held eight days after a death. The deceased one partakes of the special food and goes on its way.

Certain foods are prescribed for the souls' table, including boiled beans, patties made from ground *qhaya* (dehydrated *oca*) and water, a bowl of *quinoa* (a high-altitude grain) containing a hardboiled egg, and very large potatoes baked in the ground *(papa watia)*. On the assumption that the dead share the tastes of the living, the souls also receive a fancy dinner plate of pancakes, noodles, two kinds of meat (usually lamb and pork), and coffee or hot chocolate with a piece of bread. A candle and a bottle of *trago* also go on the table, and families with access to *qantu* bushes drape the table with garlands of *qantus*, the flower of the dead, and sprinkle the bell-shaped blossoms over the meal.

Food preparations are completed by late afternoon. For the rest of the day and the evening, *Runakuna* sit next to the table, alternately eating and chewing coca. Their *k'intus* are blown to *"Almakuna, Machula Aulanchis,"* whose day it is.

But what of the real food sitting on the table? I thought that it might be burned, recalling that the *despacho* feeds the *Tirakuna* through burning, but Luis explained that the food passes to the souls differently. He needed a *mihuq* (eater), who would consume the food while saying prayers for the dead. Luis expected Alcides, who had learned these prayers during his catechist's training, to perform this service, but Alcides never showed up. Apparently his own table was as much as he could handle. As the day wore on Luis asked whether Rick Wagner knew the prayers, hoping to press him into service. But Rick did not know them (lucky for him!), and the food stayed uneaten.

The next day I visited Luis and Rufina again, to find them stuffing themselves with the souls' food.

"Oh well," they said. "The souls didn't eat it."

During Rufina's funeral wake, Alcides ate from the ritual table while praying for her soul, as well as for the souls of other deceased family members. He did not finish the food, and Luis gave it to him to take home.

A series of Quechua texts collected by Gifford and Hoggarth includes this statement:

Those who have eaten a share [of the funeral feast] believe that they are eating on behalf of the stomach of the dead man and they will say, "I don't feel satisfied these days. It's said we are eating on behalf of the dead man's stomach."[8]

This communion of stomachs exists even among living people: "Put it from your stomach into Rick's." Felicha's remark expresses the typically Andean assumption that all matter is not only alive, but is interconnected. To be in a very distant location, like my country (so distant that *Runakuna* wondered whether it had a different sun) is to be in a state like that of the dead, who continue their corporeal life in a different mode from that of the living. Distant as they may be, the dead and the absent may on occasion be fed through the medium of the body.

Animal Fertility Rituals

Force-feeding emerges again as a ritual technique during fertility rites held for the sheep during Carnival and on the feast of San Juan, and for the llamas in early August. During the *Llama Ch'uyay*, the llamas are force-fed their *hampi* (medicine) of *chicha, trago,* sugar, soup broth, barley mash, ground *canihua,* and special herbs *(t'urpay, lloque lloque, ch'iri ch'iri, molle, t'ullma, chankaka,* and *yawar chanka).* Families who own horses usually perform the same ritual for them on the feast of Santiago, 25 July.

In the early afternoon of 6 August 1975, Francisco Quispe and his son-in-law Apolinar prepared colored tassels called *t'ikas* (flowers) to decorate the animals. As the two men cut and tied the yarn, they sat in front of the woven sack and *unkhuña* (coca-carrying cloth) they had used while preparing a *despacho* the previous night. Their chewed coca wads went into the sack. Meanwhile

While chewing coca, Erasmo (left) and his son Hipolito make tassels to ritually decorate their horses on the Feast of Santiago. The bag of coca leaves and jugs of *trago* will be consumed during the ritual and the ensuing festivities. Llamas are similarly honored in August.

Sista, Gavina, and Cipriana (Francisco's daughter and two daughters-in-law) prepared the llamas' *hampi* in a big pot.

Preparations completed, we adjourned to the corral with Francisco and his extended family: daughter Sista and her husband, Apolinar, stepsons Julian and Erasmo, and their wives Gavina and Cipriana. Francisco's wife, María, was housebound with her terminal illness. Julian Quintanilla, a friend of Apolinar's, joined us.

Although the day was miserably cold and drizzly, we had to keep the llamas company in the corral, where we sat stoically chewing coca from the ritual cloth, drinking *chicha* and *trago*, and smoking cigarettes. Someone should have been playing "Sargento," a traditional piece for flute and drum played during Carnival and animal *ch'uyay*s, but the bad weather dampened our musical inspiration. Instead, they called for the tape recording I had made during the *Uwiha Ch'uyay* (Sheep Festival) the previous June and played it over and over again. The hours wore on and the batteries wore out, but "Sargento" wheezed on.

Shortly before sundown, Julian and Apolinar removed their sandals and began to debate which male animal was the *machu llama* (old llama), or stud. Francisco pointed out the largest male, but the younger men preferred a smaller and older one. Once the men had grabbed the unruly animal, they forced three bottles of "medicine" down its throat and decorated it with tassels. Then they went on to repeat the procedure for the herd of six adult llamas and one baby. They forced as much of the medicinal brew as possible down the llamas' throats; the biggest male consumed five and one-half bottles, the baby one-half. Although three or more bottles were desirable for force-feeding a llama, five bottles were usually considered unlucky, and the men went to a lot of trouble to get the large llama to drink the last half bottle.

While the men were force-feeding and decorating the llamas, they were themselves continuously fed *chicha* and *trago* by the women. By the time they had finished, men and llamas together were stumbling around tipsily.

The herd duly decorated and surfeited with "medicine," we turned to the most dramatic of Sonqo's libations, the *ch'uyay* proper, which entails throwing whole containers of *chicha* onto the herd in a grand sweeping motion. Francisco used traditional wooden goblets called *qero*s for his *Llama Ch'uyay,* whereas Luis used yellow plastic teacups—prized new purchases from Cuzco—for his *Uwiha Ch'uyay* in 1975, and in 1980 did his *Llama Ch'uyay* out of the same bottle he had just used to force-feed the llamas.[9]

The *ch'uyay* completed, we plunged into *hallpachikuy* (forced coca chewing), cramming one another's mouths with coca and eventually depositing the wads in the woven sack. Finally, yelling, singing, and dancing, the inebriated *Runakuna* drove their equally inebriated animals out of the corral to graze nearby. The night was dark and damp, so we retreated to Julian's house to eat soup and to sing until three o'clock in the morning.

San Juan celebrations for the sheep begin before daybreak, when the rising Sun, just past the winter solstice, is believed to have special energizing powers. In 1975, as the San Juan sun rose brilliantly and seemed to tremble in the sky, Luis remarked with satisfaction, *"Inti tusun"* ("The Sun dances"). At that moment, he said, the water in the streams momentarily turned to *hampi* (medicine). From sunrise to early afternoon, families sit in their corrals with the sheep, chewing coca from the ritual cloth, drinking *chicha,* and playing "Sargento." The Carnival *ch'uyay* is held at sunset, and the herds are sprinkled with tiny red and yellow flowers called *wakankilla* while the Sun disappears behind the peak of Sawasiray-Pitusiray.

Unlike the llamas, who drink *hampi* and are decorated with tassels, the sheep get daubed with red paint and are made to chew coca. They are stretched out on a poncho facing each other in male-female pairs to "get married." Afterward, the human participants pair themselves to perform the *ch'uyay.* Finally, they drive the confused animals out of the corral, playing "Sargento" on flutes and drums and dancing wildly as the sheep fan out over the hillsides and begin to graze.

"*Urqokuna uwihatan hap'ichishanku*" ("The hills are turning on the sheep"), remarked Gavina a few weeks later as we listened to my tapes of "Sargento."

The verb *hap'ichiy* (to turn on) also refers to lighting candles or to turning on the radio. And while the hills may "turn on" the sheep, they also turn on the people, who play "Sargento" and dance to the point of exhaustion.

Ch'uño Ch'allay: Fortifying Dead Potatoes

Agustu, August First, is another occasion for *Runakuna* to spend the day sitting out in their corrals—but this time they keep company not with their animals, but with piles of *ch'uño* ready to be moved into the storerooms. In 1975 we joined Julian and Gavina, along with Francisco and María, who shared a common storeroom. When we arrived Julian was making a straw mat, and Francisco was carrying loads of *ch'uño* into the yard and dumping them from shoulder height to winnow out bits of straw. Julian eagerly asked us to break out the *trago*, which he used for a libation on the mat. We helped put the *ch'uño* in large woven sacks and lugged them into the storeroom.

After dinner we sat around for a while chewing coca, drinking *trago*, and smoking cigarettes before adjourning to the storeroom. Francisco carried a bit of incense around the *ch'uño* and the straw mats. We placed *k'intu*s on the mats and gave them libations of *trago* and *chicha*. The mats were destined to become *ch'uño* bins, rolled up into cylinders and placed on their ends.

A small bundle of *ch'uño* was placed on a bed at one end of the storeroom; each of us sprinkled *chicha* on this *ch'uño* and on the storeroom door. Then we sprinkled *trago* on the sacks of *ch'uño*. I was instructed once again to play my tape of "Sargento."

Julian and Francisco set to work pouring the large sacks of *ch'uño* into the bins as fast as possible. While they worked Gavina fed them *chicha*, and Rick Wagner plied them with *trago*. The men instructed Rick to serve the liquor as fast as he could, for they should be drinking the whole time they are pouring out the *ch'uño*. After they finished we moved back into the house and, joined by Apolinar and Sista, we prepared the August *despacho*.

Luis stored his *ch'uño* the next day, and he did it somewhat differently, illustrating the flexibility that exists in the parameters of Sonqo's rituals.[10] After a period of quiet coca chewing, he produced a small bottle of *vinu* (red wine) and a large, dead black bird he called a *malqo*. Since there was no *trago* or *chicha*, Luis made do with the wine, pouring it on a coca *k'intu* placed on the bottom of a straw bin.[11]

Luis then poured some wine on the dead bird, muttered a short, inaudible prayer, and put the bird down next to the bin. After the *ch'uño* had been poured into the bins, he picked up the bird and the bottle of *vinu* and buried them in the *ch'uño* "to guard it."

Another round of coca chewing followed, and the job was done.

Saturation, Decoration, Procreation, and Noise

Why do Sonqo *Runakuna* saturate themselves in ritual with food, alcohol, and coca? What religious ideas underlie the practices of force-feeding llamas, of feeding the dead by eating, and of sharing food with an absent person through an apparently metaphysical communion of stomachs? Odd as it may seem, we can find an answer in the *Runakuna*'s attitude toward the most obvious and tangible transformation effected by eating: the transformation of food into excrement.

Hysterical and depressed after Rufina's death, Luis predicted that he and his children would die from starvation. Why? Because without a woman in the household, he would have to send the animals away to be cared for by others, and there would be no manure in his corral. No manure means no fertilizer for the potatoes. No fertilizer means no crop. No crop means no food. Obviously, they were all doomed.

For lack of a woman the herd was lost.
For lack of a herd the manure was lost.
For lack of manure the potatoes were lost.
For lack of potatoes the family starved.
All for lack of a woman.

Of course, it would never have come to starvation, for Luis's relatives and *compadres* would have loaned him manure. However, Luis's prediction does show us how the household, agricultural, and pastoral economies are systematically interconnected, with manure serving as a crucial link. It also indicates that the system as a whole depends on the sexes' complementary and dialectical division of labor. Through their tending the animals, women provide men with the manure the men use to fertilize their fields and to produce food for their families. Women themselves use dried dung in their cooking fires. Manure is an essential element in the system of reciprocal exchanges that characterizes the *warmi-qhari*'s married relationship. The fertilizing capacity of manure facilitates transformations within this system: the transformation of seeds to potato plants, and of harvested potatoes to cooked food.

Now, you cannot sit in the corral during fertility rituals without sitting in dung. Unavoidably the little black turds stick to skirts and ponchos, to coca-carrying cloths and ritual sacks. *Runakuna* do not deliberately coat themselves with dung, but they do not try to avoid it, either. Sitting in the corral during his San Juan sheep festival in 1980, Serafeo reflected thoughtfully on our debt to the sheep: they give us wool for our clothes and meat to eat, and their dung not only serves us as fuel but is *hampi* for the potatoes. Potatoes need a lot of *hampi; ullucus* and *ocas* not as much.

The word *hampi,* roughly corresponding to our word medicine, can refer to anything that possesses special curative powers owing to its strong *sami.* *Hampi* has the power to change the state of its object. As *hampi,* manure falls

144

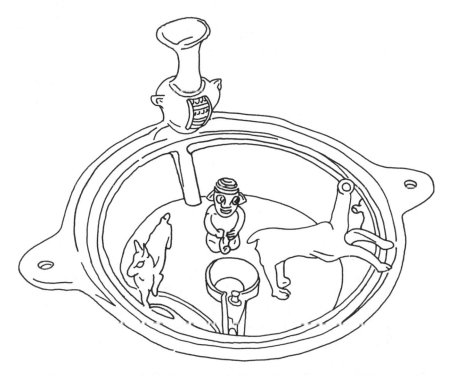

Figure 7. An Incaic ritual drinking vessel. (From the collection of El Museo Inka de la Universidad San Antonio Abad de Cuzco; drawing by Robyn Johnson-Ross)

into the same category as coca leaves, ingredients for burnt offerings, and the vast array of herbs used in traditional curing. All *hampi*, of course, must be used properly—for medicine in one context is poison in another. Feces are useless and sickening as human food, but as food for the potatoes they indirectly feed human beings as well. The *Machu Wayra* (Old Wind) from the *chullpas*, too, is said to be *wanu* (manure)—it makes humans sick but fertilizes the potato crop.

A silver and copper bowl in Cuzco's Museo Inka contains hollow figurines of a man and two llamas (see Figure 7).[12] Around the rim and between the bowl's surface and base is a circulatory system that turns the vessel into a kind of miniature fountain. From our perspective it looks like a pornographic fountain, for liquid poured into the miniature *chicha* jar on the bowl's rim, or into the hollow neck of one of the llamas, would flow around and underneath the bowl to spout from the man's prominent penis and from the llamas' anuses. Then the liquid would fall into tiny drains and recirculate through the vessel. Possibly the long hollow neck of the headless llama served as a kind of straw, so *chicha* that had circulated through the figurines could be sucked into the human body.

Now, this vessel almost certainly was intended (not to titillate an Inca's coprophilia) for use in animal fertility rituals. Similar bowls containing figures of animals or humans (but made of clay or wood and without the fancy plumbing system) are still used in the far south of Peru and northern Bolivia for drinking and performing libations in animal fertility rituals. In the context of Andean subsistence economy, a concern with animal excrement is quite understandable, and it is not surprising that in rituals focused on the animals dung is welcomed rather than avoided. Furthermore, given the fact that dung is a kind of *hampi*, it makes sense for ritual to focus on the transformative process through which this excremental medicine is produced. The Incas' ritual bowl vividly illustrates this process as a kind of corporeal transubstantiation.

In rituals for the dead, like All Souls' Day and funerals, the ritual *mihuq's* (eater's) body is a transforming vessel for the food. A transubstantiation occurs that is similar to the normal excremental process but which must be directed differently in order to nourish the dead. The *mihuq's* speech directs the food to the dead, just as the invocation in *phukuy* directs the coca's *sami* to the *Tirakuna*. The *mihuq's* body is a conduit; the food's *sami* passes through him from this world of the living to that of the dead.

When *enqas* are brought out on the eve of animal *ch'uyays*, they "graze" on coca through the medium of the participating humans, who cram leaves into one another's mouths in *hallpachikuy*. The pile of chewed wads thus produced is the *enqa's* excrement and, unlike the *hachu* produced in routine coca chewing, the wads must be carefully saved so that they may be buried in the animals' corral.

The *despacho* undergoes a similar transubstantiation. The coca *k'intus* and the other *hampi* chosen for the offering bundle are enclosed in a paper representation of the human body. As it burns, the paper is converted to food for *Pacha* and the *Tirakuna*.

During the *Llama Ch'uyay Runakuna* saturate their herds, both inside and out, with *chicha*. In *Uwiha Ch'uyay* the sheep are forced to chew coca before being doused with *chicha*. In both rituals, the humans are supposed to drink continuously, in effect force-feeding themselves while they feed the animals. As they drink and chew coca, each *Runa* offers a libation and a *phukuy* to *Pacha* and the *Tirakuna*. By the time the ritual is finished, people, animals, Earth, and Hills are all saturated—wet, drunk, and dancing. The Hills, activated in human ritual, "turn on" the animals.

Ch'uño-storing rituals are structurally similar to the animal *ch'uyays*, even though they celebrate dried-up potatoes rather than living animals. *Runakuna* treat potatoes as living, sentient beings—as female plants who give birth upon being planted. When potatoes turn into *ch'uño*, they are said to die, and *Runakuna* hope for a hard early frost to "slaughter" them quickly and mercifully. Once the potatoes have undergone a process of alternate freezing and thawing, they become hard, dry lumps of *ch'uño*. This process preserves the food value of the potatoes in a form that can be stored for several years. At Rufina's funeral wake, Luis compared himself to a piece of *ch'uño* that had "died but keeps on existing."

Ch'uño, mummified potatoes, resemble the ancestral *Machukuna*. Both have died in a desiccating sun but continue to interact with the living. *Ch'uño* is reconstituted through soaking in water; the *Machukuna* try to reconstitute themselves by sucking blood from living humans. The desiccated remains identified with *Machula Aulanchis*, the bones on Antaqaqa, are treated as fertilizing ancestral spirits and ritually honored with libations and invocations. Similarly, *Ch'uño Ch'allay* feeds the thirsty potato mummies with alcohol; *Runakuna* say that without the *ch'allay* the *ch'uño* supply would give out before February. And in this libation, similar to the animal *ch'uyay*s, the men who pour *chicha* into the *ch'uño* bins should pour *chicha* down their own throats as they do so, drinking not only for themselves, but for the mummified potatoes as well.

Music is another aspect of ritual saturation. While we doused the potatoes with *chicha* and *trago* and drank continuously, I had to make sure the tape recorder was playing "Sargento." Rituals for the household's well-being should be noisy, and the sound should be continuous and properly shaped—for music, song, and prayer identify the occasion and direct the flow of the *sami*. It matters more that the music flow continuously than that it be well-played During the 1975 San Juan ritual, the men played "Sargento" unceasingly on flutes and drums, and had to spell each other to keep from getting exhausted. At subsequent rituals the men were content to let my tape recorder do this work for them. Tired batteries were no obstacle because, after all, when men play "Sargento" they get tired too, and the quality of the music suffers. However, abrupt and discontinuous noises, such as a dog's sudden barking or twigs snapping in the fireplace, are highly unsuitable during rituals.

Decoration is yet another way of capturing and directing the *sami*'s flow during ritual. Making the llama's yarn tassel "flowers" is a ritual act performed while chewing coca over the special woven sack. Recall that the inspired craftsman is *santuyuq*, and that he imbues his product with a spiritual efficacy derived from sacred beings. Like a string of magnets activated by coca, the *sami* passes from the *Tirakuna* through the maker to the tassels and on to the llamas. This *sami*, too, must be properly directed: correct colors must be prepared for different categories of animals—old, young, male, female—and placed in the correct position on the animals' bodies. After Francisco's *ch'uyay*, Luis quizzed me on the placement of the tassels and emphasized the importance of proper placement.

Eating, music, and decoration: all facilitate a flow of vitality among different categories of living beings. Sexuality provides a symbolic idiom to express this process, although (as far as I know) actual sexual relations do not figure in any of these household rituals. The *Llama Ch'uyay* is considered pointless in a herd without a stud; in *Uwiha Ch'uyay* the sheep are paired up and "married." In both rituals the libation on the herd is performed by married couples, as though their sexuality and that of their animals were connected.

147

A snatch of ritual song—"In the llama fiesta/You make your lover cry"[13]—implicitly equates the llamas and the women, for the women should cry in sympathy as their men pierce the screaming llamas' skin, and blood drips down their ears.

In Chapter 1 we saw that the *enqa*s also embody a kind of sexuality—illustrated by Basilia's exclamation over a phallic *enqa* in the Cuzco museum and Apu Qanaqway's supernatural and highly sexualized bulls called *"enqaychu."* Moreover, it is the connection of both *enqa*s and coca *k'intu*s with light—for both should be oriented to the sunrise—that links them to the masculine energy of Father Sun.

Luis called the bird that he had left in the *ch'uño* a *malqo*, which carries sexual connotations, for *malqo* is a slangy way of referring to nubile young adults of marriageable age. Like the *enqa*s and the ancestor's skull (see Chapter 1), the dead but sexually active bird had been left to guard the *ch'uño*. Lacking *chicha* or *trago*, Luis chose the *malqo* as a suitable substitute.

Chicha itself may have connotations of semen, although Sonqo *Runakuna* never articulated this to me. During festivities on 25 December in nearby Accha, women are served *chicha* in a cow horn that they place between their legs before drinking as a token of fertility.[14] Interpreted sexually, the *ch'uyay* itself could be seen as a kind of ritual insemination that occurs near the climax of the intoxicated and noisy festivities.

The symbolic idiom of sex figures suitably in the rituals, for sexual relations exemplify the exchange of energy between different but complementary kinds of being—an exchange that generates and maintains the flow of life. Daily life is full of such exchanges. Sex is only one example; *chakra ayni* (reciprocity in agricultural labor) is another. Ritual intensifies the ubiquitous focus on exchange and its regulation by taking advantage of propitious times of the year: the dancing rays of the returning Sun at the winter solstice; the opening of the Earth in August. Through ritualized exchange, opposed but complementary categories are drawn into conjunction (living *Runakuna* and their dead, *Runakuna* and *Tirakuna*, *Runakuna* and animals, animals and *Tirakuna*) and categorical distinctions are blurred (the lover and the llama, the married couple and the "married" sheep, the tipsy people and the tipsy herds). Formerly the ritual animals were dressed in human clothing to further emphasize the equation of humans and their herds. Old people complain bitterly that their grown children no longer observe this practice.[15] *Runakuna* drink and eat for their animals and their dead as well as for themselves, and they offer their own bodies as transformers for the *samincha*. For the Sacred Places; they offer a symbolic self-sacrifice by projecting their own image onto the offering bundle to be burned.

The identification of human participants with one another (Turner's *"communitas"*) is also stressed in ritual. *Runakuna* drink, dance, and yell together. In *hallpachikuy* (forced coca chewing), the element of individual reciprocity, so carefully fostered in normal coca chewing etiquette, is submerged in the collectivity as each person participant forces coca. The communal *hachu* (chewed coca) is gathered and buried, like both the communal heap of bones in Sonqo's graveyard and the communal, deindividualized ancestors on Antaqaqa.

Andean ritual happens at an interface; it propels different dimensions of the cosmos into contact with one another and temporarily merges them. The orgiastic quality of Sonqo's rituals is hardly surprising—for it takes an out-pouring of energy to get this job done. In their barren landscape of browns, grays, and pale greens, these people who live on the edge of subsistence satu-rate themselves, their animals, their Earth. Whether they feel like it or not, *Runakuna* sing and party in the chilly rain, icy night, or blistering sun. Their stomp-dancing pounds the sensitive Earth; their raucous music carries to the *Apus* and the sky; their brilliantly colored clothing glows against the bland adobes. With all their collective energy, *Runakuna* force the reluctant world to sustain them.

Chapter Seven

Rites of the *Ayllu*

The Feast of Santa Cruz

Day after day *Runakuna* wend their busy but separate ways over the centuries-old footpaths worn deep into the rocks. Watching each other—always watching. Now, in the late 1980s, the road is changing the old landscape; some of the ancient footpaths are falling into disuse, and an occasional car or pickup truck provides a new focus for the watchers' eyes and speculations. Every vehicle is noted and discussed, and a few days later a rumor almost inevitably returns: "They were Japanese tourists on their way to Tres Cruces. They stopped in Colquepata to photograph the church and bought three bottles of orange soda in Valencia's store."

When the *guardia civil* putt-putt past on their motorbikes, the *Runakuna* stiffen a little and settle silently into their layers of heavy clothing, watching intently. And on this subject too the rumor returns: "They think Crisologo murdered his old father-in-law to get the inheritance. How stupid! The old man was almost a hundred, and he died of the flu we've all been catching lately."

Or: "They were just going around watching us. That's all."

But, at intervals throughout the year, there are comings-and-goings no rumor need explain. Announced by the low, penetrating call of conch-shell trumpets, Sonqo's authorities trudge in procession over the well-worn paths. On Catholic feast days, they join the two festival sponsors and a band of musicians to carry their *taytachas* (crosses) or *mamachas* (Virgins' images) from the local church to a tiny chapel on the peak of Pachawani. The sponsors then return home while the staff bearers make the rounds of one another's houses. They crisscross Sonqo's territory as they do so, for the order of visitation is determined by descending rank order rather than by geographical proximity. At sunset they parade—rather tipsily—back to the chapel to retrieve the sacred images and carry them back to the church by yet a different route.

None of the watching *Runakuna* can view the whole *paseo* (round of visiting) from where they stand—but seeing a fraction is enough to evoke the complete circuit in their minds. They gossip about what they have seen: "They took a long time at the *segundo*'s house. His wife probably didn't have the soup ready. And, of all things, they came outside to eat—the stove must have been smoking like crazy!"

While the entire *ayllu* quietly notices the goings-on, only a small fraction of Sonqo's population actually participates, either in the officials' *paseo* or in the feasting at the church on the following day. The two sponsors and their wives attend, of course, along with their kinsmen and *compadres* who gathered in *ayni* to help prepare for the celebrations. The staff bearers and administrative council members usually attend without their wives, joined by the *mayordomo* (church custodian) and two or three other elders who occupy places of honor. The rest of the *ayllu Runakuna* go about their usual tasks, occasionally speculating on the progress of the festivities. If the workload permits, they use the holiday as an excuse to finish early and break out a bottle of *trago*. But they do not join the formal celebration, nor do they feel annoyed by the exclusion.

The *Runakuna do* feel annoyed if the sponsors fall down on the job and fail to fulfill their obligation to the community. This is a fairly common occurrence. In September of 1975, for example, the feast of San Geronimo was cancelled because the appointed sponsors backed out. The *Runakuna* went through the day grumbling and anxious: Mamacha San Geronimo would feel sad and neglected on her day, and that was bad for the *ayllu*.The authorities tried to compensate by opening the church, dressing the *mamacha* in her crown and special garments, and holding a prayer service. But there was no music; food, chicha, and coca were not served; the courtyard was not pounded by dancers' feet; and the *Runakuna* lamented their *ayllu*'s omission.

The practice of lovingly dressing the sacred images and carrying them in procession derives both from Mediterranean Catholicism and from the pre-Columbian Andean practice of ritually dressing and parading ancestral mummies. Like the mummies, the *taytachas* and *mamachas*—little fathers and mothers—are repositories of the *ayllu*'s well-being. They connect the dead with the living, for they say the *mamacha*'s crown acts as a kind of magnet to draw the *almakuna* (souls) back to Sonqo for the Day of the Dead.

On 3 May 1975 the sponsors, community staff bearers, and a group of four musicians convened at the church to "dress" the two *taytachas*, simple wood crosses, which the day before they had carried up to the Pachawani chapel and

back. After they placed the crosses, swathed in white cloth, under an impro-
vised canopy, the staff bearers and musicians set off on yet another round of
ritual visits.

The two sponsors rushed back to their respective houses, where preparations for the afternoon's festivities were feverishly underway. Their two households were collaborating in the *chicha* making. Don Domingo, the junior sponsor, had traveled to Cuzco to buy *wiñapu* (sprouted corn); Don Victor, the
senior sponsor, whose house was conveniently close to the church, was doing
the actual *chicha* making. There I found a hive of activity, men and women
sharing the work as they ground the *wiñapu,* fetched water, and fed thorny
branches into the blazing hot fire. Domingo had arrived with the corn only the
previous day, barely in time to produce a semblance of *chicha.*

About one o'clock in the afternoon, Domingo's group headed for the
church. After they had settled around their large *chicha* jar, Victor's group entered the courtyard. The two groups arranged themselves so that the women—
with their bundles of boiled potatoes, chopped boiled *ullucus*, pancakes,
chunks of boiled mutton, and *chicha*—were seated in two groups to the left as
one faces the church. The men sat behind two tables to the women's right. The
band and *regidores* (town criers) with *varas* and *putuus* stood alongside the wall
to the right. *Alcalde, segundo, president,* and *mayordomo* sat directly behind the
tables; the rest of the men, including the two sponsors, their kinsmen, and the
elders, sat to either side of the officials, the junior sponsor to the *alcalde's* left
and the senior sponsor to his right.

This is the usual arrangement for public gatherings: men in a line to the
right; women in a crowd to the left. Inside the church, men stand to the right
hand of the images, which look out at them from the altar,whereas women
stand to the images' left. That the junior sponsor sits on the *alcalde's* left while
the senior sponsor sits on his right expresses the idea that the two are *"warmi-
qhari hina,"* "like man and wife."

In many Andean communities, each of the two festival sponsors represents a moiety, or section of the community; the moieties are related as
"upper" and "lower" or "greater" and "lesser." The sponsors' collaboration in
public ritual expresses the unification of the two parts in a single community.[1]
The dual fiesta sponsorship in Sonqo is a variation on this theme, but with a
different emphasis. Sonqo *ayllu* is modeled on the household: like the household, the *ayllu* is dualistic in nature, depending on the different but complementary activities of husband and wife.

Just as the household has its *enqas,* so too does the *ayllu* have its sacred
power objects—the *taytachas* (wooden crosses) and *mamachas* (Mama Consebida and Mama San Geronimo; doll-like images of the Virgin). Like the *enqas,*
the *taytachas* and *mamachas* are normally hidden from view, and they emerge
from the locked church only on special occasions. These sacred male and female images embody the idea of continuously enfolding oppositions that we
encountered in previous chapters. The two crosses, or little fathers, that stand
on either side of the altar are related as left and right. The little mothers also

152

form a complementary pair; Mama Consebida is described as greater (that is, major or senior) and Mama San Geronimo as lesser (that is, minor or junior).

Thus, Catholic imagery is used to express indigenous ideas of opposition and complementarity. The relationship of wet and dry seasons is suitably expressed by the celebration of female *mamachas* during the warm, wet planting season and the celebration of male *taytachas* during the sunny, dry harvest season. Early May, when the dry season begins and harvest starts in earnest, brings the Feast of the Holy Cross *(Santa Cruz)*, followed by the long ritual cycle culminating in the Qoyllur Rit'i pilgrimage. During this pilgrimage, another *taytacha*—a small painted picture of crucified Christ housed in a red wooden box—is carried in procession. The rainy season is marked by parallel rituals celebrating *mamachas* rather than *taytachas*. In late September, as the rains return, the feast of San Geronimo marks the official opening of the planting season. Although Geronimo is a male saint, a female image, Mama San Geronimo (or La Virgen de San Geronimo), is carried around the community's footpaths. On 8 December, as the rainy season reaches its height, Sonqueños celebrate Mama Consebida, La Virgen de la Concepción.

During these festivals, the junior sponsor is "like a wife" to the senior sponsor, much as Luis was "like a woman" when, during the February lull in agricultural activity, he "went around knitting." Knitting is a male aspect of the female domain of handicrafts; conversely, the junior sponsorship is the female aspect of the male domain of public ritual. In Andean relativistic thought, nothing and no one is absolutely male or female. Relative to the junior sponsor, the senior sponsor is male; but relative to the *alcalde*, both sponsors stand in a female role, for they prepare the food and the *chicha* and have it served. The *alcalde* distributes the *chicha* provided by the sponsors.

The feast at Santa Cruz followed the pattern of all ritual meals: *pututus* sounded, and three times the band played a short phrase called *alawaru* (prayer, from Spanish *alabado*), first facing the church, then the ritual table, and finally facing eastward. The women ladled food onto metal plates that young barefoot men from the sponsors' families carried to the tables. Each man served his group's food to members of both groups. Women were served but they did not eat, instead storing the food in their folded shawls. When the meal was finished, the band again played *alawaru*, and the servers knelt hatless to pray. Then the whole process was repeated.

When the second round of eating was finished, the distribution of coca and *chicha* began. While the *alcalde* called guests over to the table to drink *chicha*, the sponsors walked through the gathering dispensing handfuls of coca. After all the men had been served *chicha* individually, the company sat chewing coca and sharing *k'intus*. The serving men began their rounds with the pitchers, doling out *chicha* to each of the guests, first from one wooden goblet, then from the other, and finally from the *puchuela* (clay bowl). It is quite a feat to down these three servings, as they are pressed on in rapid succession. Several people produced plastic pitchers from the folds of their shawls and ponchos and quietly stored the *chicha* to take home.

153

The triple servings were most unwelcome, for the cold, thin *chicha* sat heavily in the stomach, and the weather was chilly with a continuous drizzle. Not a propitious day to usher in the harvest season! The *Runakuna* drew their ponchos and shawls around themselves, shivering and grumbling.

The music started up, but no one felt like dancing. Domingo had hired a man from the community of Accha to bring a battery-run record player, complete with loudspeakers and records of popular Quechua songs. By 1984 almost every family in Sonqo had one of these, but in 1975 it was a novelty, and Domingo thought it a very classy addition to the festivities. He was right as far as the record player went. The problem was the man from Accha, who complained about Sonqo nonstop. Such a barren place, and poor, with a terrible climate! How much better to live in Accha! What with the rain, the cold *chicha*, and the irritating phonograph man, nobody felt up to dancing or even talking much.

Yet no one left. Dusk was falling before the second round of food was duly served and eaten and the coca and *chicha* distributed. Only after the sponsors had carried the crosses back into the church did the guests scatter quickly and gratefully to their homes.

Nevertheless, in the days that followed *Runakuna* took great pains to assure me that they had had a wonderful time. "We know how to do things in Sonqo!" they said. Only months later did Apolinar, the *segundo*, remark privately that the feast had been boring and uncomfortable.

The *ayllu* had met its obligations at Santa Cruz. The sponsors came through with an admirable feast, but nevertheless, in ritual terms the event was not a great success. The ritual's form had been observed, but the desirable outpouring of high spirits in dance, song, and libation had not taken place—and therefore could not return to the *ayllu* as vitality and well-being. Just as a demoralized Don Luis performed his household's ritual duties halfheartedly and with scant success, a demoralized community may feel no enthusiasm for the performance of public rituals. Halfhearted celebrations only deepen the low morale, for they may leave the *taytacha*s and *mamacha*s sad and dissatisfied. Just as ritual ministration to the *enqa*s should revitalize the household, the celebration of crosses and saints, communal power objects, should revitalize the *ayllu*.

Although only a fraction of Sonqo's population attends the celebrations, the *ayllu* as a whole benefits from them, and so all the *Runakuna* have a stake in their success. Only once a year do all the *Ayllu Runakuna* gather in a community-wide fiesta. Then they celebrate, not the images in the church, but the *alcalde* and their *Tirakuna*.

Puqllay: Carnival Time

In February the rains peak and the Sun passes its zenith; the first early potatoes, *ullucus*, and *tarwi* (small beans) are ready to harvest. Peaches, maize, and wheat appear in the Sunday market. The soil is wet and warm, and men can

154

be seen with their foot plows opening the fields for next year's planting. This is the season of *Puqllay,* Carnival. Women dance with bundles of maize, grain, and fruit in their shawls. Young mothers bundle in their infants as well, who bounce wide-eyed above the maternal twirling and stamping. Sometimes, women and men form two choirs to sing back and forth:

Kay kanmi llikllay!	Here I have my shawl!
—Puqllay!—	*—Puqllay!—*
Puqllay lloqsimushán!	*Puqllay*'s starting up!
—Puqllay!—	*—Puqllay!—*
Durasnus q'epintín!	Bringing peaches!
—Puqllay!—	*—Puqllay!—*
Irampu q'epintín!	Bringing wheat!
—Puqllay!—	*—Puqllay!—*
Muyurikusunchís!	We'll go twirling around!
—Puqllay!—	*—Puqllay!—*
Kantarikusunchís!	We'll all start singing!
—Puqllay!—	*—Puqllay!—*
Muyurikusunmí!	Let's really twirl around!
—Noqapas!—	—Me too!—
Kirilla yachará!	And taste the battle![2]

The height of the rainy season is a time for offerings and ritual battles. Diane Hopkins (1982) observes that the chronicler Guaman Poma de Ayala called this season *Pacha Phukuy,* "Blowing [offerings] to the Earth," and that the chronicler Gutiérrez described the Inca king presiding over a battle in which his men fought each other with hard fruit and slingshots: "many Indians came off with bad head injuries, and some died of the wounds they received."[3] After the battle, according to Molina, the royal mummies of Upper and Lower Cuzco were brought into the main plaza and set up in two lines to receive offerings of food and *chicha* "as if they were alive."[4]

These pre-Columbian festivals of the late rainy season were easily incorporated into Spanish Carnival, a licentious and only marginally religious holiday that required a minimum of adjustment to Catholic ritual forms. Of Sonqo's community festivals, *Puqllay* contains the least Christian imagery and is still a time for boisterous sexual play and ritual fighting.[5] Although the ancestral mummies are long gone, Carnival is still an occasion for surveying community boundaries and for making offerings to Sacred Places. The Thursday before Carnival, on *Comadres P'unchay* (Comadres' Day, Feast of the *Comadres),* many *Runakuna* climb beyond the upper boundaries of their community to a high plain below a pass called Panapunku. There an ancient footpath crosses the boundary between the provinces of Paucartambo and Calca. The plain's name, Chiwchillani, refers to the incubation of birds' eggs and the development of the chicks. The borders of three districts in two provinces converge there: the districts of P'isaq and San Salvador in Calca Province and the district of Colquepata in Paucartambo Province. From Chiwchillani, Sonqo and

155

its neighboring *ayllu*s can be seen as distinct and integral places. Only from above does one grasp the *ayllu*'s geographical unity.

The jagged range of mountains rises abruptly to mark geologic discontinuity as the gray-brown soil of Colquepata meets the reddish soil of Calca. These reddish mountains are the "nasty" ones I mentioned in Chapter 1—the ones who flow in hail storms with the blood sucked from human beings.

Until 1952 these mountains had another source of blood as well, for groups of *sargento* dancers from the three districts met in Chiwchillani to dance the *tinkuy* (encounter)—and in the process went at each other with stones, slings, and staffs. Their blood soaked into the ground, and when—as sometimes happened—a person was killed, the corpse was buried where it fell. *"Amas turalláy manchankichu!"* "Don't be afraid, little brother!" sing the women.[6]

Hakuchu, turalláy, Chiwchallanita!	Let's go, little brother, to Chiwchillani!
Takispan purimusun.	We'll go along singing.
Amas, turacháy, mancharinkichu	Don't be afraid, little brother
Yawar mayupi rikukushaspa	When you see yourself in a river of blood,
Rumi chikchipi rikukushaspa.	When you find yourself in a hail of stones.

Although three districts meet on Chiwchillani, Sonqueños view the *tinkuy* as an encounter between the two provinces, in which Paucartambo *ayllu*s compete with *ayllu*s from Calca. "We're on the border of Paucartambo," Luis explained, "so we have to defend its boundaries. The border *ayllu*s meet *(topanku)* at the provincial boundaries on *Comadres P'unchay*."

In 1952 a man from Sipaskancha died there, and the *guardia civil* stepped in to prohibit what they considered a murderous practice.[7] With fighting banned, *tinkuy* survives as a competitive dance. Contingents from the various *ayllu*s arrive with the men dressed in *sargento* costumes and the women clad in their best clothes, decked with ribbons and tassels. The dance groups meet and mingle, each trying to out-dance the others. Although musicians from each community play *sargento* music, they make no attempt at coordination. The whole point is to drown each other out.

Sargento is danced in pairs: two men bob and sidle back and forth facing each other, occasionally switching the other's calves. When male and female dancers pair up, the whipping gets more ferocious. Men were expected to seek out partners from other communities, and the *tinkuy* must have originally been "fought" with sex as well as slings and stones.

Hakuchu, turáy, pasiyamusun?	Shall we wander off, little brother?
Hakuchu ñañáy, pasiyamusun?	Shall we wander off, little sister?
Wakankillasta pallaramusun.	Let's go pick our wakankilla flowers.
. . .	. . .
Hakuyá, turacháy, tusurimusun!	Come on, little brother, let's dance!
Hakuyá, ñañacháy, tusurimusun	Come on, little sister, let's dance
tinkunapatapi, chaypiña chaypiña!	On the *tinku* ground, right there, right there!

When Sonqo *Runakuna* sit up drinking, joking, and flirting on holiday nights, they sometimes recall this dancing/fighting/lovemaking encounter. I recorded the following conversation on the feast of Santiago (25 July 1984) as I celebrated with Erasmo and Cipriana. We were joined by their son Hipolito and their adopted son Simforoso, who were accompanied by their wives.

Simforoso: *Kunan noqa yachani ankiyta yá, chaymanta parlasunchis, salú! Kunan munaychata tukaypusayki, yá! Piru kunan grabanki!*[8]

Now I know how to play this [the flute] very well—so let's talk about that! Salud! Now I'll play for you real pretty, and you record it.

Me: *Yá, grabasaq kunan!*

Yeah, I'll record it!

Hipolito: *Piru tukayruraq! Kunan noqayku grabayusaqku allinta, peru qan Kumari tumayuy, listo!*

Okay, so play already! We'll record you just fine—but you gotta drink, *Compadre*!

Erasmo: *Noqapis tukamusaqmi kunan!*

I'm gonna play, too!

Hipolito: *Yá, iskayninku machukuna tukayrunqaku.*

Yeah, both the old men are gonna play.

Erasmo: *Arí, arí, machukuna.*

Yeah, yeah, the old men.

Simforoso: *Chaymi noqaq nay isti noqaq kan!*

But I'm the one who's got this!

Hipolito (impressively indicating Simforoso's flute): *Instrumento! Chaychallawan puriyku p'asña qhari maqt'a wark'anakamuyku, maqanakuyku, apaynakuyku, hina!*

The instrument! We go around with that and, girls and young men, we slingshoot each other, beat up on each other, carry each other away—whatever!

(They get excited and all start playing and talking at once.)

Hipolito: *Manayá rikunchu! Listu! Tumaychis! Tumaychis! Tusuychisyá! Listu, tukaychis kunanqa!*

Hey, we can't make anything out! Okay now, drink! Drink! Dance like crazy! Okay, now you can play!

Simforoso: *Chayta tukushani, riki? Kanmi munaycha antiwa—waw! waw!—kirrillas ki'sta salindu del piligro, oseya de antes, mana yachanichu, piru kan Chiwchillani haqay lumachallapi . . .*

157

So that's what I'll play, right? This is how the beautiful old-time—waw! waw!—warriors came marching out of danger. That must have been a long time ago, I guess. But there's Chiwchillani in that high plain . . .

Erasmo: *Haqay qhepallayá kashan.*

It's right there, behind that ridge.

In 1976 I joined the climb to Chiwchillani, where my companions anxiously kept me at a distance from the dancing. It was a memorable climb partly because I had never been so drunk and so exhausted in my life. *Comadres P'unchay* was "my" day, for I had acquired four new sets of *compadres* that year, and they were all ready to stuff me with mutton soup and *ch'uño* before seven o'clock in the morning. I had consumed three big breakfasts and at least one bottle of *trago* before we started the steep climb.

Serafeo and Valentina, Sonqo's "captains," or lead dancers, led me up the path in a tremendous hurry. Serafeo went running from ridge to hill, stopping often to rest briefly, gulp down some *trago,* and tell me the names of the Places we were passing. This surprised me, for Serafeo is normally close-mouthed with that kind of information, but later I learned that the Sonqueños *should* have approached Chiwchillani in a formal contingent, inspecting Sonqo's borders as they came. Apparently, as Sonqo's *arariwa* (ritual dance leader), Serafeo was trying to make up for this omission without arriving too late for the others. At one point his snare drum rolled down the slope and we had to backtrack for it, laughing frantically.

Arriving at Chiwchillani at about half past three in the afternoon, we met up with about a dozen Sonqueños, including *Alcalde* Eustaquio without his signs of office and a man from Sipaskancha who was courting a girl from Sonqo. The men began to put on their *sargento* costumes and preen themselves. Although the costume resembles that of the colonial Spanish soldiers who gave the dance its name, its white plumed headdress and flowing wing-like sleeves also evoke the *wallatas,* a white water bird that lives in Qesqay Qocha, the high lake not far from Chiwchillani. The dancer's bobbing step, too, reminds one of the *"puka chaki wallatascha"* ("little red-footed *wallatas"*) of which they sing:

Qhesqay Pampa wallatascha	Little *wallatas* of Qesqay Pampa
Qhesqay Pampa wallatascha	Little *wallatas* of Qesqay Pampa
Machu runaman payarusqa	Knocked out an old man
Paya warminman pasarusqa.	And knocked up his old lady.[9]

Sitting near us on Chiwchillani were groups from the adjoining Colquepata *ayllus*—Chocopia, Sipaskancha Alta, and Sipaskancha Baja. On the other side of the dance plain sat contingents from P'isaq (*ayllu*s of Kuyo Grande, Chawaytiri, and Sacaca) and San Salvador (Qamawara and Tirakancha). Each group kept to itself and mingled with the others only in the crowd on the plain below.

The Sonqo *Runakuna* seemed to feel little enthusiasm for joining the encounter. Serafeo and a few others finally went trotting down the hill with the tentative air of swimmers about to dive into very cold water. They milled around the edge of the crowd, Serafeo playing his snare drum—and shortly returned to the rest of us. None of the women from Sonqo joined the dancing, but I saw couples from other communities run hand-in-hand into the crowd. Men did not seem to seek out women from other communities.

In the days that followed, I asked why the Sonqo contingent had been so reticent about joining the dance. *"Manchakuyku"* ("We're afraid"), was one reply. *"Manan munankuchu"* ("They don't want to"), was another. Josefa shook her head disdainfully. *"Qellu Sonqokuna!"* ("Lazy Sonqueños!"), she exclaimed. Basilia added that women from Kuyo Grande are bold and wild, whereas the Sonqo women keep their distance.

Sonqo's contingent left at about half past four, heading rapidly to Qolqerí, a lower pass where the more populated part of Sonqo's territory gives way to the high *puna* no-man's-land above. There many more Sonqo *Runakuna* awaited us, sitting in the gray afternoon drizzle. Our group made a grand entrance, Serafeo tapping away on his snare drum and the Sipaskancha suitor playing his flute, while the others came whooping and leaping like "beautiful old-time—waw! waw!—warriors marching out of danger." Basilia and Alcides glared at me reproachfully as we sat down to fortify ourselves with *trago* and cold *ch'uño*. They soon left with another group. I had insulted them by not visiting on *Comadres P'unchay*.

A rainy and moonless night set in, but that did not stop us from setting off on *paseo* to visit the houses of community authorities beginning with the *mayordomo*, and then going on to the *alcalde*, the *segundo*, and the four *regidores*. Don Luis, as president, was included as the last stop. In each house, sleepy hosts hauled themselves out of bed to serve us hot soup, *trago*, and coca, after which we danced the *sargento*, doing our best not to trip in the fireplace or step on the crockery.

The *paseos* had been held every Sunday for five weeks and would culminate the following Sunday to usher in Carnival week. Ideally, young unmarried people should make these rainy nocturnal rounds, but in 1976 most of the dancers were young married couples, for most of the local bachelors were off working in Cuzco or serving in the army.

During the *comadres' paseo*, my group deviated from the proper order and visited the *alcalde* before the *mayordomo* to avoid the group that had gone on ahead of us. Finally, at three in the morning, the two contingents met at Don Luis's house. Then there came to pass a mighty battle—which I unfortunately missed, having passed out cold shortly before it began.

The *paseo* groups had coalesced around two constellations of personal bonds, based primarily on friendship and *compadrazgo*. They did not represent traditional groups within the community, nor—as far as I could tell—political factions. Probably years of submerged tension surfaced in this fight, which no outsider could reconstruct entirely—for, after all, these people had known

159

each other, and gotten on each other's nerves, all their lives. The fact that they were all dead-drunk and dead-tired must have fed their bad tempers, compounded by the knowledge that this was the day they *should* have gone fighting in the *puna*.

Alcides was among the first arrivals and ordered the later group to leave. Luis was furious, and he ordered Bernardo to beat Alcides. Bernardo refused, but Adriano, Luis's newest *ahijado*, stepped in to do the job. Adriano and Alcides are both Luis's godchildren through *matrimonio*, both were in line for the *alcalde*ship, and both had been trained as catechists. Felicha jumped up to take on her cousin Dominga, a girl her own age. Luis is said to have jumped out of bed to join the fray with a flashlight I had given him, shining it in people's eyes with his left hand and swinging at them with his right. Basilia stood by her son, and Luis ordered them both out of the house.

Interestingly, the antagonists automatically paired themselves up with their most equal counterpart. Rivals in battle, like lovers, are *yanantin* (a matched pair; helpmates). The word *ayni* (reciprocal exchange) can refer to vengeance as well as mutual aid. Any release of energy—whether constructive or destructive—calls for collaboration.

Unlike the *tinkuy,* which would have had the more impersonal quality of team sports, this brawl was deeply felt on a personal level and left its mark on the Carnival festivities the following week. There was no *paseo* the following Sunday, although it should have been the finest one of all.

On Monday, each family turned to its own ritual obligations to the sheep. Communal festivities did not start up again until Tuesday, *Puqllay P'unchay,* Carnival itself, when the *ayllu Runakuna purinku* (go around) to their authorities' houses in a mass *paseo*. On Wednesday the *alcalde* himself passes through the community, visiting his fellow staff bearers with an entourage of any *ayllu Runakuna* who want to join him.

Eustaquio, having buckled under to his mother (see Chapter 3), made an admirable *alcalde*. On Tuesday he presided behind the ritual table with the *vara* (staff of office) held firmly in his right hand. Arriving in groups of five to ten, the *Runakuna* showered him with tiny blossoms of the red and yellow *waqankilla* plant, which blooms in the very high *puna* during Carnival season.[10]

I too was showered with this natural confetti by my new *compadres* on the morning of *Comadres P'unchay;* and at about the same time, the *ayllu*'s staff bearers were sprinkling the petals over the little mothers in the church as well. As the sun set on Monday, each family sprinkled *waqankilla* over its courtyard and herds—a *ch'uyay* not of *chicha,* but of flowers.

Presiding behind the ritual table, Eustaquio served coca and *chicha* in the manner described at the beginning of Chapter 6. His mother dominated the women's scene, quite overshadowing her daughter-in-law. As Eustaquio called the guests over in turn, he articulated a hierarchical ranking for most of the *ayllu*'s adult members. Only after the guests had been served two rounds of food did the dancing start, with the older men playing a chorus of long, deep-voiced flutes. The *sargento* dancers sought out female partners, breaking the dance from time to time to accept servings of *chicha,* which flowed continuously.

Sargento is a pretty dance, with the men ducking and bobbing and the women, bent slightly over their many skirts, turning in place. This dance beautifully expresses the relationship between the sexes. Each woman carries a multicolored tasseled rope or a long fernlike branch, and as she twirls demurely—suddenly it lashes out at her partner's bare calves. He leaps to avoid it, and she tries to catch him again on the way down.

Basilia told me gleefully that "in the old times" women put thorns or pieces of wire in their tasseled ropes to scourge the men until blood ran down their legs. In 1976 I saw no bloodletting, but plenty of welts and bruises. And on both sexes—for eventually, the men turn on their female tormentors to deliver the same treatment with their own ropes and branches. Safely back in Sonqo, the *Runakuna* put their constraint aside and let the pretty birdlike courtship dance call forth a *tinkuy,* a whipping encounter. Occasionally a dancer breaks out of this violent partnership for a moment to deliver a few blows to a vulnerable neighbor, occupied elsewhere and exposed from the rear.

And they have a great time: laughing, screeching, and eventually tumbling down to rest—the woman among the crowd of women, the man joining the seated line of men.

Adriano and Alcides sat moping in silence on opposite sides of the gathering, neither dancing nor fighting. Basilia hunkered down, glowering defensively inside an incredible mountain of skirts. Late in the afternoon she skipped and twirled off lightheartedly, singing masterfully at the top of her voice. They should miss her! They should regret it when she felt too sad to dance! Basilia's contrariness did put a damper on the festivities, but the others shrugged off her moodiness and concentrated on their own drinking and mutual beating. Luis played the flute for a while and then wandered off. He missed Rufina.

Puqllay continued on a smaller scale for the rest of the week. Days and nights were quiet, but from late afternoon until twilight, dance groups converged on Pachawani and Yanqay, two promontories near opposite ends of Sonqo's territory. Dancers seemed to choose one hill over the other out of convenience or preference for the people they expected to meet there. The two groups could see each other as tiny bobbing figures of red, black, and white decorating the brown hilltops.

These twilight dances were just as boisterous as those on Tuesday and Wednesday. Couples sang to each other as they danced, alternating responses. They rested their bruised legs and took to shoving, punching, and rump-bumping, encounters with a more individualized quality of courtship about them. The cloudy night fell, and the crowds diminished, couples apparently stealing off together under cover of darkness.

On Saturday morning I left Sonqo in the cold fog to return to the United States. The next day Basilia arrived in Cuzco to see me off, chattering in excitement about a contingent of girls from Chocopia who had come to Sonqo the day before. Bold and well-dressed singers, they lured the *Runakuna* to dance again on Yanqay, near the Chocopia border, rather than on Antaqaqa, the traditional Saturday dancing ground.

Sunday was the last and final day of Carnival, *Puqllay Kachaypari* (Carnival Send-Off), and as the truck crept over the muddy road toward Cuzco, Basilia listened and watched in delight to the sounds of Carnival in the communities she passed.

'Qhawayachiwaspá	Now that it's got us looking
—Puqllay!—	—Puqllay!—
Puqllayqa ripushán!	Puqllay's going away!
—Puqllay!—	—Puqllay!—
Sapa runachawán	Now that it's left its sami
—Puqllay!—	—Puqllay!—
Saminman churaspá!	With each little man!—[11]
—Puqllay!—	—Puqllay!—
Llapa sultiratán	Now that it's made us notice
—Puqllay!—	—Puqllay!—
Qhawachiwaspá!	All the unmarried girls!
—Puqllay!—	—Puqllay!—

The Great Pilgrimage

Preparations

Corpus Christi is a movable feast, falling in late May or June (on the Thursday after Trinity Sunday). During the preceding weeks, about thirty Sonqueños prepare to embark on a great purgatorial adventure. The stay-at-homes look wistfully eastward toward the distant peaks of the Qoyllur Rit'i range, remarking sadly that they really should go—maybe next year. But the journey is exhausting and full of spiritual dangers, so one easily finds excuses not to join in. Most Sonqo *Runakuna* go on the Qoyllur Rit'i pilgrimage only two or three times in the course of their lives. A few, like Erasmo, go every year.

Ripunay qasakama	I must go to the ice
Señor Qoyllur Rit'i.	Lord Qoyllur Rit'i.
Samiykiwan saminchay	Bless me with your sami
Ñuqñu Hesusllay.	Sweet Jesus.[12]

In 1785 a miracle took place at Qoyllur Rit'i: the Christ Child appeared to a shepherd boy from the nearby village of Tayankani. After playing with the shepherd, the Christ Child disappeared into a rock, which was ever after marked with his imprint.[13] Sonqo *Runakuna* vaguely recall this story but seem uninterested in it. For them, the pilgrimage is to *Rit'i* (the Snow) and to the *Tay-takuna* (Fathers), the great *Apus* (Lord Mountains). The rock bearing Christ's image, now enclosed in a concrete chapel, is a prototype of Sonqo's own small *taytacha*—a small portable shrine consisting of a red three-sided wooden box, about one foot square and six inches deep, painted inside with a simple picture of the crucified Christ. Every year the Sonqo *taytacha* joins a crowd of *taytacha*s from other communities at the foot of Christ's image in the church. While the pilgrims perform outside the church in dance groups, or climb to the glaciers above the sanctuary, the *taytacha*s visit with one another in a kind of annual reunion. At the pilgrimage's end they are carried home, renewed.[14]

Ten months out of the year the little *taytacha* stays shut up in Sonqo's church, but seven weeks before the pilgrimage he emerges, cradled in the arms of the *huntador* ("coordinator," the pilgrimage sponsor), who carries him around the community soliciting cash contributions. In the following weeks, the *taytacha* lives as a guest in the *huntador*'s house, sitting in a place of honor in a wall-niche opposite the doorway. For the *huntador* and his family, the *tay-tacha*'s visit is a once-in-a-lifetime event—a special honor and a grave respon-sibility. Every Wednesday the *huntador*'s family holds a private *velakuy* (candle-light vigil), chewing coca and drinking with (and for) the image, much as do all Sonqo *Runakuna* with their *enqas* on the eves of Carnival, San Juan, and August First.

The *huntador*'s burden is shared by a secondary sponsor, the *priwistu* (provost), who holds a welcome-home feast for the returning pilgrims. The staff bearers do not participate in either the pilgrimage itself or in the sequence of rituals held before and after it. The *alcalde*'s usual role of ritual director is taken over by the *arariwa*, the leader of Sonqo's ritual dancers.[15]

Ritual dancing is considered a *cargo*, as it involves an outlay of time, en-ergy, cash, and the preparation of the ornate, expensive costume. The dancers are joined by a four-man band composed of two transverse flutes, a snare drum, and a bass drum. The *taytacha* is escorted by two women called *alfereces*, the only festival *cargo* held by women independent of their husbands.

The *huntador* chooses his dancers, band, and *alfereces* in consultation with kinsmen, elders, and the *alcalde*. Other pilgrims are usually related in some way to the *huntador* and contribute to his *cargo* by cooking, gathering firewood, preparing *chicha*, or carrying provisions. The *huntador* and his wife face the responsibility of feeding the group and directing its progress.

In 1975 Luis was *huntador*, and as temporary members of his household Rick Wagner and I were drawn into the pilgrimage. Our job was to keep the pilgrims supplied with hot coffee saturated with sugar, and Luis seemed im-mensely pleased by this unusual addition to the menu of boiled potatoes and potato soup.

The fourth Wednesday before Corpus Christi, the candlelight vigil moves from the *huntador*'s house to the church. The vigil consists of a three-part cycle: (1) praying; (2) coca chewing; and (3) ritual dancing. This cycle is repeated three times in its entirety and ends shortly after daybreak.

At about one o'clock in the morning, we settled in the church, with the *taytacha* sitting on the altar. *Arariwa* Serafeo, a trained catechist, led a service of prayers and hymns in Quechua:

Chakatasqa k'irichasqa	Crucified and wounded
Apu Hesus hamusunki,	Lord Jesus comes to you,
Huchasapa wawallanta	To interrogate you
Tapupayakamusunki.	His own sinful child.

Then we filed out into the cold night and huddled on the church steps, chewing Luis's coca and drinking his *trago*. After about half an hour, we returned to the church to watch the *ch'unchu*s, the ritual dancers representing people of the tropical forest.

The four dancers took their places before the altar, their high, orange-feathered headdresses throwing immense shadows, their sequined vests and aprons glinting in the candlelight. As the band played its prelude, the dancers blew a few notes on reed panpipes in their left hands, holding *chonta* palm staffs in their right.[16] Bowing, they placed the panpipes next to the *taytacha*, aligned themselves in two pairs, and launched into their dance.

The strenuous dance lasts nearly an hour. The dancers make a point of showing no fatigue as they solemnly clash their staffs and trace out patterns of *x*'s, circles, and figure-eights with skipping steps. Dancing in pairs, the *ch'unchu*s immediately repeat each skipped pattern in reverse while the repetitive music continues in a melodic line that rises and then falls, falls and then rises. The dancers, the choreography, and the musical phrases are structured in opposed yet mutually supportive pairs.[17] Underneath the melody, the base drum pounds a mesmerizing beat.

Throughout the Corpus season, both at home and at the sanctuary, *ch'unchu* music rings in one's ears. The sanctuary is crowded with delegations playing *ch'unchu*, each with a slight but perceptible difference in the melody, all supported by the same inexorable rhythm.[18]

The comical and frightening *ukuku* (bear) dancer, clad in his shaggy brown tunic and knitted mask, did not join the first church vigil. But during the second one a week later, in he barged, whooping in a falsetto voice. Yelling insults and obscenities, the shaggy *ukuku* shambled into the middle of the orderly dance, tripping up the stoic, deadpan *ch'unchu*s with his whip. Occasionally he broke away to run through the audience, squeaking lewd invitations to the women and cuffing the men indiscriminantly.

Under his mask, the *ukuku* was our friend Eustaquio, who later that year was to resist election as *alcalde*. The following week during the third vigil, Eustaquio was joined by another *ukuku*, Alcides's brother-in-law earnest Tomas Illa, who was just beginning to participate in the *ayllu*'s public functions. His first night out, this new *ukuku* was "murdered" by the *ch'unchu*s with their pointed staffs, who then dumped the "body" outside the church while Eustaquio as senior *ukuku* wailed and carried on. But no sooner had the dance

Ch'unchu dancers in feather headdresses fall back to make way for the clowning *ukuku* (bear) dancers. (Photo by Rick Wagner)

started up again when in roared the young *ukuku*, risen from the dead to scourge them all.

After each of the three all-night vigils, the company sets off in *paseo* to households that have volunteered to entertain the *taytacha* and his entourage. The *paseo* ends around noon, when the tired group arrives at the *huntador's* house, where they settle down to consume yet another meal and more *trago*.

The first vigil ended splendidly. Rufina had prepared a fine meal with the help of her three sisters and her various *comadres*. Respected elders joined them: Don Inocencio; Don Modesto, the *mayordomo* (church custodian); and Luis's brother-in-law Don Gabriel, the previous year's *huntador*. The *priwistu*, Old Marcelino "Machu" Mamani, also arrived, apparently trying with this fairly minor office to offset his reputation as "old but not elder" (see Chapter 3).

The band entered the courtyard playing *ch'unchu* music, followed by the *ch'unchu* dancers. Luis proudly carried the *taytacha* behind them. As the *ch'unchus* began to dance, the rest of the men settled down along the courtyard wall and waited to be served.

Eating—*ch'unchu* dancing—coca and *trago*. Eating—*ch'unchu* dancing—coca and *trago*. On and on it went until three in the afternoon, when Luis passed out in the storeroom, and Rufina had to emerge from her place beside the stove to take over his hostly duties. To keep the guests from leaving, she began dancing energetically with old Modesto, who distinguished his position as elder and *mayordomo* by leaping around like an enthusiastic frog while maintaining a serenely blank expression.

Flanked by community elders, Luis (second from right) chuckles at the joking *ukuku* (bear) dancer while hosting Corpus Christi festivities in his courtyard. To the left, *ch'unchu* dancers sit behind a table bearing two goblets of *chicha* and the three-pronged whip symbolizing the *ayllu*'s authority. (Photo by Rick Wagner)

But the guests were ready to leave and quietly slipped away to collapse into bed. It had been a good beginning to the Corpus season.

The Journey

The Sunday before Corpus Christi, pilgrims gathered in Luis's courtyard for a ritual meal. We set off around noon: the band in front, followed by the *ch'unchus*; Luis and Rufina next, carrying the *taytacha* and escorted by the *alfereces*; and a retinue of pilgrims bringing up the rear. Erasmo was carting along his faithful baritone horn, ready to join in from time to time when the flutists put away their instruments of plastic tubing and produced trumpets from under their ponchos.

As we trudged along the rut-scarred highway past Qoyapuqru, Basilia ran up to join us, beaming guiltily. We had expected her to stay home, for Alcides's wife Luisa was too pregnant to tend the sheep in Basilia's absence and might give birth any day. Basilia should have stayed with her, but at the last minute—there she was with us. She loved to travel and could not bear to miss the few opportunities her circumscribed life provided. Delighting to be on the move, her irrepressible commentary alternated between awe and amusement as she ambled along under a load of provisions.

We dropped down to the traditional footpath, past Wankarani and Qellu Unu, to retrace the path the plague is said to have followed as it came up to Sonqo from Colquepata. Before we descended, the company stopped and turned its gaze backward: Sonqo's church was about to pass from view. We knelt and removed our hats; the *alawaru* sounded; and the pilgrims filed up to kiss the *taytacha* proudly cradled in Rufina's arms.

We stopped again at Qellu Unu before crossing the boundary between Sonqo and Colquepata; throughout the pilgrimage this procedure was repeated every time an important peak or chapel entered our view or passed from it. And every time we met a group from another community we stopped again; the two *huntadors* exchanged *taytachas* and the two bands played *alawaru*—not in unison, but vying to see which could play louder.

Many older pilgrims could remember walking all the way from Sonqo to the glacial sanctuary, a weeklong trek marked by innumerable pauses for *alawaru*. But now Sonqueños join the other delegations from Colquepata in excruciatingly crowded and slow-moving trucks that leave the district capital in midafternoon and arrive about eleven at night in the tiny village of Mahuayani, where the final steep ascent to the sanctuary begins. As the trucks rumble out of the plaza, many of their occupants weep from a mixture of joy, excitement, and anxiety. For some, this journey is the emotional peak of a lifetime.

After resting at Mahuayani, we took the final eight-kilometer ascent by foot and timed our ascent to arrive at the sanctuary just at sunrise. We each added a stone to our packs as a *hucha* (load of sin) to be left at our destination. As we began the climb, the peaks of the snowy mountains were hidden by nearer ridges. About two in the morning, Alcides, who was along as a flutist, turned to me in excitement: "Soon we'll see the *Taytakuna* (Fathers)!"

We turned a bend in the path and there they were, indeed, their peaks shining in the moonlight. In their company the white frost forming on our shivering heads and backs seemed natural and even honorable. We stopped for the *alawaru* and continued.

We passed a stand of tall, tough grass knotted in strange configurations. Several pilgrims slipped off the path, groping behind their backs with their left hands to twist the grass leftward. Then they hurried to join their fellows. Apolinar explained that through this leftward twisting, the pilgrims leave their sins behind in the clumps of grass.

Night was lifting as we arrived at the *kalwayu (calvario)*, a large cross looming over the spring below the sanctuary. Serafeo blew into his panpipe, bowed to the snowy peaks, and skipped up to the sanctuary and back, shadowed by the mocking *ukuku*. He was joined for a second approach by the other dancers; the third time the whole delegation of pilgrims followed. We knelt on the frozen puddles before entering the cement chapel roofed with corrugated aluminum. The chapel was constructed by the *Hermandad* (Brotherhood), a Mestizo fraternity devoted to the worship of Qoyllur Rit'i, to protect the miraculous rock bearing *taytacha*'s image. There Sonqo's little *taytacha* joined the crowd of *taytacha*s from other *ayllu*s.

At the other end of the chapel a throng of people stood with burning candles, some weeping, some praying, some standing silently. Five years later I was to join them, burning a long white candle for Basilia's departed soul. But in 1975 Basilia was very much with us, and before the exhausting trek was over I felt much indebted to her humorous and sympathetic encouragement.

Outside, we found Sonqo's traditional camping spot and collapsed to rest as the sun rose higher in the sky, melting the puddles. Soon we became almost as uncomfortable from the heat of the day as we had been earlier from the cold of the night.

The valley around the sanctuary was filled with thousands of pilgrims from hundreds of communities—a spectrum of social types. Each community brought a troop of dancers, the two most common being the *ch'unchu*s, who represent wild men from the jungle, and the *qolla*s, who represent traders from the Altiplano to the south. The *ch'unchu* dancers come mainly from Paucartambo communities, which are ethnically Indian, whereas the *qolla*s are more Hispanicized.

There are many other types of dance as well—far more than I can describe here.[19] The glacial valley seems to vibrate with color and movement as the various troupes dance around the churchyard. The sounds of many bands—each playing by itself without any attempt at coordination—rise and merge in the thin, clear air. The effect is not cacophonous but strangely pleasant and exciting: a kind of mighty jingling produced by the heavy beat and rising-falling melody of many *ch'unchu* bands, together with the high, vibrating music of the *qolla*s and the blaring of many brass bands.

Other pilgrims wandered off on private missions. In penance and devotion, some climbed the last arduous ascent onto the glacier spilling off the slopes of Apu Qolqepunku. Many women stopped at the small stone shrine of the Virgen de Fatima, whom they call *awaq mamacha* (little weaving mother), to set up small backstrap looms and weave little pieces to leave as offerings. The *mamacha* guides the women's hands as they weave, and they depart newly instructed in their craft.

Nearby, pilgrims were busily building miniature house compounds of small stones. Inside the little corrals were "herds" of pebbles representing domestic animals. This is no child's game, but a stone message to the *Taytakuna* indicating objects that the builder hopes to acquire. Often the pebble houses and sheep are joined by pebble trucks, cars, sewing machines, and televisions. Literate pilgrims bypass this pebble "game" and write their requests on scraps of white paper that they slip into cracks in the stone walls of the *mamacha*'s shrine.[20]

Everywhere—at the sanctuary, on the ice, in the scree-filled slopes between—the *ukuku*s are very much in evidence, combining court jester and policeman into a single role. They enforce a ban on alcoholic beverages (for while coca is chewed, *trago* is prohibited). When the Archbishop of Cuzco passes in procession, and when he says Mass over loudspeakers, the *ukuku*s cuff pilgrims who inattentively forget to remove their hats.

On Monday night, as we curled up under ponchos and blankets trying to sleep as best we could, an *ukuku* came by yelling at Eustaquio to come up to the glacier—only to be met with snores and a grumpy refusal. Eustaquio should have joined other *ukuku* dancers to vie for the privilege of carrying down a large cross, which the *Hermandad* had planted on the glacier the previous Friday.

At daybreak hundreds of shaggy bears, carrying blocks of ice on their backs, streamed off the glacier in three lines down to the sanctuary. This ice, cut from the *Apu* himself, is described as *santu* (holy) and *hampi* (medicinal).[21]

The moonlit ascent to the glacier is perilous, and it is said that *ukuku*s have lost their lives falling into crevices or being knocked out by icy snowballs. But these are relatively minor perils compared to the spiritual danger, for the glacier is the abode of howling *kukuchi*s (see Chapter 1). As bears are believed to be immortal and capable of great physical and spiritual bravery, the *ukuku* dancers are expected to ward off the cannibalistic demons. One of the Andes' most beloved folktales tells of the young Bear Man who fought with the damned soul of an evil *hacendado* and defeated it.[22]

Without the protection of the *ukukus* and the *taytachas*, the other pilgrims would not dare to venture among the snowy peaks. Rufina warned me against returning out of season.

"*Amayá!*" she exclaimed, roused by the thought into uncharacteristic vehemence. "*Manan imapas kanchu . . . Kukuchi mihusunkiman!*" ("Don't! There's nothing there . . . The *kukuchi*s would eat you!").

After the *ukuku*s had descended from the ice, the archbishop said Mass, and the pilgrims prepared to depart. Mestizos from Cuzco set off down the path to Mahuayani, where trucks and buses awaited them.[23] Pilgrims from the *Runa* communities retrieved their *taytachas* to carry them through the longest and most exhausting leg of the journey, a twenty-hour trek across the cold *puna* to Tayankani, and on across one more steep pass to the town of Ocongate.

Several times along the way, when we stopped for *alawaru*, the *taytachas* were placed at the foot of a larger cross, and the *arariwas* danced. At dusk we settled to eat and rest in a high sheltered plain called Yana Kancha, and when the moon rose we set out again to walk until sunrise. Deep in the night, crossing another pass, members of the *Hermandad* danced the *Qhapaq Qolla* (Mighty Qolla), singing the fearful "Yawar Mayu" ("Blood River").

Ama Wayqelláy waqakunkichu
Yawar Mayupi rikukushaspa.
Warak'achallay "Q'aq Q'aq."

Don't weep, Little Brother,
When you look into Blood River.
My little sling goes "Q'aq! Q'aq!"[24]

As dawn neared, many *ukuku*s gathered to be whipped by the *celadores,* disciplinarians of the *Hermandad.*

Foreign unbeliever though I was, this nightwalk to Tayankani was an unforgettably moving experience. The moonlit snowpeaks seemed close enough to touch and yet immensely distant; the night pierced with a cold the likes of which I have never felt since; light-headed from thin air and exhaustion, I thought the figures in the line before me were swelling up and shrinking down preternaturally.

As it began to get light, the *Hermandad* and the *ukuku*s started goading the pilgrims, forcing us to hurry along with a skipping step. No one, no matter how aged or exhausted, was allowed to rest, for sunrise was near. We descended onto a large plateau above Taytankani and formed a line facing eastward. Suddenly the sun rose; the bands burst into *alawaru* and everyone, dancers and pilgrims, began running across the plain down to Tayankani in long, snaking, crisscrossing lines.

In Tayankani we rested as the *Hermandad* made a procession into the small church. Then we set out on the last leg of the trek, for the steep ridge between Tayankani and Ocongate still remained between the pilgrims and the trucks waiting to carry them on the long, uncomfortable ride home.

Once in Ocongate, Sonqo's pilgrims paid little attention to the final procession into the church, for they were tired and ready to go home. We found one of the Colquepata trucks and climbed aboard, pleased to get there first. There we sat and slept, ate, or quietly chewed coca while other groups straggled aboard, jockeying with us for space. Finally we all became as crowded and irritated with one other as we had been on the ride to Mahuayani.

For Sonqo *Runakuna,* processions organized by the *Hermandad* were not a major interest. They had come to walk among the snowy Fathers, to climb the glacial ice, and to dance in the sunrise above Tayankani, and they had already done all of this. But the Sonqo *Runakuna*'s de-emphasis on Catholic processions and rituals does not mean that they do not view them as essential to the pilgrimage. After all, the Sonqueños bring their own *taytacha* to visit the great *taytacha* in the sanctuary among the hundreds of other community *taytacha*s. As the Sonqo *Runakuna* travel with dancers and pilgrims from other *ayllu*s, all led by the *Hermandad,* so too does their *taytacha* travel with those of other *ayllu*s, all led by a larger *taytacha* from Tayankani. The Catholic ritual is part of the whole process of revitalization and renewal effected by the pilgrimage—but just as processions and church services in Sonqo benefit the whole *ayllu* while requiring the attendance of only a few, so it is with processions and church services during the pilgrimage. These are not the responsibility of the *Runakuna* who, while not participating directly or even paying much attention to the Catholic rituals, still benefit from them.

At two o'clock on Thursday morning, we crawled off the crowded truck in Chocopia, the stop closest to Sonqo, and trudged back to Luis and Rufina's house, where a widowed *comadre* greeted us with hot and welcome soup. The meal, drinks, and *hallpay* were brief, and we quickly scattered home to our respective beds.

Celebrating the Return

I vaguely recall Luis bursting into our room the next day, shouting for me to get up and go to the Corpus festivities in T'oqra—a brief interruption that hardly penetrated my deep, exhausted sleep, which lasted well into the afternoon. Luis and Rufina also rested at home, but the dancers, musicians, and a few pilgrims—including indefatigable Basilia—set out in the morning to celebrate Corpus Christi in T'oqra, along with Colquepata's other *ayllus*.

In the evening they returned home. Two days of dancing, playing, and celebrating still stretched before them. As long as the *taytacha* remained outside the church, its retinue was obliged to worship it through dance and music. On Friday the little box with its painted crucifixion traveled to the *priwistu's* (provost's) house to celebrate its official homecoming. On Saturday it returned to the *huntador* (coordinator), and Luis capped off his final *cargo* with another day of eating, drinking, coca chewing, and dancing.

Don Justino, who was serving as *alcalde* at the time, appeared at these celebrations, but he did not carry his tokens of office. As the *priwistu's* son, Justino spent his time rushing between the house, where his stepmother labored at the stove, and the line of male guests, whom he had to serve with soup and *chicha*. The authority invested in the *alcalde*, in fact, was not present; Justino was just the sponsor's son and the *chaki-maki* ("gofer"; literally, foot-hand).

Unlike the Saints' Day celebrations, it is the *arariwa* rather than the *alcalde* who serves as master of ceremonies throughout the Corpus cycle. At ritual feasts, the *arariwa* occupies the place of honor to the right of the *huntador* at the ritual table. Guests who want to leave briefly to urinate and couples who wish to dance must ask the *arariwa's* permission. He directs the serving of *chicha* while the *huntador* distributes handfuls of coca leaf.[25]

During the Friday festivities, the usual two rounds of eating, coca chewing, and *chicha* drinking were supplemented by a procedure resembling *ch'uyay*, the ritual libation at animal fertility ceremonies. Once the dinner plates were collected, the *priwistu's* wife emerged from the house and stood at her husband's left. The *arariwa* gave them each a *qero* of *chicha* and, turning to face east, they crossed themselves and prayed rapidly and inaudibly. Then they tossed the *chicha*—not on their herds this time—but down their own throats. Luis's and Rufina's turn was next, followed by *Arariwa* Serafeo and his wife, Valentina. Other married couples followed suit.

The next day, after Rufina and her assistants emerged from the house, the same procedure was repeated. But then Luis opened a big coca bundle on the ritual table and the company plunged into a *hallpachikuy* (forced coca chewing), stuffing one another's mouths in a giggling, scrabbling free-for-all. Rufina's brother Domingo, who had been busy serving, called for dancing, and though it was getting dark, they hung a lantern on a pole and danced the *sargento* in the courtyard until ten o'clock. The close companionship forged through six weeks of tiring ritual was drawing to a close.

To my great annoyance, I did not see the final step of this long ritual sequence. Luis's entourage returned the following day to eat yet another ritual meal before escorting the *taytacha* to the church, where he would rest for another ten months. As Luis placed the box with its painted Christ on the altar, he would pass his *cargo* to next year's sponsor. I tried to tag along as the dancers and the band filed out of the house, but Luis shooed me away, telling me to go home and cook. In about an hour he returned, glad to be finished with his *cargos* and feeling very pleased with himself.

Processions and Power Objects

There are many aspects to long, complex ritual practices like Santa Cruz, Carnival, and the pilgrimage to Qoyllur Rit'i, and many perspectives from which to view them. One of the basic functions of these rituals is to maintain the connection between the *Runakuna* and their Sacred Places, so necessary to the existence and perpetuation of the *ayllu*.

In their private family rituals, *Runakuna* communicate with the Sacred Places to ensure the welfare of their animals, their *ch'uño*, and the souls of their dead. Blowing over coca and food; pouring out alcohol; burning *despachos*; force-feeding; invocations and music; ritually correct decoration: these are the *Runakuna*'s ritual techniques for communicating with *Pacha* and the *Tirakuna*. Their power objects, *enqa*s and *istrilla*s, store vitality and well-being by forging a connection between the household and the Sacred Places.

In communal festivals, it is not the household but the *ayllu* as a whole that commands ritual attention. In these community-wide celebrations another ritual technique, the procession, takes on great importance, bringing the *ayllu*'s representatives into direct contact with their territory. *Runakuna* communicate with their Places by visiting them. During Carnival they "play"—that is, dance/fight—on Qolqerí, Pachawani, Yanqay, and Antaqaqa, four of their highest and most powerful hills. Their *paseos*, moreover, lead them crisscrossing Sonqo's territory, as they visit the *varayuqkuna* (staff bearers) in descending rank order.

The pilgrimage to Qoyllur Rit'i accomplishes the same thing on a larger scale, for by visiting the Lord Mountains, *Runakuna* confirm their relationship with Sacred Places of regional importance and integrate themselves as an *ayllu* within a set of regional *ayllu*s. Their power object, the *taytacha*, begins his ritual travels within Sonqo, for he is carried around the community for contributions, then moves back and forth between the *huntador*'s house and the church, and finally visits other households on *paseo*. After weeks of preparation, the *taytacha* sets out on a procession that transcends the community, leading the pilgrims through a landscape of greater and more powerful Places. Back in Sonqo, he again moves through the community, from *huntador* to *priwistu* and then back to the church.

During Carnival season, it is the *alcalde* himself who serves as the *ayllu*'s icon, its transmitter of vitality between *Runakuna* and *Tirakuna*. The roles of sponsor, ritual leader, and mediating icon are combined in the *alcalde* as the *ayllu*'s human representative. On Carnival Tuesday, the *Runakuna* visit their *alcalde* at his house—just as on Saints' Days they visit the images in the church—and during the days that follow he leads them dancing on their sacred hills.

On a plane of immediate experience, processions and pilgrimages infuse meaning into the most mundane activities: walking and watching. To walk long distances in the freezing cold with mountains for company is the *Runakuna*'s lot in life. Pilgrimage intensifies this experience to reveal spiritual potency in the most routine activity. In processions, the basic activity of walking Sonqo's footpaths is given a public structure and a deeper significance. *Taytacha*s and *mamacha*s emerge from their "house" (the church) to traverse the paths, and after they are put away the staff bearers continue to walk in *paseo*. The mere fact of walking is experienced as an affirmation of the *Runakuna*'s connection with the Sacred Places, so that walking itself is an affirmation of community.[26]

People who stay at home see only pieces of the ritual cycles, but from these pieces they reconstruct the rest through imagination and gossip. They know that in other years their own households will be drawn into the festivities, and that the other *Runakuna* will be watching them. Did this year's *huntador* do better than last year's? And will they, when their turn comes, outdo everyone else as they wend their colorful way, pilgrims under the eyes of many watchers?

Chapter Eight

Yawar Mayu
Blood River

Ama Wayqelláy waqakunkichu
Yawar Mayupi rikukushaspa.
Don't weep, Little Brother,
When you look into Blood River.

The Violent Encounter

Runakuna eat little and drink no alcohol during the pilgrimage to Qoyllur Rit'i. Ritual force-feeding takes place back in the *ayllu*, before the pilgrimage starts and after it ends. During the pilgrimage itself, *Runakuna* pour out their energy by dancing; by walking long, exhausting distances in the cold; and by letting their blood flow. The pilgrimage is, as they say, a *"sacrificio."* Occasionally pilgrims are swallowed up by the glacier and lost.

Carnival, too, calls forth a *yawar mayu* (blood river). The mutual blood-letting inherent in the pretty *sargento* dance formerly was brought to its logical conclusion in the *tinkuy* on Chiwchillani, leaving the satisfied mountains "fed" with blood and corpses. The mountains need sacrifices like this, and when for some reason they go hungry or are irritated, they have ways of showing their displeasure.

In 1980 the Sonqueños' pilgrimage to Qoyllur Rit'i was "ruined" (*"malograpun"*). I had gone to the sanctuary directly from Cuzco, having planned to meet the delegation from Sonqo there. The night passed, the sun rose, the icy puddles began to melt—and still the Sonqo *Runakuna* did not arrive. About ten o'clock in the morning, I finally found them—strangely disunified, withdrawn, and downcast.

They arrived late to start with, for their truck had been delayed in Colquepata. Sunrise had already passed before they arrived at the *kalwayu* and settled down to rest until their final procession into the church. But the grand dancing entrance, the culmination of weeks of ritual preparation, was denied them when a rock came rolling down the mountain and crushed Hilario Quispe's foot. The *Hermandad* had to be called, a medic came running, and Hilario was bundled onto a stretcher to be carried back down to Mahuayani. From there he was taken by car to Cuzco in what must have been a long, painful ride. Half of the dancers ran down to Mahuayani with the stretchers, and the rest of Sonqo's pilgrims milled around in dismay and confusion.

This was very bad. Obviously the falling rock was bad for poor Hilario with his crushed foot, and obviously it wrecked Sonqo's parade into the sanctuary. But it was worse than that—for as far as *Runakuna* are concerned, no rock rolls randomly, least of all at Qoyllur Rit'i. The rock was a sign from the Mountain/Saint that Sonqo's delegation was unacceptable.[1] It announced, publicly and unequivocally, that for some reason the *huntador* had failed in his cargo. The *Hermandad* felt unsure as to whether Sonqo's *taytacha* should be allowed into the sanctuary. After a worried consultation they relented, and the *huntador* and the *arariwa* quietly carried their icon into the church and placed him on the altar.

The rest of Sonqo's pilgrims dragged themselves into the sanctuary grounds, only to find their usual camping spot thoroughly occupied by another delegation. I met up with them as they were hunting for a free plot of ground to park their weary bodies in.

Almost an hour passed before anyone told me what had happened. The Sonqo delegation curled up in twos and threes to eat a little, sleep, or settle into depression—leaving me in complete perplexity until Erasmo roused himself to go looking for medicinal herbs. Before setting off he mentioned the accident, almost as an aside.

The delegation completed the pilgrimage and finished the entire ritual sequence, but in poor spirits. Back in Sonqo I encountered an undercurrent of consternation as I heard *Runakuna* speak pityingly of the ruined cargo and Hilario's foot, wondering what had brought on the disaster.

Hilario's injury signified his *ayllu*'s disgrace. Disgrace is no small issue here, for the element of competition is very strong at Qoyllur Rit'i. Every band tries to drown out the others; every dance group tries to create finer costumes and to dance better and longer than the others. Different types of dancers represent different kinds of community. The competition between the provinces of Paucartambo and Quispikanchis formerly found expression in a final ritual battle between *ch'unchu*s and *qolla*s—jungle Indians vying with highland traders.[2] Up on the glacier the *ukuku*s sort themselves out by province, and there too a competitive element comes into play. In fact, no encounter at Qoyllur Rit'i lacks an undercurrent of competition: even when two delegations meet on the trail and courteously greet each other's *taytacha*s, their bands vie to see which can play louder. In 1980 the Mountain eliminated Sonqo from this huge, multifaceted competition.

It may seem paradoxical that competition enters so strongly into an event that serves to integrate *ayllu*s over a large region, and whose overall effect is to produce an overwhelming sense of "comunitas," an ecstatic submersion of individual selfhood into a larger whole.[3] Yet it is exactly the competition—the clash of *ayllu* with *ayllu*, province with province, *puna* people with valley people—that explodes in a huge jingle of sound and blaze of color, in an intensity of activity and noise, which vibrates for a few days in the sun and ice of the *Apu*'s glacial solitude.

As they meet in a multitude of overlapping encounters, the dance groups work themselves into a more and more excited buzz of activity. The excitement reaches its climax on the plain above Tayankani as night yields to day; as the warm rays of the rising sun strike the ice of the snowy peaks; as the bands blare in unified cacophony and the shouting pilgrims run across the plain in crisscrossing lines—all converging and diverging, converging and diverging.

It comes as no surprise that the greatest event of the ritual year requires an ecstatic outburst of energy. As in household rituals, the collective outpouring of energy is what makes the ritual "work"—this is what catches *sami* and keeps it circulating (see Chapter 6). Household ritual accomplishes this goal through the techniques of coca chewing, libation, force-feeding, decoration, dance, and *despacho* burning. At Qoyllur Rit'i, *sami* is circulated through a collective sacrifice of energy and sound, and through a *yawar mayu* (river of blood) flowing under the whips of the *celadores* (disciplinarians of the *Hermandad*) and from wounds incurred in ritual fighting.

The *tinkuy* (ritual encounter) is a central focus of community-level celebrations that transcend the private rites observed within each household. Through *tinkuy*, social unity is created dialectically and expressed in terms of complementary opposition. Although *tinkuy* refers to ritual dance-battles, the word has wider applications. It is not easily translated into English ("dialectic" conveys a similar meaning but is far too abstract). When streams converge in foaming eddies to produce a single, larger stream they are said to *tinkuy*, and their convergence is called *tinku* (or *tingu*). *Tinku*s are powerful, dangerous places full of liberated and uncontrollable forces. There, *amaru*s (dragonlike serpents) may emerge from the underworld; there, one may be overcome with sleep never to awaken; and there, the brave and lucky may find personal power objects. In the *tinku* battle, antagonists meet in a violent union. Carnival *sargento* is a *tinku*—simultaneously a dance, a fight, and a love affair.

The word *puqllay*, very inadequately translated "to play," possesses the same undercurrent of violence as the word *tinkuy*.[4] The Quechua term for Carnival, the season for play, *Puqllay* is a time for battles, whipping contests, and lovemaking, a time when the normally restrained flow of mutual endearment and reassurance is reversed and floodgates of hostility and lust are opened.

However, these floodgates are opened in a controlled and limited way for, violent though it may be, *puqllay* is play nevertheless, just as *tinkuy* is ritual battle rather than unrestrained brawling. Like a football game, *tinkuy* and *puqllay* take place between clearly defined teams, at an appointed time, and for a limited duration.

In the *comadres'* brawl at Luis's house, antagonists followed the culturally determined "habitus" for fighting, automatically turning to their "opposite number" as in a *tinku*. But the ritual frame, which might have given this Carnival fighting a higher meaning, was lacking; violence erupted in a personal quarrel rather than in a ritual battle, and its ultimate effect was divisive rather than unifying. The *tinku* and the brawl do not necessarily contrast as "make believe" fighting and "real" fighting. The combat in a *tinku* is real enough, and the Earth and the Mountains are actually believed to consume the victims' blood. What the ritual frame of the *tinku* accomplishes is a raising of the combat to an impersonal, or community, level. On the other hand, when *tinku* fighting is prohibited and replaced by competitive dancing, as it now is on Chiwchillani, the dance serves as a metaphorical battle, with the ritual frame reminding the dancers of its more violent analog.

Warfare of any kind expresses a group's social boundaries and is also a form of communication between the opposing groups. In *tinkuy*, one experiences an opponent's similarity to oneself as well as his or her difference. If there were no basic similarity between the combatants, they could not join in battle; but if there were no differences between them, they would not have a reason to fight. Many characteristics of the Andean *ayllu* (as discussed in Chapter 3) are expressed by means of the *tinku:* the *ayllu* coheres as a faction[5] and defines its boundaries[6] while simultaneously being incorporated into an *ayllu* of a higher order.

By its very nature, then, the *ayllu* needs the *tinku* to define itself, for the encounter affirms the community's separateness while integrating it with other *ayllus*. Together, the encountering *ayllus* "feed" the source of their vitality and well-being, the Earth and the Sacred Places, with an outpouring of their own blood and energy, liberated through the *tinku*.

Seen in this light, hostility and violence are neither unequivocally negative nor ultimately destructive. The loss of life's blood in ritual battle is necessary for the perpetuation of life; it is part of the reciprocal relationship *Runakuna* maintain with the *Tirakuna*. The *ayllus* who meet in Chiwchillani (the Incubation Place) join in a shared sacrifice and thereby express their unity in opposition.

In other contexts the word *tinkuy* may have less violent connotations. The mixture of ingredients in cooking or the preparation of medicines is *tinkuy*. In some central Peruvian communities, two sets of affines are said to *tinkuy* in the houseraising ritual for a newlywed couple.[7] Each affine contributes specific structural elements for the framework of the new building. The ritual should be a happy occasion, with the two sets of in-laws meeting in goodwill rather than in animosity. In the same region, Cesar Fonseca reported that the sprouting plants are said to *tinkuy* as the seedlings emerge from beneath the ground to meet the open air.[8] Similarly, Sonqueños often use the word *tinku* as an adjective to mean "of middle-size," "between big and little."

In both violent and peaceful modes, *tinkuy* signifies a mixture of different elements that brings something new into existence. And this new being—the *ayllu*, the new household, cooked food, medicine, sprouting plants, even the growing animal "still just middle-sized" *("tinkuchallaraq")*—is endowed with vitalizing force.

There is an underlying similarity between *tinku* (the encounter) and *ayni* (reciprocal exchange; see Chapter 2). Both *tinku* and *ayni* bring equal but opposite parties into relationship with each other; and both may have peaceful or violent manifestations depending upon the contexts involved. In its most general sense, *ayni* refers to the exchange of equal or equivalent behavior. Usually *ayni* indicates an amicable relationship of mutual aid, involving reciprocation of goods and services. But offenses as well as services can be repaid in kind, and antagonists as well as helpmates are bound together in an *ayni* relationship of mutual give-and-take.

The gentle stream of formal endearments and stylized courtesy ("My Father, My Mother, My Dove, My Little Heart, Yes indeed you're right, Yes indeed, Of course, Thank you, Thank you *ever so much*, My Dove Heart . . .") flows across an undertow of potential violence. Outside the clearly defined framework of ritual, this violence is difficult to check, for the antagonists' *ayni* relationship perpetuates hostilities. There are two affective tides in the affairs of *Runakuna:* one that draws people together in cooperation, and the other that separates them in hostility. Once the tide has turned it can seldom be stemmed until it has run its course.

Crosscurrents in the Flow of Life

Whether hostile or friendly, exchange is the mechanism moving the flow of life. The circulation of *sami,* or life force, underlies all cultural activities from religious ritual to economics to politics. In this worldview, all existing things—people, llamas, mountains, potato fields, houses, whatever—are imbued with life. The life force can be transmitted from one living thing to another. The flow of *sami* depends upon a material medium; there are no disembodied essences in the Andean universe. In this, *sami* resembles the Polynesian *mana* and our own concept of energy.The flow is neutral in itself and must be controlled and directed so that all things attain their proper mode and degree of liveliness.[9] All activity revolves around this central problem: controlling and directing the flow of life.

Reciprocity is like a pumping mechanism at the heart of the Andeans' circulatory cosmos. The Incas organized the economy of their empire around this idea, exacting taxes in labor rather than in goods or currency, and facilitating the exchange of produce among different ecological zones. Although the Inca state is long gone, an emphasis on energy exchange persists in smaller-scale reciprocity relations among *Runa* households. Within the household, husband and wife are bound in a relationship of mutual aid; and through the *cargos* each household enters into a relationship of reciprocity with the community as a whole.

Two individuals or groups of individuals are needed to effect an exchange, to keep the pump of reciprocity moving; this manifests itself in the dialectical dualism pervading Andean activities. Viewed processually, the many pairs of dual oppositions that appear throughout this book are human activities participating in a dynamic circulatory cosmos (and not, as they may seem when abstracted from their processual context, Platonic ideas floating in a realm of pure mind). These oppositions bear witness to a pervasive Andean tendency to think and behave in terms of dialectical oppositions ingrained as "habitus" at the level of mundane and semiautomatic activities like farming, cooking, and coca chewing. I believe this habitus takes shape largely through daily activities that are given cultural meaning by a highly sexualized worldview. Thus, dialectical opposition in ritual draws upon tendencies of action and thought that have already been ingrained in participants living out their lives as members of *Runa* society. Cosmos, community, household, and individual are realized through the fusion of opposites, like the *warmi* and *qhari,* each of which contains the other.

In Andean communities, complementary opposition is often expressed in social organization. For example, Inca Cuzco was divided into upper and lower halves, each of which was further divided into two sections (like the *despacho*'s four coca *k'intus*, which combine first into two and then into one large *k'intu* representing the whole person). The community of Chuschi (department of Ayacucho) is divided into upper and lower halves, each of which is governed by a separate set of authorities. In other communities, several *ayllus* combine into two sections whose members fight an annual *tinku* during Carnival.[10]

Dual organization is rather weakly expressed in Sonqo. The *surt'is* of the sectorial fallowing system are divided into upper and lower sections; most saint's day festivals require a pair of sponsors, who are "like man and wife." In contrast to communities like Chuschi, Sonqo's population is not divided into two moieties, nor does Sonqo participate in a dual organization at the district level.[11] The mythic imagery of the *ayllu*'s oral tradition employs not a dual, but a tripartite, representation of three ancestors/authorities associated with three Sacred Places.

On the other hand, complementary opposition is strongly expressed in Sonqo's ritual symbolism. During the *ayllu*'s public rituals, the list of mutually enfolding oppositions seems to expand ad infinitum: women on the left, men on the right; women in a crowd, men in a line; *mamachas* and *taytachas*; left and right *taytachas*; lesser and greater *mamachas*; *taytachas*' feasts during *chiraw* (dry harvest season), *mamachas*' feasts during *poqoy* (wet growing season); junior and senior sponsors; *alcalde* and *arariwa;* low-pitched and high-pitched *pututus* blown by junior and senior *regidores*—the list could go on.

Such a noncontextual listing of binary oppositions unavoidably presents as static and absolute what are in actuality fluid and context-dependent relationships. For example, the two sponsors for saint's day fiestas are both men but, relative to the senior sponsor, the junior sponsor is female, for the two are *warmi-qhari hina* (like a wife-and-husband). Similarly, in Andean cosmology the vertical mountains are male relative to the generalized, horizontal Mother Earth; but relative to Father Sun the mountains belong to the female sphere of *Pacha*. Relative to their women, the men of Sonqo are male; but in the larger context of the national society, *Runakuna* relate to the *Mistikuna* in a female mode: their public activity is confined to the protective privacy of the *ayllu*, whereas the *Mistikuna* participate in a hierarchy of national offices. As Indian peasants, *Runakuna* provide an ancestral substratum for the Peruvian nation; their identity, relative to the nation, is collective rather than individual.

Triads figure just as prominently in Sonqo's ritual practices and in its mythic history: the *ayllu* has three sets of three ancestors—three *Machukuna*, three original *Runakuna*, and three Anton Quispes. The ritual table is set with: (1) a three-pronged whip representing the *ayllu*'s authority; (2) three drinking vessels (the two tall vertical *qeros* and single low horizontal *puchuela*); and (3) a coca *unkhuña* tied properly so that three tasseled corners, its "two heads and one foot," protrude. Public fiestas are dominated by three ritual actors: two sponsors and an *alcalde;* or a *huntador,* a *priwistu,* and an *arariwa.* There is a total of three *taytachas*, for in addition to the two crosses celebrated within Sonqo during the feast of Santa Cruz, there is the painted icon of Christ, a *taytacha* who travels outside the *ayllu* during pilgrimages. And in the *tinkuy* at Chiwchillani, three districts from two provinces meet in competition. Again, the list could go on.

There is a connection between the triadic and dyadic groupings. Examined more closely, each unit of three divides into a binary opposition of two against one, in which complementary elements are nested within other oppositions of a higher order.[12] The asymmetry—or *puchu* ("too-muchness")—of the triad creates a dynamic tension of inside against outside, male against female, even against odd. *Mink'a,* the asymmetrical aspect of reciprocity, is expressed in the triads—the state of unbalance that keeps the social seesaw moving up and down.

The *ayllu* depends on its ritual work to bring about the proper oppositions in a controlled way. Ritual recognizes that potential for violent conflict is inherent in every opposition and puts the violence to use within a limiting and controlling frame.[13] Within this ritual frame, competitive and violent encounters function as a particularly hard collective push to keep the flow of life moving on.

Joking Together/Fighting Together

Outside formal religious ritual, competitive and violent encounters occur on a smaller scale as "cultural performances."[14] For example, the delicate balance between peaceful collaboration and hostility is beautifully expressed in *chansanakuy* (joking together), a stylized form of Quechua repartee that often arises spontaneously in animated group situations.[15] While their companions listen, two people take on a pair of opposed social roles: *maqt'a-p'asña* (boy-girl), *Runa-Misti, kuraq-sullka* (senior-junior), *machu-wayna* (old man-young man). The pair's repartee is played out in terms of these opposed and complementary social roles (which need not *necessarily* correspond to real-life roles; occasionally two men vie as *maqt'a* and *p'asna*, two *Runakuna* as *Runa* and *Misti*). The roles may change in midstream and defuse the mounting tension—*maqt'a* and *p'asna* metamorphosing into *Runa* and *Misti* or into *kuraq* and *sullka*. The pair may reverse roles and begin anew, or a member of the audience may leap into the fray to displace one of the competitors.

In *chansanakuy* one hears Quechua used with eloquence and wit, for *Runakuna* place great store in the ability to excel in this quick, elegant repartee. I regret that I have never been able to record any of these episodes, for I view *chansanakuy* as a paradigmatic summing up of social relations as *Runakuna* know them. *Chansanakuy*, to use the phrase popularized by Geertz, is "deep play."[16]

Chansanakuy tends to develop either in small confined groups or in open public places like markets where people get acquainted and provide general entertainment by calling back and forth in a stylized repartee. The stereotyped roles protect the *Runakuna*'s private selves while providing a chance for them to show off publicly. In *chansanakuy*, possible human relationships are automatically defined in terms of complementary opposition, showing how deeply the dialectical tendency is ingrained.

Chansanakuy provides possibilities for opponents to use the stereotyped social roles to tease each other personally; this is part of what gives *chansanakuy* its spice. When one opponent repeatedly hits home in a personal way, without defusing the tension through role reversal or transformation, suddenly the jokes can become insults and the two will go at each other with fists as well as words.

"*Hinapuni, Comadre*" ("That's just how it is, *Comadre*"), Balvina sighed when I described such an incident to her. "*Chansananku—maqananku—chansananku—maqananku*" ("They joke together—fight together—joke together—fight together").

I had been describing the funeral wake for Josefa's very old father. Mourners at funeral wakes are expected to participate in *chansanakuy*, for the tense and amusing interplay of opposed roles helps pass the long, tiring night, diverts the bereaved, and entertains the visiting *almas* (souls). On a more abstract level, this social interaction mirrors the spiritual situation in which the mourners find themselves. During funeral wakes, two categories come into contact: the living and the dead, whose opposition and interdependence is fundamental to the cosmic order. The living and the dead occupy parallel worlds (states of existence) that interpenetrate and draw vitality from each other. In its dialectical structure and in the emotional tone it evokes, *chansanakuy* expresses this dangerous—but necessary and inevitable—interpenetration. In psychological terms, stylized joking during the wake, as secondary process, co-incides with mourning at the level of primary process. As Bateson says:

Consciousness talks about things or persons, and attaches predicates to specific things or persons which have been mentioned. In primary process the things or persons are usually not identified, and the focus of the discourse is on the *relationships* which are asserted to obtain between them.[17]

At this particular wake Crisologo, the deceased's son-in-law and a *chansaq Runa* (good joker), took on Octavio, a soft-looking, pretty young man who had just returned to live in Sonqo after several years in the city. The *Runakuna* were curious about him, and as if to demonstrate his *Runa*-ness he came decked out in a brand new fancy poncho and a gorgeous *chullo* (cap) decorated with an amazing quantity of buttons, beads, and tassels.[18] Crisologo faced Octavio wearing an old felt Mestizo-style hat and launched into a *Misti-Runa* routine, giving Octavio a chance to play the *Runa*. Then he deftly switched his battered felt hat for the betasselled *chullo;* now Crisologo was *Runa* (in Octavio's *chullo*) and Octavio was *Misti*. As they bantered back and forth the spectators howled appreciatively, and Crisologo kept breaking out of his role to exclaim in admiration, "How well he's answering!"

Crisologo tossed back the *chullo* and grabbed Josefa's flat fringed woman's hat: now he was *p'asna* (girl) and Octavio was *maqt'a* (boy). Everybody giggled to see the lean middle-aged man peer coyly from under the fringes, flirting brazenly with this newly returned bachelor. But since Octavio was an eligible bachelor and knew himself scrutinized as such, the play penetrated too deeply. When *p'asna* Crisologo started speculating about the size of this *maqt'a's* "eggs," Octavio exploded and had to be restrained by four men at once.

"*Maricón,*" he yelled at Crisologo and the other men who had laughed at him.

Maricón is an insulting Spanish term for male homosexuals, roughly equivalent to the English "queer." I have not heard the term used in Sonqo by monolingual Quechua speakers. Crisologo had broken through Octavio's pres-entation of self as *Runa* and as he-man, and had beaten him at a quintessen-tially Quechua game of oneupmanship.

But he had carried the game too far; the delicate interplay had broken down. This was bad, especially at a funeral wake. But it was not unexpected either, for the more exciting the *chansanakuy* the more likely it is to break down into violence. As Balvina commented, "*Chansananku—maqananku— chansananku—maqananku.*"

The phrase communicates a deep sense—typical of *Runakuna*—of the fragility of social order. Violence is accepted as necessary to life, but it is also feared. Virtually every encounter, from conversation to ritual battle, occurs within some kind of stylized, formalizing framework to keep its inherent con-flict under control. When these ritual frames are not maintained (as is likely during periods of rapid social change), the delicate equilibrium of social life is prone to collapse. When this happens, as in the *comadres'* brawl, deeply ingrained tendencies of thought and action are played out without restraint.

In their celebrations the *Runakuna* get very drunk and excited, finally dropping in exhaustion. A casual visitor might see only a bunch of Indians drinking themselves into a holiday stupor. Their behavior may not appear fundamentally different from the market-day drinking that makes them boisterous, then quarrelsome—and finally leaves them keeled over in the gutter or passed out on the road. Yet the intense orgiastic outpouring of spirit in the controlled context of ritual *does* differ fundamentally from the desperate market-day drinking of depressed and angry peasants—just as a ritual battle differs fundamentally from a brawl. Both ritual fighting and festive drinking are sacrifices of one's *sami*. Both express social differences while simultaneously unifying the participants. The blood, energy, and sound poured out in the *tinku* eventually return to the combatants, whereas what pours out in feuds and drinking binges is lost forever. The *tinku* battle and the brawl tend to activate the same cultural habits, the same modes of social interaction. Different as these contexts may be in terms of meaning, the *behavior* involved is similar. But while the brawl and the drinking binge may be played out according to the same cultural forms as, respectively, the *tinku* battle and the communal festival, the ritual frames that give cultural meaning to these behaviors are missing. *Chansanakuy* collapses into *maqanakuy*. This is not a "deep river" sweeping through familiar channels of ritual structure, but a tidal wave.

Hallpay, the shared chewing of coca leaves, is one of the most pervasive of these framing cultural performances. The exchange of coca leaves, accompanied by the invocation of deities, puts a peaceful definition on social interaction; within this context hostile behavior is virtually unthinkable. But as coca becomes scarcer and subject to more stringent controls, this ritual frame is increasingly difficult for *Runakuna* to maintain.

Chapter Nine

Coca and Cultural Identity

Waiting for the Incas

"Malogradu kani," said Don Luis. *"Malogradu kani"*—"I'm ruined."

Outside the house, his August First *despacho* was burning. The *Tirakuna* were eating. Inside, Luis, Balvina, and I were sharing coca leaves and shots of *trago*. The children were already sound asleep.

"What? Why are you ruined?"

"The Incas wouldn't recognize me."

We were talking about the *pachakuti*—the "world turnaround"—when the Incas would emerge from Paititi with golden corn and reinstate the *Runakuna* as masters of the land.[1] How would the Incas recognize the *Runakuna*? How would they distinguish *Runa* from *Misti*?

In previous conversations, Luis had stressed literacy as the distinguishing marker dividing *Runa* from *Misti*. The Incas, he had declared, did not know writing. They knew how to speak; their speech moved boulders into walls and straightened rivers in their courses. It was the *Castellanokuna,* the conquering Spanish, who came with writing and drove away the Incas. Today, the *Mistikuna* know how to read and write, and—though rocks no longer move at their bidding—*Runakuna* still know how to speak.

But the present conversation had turned to a more visible marker: the Incas would recognize as their own only people wearing *Runa p'acha* (*Runa* clothing). Luis snuggled into his striped poncho, pulled his *chullo* over his ears,

184

and stretched his bare, gnarled feet toward the fire. The night was very cold. Balvina sighed and poured another round of *trago*.

"You don't look ruined to me, sitting there in your *Runa p'acha*," I said.

"Oh, I'm ruined all right," Luis responded matter of factly. "Look at my pants." His faded dungarees, rolled up almost to the knees, had been purchased with money in the Cuzco market. (In fact, I had paid for them, a parting gift to Luis before I left for the States in 1978.)

"This isn't all llama or alpaca wool, either," he added, fingering his poncho, "and this pink yarn in my *chullo* is synthetic."

"They might not mind that," Balvina said. "We made them ourselves."

"The Incas know only llama and alpaca," Luis responded, sadly and emphatically.

"Could you change back?" I asked.

"It wouldn't matter," said Luis. "Once you're ruined, you're ruined. I can write my name and I know a little Spanish. That can't be changed now." He paused. "Anyway, it's good that I can sign my name."

He got up and started poking at the fire.

"*Hinalla kashan, Comadre!*" he exclaimed heartily. "That's how it is!"

The next afternoon, as we sat in the courtyard spinning, Luis returned to the subject of *Runa p'acha*.

"The boys have to change to *Misti p'acha* (Mestizo clothing)," he suddenly remarked. "They need it when they go to school."

"Is the *Runa* way of life *(Runa kawsay)* going to disappear, then?" I asked him.

He was silent for a while, then stopped spinning and opened his coca bag.

"Are you sad about that?" he asked, offering me a *k'intu*.

"Yes."

"Don't be. We'll be fine. The girls haven't changed their clothes. As long as the women stay with the *Runa p'acha*, our way of life won't disappear."

He accepted my *k'intu* and smiled placidly, seeming pleased with his solution. "It's going to be all right," he said. "*Allinmi kanqa.*"

Sitting next to us, round-faced, motherly Inucha was weaving a skirt border. I figured her age to be about thirteen, but she had already lost track of her years. Although she had put in some time in school, she never seriously tried to learn to read and what Spanish she learned to speak she had already forgotten. She loved her animals and animal husbandry and showed a good aptitude for weaving, which her *mamas*, Balvina (stepmother) and Gavina (mother's sister), encouraged by taking the time to criticize and discuss her handiwork. Had she lived, Inucha would probably have been the kind of woman Luis had in mind when he spoke of the women staying with *Runa p'acha*.

He certainly exerted what influence he could to keep her that way. I wonder whether she forgave him for refusing to let her accompany us to Cuzco in August of 1984.

The morning we left, Inucha was up and ready to go long before us. I found her already outside the house, seated next to a neat bundle, waiting for us in her best *Runa p'acha*. Luis looked dismayed when he saw her and remained firm in his decree that she stay home. He and I set off, and she trailed after us in the morning twilight for half an hour, wailing desolately at the top of her lungs.

"Shut up and go home!" Luis yelled over his shoulder. "You sound like a *kukuchi*!"

Finally, she turned back and returned to her animals and her weaving. Two years later Inucha died in the cold of June without (as far as I know) ever having seen Cuzco.

In Luis's eyes, Sonqo is an *ayllu* of "ruined" men, redeemed by some (but not all) of their women. The Incas' demands for cultural purity are stringent: one must reject the things of the *Castellanokuna* (the Spanish)—their language, their literacy, their money, their clothing. It is not easy for a man in Sonqo to keep this cultural faith, and few of them do so.

As a young man, Luis occasionally walked to the Paucartambo market with Erasmo. On one of these trips they heard amazing news that affected Luis deeply.

An *hacienda Runa* had been looking for his master's lost cattle. His search took him far away toward the *yunga* (high jungle), where he met an Inca. He was a pure *Runa*, without a thread of sheep's wool on his body or a word of Spanish in his head, so the Inca led him to the top of a high hill and pointed out Paititi, a shining golden city nestled in the depths of the forest. There the other Incas were waiting out the present age, waiting for their *timpu* to come around again. Then the Inca went away, but not before giving the *Runa* two ears of golden corn as harbingers of riches to come after the *pachakuti*.

And what did that silly *Runa* do? He hid the corn, which was too heavy to carry alone, and went running back like a faithful hound to tell his *hacendado* (lord of the manor). Of course, the *Misti* patron was eager for the gold, and they immediately set out to fetch it. But they never found it, for a fog rose out of the forest, thunder roared, hail and rain poured down, and the two barely got back home alive.

Luis was furious when he learned that Erasmo had recorded this anecdote for me on tape, along with some *kwintu*s (stories): "The Sons of the Bear," "The Condor Son-in-Law," and "The Fox and the Mouse." That was no *kwintu*, Luis fumed. It was "true" *(chiqaq)*; it happened in his own time, not even twenty years ago!

The story of a *Runa* favored by the hidden Incas and then rejected for his association with a *Misti* seemed like a miraculous proof for Luis's cultural faith. It is a hard faith to maintain, and Luis needed miracles. Even so, he felt that he had fallen away: *"Malogradu kani."* "I'm ruined."

Erasmo, in contrast, seemed a bit skeptical about the gold-bearing Inca, but his skepticism did not worry him. Much as potato farming bored him, the city and its ways did not attract him. Not that he was uninterested in money and the technological wonders it can buy, but his deeper involvement lay with the study of coca leaves and the interpretation of dreams. Outside Sonqo, his wanderings usually stayed within the sphere of *Runakuna*. He generally kept away from Cuzco, where he was once hit by a car.

In 1984 Erasmo ventured into the city for the first time in years, lured by the prospect of my buying him a tape recorder. It was strange to meet him in the tiny room rented by Luis's taxi-driver son José. I found him sitting shyly on the edge of the bed, surveying José's *artifactos* (television, kerosene stove, knitting machine) with some amazement. He had removed his poncho and tasseled *chullo* for the trip and was dressed in a borrowed jacket and dungarees. I stopped short as I entered the room, struck by the incongruity of seeing him in Cuzco. He seemed diminished not only in stature but in charismatic presence as well.

At that moment Erasmo jumped to his feet and laughed. "How strange to see you in Cuzco, *Comadre!* You look smaller. In Sonqo you're a *hatun warmi* (big woman) but here you look just—just regular."

We went out to buy him his tape recorder. We went to store after store without finding a decent machine at a price I was willing to pay. We felt awkward as the sale clerks, in store after store, eyed us curiously. Finally we got discouraged and Erasmo declared us unlucky.

We went to my rented room, and Erasmo pulled out his coca bag.

"Hallpakusunchis kunan, Comadre" ("Let's chew coca now, *Comadre"*), he said, with the old gleam in his eye.

He carefully prepared a *k'intu* and blew over it, calling on Cuzco, Sapphi Street, and the Inca fortress of Sacsahuaman. We exchanged *k'intus*, began to talk, and the time passed.

Suddenly Erasmo started to his feet.

"Yaw, *Comadre!* It's getting late! Don't you know of any other stores?"

I had thought of one more store, so we set out again. There we immediately found what we wanted. The salespeople were friendly and volunteered to write out a receipt in Erasmo's name in case the *guardia civil* questioned him during the trip back to Sonqo.

It was dark by the time we left. Erasmo carefully wrapped the new acquisition in his carrying cloth and slung it over his back. Then he set off, scurrying along the sidewalk.

"We have to get inside, *Comadre!* The *suwakuna* (thieves) will be out!"

We made it back without encountering any *suwakuna*. Erasmo lovingly placed his treasure in the center of the room and strutted around it.

"You see, I did it! Didn't I tell you I could do a good *phukuy*?"

He sat down and looked a little awestruck. "I did it with the coca," he said again.

The Incas' demands for cultural purity are not unequivocally negative. *Runakuna* speak Quechua, the Incas' language, and they cultivate, respect, and preserve the power of the spoken word; their rejection of money is a refusal to bypass human reciprocity; they recognize that in weaving their *Runa p'acha* they maintain a fine and ancient tradition. Although their speech no longer moves boulders or changes the course of rivers, they still know how to communicate with their landscape through the medium of coca leaves.

"We are Incas!" they sometimes say.

Of course, viewed through a social historian's glasses, the *Runakuna* are not Incas. Their *Runa p'acha* is a version of colonial Spanish dress. The man's knee breeches and vest and the woman's full skirts certainly would not have been recognized by the Cuzco Incas; nor would the Incas have recognized the old colonial churches and arched stone bridges as their handiwork. The *Runakuna*'s Christian names would make no sense to the Incas, and the mixed Spanish and Quechua surnames betray centuries of miscegenation. The Incas would find *Runasimi* (*Runa* speech) mixed with unfamiliar vocabulary—such as *"Yusulpayki"* ("Thank you"), which is neither Spanish nor Inca. *"Yusulpayki"* is derived from Spanish *"Dios se le pague"* ("May God pay you") and hybridized with the Quechua interactive suffix *-yki* (I-to-you). Ritual activity, like language, would have incorporated a great many unfamiliar elements. They might find coca used more widely and in a greater variety of contexts than they had used it themselves.

Language, clothing, coca—these signify for the *Runakuna* their separateness and historical integrity as a people in a society whose origins lie neither in the Incas nor in Spain, but in the Spanish conquest of the Incas.

Coca, the leitmotif announcing harmonious social relations and ritual reciprocity with the land, expresses their cultural separateness. Coca's ritual symbolism epitomizes the premises of the *Runa*'s worldview. Viewed in a larger historical and sociopolitical perspective, coca also epitomizes the intensifying dilemmas of the *Runakuna*'s ambiguous cultural situation.

Coca and Cultural Identity

The debate about coca chewing[2]—symbolically a debate about cultural difference—is as old as the Spanish Conquest. Coca had been chewed for millennia before the conquest and, judging from the archaeological evidence, held much of the same ritual symbolism in pre-Columbian times that it does today. After the conquest coca took on new significance, becoming a marker of indigenous identity as Andean and Spanish cultures met in a brutal and tragic encounter.[3]

Some colonial chroniclers assert that, prior to the conquest, coca was reserved for the upper classes and for special ritual occasions, its production and distribution being carefully controlled by the Inca nobility. However, careful study of archival documents by Murra[4] and others indicates that the pre-Columbian coca trade was subject to fewer controls than the chroniclers would lead us to believe. It seems probable that, whereas coca was a sumptuary item—like honey, timber, arid feathers, which also came from the lowlands—its use was not restricted to the nobility.

Although coca was not new to the common people, its role in their lives after the conquest was far from benign. Coca, making it possible to drive Indian miners at a (literally) more killing pace than would otherwise have been possible, contributed to the shocking death toll exacted by the notorious mines of Potosí, Huancavelica, and elsewhere. As Spanish colonists took over the confiscated coca plantations of the Inca nobility, coca became a market item cultivated for sale to native people. During the sixteenth and seventeenth centuries, coca production increased forty- to fifty-fold, according to one estimate.[5] Colonial economic interests profited greatly from the leaf and, in the hands of these interests, coca exacerbated the suffering of the conquered population. Ironically, thousands of highland Indians, doing forced labor in the tropical coca fields, died cultivating a crop destined for sale to their own people.[6] The myth that Mamacha Santísima María invented coca chewing while mourning for her lost child tells us that *hallpay* was invented in grief to alleviate grief. In this sense, the myth is most accurate.

While many colonists cashed in on the native market for coca, missionaries quickly recognized coca's importance to indigenous religion and called for its extermination. By 1551 coca had been condemned by the first ecclesiastical council in Lima. By the end of the century, however, the Catholic Church had reconciled itself to coca, whose taxation provided a good deal of revenue.

In 1573 Viceroy Toledo removed official controls on coca cultivation. Through the next three centuries, coca was accepted as a necessity of life by the economic interests controlling Peru, even though chewing coca was considered a lower-class habit.

Paradoxically, it was out of this historical situation—the colonial holocaust of disease, taxation, forced labor, and forced religious conversion—that the cultural identity of the *Runakuna* took shape, and that coca use came to signify Indianness. Indigenous culture was stubbornly retained after the conquest, but in a context that transformed it.

Today, one may view the *Runakuna* from two different but related perspectives. One may view them as the cultural product of a historical dialectic of oppression and resistance—a continuing dialectic that the *Runakuna* help perpetuate by clinging to their traditions. On the other hand, they may be viewed as survivors in a long struggle to maintain their own way of life, to live as a separate *people*, albeit a conquered one.

Both perspectives have validity. The paradoxes surrounding coca—through colonial history and up to the present context of social upheaval and international narcotics traffic—epitomize the paradoxes in which the *Runakuna* are caught. These paradoxes, in fact, created them.

The coca plant is a hardy bush *(Erythroxylum coca)* that grows on the steep eastern slopes of the Andes. This is a difficult tropical region of extremely high rainfall and poor, highly eroded soil. Coca thrives there: once the bush has matured it will produce up to four harvests a year. It is, moreover, resistant to insect pests and needs relatively little care. Coca leaves are harvested by hand on commercial plantations or small household plots, after which they are dried in the sun or in heated sheds, then baled for shipment to highland markets.

The debate over coca chewing generally focuses on its medicinal aspects. It has been argued that coca chewing aids in high-altitude adaptation, but there is little good evidence for this position.[7] However, coca chewing does ameliorate the nutritional effects of living almost exclusively off potatoes in the high Andean *puna*. Coca leaves contain vitamins A and B_1, calcium, iron, and phosphorus, and the calcium carbonate chewed with the leaves contains vitamin C. These vitamins and minerals are badly needed in high-altitude communities where any kind of green vegetable is hard to come by.[8]

There are some indications that coca chewing after meals helps regulate glucose metabolism, a particularly important function in people subsisting on a heavily carbohydrate diet.[9] This hypothesis makes intuitive sense in terms of my experience in Sonqo. Contrary to those who argue that coca must foster malnutrition by suppressing the appetite,[10] coca is chewed *after* meals as a complement to, not a substitute for, food; as a "hot" substance coca is thought to balance the "cold" potatoes."[11]

When masticated with calcium carbonate, coca's effect is rather similar to that produced by a cup of coffee and an aspirin tablet. Coca produces a feeling of clear-headedness conducive to work and concentration while relieving fatigue and dulling sensations of hunger and thirst. Chewing coca slightly elevates the heart rate and produces a mild vasoconstriction in the extremities that helps maintain the body's core temperature.[12] As a "hot" substance, coca is considered good medicine against cold and ailments thought to be caused by the cold. Coca also settles an upset stomach and—as many tourists to Cuzco learn—coca tea is a time-honored remedy against the dizziness, nausea, and headaches caused by the high altitude.[13]

The way in which coca produces these effects and how, pharmacologically speaking, coca's effects compare to those of cocaine, is not well understood. The coca leaf contains several alkaloids (basic compounds synthesized from amino acids that affect the nervous system) in the amount of .5 to 2 percent of the leaf's weight depending on the species of plant; cocaine accounts for from 50 to 90 percent of this alkaloid content. Pure cocaine and cocaine salts are extracted from the leaf through a complex process of several steps involving gasoline or kerosene and various difficult to obtain chemicals.[14] The proportion in weight of leaves to extracted cocaine is approximately three hundred to one.[15]

Ingested, cocaine produces a physiological state characteristic of excitement, which prepares the body for exertion, flight, or aggression.[16] However, the *Runa* who chews coca leaves is not ingesting pure cocaine, for the *llipt'a* (compressed ash chewed with coca) activates the leaf's other thirteen alkaloids as well. There is some evidence that cocaine absorbed through the digestive tract, as in coca chewing, is broken down into ecgonine and benzylecgonine before it reaches the bloodstream.[17] Both of these are far milder in their effects than cocaine. Given the limited state of knowledge, it is not yet possible to compare coca chewing with cocaine ingestion in quantitative terms. It is clear, however, that—physiologically speaking—coca chewing is more comparable to our consumption of caffeine in coffee, tea, and soft drinks, and to our over-the-counter pain relievers, than it is to the recreational use of cocaine in its highly refined and concentrated form—the product of Western technology and imagination.

Cocaine was isolated from the coca leaf in Germany in 1860 and became the wonder drug of the late nineteenth century; it was touted as an anesthetic, a cure for opium addiction, and a general tonic. Many coca preparations were sold on the open market, including a coca "wine," cigarettes laced with co-caine, and sprays and ointments. The good old American soda fountain origi-nated as a dispensary for Coca-Cola, originally a tonic for headache and fatigue.

By the turn of the century, public and medical opinion was turning against the great white cure-all. The Coca-Cola company replaced cocaine with caf-feine in 1906, and in 1914 the Harrison Act severely restricted the sale of co-caine. In 1922 cocaine was officially declared a narcotic, and Congress banned the importation of most cocaine and coca leaves.[18]

It hardly seems coincidental that after the leaf's powerful derivative was outlawed in North America and Europe, the debate over native coca chew-ing—which had lain dormant for over three centuries—took on new force in Peru and Bolivia.

In the 1940s, Carlos Gutiérrez Noriega, a Peruvian physician, spearheaded a passionate movement dedicated to the eradication of coca chewing.[19] The dullness and apathy attributed to Indians—their poverty, ill health, and even illiteracy—were blamed on coca chewing. The leaf had supposedly produced a population of passive zombielike drug addicts. In 1950 a United Nations Commission of Enquiry officially concurred in this opinion, concluding that coca chewing had negative physical, moral, economic, and social effects. Its recommendation was a fifteen-year phasing out of coca cultivation. The com-mission's report was based on a two-month fact-finding tour, most of which was spent talking to Mestizo officials—the very segment of Andean society most antagonistic to coca-chewing Indians and most eager to show their su-periority to them. It seems not to have occurred to the commission to talk to the coca chewers themselves.[20]

The UN's recommendation to ban coca elicited a strong response. Carlos Monge, former surgeon general of the Peruvian Army, challenged the com-mission's findings at a meeting of the United Nations in 1950, and it was not until 1961 that Peru and Bolivia, signed the Single Convention on Narcotic Drugs, which called for the abolition of coca chewing and the eradication of coca cultivation within twenty-five years.

Defenders of traditional coca chewing tend to be as passionate and dedicated to their cause as coca's detractors, with both sides convinced that they are promoting the welfare of indigenous people. In countries where coca chewing is a hallmark of Indianness, it is hard to sort out scientific opinions about coca chewing from social attitudes toward Indians. In an atmosphere of condemnation, the fact that the Indians themselves say that the coca leaf is beneficial and socially meaningful is simply taken as evidence of their "addiction." Proponents of coca chewing, on the other hand, are inclined to take the Indians' word for it and leave it at that.

In my opinion, evidence on both sides seems rather weak. Long-term coca chewing does not seem to be very bad for the health, but it does not seem to be essential to good health either.[21] Even assuming that a lifetime of heavy coca chewing might be somewhat damaging to the health, it is certainly less so than a lifetime of heavy drinking, smoking (especially at 3,500 meters above sea level), or consuming sweet carbonated beverages. It is interesting that the passion evoked by the coca issue is not excited by alcohol, whose consumption spans all segments of Andean society.

The passionate focus on health issues has obscured a more fundamental problem: the heart of the debate is not coca itself, but the cultural separateness of the people who chew it. It is harder to know where one stands regarding cultural differences than it is regarding health issues. To what extent can human beings coexist while living different ways of life? Is it possible to create a truly pluralistic society? We hardly know how to start talking about these questions, while throughout the world people go on fighting and dying over cultural differences.

The twenty-five years specified by the Single Convention on Narcotics have come and gone. Far from being eradicated, coca cultivation has increased—not because Andean Indians continue to chew coca leaves, but because cocaine is the latest "boom" in the international drug trade.

North American friends often respond to my interest in coca chewing with snickers. They joke about my research "high in the Andes" and make cute inquiries as to whether I couldn't bring *them* some. They react, in other words, as though I were talking about cocaine, and they transfer their attitudes about cocaine to the leaf from which cocaine is derived.

Young tourists in Cuzco often rush out to buy coca leaves and are disappointed when they feel little effect. In Sonqo, the careful, elegant Francisco Quispe spoke to me about my "countrymen" *(llaqtamasikuna),* whom he had seen in the ruins at P'isaq stuffing wads of coca leaves into their mouths with no concern at all for propriety, or for the respect due the leaf itself.

"They were like horses," Francisco said with quiet disgust.

It was less difficult to explain to Don Francisco what my "countrymen" were so excited about than it is to explain to them the nature and meaning of coca use in its traditional context. In fact, by 1985 cocaine had entered the *Runakuna*'s consciousness. At this writing, the *Runakuna*'s access to coca is severely restricted; narcotics-control measures aimed at stemming cocaine production have restricted the legal transportation of coca and taxed it heavily. As a result, there is a new black market of coca leaves destined for traditional use but sold outside the legal channels.

These restrictive measures are not deliberately aimed by policymakers at traditional users of coca. The "war" has been declared on drug traffickers, not on coca chewers, but traditional chewers are affected nonetheless, caught up as they are in the general web of deception and violence. According to patterns of seasonal migration, many highland Indians descend to work in lowland coca fields during slack periods in their own agricultural cycle. Traditionally, they returned home laden with coca leaves for their own use and for sale to neighbors. This is now a risky practice. Transportation of coca has been highly restricted, and a cargo of coca beyond that needed for immediate personal consumption is subject to confiscation. Thus, while purchase of coca for traditional use remains legal, *Runakuna* find that getting it home is a more difficult matter. To compound the problem, coca is no longer sold at the local Sunday market in Colquepata, and the *guardia civil* search virtually every truck for black-market coca leaves. *Runakuna* find themselves making do with less and less.

The guards explain to them that restrictions are necessary to stop *narcotraficantes* (drug traffickers), who make cocaine from coca leaves to sell in the United States and Lima, where it ruins people's lives. In 1985 I found many *Runakuna* anxious to talk about this problem. They were quite willing to believe that cocaine was a bad thing and that *narcotraficantes* were terrible people.

"But our coca chewing is separate from all that. We are accustomed to it, and have never had anything to do with cocaine. Why should we be deprived of our coca because of those *narcotraficantes?* There is no justice in this."

And: "Here we are doing without coca. Has this affected the supply of cocaine in your country?"

In 1975 few of Sonqo's *Runakuna* had heard of or had any notion about the United States. Today (late 1980s) they know that the United States is where people buy cocaine—and that because of this the *Runakuna* must work their fields all day without chewing coca leaves or exchanging *k'intus* in *hallpay*, and that their burnt offerings are now meager, composed of carefully hoarded leaves. Suddenly, the *Runakuna* have been made aware that what happens in North America penetrates to the very center of their lives, and this makes them angry.

They carry on without coca, of course, compensating with alcohol and cigarettes, and with the ubiquitous phrases of endearment and reassurance spoken to indicate harmonious social bonds. But the cultural balance has been thrown off, and the ritual frame that gives life coherence and meaning is being pulled away from them.

Of course, the ritual frame is being pulled away from them anyway; and they are turning away from it. The forced deprivation of coca only complicates an already complex and confusing situation. It forces on *Runakuna* what should be one of the more significant choices they make about themselves: whether or not to chew coca. This choice expresses—and expresses consciously—who the *Runakuna* are, or at least which of their available cultural skins they are wearing at the moment.

Having invested much time and thought in understanding coca chewing, I would like to see the *Runakuna* continue their tradition. *Hallpay* is a window onto a way of life that, as an ethnographer, I readily embraced for its own sake. Learning the *Runa*'s way of life seemed to satisfy the quest Malinowski laid out in *Argonauts:*

Perhaps man's mentality may be revealed to us, and brought near, along some lines which we have never followed before. Perhaps through realising human nature in a shape very distant and foreign to us, we shall have some light shed on our own.[22]

This quest is admirable but also selfish. My experience in Sonqo broadened my vision of human nature and it seemed to give me a way of coping with my own lack of cultural and religious faith. I came to feel about Andean culture the way one feels about a friend whose different and unexpected attitudes toward life deepen one's own experience and character.

But the hardest discipline of friendship is to allow the other to change in ways one dislikes and which no longer suit one's own needs. My appreciation of coca chewing, and the fact that I have gleaned some personal fulfillment from studying it, gives me no particular right to declare that *Runakuna* should continue to chew coca; likewise, no one else has a right, out of distaste or unconcern for their culture, to order the *Runakuna* to stop.

When Don Luis asks me if I am sad to see their way of life disappearing, I answer "Yes" without hesitation. I can say unequivocally that if their language, their ancient and marvelous arts of weaving and speaking, their appreciation of human reciprocity, and their intimate relationship with the land are lost, the world will be diminished.

But I would not be sorry to see *Runakuna* eased of their grinding poverty, to see their health improved, and to see them living less constrained lives, socially and politically. I am not sure we can have it both ways.

The Future Comes Up Behind Us

Runakuna experience a world full of circulating currents. The *sami* circulates through the world and vitalizes each thing according to its proper nature. Blown from coca leaves, the *sami* returns to the giver, just as streams flow down the mountainside into the deep tropical forest and from there return again to Sonqo. Some of the streams' vitalizing water evaporates into the air and returns as rain; some, the *Runakuna* say, flows back underground to break through the Earth's crust in Sonqo's *puna* marshes. The Wind, a river of air, roars out of his cave in the *puna*, rushes, about the mountainsides, and returns again to his home. The river of blood circulates through the human body. Human energy flows out in labor and returns in *ayni*. Generations pass into the same soil from which their ancestors sprang and from which they will nourish future generations. Time moves ahead like a river to drop from view into that subterranean interior that contains both past and future. Future time does not lie ahead of us, but comes up at our backs. It wells up from under our feet; it catches us by surprise like a wind blowing from behind.

The Andean cultural vision of a circulatory world, in which all action eventually turns back on itself, is one of many possible human ways of experiencing the world and of acting within it. We might learn from it if we would rein in the Enlightenment Brigade (charging onward in the name of progress and "development") long enough to pay attention. But I do not expect this to happen.

I would like to believe that *Runakuna* will improve their lives materially and be drawn into the life of their nation on a more equal footing without losing the distinctive knowledge, skill, values, and style that make them a unique people. To accomplish this goal, *Runakuna* would need time—time to learn what options exist for them, time to judge which kinds of gain entail which kinds of loss, and time to choose accordingly. Given enough time, the *Runakuna* might change from within, instead of continually having to address external influences out to rescue, reform, or subjugate them (or simply to run them down in pursuit of some other goal).

Time is exactly what the *Runakuna* do not have. At this writing (in 1987), much of Peru has been engulfed by a tidal wave of violence. A few hundreds of miles from Cuzco communities not unlike Sonqo and villages not unlike Colquepata lie desolate as ghost towns—their inhabitants massacred, "disappeared," or fled to Lima. Bodies lie tumbled together, not in the cemeteries of their *ayllus*, but in mass dumping grounds of peasants massacred in guerrilla warfare.[23] So far, Sonqo has been relatively untroubled by this violence, but it is hard to predict what lies in store for the *Runakuna*.

Andean ghosts are hardy souls. The deserted towns will probably revive when the violence finally subsides and refugees return bringing with them *hawamanta Runakuna* (outsiders). The cycle of destruction and renovation—or something like it—has all happened before, as Andean oral tradition attests.[24] Eventually the *Runakuna* will emerge from this harsh transformation, and only then will we know how much has been lost, gained, and suffered.

Epilogue

Rufina's Children

Don Luis's first grandchild, a boy named Eldder, was born in 1981 in a tiny rented room off the crumbling courtyard of what was once the fine, large home of a wealthy Cuzco family. José and his wife, Emilia, shared a water spigot and a toilet with three other families who rented rooms off the same courtyard. The landlord, who lived on the second floor, continued to use an aged plumbing system that leaked into the rented windowless rooms below. When I ate with José and Emilia during my 1984 sojourn in Cuzco, we had to whisk aside our plates when the water ran upstairs, to keep whatever was dripping from the ceiling from flavoring our dinners.

The room, which I estimate to be about eight by ten feet, contained a bed, a bench, a kerosene stove (which lit in a burst of flames and fumes), a knitting machine, shelves and cartons of clothes and food supplies, a blender, and a television set. An electric light bulb over the door provided the only light. The TV set ran almost constantly with sports programs or with Brazilian soap operas about the complicated troubles of wealthy cosmopolitan families.

In spite of the clutter and fetid smell, I spent many pleasant evenings there. Friends and neighbors often came over and crowded onto the bed and bench to watch TV—cheering for the Peruvian Olympic Girls Volleyball Team or exclaiming in awe and amusement over the travails of the soap opera heroines.

Emilia likes to recall Eldder's birth. In spite of the pain, it was a good experience. Her mother was visiting from her home village of Cachín in Calca, and her father-in-law was visiting from Sonqo. The two attended Emilia in her labor, comforted her, and swaddled her tightly to force out the afterbirth. Emilia says she trusted their experience and felt calm and well attended. The birth of her second child was a different kind of experience. She and her husband were alone when she went into labor, and José, frightened by the memory of his mother's death in childbirth, bundled her into his blue Volkswagen taxicab and took her to the hospital. Emilia speaks sadly of the loneliness she felt there, left by herself for hours at a time, and what relief she felt when José arrived with a big pail of soup.

Eldder's name was suggested by an American passenger in his father's taxi. Wanting something foreign and exotic, José asked a fare (apparently a Mormon missionary) to suggest a name for the new baby. He learned that "elder" meant *viejito* in Spanish (*machula* in Quechua), and this struck his fancy. Now he and Emilia wonder whether they chose well.

Emilia is an energetic, good-humored, and sympathetic young woman who wears her hair in braids and dresses rather severely in slacks or in a dark blue skirt and sweater. She uses her knitting machine to make sweaters for sale, and is ambitious for her husband and children. She points out happily that her children's surnames—Gutiérrez Cruz—are both Spanish and will not betray their Quechua origin.

She is not at all the kind of woman Luis had in mind when he spoke of the *warmikuna* preserving the *Runa*'s way of life. I think she and Luis regard each other with some dismay—but he recognizes that she is good-hearted and a hard worker, and he makes no complaint. For her part, Emilia knows of my long-standing affection for her father-in-law, and if she has criticisms, she makes them outside my hearing.

Emilia is not so discreet when it comes to Sonqo, however. Sonqo is just too cold for her, and the custom of using dried dung for cooking fuel turns her stomach. She cannot stand to spend more than a few days there at a time. Cachín, she explains, is a lower, warmer community, where firewood is available for fuel.

José works hard in his little blue taxicab. He usually leaves the house by seven in the morning, breaks for a midday meal, and continues driving until eight, nine, or ten at night. The long hours at the wheel aggravate a kidney ailment, begun in the army by a sergeant's ill (or well?) placed kick. He seldom drinks, for he holds liquor badly and knows it would interfere with his driving. He almost never chews coca: "Why chew coca in Cuzco?" he asks.

José has managed to combine good luck, hard work, and a winsome personality. He was trained as a chauffeur in the army and afterward was hired by a Colquepata truck driver, who took a liking to him. A Cuzco *compadre*, who had taken in his brother Bernardo as a domestic servant, helped José raise the down payment for his own taxi. For a boy from a *puna ayllu*, "Pepe" is doing very well. He is an up-and-coming *cholo*, making the transition from *Runa* to *Misti*. In Sonqo José would have headed a group of *ermanus* (siblings) who held land in common and cooperated in working it, but he cannot maintain this role while working as a taxi driver in Cuzco. Although Rufina had hoped that

José, as her eldest, would "finish everything," it seems that if any of her sons stays in Sonqo and completes the *cargos*, it will be nineteen-year-old Esteban. At sixteen he served as junior regidor, proudly blowing a *pututu* from the hill-top named Yanqay. Seeing his son look forward to service as senior *regidor,* Luis went to the trouble and expense of buying back his family's ancestral *pututu*, a huge white conch shell named Wayna Ausangate that had been sold years before by his loathed stepfather to a Colquepata *Misti*.

Esteban is growing up. He is beginning to take a man's place in the as-semblies, fields, and houseraising *mink'a*s, and he smiles in pleasure when the older men offer him coca *k'intu*s. He sleeps separately from his family in a small house adjoining his father's house compound. When assemblies are called, he usually attends on his father's behalf.

"I'm old now," says Luis. "Let the young men worry about the assemblies."

Although Esteban is far from stupid, he never made it through primary school. He explains apologetically that the teachers beat him for making mis-takes, and this made him so nervous that the answers always went right out of his head. He is an affectionate boy and good company, always glad to guide me around the paths and places of his *ayllu*. He enjoys listening to stories and has begun telling his own versions for my tape recorder. His father listens care-fully, adding criticism and praise.

José and Bernardo worry that Esteban will "get stuck" in Sonqo, and they would gladly help him move to Cuzco. Luis says his son should do as he pleases, but he obviously thinks Esteban should remain in the *ayllu*. Ready to retire into his elderhood, Luis seems relieved that one of his sons has turned out *"manan allin umayuq"* ("not possessed of a good head")—in other words, unintelligent—and is therefore ill fitted for city life.

Esteban was very fond of his sister Inucha, who was three years younger than he. Had she lived to grow up and marry, they probably would have built houses in adjoining neighborhoods and collaborated closely in farming, herd-ing, and the *cargos,* much as Don Luis did with his sister Basilia.

Esteban does maintain regular contact with his older sister Felicitas, now married to a *Runa* from Colquepata, but their relationship seems to lack the ease and intimacy he had with Inucha. Felicitas (whose childhood nickname was Felicha) is far less contented than Esteban with life in Sonqo. She enjoys visiting José in Cuzco and brings Eldder's two-year-old cousin Mario. Mario is Felicitas's second child; the first, born only a few weeks after Eldder, died suddenly of a cough at the age of two.

A strikingly handsome young woman with smooth, sharp features, Fe-licitas disappeared for a few years in her teens—lured to Killabamba to work as a cook in a placer mining camp. She says she liked it and proudly displays the sweaters she bought with her wages. In Killabamba she wore slacks, but after her furious father and Eldder brother José found her and marched her back to Sonqo, she returned to wearing the heavy black skirts, woven mantle, and flat fringed hat—to *Runa p'acha*. Felicitas and her earnest young husband, Saturnino, work hard to raise cash crops and make money for factory-made

Esteban, at seventeen, poses with his fancy poncho and loud-speaker, which is hooked up to an automobile battery. A record of popular Andean songs *(huaynos)* leans against the battery-powered phonograph. Loudspeakers are all the rage among the Sonqo *Runakuna,* many of whom enjoy blaring music at one another across the mountainside.

clothes and *artifactos,* their consuming interest in life. Their notions of gringo wealth know no bounds, and Felicitas fantasizes that someday I will land in front of her house in my private airplane.

José often sees his brother Bernardo, who lives in Oropesa, a breadbaking town near Cuzco. Rufina had expected this second son, not José, to become successful in the city. A good student, Bernardo was declared *allin umayuq* (intelligent), and therefore was sent in his teens to work as a domestic servant in Cuzco, where he could attend high school at night. He began as a kitchen boy in the Cuzco house of Sonqo's schoolteacher, but he did not last there (he drank up the milk and worked poorly). Finally Bernardo found his niche with a shopkeeper from Huancarani, a generous, cheerful man, himself only a generation away from the countryside.

Bernardo lived in this household for years, raised almost as one of the family. But once past adolescence, he could not find a steady footing in any other kind of work. He shunted between his patron's brother in Lima, his own brother José in Cuzco, and his father in Sonqo, until he got a fifteen-year-old girl in Oropesa pregnant and moved in with her family as son-in-law and

Christmas Eve in Cuzco: Dressed in *Misti p'acha* (Mestizo clothing), Luis (second from the right) celebrates with the author (right) in José's new apartment. José (left) tries to get little Madaleyne to hold still for the camera. (Photo by András Sándor)

baker's assistant. In December of 1985, his young wife had a daughter—another addition to Eldder's expanding group of cousins.

Eldder was a brash four-year-old the last time I saw him, in December of 1985. His family was in much better quarters, having moved to an apartment in a new house closer to the outskirts of town. They now have a living room, which contains the knitting machine, a larger television set, a bench, a table, a few straight-backed chairs, stores of corn and potatoes, and several chickens. A ladderlike staircase leads to a spacious loft complete with casement window, double bed, and chamber pots.

There are problems with their new apartment. The landlord does not want them cooking there, so Emilia prepares their meals on a Primus burner inside a corrugated aluminum shack in the courtyard, where a spigot provides their only running water. Nevertheless, this cleaner and larger apartment is a vast improvement over the stuffy, leaky little room where Eldder spent his first three years of life.

Eldder has started kindergarten, and Emilia proudly reports that the teacher describes him as *"bien inteligente."* He is an active, talkative little boy, who looks very fine scampering around in his sneakers and blue jeans, with his black hair slicked back. When his mother hugs him, calling him her *"gusanito"* ("little worm," an endearment), Eldder squirms free and proclaims, "I'm not a little worm! I'm a big snake!"

200

The next generation: Little Eldder walks with his mother on a Cuzco street.

Luis visits José every four to six weeks. He puts aside his poncho and *chullo* for these trips; he tries not to embarrass his son by looking like an Indian, although his shuffling, lopsided walk betrays a lifetime of carrying heavy loads. Luis's round face lights up at the sight of his grandchildren. He reaches out to embrace Eldder with the indescribable gentleness. *Runakuna* extend to children they love, calling to him in Quechua, *"Imaynallan Hawayniy, Machhucha?"* ("How's my grandchild, little guy?").

Eldder tenses and pulls back in mock perplexity. *"Como? Que dices? No entiendo!"* ("How's that? What did you say? I don't understand").

Luis sighs, his features withdrawing into detached repose.

"Hablamos Quechua con el Papa Grande" ("We speak Quechua with Grandfather"), admonishes Emilia.

Eldder's parents say they don't understand why he refuses to speak Quechua; they converse with each other in a mixture of both languages, but more in Quechua than in Spanish. When I say that it's a shame the boy can't talk to his grandfather, Emilia agrees rather halfheartedly.

"But *Comadre*, he's not going to stay in Peru. At least we hope he won't. We don't want him to stay here and live like us in this poverty. We hope he'll go away to the United States. It's English he needs to learn, not Quechua."

In December of 1985 José drove me in his taxi to visit the Inca ruins at

Ollantaytambo, and little Eldder came along for the ride. We visited Randall and Wendy, an expatriate couple who left America to settle in Peru, and who ran a hotel in Ollantaytambo.

Randall greeted Eldder in Quechua, and Eldder stared back sullenly.

Unconstrained by ideals of ethnographic detachment, Randall turned to José and minced no words: "What a disgrace! You say you're from Colquepata, and your son doesn't speak Quechua! How is this possible?"

José shrugged and looked away. The rebuke seemed to roll off his back.

But it had not. Two weeks later, when Luis visited Cuzco again, I found Emilia packing a bundle of Eldder's clothes. Her son was going to Sonqo.

"My husband's been upset for days," she said, "thinking about what that Señor Randall said to him. We've decided that the children have to learn Quechua, and that they should know where their parents came from."

Eldder played in silence, running up and down the staircase with a toy truck, glancing from time to time at his mother's preparations.

José still seemed restless. Helping me with some errands a few days before I left Cuzco, he mentioned that he would like to sell the taxi and buy a truck. The taxi was fine—but he liked driving in the countryside. With a truck he could haul produce between Cuzco and Sonqo, and between Cuzco and Cachín. Emilia could go along with him, driving back and forth between the city and their *ayllus*.

"Now *that* could be a good life," he commented wistfully.

Afterword to the Second Edition

"No Somos Indios Ahora"

The meaning of two central terms in this book—*runa* and *ayllu*—will change rapidly and perhaps drastically in the next fifty (or even twenty) years.

(Introduction, 1988)

17 July 2000
Late morning, clear July weather, a little wind. I'm on my way to Sunday market in Colquepata. Shafts of sunlight are falling across the brown treeless slopes of Towlakancha. They strike a rocky pinnacle, Ixchinu, who casts the same cold shadows as ever. It seems a timeless scene, as it might have been generations ago. Far up on the hillside I notice the familiar cone-shaped form of a seated shepherdess. It's Doña Balvina tending her sheep, a small figure of black and red. She sits almost motionless, watching for hours on end, watching . . .
She's watching the cars go by. Counting—Two hundred ninety-seven, two hundred ninety-eight, two hundred ninety-nine . . .

Indeed, some things have changed. The road is not only passable; it is used. Felicitas complains that the traffic keeps her awake all night. She and Saturnino regret having built their house so close to the road. Cirilo tells me that in an hour spent waiting for me in Colquepata plaza he counted one hundred cars.

One hundred cars in an hour! This was extraordinary, for a normal day sees only three or four cars pass through Sonqo. Most regular commerce, including Colquepata's new bus service, still plies the old route via Huancarani. But mid-July is festival season in Paucartambo. The previous week saw hundreds of vehicles—cars, vans, pickup trucks, motorcycles, even bicycles—winding through Sonqo on their way to the feast of *Mamacha Carmen*, patron saint of Paucartambo, on July 16. Now, on the seventeenth, throngs of festivalgoers were returning to Cuzco by the shortest route—and this was our road, the "high road," now nicely graded and in good repair. All the unaccustomed traffic was fun for some, annoying for others and for many, it seemed, a ray of hope. People wondered out loud whether the road could become a regular tourist route carrying foreign visitors (and their money) from Cuzco to Paucartmbo and the tropical forests beyond.

In the Introduction I warned that the *Runakuna* were "standing on the brink of their next transformation." I was right about the transformation but I was wrong about "standing on the brink"—for they were already diving off. Profound changes have occurred in Sonqo since the first publication of this book in 1988. Some of them seem to confirm my earlier interpretations; others imply more radical changes in mentality and cultural orientation than I expected.

Immersed in writing, teaching and parenthood, I let many years slip past before I visited Don Luis for a few days in March 1995. For Peru, 1985–95 was a disastrous decade of violence and economic collapse. Cuzco was spared the worst of the violence but not the economic hardship. Rural potato farmers were hit hard by the end of market subsidies; this, combined with the high cost of transportation, made marketing and travel almost impossible. Sonqueños were thrown back temporarily and unwillingly on subsistence strategies.

When I visited Sonqo in 1995 things were just beginning to pick up again. It seemed to me then that surprisingly little had changed since my last fieldwork in late 1985. I noted that the herds of sheep, llamas, and alpacas were diminished in size and economic importance. A government-sponsored development project had built a latrine for every household. But there was nothing as visible and startling as the demographic shift I had witnessed between 1980 and '84 when the road was completed and the *surt'i* fallowing system decisively collapsed. I realize now that I did not perceive other profound alterations, including a dramatic rise in alcoholism and a (not unrelated) turn to evangelical Protestantism. Nor, in my too-brief sojourn, did I perceive that Erasmo was seriously ill.

I returned in the year 2000 during a phase of exuberant dry-season construction.[1] Tile-roofed two-story houses had replaced many of the old one-room thatched dwellings, and more were going up. As I passed through Chocopia and entered Sonqo I also noticed that most house compounds had outdoor water faucets and that wire fences ran along the margins of some of the fields. During the following two weeks it became abundantly clear that Sonqo was no longer the *Runa* community it had been twenty years earlier.

Runa, Misti, and *Mestizo*

In 1999 David Edwards, a student in my university department visited Sonqo with a video camera.[2] He taped a message from Don Luis, including these words:

Inka kanman karan, kanman, ankhayna Runalla kaykuman karan. Intunsis Mistikama kunan kanku. Misti chay kapushan paykuna munanayuq. Inkataq manan. Inkaqa ahinallan karayku, coca hallpaq, aha tumaq, ahata vasupi tumaran Inkaqa. Akhna karayku, kunan manan, Español-Mistillaña kunanqa.

If there were still Incas, as there should have been, then we really would be *Runa*. But instead they're all turning *Misti*. They're filled with desire to be *Misti*, not Inca. We were like Incas, chewing coca, drinking chicha, drinking it from (ceremonial) tumblers.[3] That's how we were, but no longer—now we're Spanish *Mistis*, we're altogether *Misti* now."

In its widest extension, the word *runa* means *person;* it refers to human beings in general. Luis, however, uses the word in a more restricted sense: "*If there were still Incas . . . then we really would be* Runa." Here, the word *Runa* refers specifically to indigenous people who consider themselves inheritors of Inca customs and life ways. During my fieldwork in the 1970s and '80s, Sonqueños used the word *Runa* in this sense. I was not a *Runa,* for example; I was a *Gringu.* In the year 2000, old-timers like Luis still used the word *Runa* with its restricted sense but their children and grandchildren did not. The younger people even substituted *indio*—a word loaded with socially negative connotations—when speaking of indigenous Andeans, decisively distancing themselves from the life ways of their parents. In this chapter, I use *Runa* and *Runakuna* (with a capital *R*) in the restricted sense, as I have used them throughout this book. *Runa* refers to the way of life I came to know between 1975 and 1985; it does not refer to most of Sonqo's inhabitants in the year 2000.

When I asked Cirilo why his generation no longer wore *chullu*s he replied, *"No somos indios ahora"* ("We're not Indians now"), inserting the Spanish phrase into our otherwise Quechua conversation. Indeed, *Runa p'acha* seemed to be going the way of thatched houses. Only older men wore the once ubiquitous knitted *chullu* caps with earflaps; ponchos had given way to close-fitting jackets; and many younger women preferred colorful *mestiza* skirts and bowler hats to the black skirts and flat fringed *monteras.*

As *"Runa"* (in its restricted sense) loses its salience so does *"Misti,"* for the terms *Runa* and *Misti* are mutually defining in their opposition. Cirilo and his generation consider themselves *Mestizo.* They think of themselves and the Colquepata townspeople as sharing a similar heritage, values, and aspirations. This is not to say that the old distinctions of wealth and social hierarchy no longer exist, but that younger adults no longer want to express these differences in terms of the culturally oppositional *Misti/Runa* vocabulary. Couples in their twenties and thirties are struggling to break out of their dependence on subsistence farming and live as members of a modern nation, from money *(ah, there's the rub!).*

In the introduction to this book I wrote that the district capital no longer provided a paramount social and cultural focus for the rural *ayllu*s: "today's

Potato harvest 1995: Cirilo entered into a sharecropping arrangement with a
Mestizo market woman from Colquepata.

social forces are centrifugal, and Colquepata's hold has loosened (page 15)."
By the year 2000 this process had reversed itself. Community *ayllu*s are losing their internal coherence and *comuneros* are drawn more strongly to participate in the economic and ritual life of the district capital. They find it advantageous to activate ties of kinship or marriage to gain a foothold in town.
Esteban, for example, has built a second house there "to store produce on the
way to market and to shelter the children." His children will attend school in
Colquepata and will need a place to spend the night. Felicitas, who lives in
Chocopia with her husband, also has a second house in town. The town itself
is developing a more prosperous air. The main street is paved; the center of
town has electricity, running water, and telephones. The small one-room one-
man medical post has been replaced by a Health Center staffed by two nurses.
A bus runs once a day between Colquepata and Cuzco. The church has been
cleaned and its doors painted; a rose garden grows in the plaza. The mayor's
business card proudly proclaims:

MUNICIPALIDAD DISTRITAL DEL COLQUEPATA
PAUCARTAMBO-CUSCO
Capital de la Papa y del Chuño

Civic spirit with a humorous twist: "Potato and Chuño Capital!" (If you've got it, flaunt it!) Morning and evening the municipality broadcasts radio programs to the surrounding countryside, playing *wayno* music, announcing news items, and broadcasting health advice to *"Hermano Campesino"* (Brother Peasant).

The *Ayllu*

The radio was playing as, the day after my arrival, I sat on the grass talking with Cirilo. (Sometimes I slip up and use his old baby name, Cirilucha—"Little Cirilo." This makes him wince and his wife laugh. I have to remind myself that the toddler whose matted hair I cut years ago is now a grown-up married man with four children.) We leaned our backs against his little thatched house and talked about the new one he was building down by the road—a big one with several rooms, an upstairs, and a tile roof. He mentioned that when I went to Sonqo I'd see lots of new houses, lots of new construction.

"What?" I said. "Aren't I in Sonqo now?"

"Well yes, but we're a separate *sector* now. We've formed an *anexo*—Mama Samana, *anexo del Sonqo*. We have our own president and our own *local* (community center)." He pointed to a whitewashed tile-roofed building on the slopes below the road.

"Are there other *sectores* (sectors)?" I asked.

He listed Qoyapuqru, Pillikunka, and Intiqkancha, names familiar to me as neighborhood-level *ayllu*s. He started to include Qhalipampa in the list but hesitated—"It's still only a *barrio* (neighborhood). They haven't gotten organized." He described Qoyapuhru as the *barrio central* (central neighborhood) with the greatest concentration of new houses. I asked whether that was due to the proximity of the church. He shook his head.

"They're mostly *Hermanos* (evangelical Protestants) over there.[4] In Qhalipampa, too—they all turned Protestant over there after Erasmo died."

Here is the story, insofar as I can tell it, of how Sonqo Ayllu lost its coherence:

Earlier in this book (Chapter 3), I searched for a common denominator underlying diverse manifestations of the Andean *ayllu*. I settled on a general definition:

ayllu refers to the collection of several individuals into a group that is distinct from (and thus potentially opposed to) other groups that might be formed in the same context. *Ayllu*-mates are united by a common focus—and this focus may be an ancestor, a Sacred Place claiming their common allegiance, an individual claiming them as kinsmen, a common specialization, or even a shared task. (page 87)

Ayllu-mates cohere as a group through their practices. *Runakuna* were focused on Sonqo as a living place, a multifaceted entity that motivated a complex of interrelated practices. The place supported them in the form of pastureland and cultivated fields; they sustained the place through ritual practices like *hall-pay* and material ones like crop rotation. This unity between people, productive activities and the place was based in an ideology of reciprocity. When people no longer agree on a common focus and are no longer motivated to share common practices, the *ayllu* loses its coherence.

During the past twenty years Sonqo has been undergoing fundamental changes in its communal orientation. The road—key in bringing change to Sonqo—is but one factor among many. In the 1980s Sonqueños began traveling more frequently to Cuzco; they purchased radios and watched TV in town. A barrage of media images revealed a brave new world of happy consumers. Younger people were more likely to speak Spanish and have at least minimal literacy. Alcohol was more easily available while coca leaf was harder to come by. At the same time, local agriculture was being transformed. Low-interest government loans provided opportunities to raise cash crops (mainly barley, oats, and early potatoes). Meanwhile, pasturelands were infested with *alikuya*, a parasitic liver fluke. As their livestock deteriorated, demoralized herders looked for other means of subsistence.

Internally, Sonqo *Ayllu* was not unified. I think the expropriation of *haciendas* during Agrarian Reform—welcome though it was—left a vacuum where local factionalism flourished. Sonqueños no longer had to unite to protect *ayllu* sovereignty against the predations of *hacendados*. Although economic collapse and social unrest in the early 1990s forced them back into old subsistence strategies, their aspirations had changed and old systems of *ayllu*-wide coordination had been decisively altered.[5] With Peru's economic recovery in the late '90s, international development agencies became important players in the local scene, and Sonqueños were confronted with more opportunities and life-altering decisions. Many converted to evangelical Protestantism, further dividing Sonqo along religious and social lines. Today the community is severely fragmented, divided between Catholics and Protestants, and between those who favor development projects and those who do not. With no common focus, the old Sonqo is dysfunctional as an *ayllu*, and a new type of group coherence is emerging at the neighborhood level.

The demise of the *surt'i* system (see Chapter 3, page 84) has played a crucial role in this process. In the *surt'i* method of communal crop rotation, everyone planted in a few adjacent sections *(surt'is*; from Spanish *suerte)* of *ayllu* lands and left the others sections to rest.[6] This ensured that fallow fields were clustered together as common pastureland. Animals grazed on these "commons" without ruining the crops, and their manure enriched the resting soils. Similar sectoral fallowing systems are found throughout the Andes and probably date from pre-Columbian times.[7] Such a system necessarily defines a community's boundaries because all the component sections must work together as a single unit. Thus Sonqo's territory had to include all eight *surt'is*, and its population had to include all the households that cultivated them. But by the 1980s, cash crops and chemical fertilizers were making this kind of community-wide coordination seem burdensome and unnecessary. Diminished by liver flukes, smaller herds needed less pasture; new fertilizers allowed farmers to shorten the "rest" periods they allowed their fields. *"Variapushayku,"* they explained. "We are varying (the cycle)."

Sonqueños just were beginning to "vary" when I arrived in 1975. I inquired very little about their land-use because (as I mention in the introduction) even my mild queries about potato varieties incited threats from the local Agrarian Reform agent. Truth to tell, it didn't take much to deflect me from this line of inquiry—and so I missed my chance to study the *surt'i* system in action. When I returned in 1978 and '80 the system was decisively collapsing and by 1984 it was gone. Fortunately, Colquepata was the site of an important study of agricultural change during the 1980s, under the direction of Enrique Mayer, Stephen Brush, and Cesar Fonseca. Karl Zimmerer, a cultural geographer on that project, continued his research in Colquepata until 1990. I draw on their work as well as my own hindsight in reconstructing the system and the processes involved in its demise.

In Sonqo's *surt'i* system, *ayllu* lands were divided into "outer" *("hawa hallpa")* and "inner" *("uray hallpa")* zones. Each of these zones was divided into eight *surt'i*s. Households had usufruct rights to *chacras* scattered throughout all sixteen sections. The outer *hawa* zone consisted of high potato fields where a single year of cultivation had to be followed with seven years of fallow. Therefore, in any given year, only one *hawa surt'i* was under cultivation; the other seven "rested" and served as pastureland. The inner *uray* zone extended down the slopes to the valley bottom and permitted more intense cultivation of several crops, including beans, *tarwi*, and barley. Most fields in this *uray hallpa* followed a three- or four-year crop rotation followed by four or five years of fallow (for example, *potatoes ullucus beans barley–fallow–fallow–fallow–fallow*). Because not all lower fields followed the same cycle, rotation in this zone was not as neatly coordinated as in the upper zone; nevertheless, in any given year, cultivated land was concentrated in four sectors with the other four lying fallow.

Don Luis referred to this year-by-year movement of crops across the *ayllu* as *muyuy*, which means "rotating" or "circulating around." "Previously it all circulated around together; now we're varying" *("Ñawpata kuska muyupun; kunan variapushayku")*. Sonqueños use the same word, *muyuy*, to describe the motion of the sun, as well as the circulation of water, as in a stream that flows down into the jungle and then runs back up underground to its place of origin. As Esteban commented (in July 2000), "The Sun is just circulating, and water does the same, just circulates" *(Muyushallan Inti. Imayna muyu kasqanta unu muyullantaq)*. As the sun and the rivers circulated, so did the crops.[8]

Communal agriculture requires the coordination of tens or even hundreds of individual households. Some Andean communities strictly control their crop rotation schedules, while in others de facto systems function through implicit agreement, governed more by tradition than by central authority. In Sonqo, as far as I can tell, the *surt'i*s were flexibly defined through the informal consensus of more than eighty competitive and often quarrelsome households. While *ayllu* members agreed as to the general areas that should be planted and left in fallow, each couple thought very concretely in terms of their own particular fields and those of their closest kinsmen. Even older people who participated in the system gave me inconsistent lists of *surt'i* names, apparently using their own fields as reference. The informal and semiarticulated nature of the system may have contributed to its rapid collapse, and certainly contributed to my overlooking its importance early-on in my fieldwork.

The *alcalde* redistributed land that was coming out of its fallow phase in a ceremony called *Chakra Mañay* (Lending Out the Fields; see Chapter 3, page 80) during Carnival Week. This was the one occasion when *Ayllu Runakuna* would gather to ritually validate the distribution and use of their lands. Presumably the details of this *mañay* had been hashed out beforehand; the public ceremony validated these implicit agreements and sanctified them with coca leaf and *chicha*. I first learned about *Chakra Mañay* from Juan Nuñez del Prado, a Cuzco anthropologist who witnessed the ceremony during a visit to Sonqo in the mid-1960s. I looked forward to watching it in 1976, for Sonqueños assured me that it would take place. But Carnival Week came and went—with no *Chakra Mañay*.

"Yes," admitted Don Luis, "I said we *always* hold *Chakra Mañay*, but—oh well!—not this year . . ."

It may be that my presence, or the presence of Agrarian Reform agents in Colquepata, discouraged such a public statement of land distribution. I think it more likely, however, that the *surt'i* system was already breaking up under the influence of barley and early potatoes. Probably the authorities avoided this public test of moral authority.

Early potatoes—delicious *maway papas*—are a delight of the Carnival season. How good it is to eat little fresh potatoes after weeks of nothing but *ch'uño*! *Maway papas*, moreover, command a high price on the Cuzco market because they are harvested two months or more before the regular potato crop. According to Karl Zimmerer's book *Changing Fortunes*, commercialization of early potatoes propelled Colquepata into a "radical reconfiguration of farm space."[9] Although cold and barren, the district is a good environment for *maway papa*. Its hillsides are dotted with boggy patches called *wayllar* that provide excellent pasturage and, when developed as raised fields *(wachu)*, can be cultivated during the dry season without irrigation. It was one of these *wachu* fields that Erasmo was building back in 1980 when he braved the "haunted" bog and carved out canals six feet deep. During the 1970s Agrarian Reform agents encouraged early potato farming with low interest loans in hopes of integrating Colquepata farmers in the market economy. With their herds debilitated by parasites, many households made the decision to concentrate less on livestock and embrace the new cash crops. With the road near completion, the decision was both reasonable and in the spirit of the times. Children, who had once herded together in small groups, were now attending school and many younger mothers were unwilling or unable to shoulder the burden themselves.

Meanwhile, the Cerveza Cuzqueña brewery was promoting barley by offering loans of seeds and fertilizer to be paid off with proceeds at harvest time. Indeed, as early as 1978, I heard people bemoan late frosts that ruined the crop and left them in debt to the brewery. Nevertheless, during the 1980s Colquepata developed into a center of barley cultivation. Household by household, families made the decision to "vary" from the communal cycle and plant where it suited them. By the time the "barley boom" had passed, the *surt'i*s were only a memory. In the year 2000, Sonqueños shrugged when I asked why there were fewer barley fields, commenting that Sonqo gets too much frost.

It was clear by the early 1980s that the new crops would leave a deep and lasting mark on life in Sonqo. In 1984 I sat with Don Gabriel and his son Vicente in a barley field near their house in Qoyapuhru. We reminisced about an afternoon nine years earlier when I had introduced myself to Gabriel in that very field. He'd shown me the fine points of harvesting potatoes while we waited for Basilia to come home from the sheep pasture. At that time the field had grown potatoes, now barley. I asked whether the field would rest the following year. Vicente answered that it no longer rested at all. They just alternated barley and potatoes without fallow. In this, they were following the general trend. "Doctoring" fields with commercial fertilizer could keep them producing crops year and after year. With the herds dwindling, there was less organic manure available anyway. He commented, however, that the soil quality was deteriorating.[10] Other Sonqueños also noticed this problem, but already in 1984 they felt unable to return to the old slower methods of cultivation. They pointed out that their population had increased and felt that the long fallow periods could not support them any longer. "When I was a boy there were thirty households, now there are eighty," said Gabriel.[11]

As farmers used chemical fertilizers to shorten the long fallow period of high *hawa* fields, the limits of the *uray* (lower) zone moved upward.[12] Only the very highest potato fields continued to follow the old cycle. Managing even small herds became more difficult once cultivated fields were scattered throughout Sonqo rather than concentrated in the *surt'i*s. The demographic shift I observed in the early '80s reflected this new situation as some households moved up to less cultivated elevations in order to pasture their animals, and others moved nearer to the road and closer to Colquepata to take advantage of new commercial opportunities. In 2000, herders at lower elevations had to be constantly alert to see that the animals didn't wander into their neighbors' *chakras*. For the first time, wire fences were appearing along fields and *ch'uño* beds to keep the animals where they belonged. And llamas and alpacas were on the way out. Don Luis had slaughtered his last llama a few months before my visit.

"That llama just liked to dance too much," he explained. "It kept getting away from us. There's not enough open space *(campo)* for llamas and alpacas."

Thinking back to the *surt'i* system, Vicente mentioned that sibling groups used to collaborate, working fields together and thus moving as a unit through the eight-year rotation cycle. *"Kunan variapushayku"* ("Now we are varying"), he said rather regretfully. Varying from the *surt'i* system not only meant breaking the rotation cycle; it meant breaking up the sibling group as an economic unit. Both barley and early potato cultivation de-emphasized the carefully orchestrated teamwork required by in-season potato fields. Barley was less-labor intensive than potatoes, so households had less need to call on reciprocal labor. Early potato cultivation, while very laborious, had a similar effect:

families themselves could provide much labor, since a variety of intensive but minor tasks like canal grading, repeated weeding, and careful monitoring did not mandate the work teams that typically were filled by extra-household recruits.[13]

Thus there was less need for *ayni* among brothers, sisters, *qatay*s and *qhachun*s. And—a crucial point—in the carefully calculated system of balances that governed household economy, less *ayni* seemed like a good thing. Now they could husband valuable time and energy for their own needs.

The aim was to make money. New crops not only produced cash income, they also produced a continuing need for cash outlays. Barley farmers had to take whatever price Cerveza Cuzqueña offered and many were perpetually in debt to the brewery. Early potato crops called for "working capital" *(capital de trabajar),* a new item in the farmers' lexicon.[14] Boggy *wachu* fields were not self-sustaining: diseases and pests throve in the humid soil, seed potatoes were of poor quality and, bit by bit, repeated cropping depleted the soil. To keep *wachu* fields going farmers had to buy seed every year, along with insecticides and chemical fertilizer, from outside sources. And for this, they needed money. Part of the profits—or loans when profits were insufficient—had to be inverted back into the field to produce the next crop of *maway papa*. Money, moreover, made it possible to eat high prestige foods like rice and noodles,[15] and to acquire radios, televisions, and factory-made clothing.

One of the most striking differences between Sonqo in 1975 and Sonqo in 2000 was the prevailing preoccupation with money. This is not to say that in 1975 Sonqueños felt contented and prosperous. No indeed—they felt marginalized. They knew themselves to be dependent on money and were frustrated by their lack of access to it, for their so-called "subsistence economy" was not really self-sufficient. Writing about highland potato farmers, including those in Colquepata, Mayer comments,

Contrary to old and persistent notions that subsistence production and consumption are carried out with local resources, our results shows show that subsistence agriculture also has a strong monetary component and that this cash investment is often lost.[16]

212

For example, Sonqueños' agricultural tools—hoes and foot plows with iron blades—must be purchased with money. Kerosene, candles, school supplies—all cost money. What changed between 1975 and 2000 was not so much the need for monetary income as the quality and depth of the preoccupation with monetary income. They have begun to perceive themselves as truly impoverished in relation to the rest of the world. They know that the *Mapa de la Pobreza* (Poverty Map), published by the Peruvian National Institute of Statistics and Information in 1999, classifies them as living in *extrema pobreza* (extreme poverty).[17] This puts them first in line for aid programs, but it is also a demoralizing way of having to think about oneself.

A startling reversal of values was brought home to me as I talked with Cirilo, catching up on the news about old friends and acquaintances. It pained me to learn that an old friend, whom I'll call Don Leopoldo, had succumbed to alcoholism and was in a bad way.

"*Aynillapin purin,*" Cirilo commented in disgust. "He just goes around in *ayni.*"

My thoughts went back to a rainy October day in 1975 when I helped Luis plant a potato field. Our work party included a tattered old man whom I had not previously met. Later I asked Valentina about him:

"*Qulqipaq llank'an payqa,*" she answered disdainfully. "He works for money."

That meant that he was really down and out, a *wakcha* with no reciprocity network. Now, twenty-five years later, it was *ayni* that marked Leopoldo as having hit rock bottom.

"At least," added Cirilo, "he gets a meal that way." Leopoldo has no one to cook for him since his wife died in 1997. Calling this *"ayni"* was a euphemistic way of saying that he has to work for food.

Ayni does continue to play an important role in people's lives, but the social value placed on *ayni* versus wage labor has changed. In Cuzco, Emilia spoke in the same vein as she proudly showed me the house they were building in the outskirts of Cuzco."I'm happy to tell you that we didn't call on *ayni* to build this house. We paid all the workmen or did the work ourselves." It was a statement about money's power to liberate us from social compromises. I was not particularly surprised to hear this from fiercely independent migrant like Emilia. Social reciprocity provides a safety net for the urban poor in times of economic crisis—important, yes, but a safety net, not the preferred way of life. I was less prepared to hear the same sentiments from Cirilo. His comment indicates that he shares Emilia's orientation: *ayni* is a strategy of last resort. The words underscored, more than his absent *chullu,* that *"No somos indios ahora."*

In spite of the diminished value placed on *ayni,* the *faena* (work party) remains a central feature of communal life. Don Crisologo was eager to show me the reservoir that the men of Mama Samana had built for their system of piped *aqua potable* (drinking water). We rested beside it on the high hillside, enjoying a view (see photo, page 2) across the valley to other Colquepata communities—T'oqra, Miskawara, Chocopia and beyond them, Sayllapata. I commented that I'd been hearing about a lot of new *sectores*.

"Yes, lots of new ones are being born," Crisologo commented, with a sweeping gesture that took in the horizon.

The situation in Sonqo is hardly unique. Other communities, too, turned to cash crops in the 1970s; left their sectoral fallow in the '80s; and divided into *sectores* in the '90s. New communities are "born" from the fissioning of old ones, a process that seems likely to continue for some time. Several longtime *ayllu*s like Sonqo, Chocopia, and T'oqra, are still in the process of fissioning and forming *sectores*, each with its own *local* (community center), *estadio* (soccer field), and elected authorities. I noticed a tendency for people to identify themselves as members of a *sector* rather than the larger community—as when Cirilo asked me when I would "go to Sonqo."

The processes currently taking place in Sonqo—while they surprised me—seem consistent with my interpretation of the *ayllu* concept in Chapter 3. I said that *ayllu*s are fluid and reformulate themselves over time in response to changing situations (page 88). In 2000 I found Sonqueños regrouping at a new level of organization, coalescing around new activities and new religious orientations. In Chapter 3 I also described Sonqo *Ayllu* as a topographically distinct place. Seen from above, Sonqo is a many-armed ridge, cut by water courses, stretching from the Panapunku divide down to the Qenqomayu River. Within Sonqo *Ayllu* are nested the named ridges, ravines and flat places—neighborhood *ayllu*s where houses are located. Topographically speaking, *sectores* are intermediate between Sonqo *Ayllu* and its component neighborhood *ayllu*s. Each *sector* is a distinct named place that contains lower level *ayllu*s and is contained within a higher level one. The *sectores* are clusters of neighborhoods and Sonqo *Ayllu* is a cluster of *sectores*.

The *sectores* do not seem to correspond to the old *surt'i*s.[18] Unlike *surt'i*s, which were units of cultivation and pasturage, *sectores* are residential units inhabited by like-minded people. Josefa and Crisologo, for example, were in the process of moving to Mama Samana from their longtime residence in Qoyapuqru. They complained that Qoyapuqru is just too crowded and too dominated by evangelical Protestants. They were enthusiastic about development projects that were making more progress in Mama Samana. In contrast, Gavina and her two unmarried daughters had converted to Protestantism and were in the process of moving from Mama Samana back to their old house in protestant Qhalipampa.

Land rights will have to be redefined if, as seems probable, the *Ayllu* continues to break down into sectors. Sectoral fallowing needed an extensive territory in order to encompass an entire rotation cycle. Once the *surt'i*s disappeared, the community was able break up into smaller residential groups. Each household, however, continues to claim plots of land scattered across Sonqo's territory. Families in Mama Samana, for example, cultivate fields in all the other sectors, and residents of other sectors cultivate fields in Mama Samana.

At minimum, I expect there will be a reshuffling of claims as households consolidate their holdings within their own sectors and relinquish others.

The Pillikunka house where I lived in 1975 provides a good example of this reshuffling. The right to live in Pillikunka came to Luis through his wife Rufina Quispe, who inherited it from her father (a lineal descendent of Pillikunka Anton Quispe). After Rufina's death, Luis moved back to Towlakancha where he had spent his childhood, expecting Esteban to inherit the Pillikunka house. When Esteban preferred to live in Mama Samana, Luis "sold" *(vindiran* from Spanish *vender)* Pillikunka to Rufina's younger brother Domingo. The word "sold" implies a monetary transaction, which surprised me. I asked Esteban about it—could individuals now buy and sell land? Wasn't it up to the *ayllu* authorities to reallocate land-use rights? He replied that the authorities didn't mind as long as all the parties were in agreement.

The transaction is interesting because, on the one hand, it is completely consistent with traditional land-use patterns and, on the other hand, it points toward a redefinition of land as private property. Luis didn't "sell" to just anybody, for Domingo Quispe has a reasonable claim to live in Pillikunka through his father (and father's fathers before him). One might argue, furthermore, that Luis was selling the house but not the land it stood on. However, Esteban did not articulate this distinction between house and land during our conversation; instead, he went on to talk about a privatization program that would divide land along the road into numbered *lotes* or privately owned parcels.

What a stark contrast between *lote* and *wasitira,* two terms referring to the same piece of earth! It's not conceivable to sell one's *wasitira* (House-Earth; see Chapter 1, page 29). You can abandon your *wasitira* and let her fall into dormancy, and you can return to reawaken her—but you can't sell her any more than you can sell your mother. *Lote* is real estate; *wasitira* is a material being with moral and affective dimensions. Private property will require Sonqueños to separate, or compartmentalize, these two aspects of their relationship to land.

Privatization is consistent the neoliberal ideology characterizing Peruvian government policies for the last two decades. According to Mayer, "As a 1980s political movement, neoliberalism reacted against too much state intervention, protectionism, state-owned enterprises, and collective production systems" instituted by Velasco's Agrarian Reform.[19] Privatization seems highly problematic in a community like Sonqo, especially given Sonqueños' current desperation for ready cash.

But what is causing this exuberant "birth" of new sectors? The demise of sectoral fallowing is only part of the story. While the *surt'is*' disappearance opens the way for a community like Sonqo to break up, it does not necessarily mean that the community *will* break up, nor does it dictate how such a breakup will happen. No, the story of the *sectores* is intimately connected to development programs, particularly to the activities of IMA, Instituto de Manejo de Agua y Medio-Ambiente (Institute for Water and Environmental Management), a Peruvian-Dutch collaboration.

Felicitas's husband, Saturnino, was serving as *Presidente* of Picchu, one of Chocopia's *sectores,* and complained (rather proudly) that the duties consumed his time. Don Luis thought his *qatay* was exaggerating: "That's just a lot of talk. He's only a 'little president'" *("huchuy prisidinti").* Nevertheless Saturnino threw himself into the work, displaying with pride a seedling tree nursery that Picchu had started with the help of IMA. It is at the *sector* level that development projects like this have taken hold.

Other development and aid programs have been—and continue to be— active but none has had the impact of IMA in galvanizing a new type of community organization. Beginning in the 1980s, a program called Vaso de Leche (Glass of Milk) promoted women's organizations and provided nutritional supplements for children. Plan International, an affiliate of Save-the-Children Foundation, provides construction material for the new two-story houses. It also encourages small animal husbandry by distributing rabbits and baby chicks to families with children, and sponsors an "adopt a child" program, in which North American and European contributors establish long-distance bonds of "friendship" with specific children.

The National Fund for Compensation and Social Development (Fondo Nacional de Compensación y Desarrollo Social or FONCODES), a rural development program initiated by the Fujimori government with collaboration from international development organizations, is responsible for the new outhouses dotting the landscape. In the early '90s, each community in Colquepata District was given a choice whether to participate in this project. Sonqo voted yes, and now every house has its solid adobe outhouse with tile roof and concrete commode (but no door). Chocopia was slower to agree, so their latrines were installed a few years later. They are bright blue corrugated metal, with holes in the floor instead of commodes (and yes, doors). The boundary of the two communities is clearly indicated by the style of latrine. If the latrines are blue, you know you're in Chocopia.

IMA, in contrast, sponsors long-term projects including piped drinking water, reforestation, greenhouse gardens, and small fish hatcheries. These projects call for sustained and committed collaboration among the beneficiaries. To attain this commitment, IMA will work at any level of organization. Their policy, explained Percy Alvaro Valencia, IMA's agent for Sonqo, is to work with the entire community if possible. If the community as a whole doesn't cooperate, then they will work with sectors or groups of families. If this fails, they will work with individual families rather than give up and leave. The hope is that the rest of the community will join the project once they witness its benefits.

Of all the Colquepata communities, Sr. Alvaro found Sonqo the most difficult. He described it as fragmented by internal dissension over religion. "They've lost their cultural framework," he said, bemoaning the loss of a common ritual life, as well as the demise of the *surt'i* system with its common pastures. In spite of these difficulties, small groups within Sonqo have coalesced around particular projects. Calling themselves Mama Samana, fourteen families announced their willingness to collaborate with IMA. They went to work building a system of piped drinking water and, indeed, other *sectores* organized themselves and followed suit.

The running water is an impressive achievement. It begins with an above-ground pipeline that brings water from the high springs around Lake Qesqay to a concrete reservoir above Mama Samana.[20] From the reservoir, water passes through narrow buried pipes to individual homes and, with a twist of the spigot, gushes into bright blue concrete basins. Unused water runs out the bottom of the basin to soak back into the ground. The system is a great improvement as long as it works. Its Achilles' heel is the flimsy plastic piping material, for leaks develop easily. About twice a week one of the IMA-trained plumbers, Vicente or Esteban, walks the pipelines searching for the telltale wet spot. Once he locates the leak, he digs down to the pipe, patches it and covers it up again. Maintaining the system and financing replacement parts will be quite a challenge.

During my visit, the Mama Samana sector held a *faena* to build a kitchen adjoining the community center. The Mothers Club *(Club de Madres)* prepared a big salad, followed by a hot drink of thin sweetened gruel provided by one of the aid projects. The salad introduced me to another IMA project—greenhouse gardening. The Mothers proudly ushered me into a vegetable garden surrounded by an adobe wall and roofed with translucent plastic. I was amazed to find several kinds of peppers, tomatoes, lettuce, and herbs flourishing more than 12,000 feet above sea level. Several families were raising their own kitchen gardens under plastic sheeting as well. Esteban even rigged up a sprinkler system for his. In addition, IMA helped him construct a pond to raise trout; he feeds them with earthworms he grows in a pile of manure.

Fish and vegetables are welcome additions to Sonqo's carbohydrate-heavy and marginally adequate diet, yet conversation centered on whether the projects could make money. The Mothers Club hoped to eventually market their produce although (since they would compete with vendors from regions with warmer climates) it would hardly seem worth the trouble. Esteban fantasized that one day he might be able to set up a kiosk at the side of the road and make his fortune selling fried fish to tourists. Improving their own diets was a secondary consideration.

Clearly, I am troubled by this preoccupation with money. To what extent is my disquiet warranted by circumstances, to what extent is it motivated by nostalgia? After all, I attended college and graduate school in the 1960s and early '70s. I was close to people who "opted out" and tried to live off the land. For me, in 1975, it was marvelous to learn about the *Runakuna*'s intense bond with the land, and to see how they ingeniously supported themselves in their difficult environment. But my nostalgia has nothing to do with their reality. Obviously Sonqeños need money. They won't be able to overcome their marginal status in Peru without participating more fully in its economy. Obviously they want access to goods that make life more comfortable (or, at least, less miserable). The prerequisite for these improvements would seem to be an adequate subsistence, yet my examples show how *allin kawsay* (living well, adequate subsistence) has taken second place to getting money. They need cash to maintain their market participation, get out of debt, and obtain "modern" amenities. But cash is hard to come by. Potato prices were so low that farmers could not break even, much less make a profit.

[The] inefficient allocation of resources arises from cash scarcity and the logic of recuperating cash through market activity. . . . Commercial production is prioritized over subsistence production, which ends up being less efficient and more expensive than commercial production. Furthermore, farmers' desperate need for money forces them to sell their cash crop below cost in order to recuperate their cash outlay. No "subsistence first" rationale is evident here.[21]

The Spanish phrase *"Nuestro trabajo no vale"* ("Our work is worth nothing") entered frequently into conversations. There was a pervasive sense among Sonqueños that their backbreaking labor is not valued by the nation as a whole. They themselves were less willing to regard their work in terms of its social value as an interaction maintaining the flow of reciprocity. Ironically, literacy and access to mass media have brought about a reorientation toward urban values that leaves them deeply frustrated.

"Allinmi Kanchis Kunan!"—*Conversion to Evangelical Protestantism*

Where were the *Tirakuna* while all this change was going on? Right where they always were, of course, yet they must have seemed uninvolved in Sonqueños' lives. *Runakuna* performed rituals for their livestock on the Feast of San Juan (24 June), in August, and during Carnival. They fed Tirakuna and Pachamama, and celebrated them with music, coca, and alcohol—yet the animals did not thrive. Their coats were scant and scruffy; their bodies thin and ravaged by parasites. Traditional ritual practice, much of which is directed to animal welfare, cannot have seemed particularly effective. As herding diminished in importance those rituals would have lost their urgency anyway.

Another demoralizing development was the loss of their Mamacha's crown. Sonqo's tiny and otherwise undistinguished church possessed a lovely old statue of the Virgin, their *Mamacha*. She was clothed in special raiment and crowned with a circlet of silver with which she called ancestral souls back to their families on the Day of the Dead. In 1979 thieves broke into the little church and stole the crown. Church robberies periodically occur in southern Peru; few of the stolen objects are recovered and the *Mamacha*'s crown was no exception. Probably it was melted down or sold in some antique shop to a well-heeled tourist. Don Luis mourned the crown as he mourned Rufina, for who would call her home on the Day of the Dead? Crown or no crown, Sonqueños went ahead and set out feasts for the souls on November First. They have continued to do so over the years, but with a lingering sense that the an-cestral connection has been diminished.

Coca, another connection to the ancestral past, is in short supply as well. The situation I described in Chapter 9 remains essentially unchanged. Coca leaf is not illegal but its transportation is so restricted and heavily controlled that people often do without it, hoarding their meager supply for ritual and medicinal purposes. Alcohol, on the other hand, is easily available. The drink of choice in 2000 was *alkul*, extremely low-grade alcohol cut with water. *Trago* (made from sugar-cane) had become an expensive luxury. I wrote about the question of alcoholism in Chapter 5:

I would not call more than a few Sonqueños chronic drinkers; rather, they are oppor-tunistic drinkers. When alcohol is available they like to drink it, and they often con-tinue drinking as long as the supply lasts. In ritual, intoxication serves important reli-gious purposes; but in many other situations, getting drunk is simply a temporary escape from life's hard work and sorrows and an excuse to release pent-up feelings. As long as opportunities to drink are limited, the situation contains its own check; when the booze runs out everything returns to normal. But as the availability of *trago* increases with improved transportation and access to cash, opportunistic drinking easily turns into chronic drinking. Alcoholism is not now [1988] a serious problem in Sonqo, but the potential is there. (page 124)

The potential became reality with a rapidity I did not expect. *Alkul* became cheap and available as, simultaneously, the ritual practices that framed alco-hol as sacramental seemed less effective.

Drinking *alkul* can be risky. I learned that Inucha died, not of a respiratory ailment as I first thought, but of alcohol poisoning. It happened while she was staying with *compadres* in Chocopia to pasture their herd along with that of her father. She arrived at their house one evening upset and crying, having been "frightened by a *kukuchi*" as she drove the sheep home after dark. They plied her with alcohol to ward off her fear until she collapsed and died.

Leopoldo's wife, whom I'll call Doña Elvira, died in 1997 after drinking for three days straight during Carnival. This surprised me, for I had known her well. She was a quiet young woman, a superb weaver, who disliked drinking alcohol. I remember how she would turn away and pretend to be busy in hopes of avoiding the *copita* of *trago*.

"That changed," Josefa told me. "It got so that she even took a secret bottle with her when she went herding. She'd come home from the pasture roaring drunk."

This is almost unthinkable behavior for a *Runa* woman—yet I had to sym-pathize as I sat there with the July wind piercing through my jacket. Life in the *puna* is just too cold and exhausting. Something has to make it bearable.

But let me back up a bit. What do I mean by "alcoholism" and why do I think it related to Protestant conversion in Sonqo? I use the term "alcoholic" as Sonqueños use the word *machaq runa* (a drinker, a drunk) to describe a per-son whose chronic drinking interferes with work, family life, and social rela-

219

tions. I have not attempted to measure alcohol consumption, nor was my visit long enough to count the number of *machaq runa* in Sonqo. Sonqueños themselves said that drinking was a problem, especially among men, which is consistent with my impressions.

My own generation was particularly hard hit. In 1975 this was the new generation; these were the dancers, musicians, cooks, and junior sponsors for *ayllu* fiestas and Qoyllur Rit'i. These were couples starting their families and optimistically turning to the new opportunities opened by the Agrarian Reform. They were the ones most eager to "vary"—to try new cash crops, new rotation sequences, new fertilizers and insecticides (as well as the loans that made all this possible). In 2000, with shock and sorrow, I found my age-mates not only disillusioned and worn-out but, in several cases, incapacitated by alcohol.

I've mentioned Leopoldo and Elvira, but there were many others. There was Guillermo (a pseudonym), for example, who danced *ch'unchu* on the Qoyllur Rit'i pilgrimage in 1975. He was a reserved young man in his early twenties who had already served as the Sonqo's secretary, making good use of his six years of elementary school education. He seemed destined to thread his way through the *cargos*, serve the *ayllu* as a responsible authority and emerge finally as a *kuraq tayta* (elder). By 1985 he had married, set up his own household, and was still active in civic affairs. Although I saw him drink heavily at a fiesta, he kept his good humor and danced indulgently with several delighted children. I do not know just when alcohol took over, but in 2000 I found him greatly changed. A widower since 1990, he had not remarried and lived alone. It was said that no woman would have him because he drank so much. I was startled to find his mother-in-law's face disfigured by a big scar, a memento of one of his drunken outbursts. His son, now twelve, was being raised by his wife's parents with whom (as the scar attests) he maintained a difficult relationship.

Apolinar, another *ch'unchu* dancer, followed a similar trajectory into alcoholism. Like Guillermo, he had finished primary school, was beginning his *cargos,* and had qualities of leadership. He enthusiastically turned to early potatoes and barley in the '80s, believing that he could turn a profit "living right here in Sonqo. I don't need to move to the city." In 1985, however, gossip warned that he could get "ugly" *(millay)* when he drank. In 1995 it described him as a chronic drinker and wife beater.

And in the year 2000? He bounded through the door of his house, where I sat chatting with Sista, his wife.

"*Allinmi kanchis kunan, Comadre!*" he exclaimed, dispensing with the usual formalities. *Allinmi kanchis:* "We're well now!"[22]

He was eager to tell me how bad he'd been, how drinking had obsessed him, how he beat his family and alienated everyone else. "Drinking was going to kill me," he said. Sista murmured agreement—"That's right, *Comadre*. That's how it was!" But all was changed now that they were *Hermanos. "Allinmi kanchis kunan!"*

And so I returned to Sonqo to find my age-mates drunk, dead, or Protestant. Apolinar and Sista's story was not atypical, for the late '90s found many houscholds disintegrating under the ravages of *alkul* and physical abuse. Desperate people hoped to turn their lives around by converting to evangelical Protestantism, which forbids the consumption of alcohol and condemns domestic violence.

"Hmph!" snorted Don Luis when I recounted my conversation with Apolinar and Sista. "We'll see how long it lasts!"

Indeed, Protestant conversion in Sonqo is less than ten years old and it is too soon to know how the trend will develop. Whatever happens, the conversions signal a watershed in Sonqo's history.[23]

The decision to convert is a family affair, spreading along extended kinship lines and bringing converts together to live in the same neighborhoods. Wives often take the initiative in hope of getting their husbands to stop drinking. Valentina, for example, was hoping to persuade Serafeo to join the *Hermanos*.

"He hasn't agreed yet but she's working on it. He'll come around eventually," Sista told me.

The central figure in the conversions is Florencio Quispe Churata, husband of Apolinar and Sista's daughter Lucia. Florencio was Sonqo's first convert and has become spiritual leader for the Protestants. He greeted me warmly when I visited his house and said that he remembered me from his childhood. I admitted that I didn't remember him and he replied that it was just as well. "I was a bad kid," he said. "I got into trouble all the time."

Florencio told his history eagerly, describing a bored, angry, dishonest boy whose life was changed by (ironically!) the Catholic priest in Colquepata.[24] It was the priest who taught him to read the Bible in Quechua and this, he said, gave direction and purpose to his life. Like many teenagers he went to work in Cuzco for several years, and there he was drawn to Seventh Day Adventists who shared his passion for Bible reading. In 1993 he converted to Adventism, and in 1994 returned to Sonqo and married Lucia.

He was not Sonqo's first Adventist. A middle-aged widow had converted a few years earlier, but she suffered from such ostracism that she gave up and returned to her old *Runa* ways. Florencio, too, encountered hostility. The *ayllu* met in assembly to discuss his case and voted to expel him. But he defended himself.

"Look at me!" he said. "You all know me, and know how bad I was. I was lazy, I lied, I stole. But now that I'm an *Hermano*, I've reformed. I'm a different person: I work hard, I don't drink, I'm honest, and I live peacefully with my wife.[25]

He prevailed. The *ayllu* knew him and had to admit that his behavior had changed for the better. So he stayed, and "little by little" a congregation of converts gathered around him. Now in his thirties, Florencio exudes a quiet sense of moral authority. His personal magnetism reminded me of Erasmo (without the playfulness). As we talked, he asked probing questions in a natural and

"They're building a town there!" Tile-roofed houses surround the church in Qoyapuqru, viewed from above.

unintrusive manner. To my surprise I found myself talking freely about my personal life.

Florencio and Lucia live in Qoyapucru, the *barrio central* (central neighborhood). This was the sector Cirilo had in mind when he spoke of my going "to Sonqo." It's also the neighborhood that Josefa and Crisologo described as "too crowded and too many *Hermanos*."

"You won't recognize it," they told me, "They're building a *llaqta* (town) there." Indeed, the change between 1995 and 2000 was remarkable. Thanks to Plan International, half a dozen two-story houses had sprung up, a few with TV antennas sprouting from the red-tiled roofs. They stood side-by-side along the road, reflecting the Protestants' more gregarious and commercial orientation. At least three Qoyapucru households, Florencio's included, had set up small dry-goods stores. I accompanied Lucia to Qhalipampa to assist in the *wasichayay* (house-raising) for her cousin Toribio, and found that a similar process of building and concentration was going on there as well.

Toribio's *wasichayay* was attended entirely by Protestants. It was striking how little Protestants and Catholics had to do with each other. The folks in Mama Samana told me that the *Hermanos* were *Adventista* (Seventh Day Adventist). They said I'd encounter a dull and dismal life over there. Not only did *Hermanos* forswear drinking, they also refused to chew coca or eat red meat. Sheep, pigs, and *quwis* (guinea pigs) were all off-limits. And of course, they made no offering to *Pachamama* and *Tirakuna*: "*Manan samichanku!*" ("They

222

don't offer the *samincha!"*) So I was surprised when *Hermana* Sista offered me a *k'intu*.

"Oh we're not *Adventista* anymore," she explained. "We're *Maranata*. We can chew coca and eat meat. We're only forbidden to drink alcohol."

Maranata! (Aramaic,"The Lord is coming!"), a cry from St. Paul's First Epistle to the Corinthians (16:22), is the name of a Pentecostal movement that originated in Sweden during the late 1950s. According to one of the few sources on the subject,

> Its leaders were influenced by a minor revival among Swedish Pentecostalists, as well as by conservative Protestant preachers in Norway and the United States. Stress was laid on the extensive use of tongues, revivalist songs and prayers for the sick. The importance of local congregational independence—free from denominational or state hierarchy—was perceived as paramount. As Dahlgren comments, "Maranata did not claim to present any new doctrine, on the contrary it regarded itself as the true Pentecostal movement."[26]

According to a website maintained by Swiss Maranata missionaries in Puno, the movement has been active in southern Peru for the past thirty-five years and has established 185 congregations.[27] Although I did not locate the Maranata missionaries who visited Sonqo, they were said to have called on people in their homes and behaved with respect for local customs ("Like you, *Comadre!*"). They emphasized the importance of leading a good life while waiting for the Second Coming of Christ.

It can hardly be a coincidence that Pentecostalism swept Sonqo a few years before the turning of the millennium. Expectations of apocalypse, as predicted in the New Testament's Book of Revelations, tapped into a deep vein of millennialism. Apolinar told me in 1978 that he expected *Pachakuti* in 2000, and he must have felt a sense of crisis as the year approached. Pentecostalism affirmed an old idea—periodic destruction and renewal of the world—and gave it a modern context. The new religion thus solved a dilemma for people who expected a *Pachakuti* but knew themselves to be "ruined" for any second coming of the Incas.

As Maranatas, moreover, they were not required to totally change their way of life. Lucia embraced me as *"Comadre!"* with tears of joy. It mattered not at all that our bond was forged by *rutuchikuy* (that evening in 1975 [page 12] when we unwittingly accepted Apolinar's dinner invitation and found ourselves cutting baby Lucia's hair). The First Hair-cutting is certainly not a Protestant—or even a Catholic—ritual, yet Lucia and other Protestants honor the bonds thus created. Lucia knew I valued the *Runa* customs and took pains to show me that they were not forgotten.

"We still live the same way, *Comadre*—we chew coca and we sing songs to the same music. The difference is that we pray only to God" *(Diosninchis).*

"That's right," Florencio added in Spanish. *"Los imagenes son falsos. Hay un solo Padre Dios"* ("The images are false. There's one single God the Father").

Lucia, holding her baby, poses in *runa p'acha*. In contrast to the skirts of 1975 (see photo, page 30), Lucia's skirt displays a new tendency to cover the whole garment with colorful embroidery.

Music is important to the Maranata movement, something that gave Lucia evident pleasure. She showed me a Maranata song book with old *wayno* melodies set to new Quechua lyrics along the lines of "Jesus Loves Me." Singing quietly to herself, she dressed in fine *Runa p'acha*, her own handiwork, and we set out for Toribio's house raising party .

Lucia dances as we walk along, singing snatches of Maranata songs, her heavy skirts swishing, her baby bouncing snugly on her back. Bundled in with the baby is a two-liter bottle of Coca-Cola—"so we won't get thirsty."

Dogs run up barking behind us. We shoo them off, and I turn around to watch them run back down the road. The church seems out of place in the row of Protestant houses. I look below the road to the old house compound where Basilia and I spent many good hours, squeezing ch'uño *and talking. From there one can see the rounded promontory of Yanqay where the* Runakuna *danced during Carnival week, the sounds of their*

music carrying for miles. Below it stretches Waska Wayllar, a fertile bog, treacherous ter-
ritory in the rainy season.

We turn again and continue on our way. Below us the schoolyard comes into view.
Above us looms the ridge named Orqokancha, where the Puma ancestor emerged at
the beginning of this world. The ridge ends in the promontory of Pachawani, whose little
chapel receives the crosses and saints' images on feast days, and where a diminished con-
tingent of dancers still gathers for Carnival pukllay. *At the other end it runs into An-*
taqaqa, home of the ancestral Machula Aulanchis.

We round another curve and step easily across the irrigation canal, reduced to a
dry-season trickle. Its water runs steeply downhill and crosses the Chaupi Ñan trail.
Generations of footfalls have worn this old Central Path deep into the rock. In 1975 this
*neighborhood was the "barrio central," or, as Crisologo once put it,"*kikin Sonqoq
sonqon*" ("The very heart of Heart"), a play on words, for sonqo means heart. Now*
the old deserted church stands silently with its roof caving in—a ghost town of sorts. The
lumpy cemetery is still home to Sonqo's almakuna, *for the dead continue to be buried*
there. I can see new graves, fancy ones with adobe monuments. Rufina's "house" and
the wooden cross twined with qantus and marigolds are long gone; her bones have been
mixed into the collective grave of her ayllu. *I think of Basilia's bones, which never joined*
them. And Erasmo's, interred there in 1996. Yes, Erasmo.

Lucia hums to the baby on her back and calls me. "Haku, let's go, Comadre. This
will make you sad."

We pass two new houses built right up against the road. One more curve stands be-
tween us and the house compound in Pillikunka where I lived in the storeroom. An-
taqaqa is coming fully into view. From Pillikunka we'll be able to see Toribio's house
in Qhalipampa, our destination. Beyond Qhalipampa the road crosses a stretch of red
rocks named Qolqe Horquna, and passes out of sight around a bend as it enters
Sipaskancha Alta.

"What do you think of your old house, Comadre*?" Lucia asks me, smiling.*

My house? Where? But yes, now I see that we're looking at Pillikunka. I didn't rec-
ognize it.

"Domingo Quispe lives there now," says Lucia. "He keeps building and building."

It's impressive. Three new tile-roofed structures have replaced the low thatched
house with its small courtyard and storerooms. It's like an adobe apartment complex
built right into the hillside.

We keep walking. We can see Toribio's new house in Qhalipampa where people are
already hard at work. The new building dwarfs the little house next to it where Toribio
spent most of his childhood. Slightly nearer to us is the deserted compound where Lucia
lived as a baby and, a little bit closer still, there is Erasmo's house. Many times I looked
over the wall from Pillikunka to see Erasmo sitting by his open door, chewing coca or
knitting a chullu. *The door stands open now as it did before.*

"They turned Protestant after Erasmo died . . ." Erasmo's death after a year-
long wasting illness seems to have come at a critical juncture in Sonqo's

history, and provided yet another impetus for people to make radical changes in their lives. His brother Julian fell sick and died around the same time. They were close in age and resembled each other so closely that Erasmo sometimes joked that they were twins. As young men, he and Julian traveled together by foot to the eastern forests and, as they crossed the cordillera, *Rayu* (Lightning) came and left them lying stunned on the ground. Thus they received their vocation as *hampichiq* (medicine men)—an event that eventually would explain the manner of their deaths. Their wasting illness was a sign of failure; *Rayu* felt let down and he was punishing them. And so *Rayu* and *Tira* (who seemed interchangeable in this context) consumed their hearts. They wasted away; their legs were like sticks; they coughed and gasped for breath.

In Erasmo's case, Esteban told me, *Rayu/Tira* had some help:

"Runakuna phukuranku wañupunanpaq," he said. "People did *phukuy* to make him die."

I knew that Erasmo inspired ambivalent feelings but such a depth of hostility amazed me. According to Esteban, Erasmo took advantage of his turn as Sonqo's president to sell a communal stand of eucalyptus trees for his own profit. (Yes, I remembered those trees—they were nothing but trouble. Don Luis was nearly impeached over them in 1975 [page 92]. I commented on this to Esteban. "You're from the old times!" *(ñawpa timpu)*, he exclaimed.)

Erasmo's presidency fell in the early '90s, a very bad time in Peru as a whole, for political instability bred a general atmosphere of violence. Sonqueños' dreams of commercial success were punctured, and they were more factionalized than ever. It's surprising that Erasmo took on the office, for he had never seemed interested in administrative *cargos*. Whatever the facts of the eucalyptus scandal, it left many Sonqueños bitterly angry and may have contributed to Mama Samana's initial separation from the community. For traditionalists, Erasmo's demise was reaffirming; it demonstrated that they actually could affect events through coca *phukuy*. But for his family and neighbors in Qhalipampa, it seems to have had the opposite effect, demonstrating that his ritual knowledge and skill amounted to nothing in the long run.

I felt stricken with the reality of Erasmo's death as we approached the open door of his house. Lucia quietly steered me over to the house-raising party, not wanting me to get sidetracked. It was awhile before I could excuse myself and go back to visit Cipriana. Hipolito and his wife slipped away from their house-raising tasks to join me and we sat with Cipriana by the fireplace, there in the dark little house where we had heard many good stories. Cipriana had grown deaf and we shouted to help her hear us. I rather apprehensively got out the gifts I had brought—a photo album, tapes of Erasmo's stories, a small cassette player. A *gringo* gift—I wondered whether they would find it appropriate. To my relief, they eagerly seized on the photos—laughing, sighing, reminiscing. Hipolito slipped a tape into the player and pulled out his coca bag. His eyes grew moist from time to time as we listened, but I was the one who cried.

They were all *Hermanos,* just as Cirilo had told me. "It's a better way to live," Hipolito assured me, offering a *k'intu.* Cipriana, straining to hear, agreed. We shared our coca leaves with the familiar phrases—*Hallpakusunchis! Yusulpayki, Urpicháy!*—but there was no blowing over the leaves, no invocations. I asked whether they had forgotten *Pachamama* and the *Tirakuna.*

"*MANAN! Manan qunquruykuchu! Pero es espiritual!*" ("No! We haven't forgotten them! But it's spiritual!"). Again, a Spanish phrase inserted into the Quechua conversation.

We talked about Erasmo's illness. "It was *Rayu* (Lightning)," they told me without self-consciousness. I had expected them to offer a different interpretation, but they too told me about the brothers' youthful encounter with *Rayu,* the failed vocation, and the slow cruel punishment. They didn't seem to feel any inconsistency between this interpretation and their conversion to Protestantism. With a sinking heart I realized that the diagnosis of failure and punishment was Erasmo's own. He must have died in a depressed and hopeless state of mind.

I returned to Toribio's *wasichayay.* The men were up on the roof of the new house, laying orange tiles; the women had finished peeling potatoes and were inside the old thatched house cooking and talking. Gavina, Toribio's mother, presided over the activities, directing her daughter in law and other young women. She said she and her teenaged daughters would move back from Mama Samana to live next to Toribio. Her brother Domingo and sister Valentina had both converted and—since Domingo had moved to Pillikunka—they both lived nearby.

While Gavina's move was part of a general reshuffling of *ayllu residence* into separate Protestant and Catholic sectors, it was motivated by more than Protestant fellowship. Julian, her husband, died back in Mama Samana and the aftermath of his death was horrible for her. She could no longer bear to live in that house because "after he died the *ñak'aqs* came."

"The *ñak'aqs* (slaughterers) . . . are supernaturally evil Mestizos who fall on nighttime travelers and kill them with their knives. They may mesmerize the victim with their flaming eyes and extract their body fat" (Chapter 3, page 88). In the year 2000 *ñak'aq* also referred to the two nurses who staff Colquepata's new Centro de Salud (Health Center). A long-standing Peruvian law requires autopsies for anyone who dies outside a hospital. The regulation is seldom enforced in remote communities—but Sonqo is no longer remote. News of a death brings the medical *ñak'aqs* hurrying by car from Colquepata to perform the autopsy right in the family house. Catholic and Protestant alike spoke of the experience with horror, dread, and anger. Some, like Gavina, were deeply traumatized by the experience. She felt an unwholesome presence hanging around the house and was afraid to live there. Balvina and Luis, who lived just up the hillside, agreed. "Even the dogs are afraid of that house! Julian's *alma* just doesn't leave it alone."

According to Sonqueños, the nurses' verdict on Julian was that he drank too much; on Erasmo, that he died of old age.[28] I was not able to confirm this report, but it seems that they made no connection between the two brothers' deaths. Protestant and Catholic shrugged off the *ñaqk'aq*'s report and agreed that they knew better—*Rayu* and *Tira* had done their worst. And they agreed on another point—it was best to avoid the *ñak'aq*s in the Health Center. "We just doctor ourselves right here with *cura hampi*" (traditional herbal remedies).

One of these herbal remedies is coca leaf, the quintessential *hampi*. Protestants still feel the need of it; in fact, I found the Protestants better supplied with coca than the Catholic traditionalists. Coca wards off the *qayqa* atmosphere surrounding a corpse and consoles the mourners in their grief. When Balvina attended Julian's funeral wake she was surprised to find the *Hermanos* chewing coca. "The body was stretched out on one side of the room and the mourners were sitting on the other. They didn't drink but they sure chewed a lot of coca" *(waputa hallpanku)*.

But to return to the house-raising party—a happy occasion. Domingo Quispe was up on the roof with the five younger men, instructing them as they laid the tiles. He called down to me that I should take their picture. The day passed in the familiar rhythm of a *wasichayay*. Men put up the roof beams and set the tiles in place. We women cooked and cooked and cooked. First we prepared the midday meal, which was served in Gavina's small house; then, we set to work on the celebratory dinner that would inaugurate the new house. It was late afternoon before the work was finished. Eagerly we passed over the threshold, men seating themselves in a line along the wall opposite the door, while we women gathered around the pots of food. We carried them over from the old house, for there was still no *q'uncha* in the new one.

Although, overall, the day's activities were familiar, there were differences—no cross went up on the peak of the roof; no *despacho* had been offered the night before. Offerings to the *Tirakuna* were replaced by lengthy prayers before meals. At midday, Don Domingo offered a litany of thanks—for the food, the new house, even my presence. *"Amen!"* murmured the hungry workers as Gavina served the soup.

The evening meal began with a longer prayer. Men and women stood up quietly and removed their hats. Domingo's prayer built in intensity until the others were moved to join in, eyes turned upward, arms raised to about eye level with the palms of the hands facing each other about eighteen inches apart. Each person prayed in his or her own words in a fervent, open manner that bore no resemblance to the high-pitched stream of endearments that characterizes traditional Quechua requests. Nor did it resemble the private breathy words whispered over coca leaves. These prayers built in speed, volume, and intensity so that they soon blended together into a babble of voices, still in Quechua but far too fast and mixed for me to follow. When Domingo finished and dropped his hands the others subsided into *Amen*s. We sat down and Gavina quickly served the soup, which was growing cold. After we ate, Toribio handed out coca leaves. We shared *k'intu*s but offered no *samincha*.

And then the drinking started. Yes, we drank in quantity. Lucia's big bottle of Coca-Cola was joined by at least five more two-liter bottles—Fanta, Sprite, and more Coke. Toribio set to work serving them with the familiar cere-mony—*"Tomakuy!"* *"Salud, tomanki!"*—again without libations to *Pacha,* or *t'inka* to the *Apukuna.* No alcohol, no getting drunk—but an ordeal nonethe-less. We chugged down cup after cup of the sticky-sweet liquid, night fell, the big fireless room grew cold, the drinks made us shiver, but no one left until the bottles were empty. I was exhausted by that time, and my head was spin-ning. (I had an incongruous image of myself as a whale that had swallowed the ocean, beached 12,000 feet above sea level.)

Somehow I made it back to Mama Samana. Gavina's daughters led me fearlessly through the night, singing quietly and steering me over the rocki-est places. I had stomach cramps the next day and Luis complained wrath-fully—those *Hermanos* were foolish enough to drink *gaseosas* in the cold! "You'd have been fine if it'd been *trago,*" he said, conveniently forgetting my history of sick hangovers.

Ñawpa Timpu / Qhipa Timpu (The Time Before / The Time Behind)

"Ay Comadre," sighs Felicitas. "It makes me sad to see your hair turning white!" She's almost forty now. I still think of her as the thirteen year-old girl who used to drive me crazy. Now her tenderness startles me and I look at her with new eyes. Yes, she's close to forty. And she turned out all right.

I never expected to hear myself described as *"ñawpa timpumanta"* (from the old times, the previous age). Yet I was, and it took me by surprise. It was strange to think of myself as an "old-timer," but the strangeness went deeper than that. *Ñawpa timpumanta* is a phrase that I associated with the *Machus,* as in the phrase that introduces Luis's narrative on page 38 of this book: *"Ñawpa timpu runakuna kasqa"* ("They say there were people in the previous age"). In this context *ñawpa timpu* referred to a different age, lit by a different sun and inhabited by a different kind of people. Literally *ñawpa timpu* means the "the era ahead." Travelers who go on ahead of us are *ñawpa.* Time, too, goes on ahead of us; we watch the past dwindle into the distance until it drops out of sight. Rarely, in my experience, was *ñawpa timpu* applied to the human past—and when it was, it referred to times long gone by and hardly remembered. *Ñawpa timpumanta* might describe an old, truly ancient person, almost the last of her generation. Happily, I haven't reached that point yet.

Yet there I was, *ñawpa timpumanta.* I was *ñawpa timpumanta* when I re-membered the eucalyptus trees; I was *ñawpa timpumanta* when I recognized difficult *pallay*s woven into old textiles by fingers long buried; I was *ñawpa tim-pumanta* when I asked why people didn't herd llamas anymore. I was *ñawpa* *timpumanta* because I was contented to stay with Luis and Balvina in their tiny thatched house. And because I was *ñawpa timpumanta* I could tell people about parents, grandparents, and siblings they never knew. I was, unexpectedly, a resource. I could tell forgotten stories; I could help piece together forgotten details of Luis's term as *presidente*. *Ñawpa timpu*, the era of *Runakuna*, referred to a way of life that had passed. *"No somos indios ahora."*

The phrase *ñawpa timpu* poignantly expresses how, in a few decades, life in Sonqo changed in fundamental ways. Protestant conversion is the most radical expression of these changes. Change also comes through many other less drastic choices—like preferring one dance over another, or trading one's poncho for a jacket. Nevertheless, every choice contributes—both as response and cause—to cultural reconfiguration. Choices respond to changing circumstances and, in turn, shape the course of change. I will end this visit to Sonqo by exploring a nexus of interrelated choices that Sonqueños are making about their lives.

The Dancer from the Dance

"No somos indios ahora," says Cirilo, tugging at the visor of his baseball cap and zipping up his nylon jacket. But later he shows me a photo of himself dressed in a chullu, *woven belt, brightly embroidered vest and old-fashioned short pants. He keeps this* Runa p'acha *for civic ceremonies in Colquepata, like inauguration of the new Health Center, he explains. It's his dance costume. The name of the dance? He pauses, unsure how to answer.* "Campesino" *(Peasant), he finally replies.*

For the past five hundred years—ever since medieval mumming met up with Inca ritual performance—festival dance in the Andes has provided a vibrant arena for the negotiation of cultural identities. The rapid urbanization of the Peruvian population during the past two decades has not diminished its vigor. If anything festival dance is flowering; dance troupes are proliferating, new songs are being composed, and new dance characters invented. In her study of Mestizo dance in Cuzco, Zoila Mendoza comments, "the performance of dances during the fiesta is a key public context in which identity is defined. Dancers are in view, are in public space, interact with and embody discourses of personhood and social order."[29] In a rapidly changing society like Peru's, participation in dance troupes provides a context for the expression of new social identities and formation of new social bonds. Because the dance tradition developed in the countryside, participation in dance troupes also provides urban migrants with a way to explore and redefine their indigenous roots.

In countryside and city, costumed dancers represent outsiders of various kinds. For example, during the celebrations for their patron saint on August fifteenth, Colquepata townspeople perform *awka chileno* (enemy Chilean), *qhapac negro* (mighty black man), and *ch'unchu estranjero* (foreign savage). Until recently, young men in Sonqo learned four dances: *wayri ch'unchu, ukuku, sargentu,* and *majeño. Wayri ch'unchu*s represented savage jungle chieftains who, accompanied by *ukuku*s (bears), danced for pilgrimages like Qoyllur Rit'i. *Sargentu*s danced during Carnival and during the *tinkuy* on the high plain of *Chiwchillani.* Their flowing white sleeves and plumed hats imitated Spanish soldiers (and also resembled the wings and plumage of the wallatas bird celebrated in Carnival songs). The comic *majeño* figure originated in imitation of muleteers from the valley of Majes. *Majeño* was a *misti* dance favored by Paucartambo *hacendados* during the early twentieth century. Sonqueños adopted the dance after the expropriation of *haciendas* in the 1970s. In 1975 they simply identified *majeño*—with his comically brutal white face and elegant riding clothes—as a *hacendado.* Sonqo's *majeño* troupe danced for civic events, like the Mother's Day celebration hosted by the local school.

All these dance characters represent potentially hostile foreigners; some, like *awka chileno,* are figures from other time periods; others, like *saqra,* represent nonhuman creatures with dangerous powers. Festival dance "domesticates" these outsiders by bringing them together in a ritually charged context. By ritually merging figures from different time periods and existential planes, the *ayllu* defuses the outsiders' threat and absorbs their power. Deborah Poole comments,

These masked and costumed personas portray outsiders whose qualities of difference or "otherness" . . . vary along both temporal and spatial axes . . . Their participation in the present is construed as a necessary prerequisite for the successful realization of traditional ritual events, in particular religious feasts and pilgrimages. The importance of dance to these events has very much to do with the ways in which their choreography and costumes visually mediate the past—from whence a fiesta or miracle tradition comes—and the future, which is guaranteed by the ensemble of fiesta, dance, and miracle.[30]

In an urban context, this theme of *outsiderness* takes on an additional layer of meaning. The dancers themselves are outsiders, for they belong to urban lower classes and many are recent arrivals from the countryside. These city dwellers reformulate rural dance traditions to suppress their more overtly "Indian" elements, as Marisol de la Cadena demonstrates in her study of Cuzco's "indigenous mestizos." By "de-Indianizing" their dancers, the performers celebrate their indigenous origins and simultaneously distance themselves from Indianness. De la Cadena describes this stance as "inclusive otherness"— "namely, setting some distance between oneself and Indians while reproducing indigenous culture."[31]

Urban attitudes feed back into the countryside. They bring us back to Cirilo who, although he lives among potato fields and sheep pastures, is very much caught up in urbanizing processes. Taking "inclusive otherness" to an extreme, he comes into town and performs *campesino.* The foreigner he rep-

231

resents is not from a distant place or a mythic time; it is himself—Cirilo as he might have been, but chooses not to be. By donning *Runa p'acha* as a costume he projects it back into the *ñawpa timpu,* "visually mediating past, present, and future." Reversing the directionality of traditional ritual, which draws the past into the present, Cirilo's performance of *campesino* projects the present (or almost-present) into the past.

Protestants refuse to join in the festival dances. After all, *"los imagines son falsos."* Their refusal has affected Sonqo's traditional celebrations. Most of the *ch'unchu* dancers have converted to Protestantism and the *ayllu* sent no delegation to Qoyllur Rit'i in 2000. Although Cirilo danced *ukuku* once at Qoyllur Rit'i, he does not expect to go again.[32] Carnival, too, is a smaller affair because *Hermanos* do not participate. "There were only a few of us," said Balvina mournfully.

Although the *ayllu* fiestas are in disarray, Catholic traditionalists still find satisfaction in Colquepata's patronal feast. According to local reports, the celebration of *Mama Asunta* on August fifteenth is growing, perhaps as a ripple-effect from the burgeoning popularity of Paucartambo's *Mamacha Carmen.* Migrants from Colquepata's rural *ayllus,* and their city-bred offspring, return from Cuzco and Lima to celebrate *Mama Asunta.* Cirilo's nephew Eldder, born and raised in Cuzco, looks forward to joining the *qhapac negro* (mighty black man) dance troupe some year soon. He never did grow comfortable with Quechua, and finds it easier to identify with Colquepata than with Sonqo. His sister Madeleyne would like to dance *p'asñacha* (little maiden). Yes, women have joined the dance troupes. *P'asñacha* wears a version of *Runa p'acha,* though the layered skirts are made from light material and reach only to her knees. The dancer moves lightly, hips moving seductively. *Wira warmi*—fat substantial woman, loaded with ponderous skirts and a heavy bundle—is an outmoded ideal from her grandmother's time. If, as Bourdieu and Connerton say, social memory is learned and expressed in bodily habitus, then *P'asñacha* has forgotten much. But she must need to keep some connection with the past, or else she would not be there dancing in Colquepata.

Women's Mobility

Wira warmi, the old feminine ideal, was embodied in the way a *Runa* woman hunkered down by her burning *q'uncha,* hands moving busily as she cooked food and nurtured children It was embodied in a woman's heavy conical form and her rocking, swishing gait. In Carnival, *sargento* dancers asked the *Alcalde's* permission—*Lisinciayki, Taytáy!*—to dance in couples, "with the men ducking and bobbing and the women, bent slightly over their many skirts, turning in place"(page 6). I wrote in Chapter 7, "This dance beautifully expresses the relationship between the sexes" (page 161). Women stretched their arms in a horizontal gesture over their twirling skirts, flicking betassled ropes at their partners' legs. Today, in cities and towns, female dance troupes do not express

232

this horizontal/vertical gender complementarity. They dance in rows, bobbing up and down, as they move forward down the street. As public performers, they display a new kind of female assertiveness and mobility.

This new mobility characterizes rural wives as well as city bred girls. The *faena* for Mama Samana's community kitchen provides some good examples:

It was a small *faena* for only seven men from Mama Samana's fourteen households attended. Three women showed up to represent their absent husbands and went off to gather firewood. The oldest men—Don Luis, in his seventies, and Don Melcanor, the sector *presidente* in his late fifties—watched and directed the younger men. The first step was to make a big mud puddle by digging a broad shallow hole and filling it with water diverted from the plastic pipline. Then they set to work treading straw into the mud and plopping the straw-mud into wooden forms to shape the adobe bricks. It was kind of fun, but hard work nonetheless. By noon they were hungry and ready to eat.

Fortunately three more women had arrived to help with the cooking. Inside the community house these *Mamakuna*—members of the *Club de Madres* (Mothers Club)—were hurriedly preparing a meal. A big pot of water was boiling on a *q'uncha* near one end of the room. It was only for *mate* (hot drink), Josefa explained, for there had been no time to cook soup. They all had too much to do that morning. The latecomers had only just arrived back from a trip to Cuzco. Other women, including Cirilo's and Esteban's wives Juana and Ernestina, were attending a meeting at their children's school in Colquepata. But the Mothers lost no time worrying about the lack of soup. Out came a big bundle of greens from their solar garden. Quickly they washed the salad in a bucket, tossed it in a big plastic basin with some salt and—presto!—lunch was ready.

The men came in and sat down a in a line along one wall. Two of the younger women sat on a bench along the opposite wall, while the others sat on the ground near the *q'uncha* or around the salad bowl. Josefa doled out plates of salad and the men accepted with the familiar gracious thanks. Although I was later to hear some male grumbling about the unsatisfying food, the men expressed no discontent with the meal as they ate. They seemed proud of the homegrown greens and helped themselves to seconds, urging me to do the same. Soon there was not a scrap of lettuce left in the basin. The Mothers then produced a big bag of sweetened powdered "oatmeal" donated by the Vaso de Leche program. (They called it *kwakir*, derived from the Quaker Oats brand name; the ingredients were listed as finely ground wheat, barley, beans, and quinoa.) They mixed it with the hot water and served it up in metal mugs. The men finished their oatmeal *mate*, excused themselves and went out to chew coca in the warm sunshine. The women stayed inside to wash up the mugs, in very high spirits. Outside, Don Melcanor had very little coca to distribute, and three of the younger men had brought none of their own. After a brief and subdued *hallpay* they went back to work.

Inside, I was feeling confused. The Mothers were trying to decide whether to play soccer or take me to see their garden. Finally they decided that they

It's more comfortable to work sitting down: Juana sits by her *q'uncha* to prepare dinner, while children play at her side.

could do both. I agreed to join them, feeling sure that I'd misunderstood something. Maybe their children were going to play soccer. We climbed up the hillside to see the garden, where we were joined by Juana and Ernestina who had returned from Colquepata. As mentioned earlier, I was duly impressed by the solar greenhouse, which seemed like Shangri La hidden in Sonqo's dry and barren terraine. But the biggest surprise was yet in store—for it was indeed the Mothers who played soccer. They had a wonderful, boisterous time, and played remarkably well. There was no doubt that these women "knew how" to use their feet! After awhile I moseyed up the hillside to see how the men were taking it. They were busy, studiously ignoring the game, their attention focused on a new mold for adobes that wasn't quite the right size. I went back bemused to watch the darting, kicking, laughing women. Well, wonders will never cease! These Mothers fed their men salad and then ran off to play soccer. And the men put up with it.

Wira warmi is not gone completely, for in the interior of their homes most women prefer to maintain the hearth and to cook as their mothers did. Waist-high wood-burning stoves with adjoining counterspace would fit easily in the new houses. This would move food preparation off the dirt floors and allow the cook more mobility. Women know that this is the "modern" way to cook, yet they continue to build their low clay *q'uncha*s (which look rather like small kilns with a round opening on top for the soup pot). They explained that they find it more comfortable to work sitting down, with ingredients and cookware on the floor within arm's reach. In Cuzco, Emilia expressed the same sentiments. She proudly showed me the *q'uncha* in her new kitchen, asserting that food cooked there was healthier and tasted better than food cooked on a kerosene or gas stove. So it is that Mother ("all hands and no feet") and her warm round stove abide at the center of the new houses as they did in the old ones. And food preparation stays where it was, on the ground.

Mother House / Mother Earth

Wira warmi was embodied in the house itself. "A house should be warm and protective—'like a mother hen who keeps her chicks under her wings,' Luis once told me, his face lighting up as he spoke" (page 53). In a similar metaphor, the house was also conceptualized as a nest. Basilia uses this metaphor—" *when you came to my little house, when you came to my little nest"*— in the song that ends this book. Denise Arnold's marvelous article on Aymara house-raising rituals tells us that Bolivian Aymara, too, describe the family house as the "Mother-Nest." The warmth and closeness of the small one-room houses, their comfortable disorder of cloth and crockery, the crowding together of their inhabitants: these fostered a nestlike experience. If the interior of the house was rather smothering, it was also comfortable and secure. It was a place for rest, safety, and nourishment; all other activities (except, of course, cooking) were carried on outdoors. As far as *Runakuna* were concerned, *Wasitira* (House-earth) really *was* a living female. As I explain in Chapter 1 (page 29), she was a localized version of *Pachamama*, one of the *Tirakuna*. She was a self-contained microcosm whose door was *Inti haykuna* (east; literally, the Sun's entry place; see page 138). From her interior perspective, the door was East whether or not it faced East as celestially defined. Within her vigilant walls the insiders created an separate intersubjective reality that outsiders could not directly perceive or share. The Incas were said to be hidden inside *Paititi* "just as we are hidden inside a house."

In many societies, particularly those that rely more on the spoken than the written word, important cultural ideas are encoded in architectural structures. Examples range across the world from the medieval cathedrals of Europe to the remarkable house-villages in the Orinoco and Amazon Basins.[33] They include humbler examples as well:

The cosmological significance of the simple and undifferentiated houses of (Aymara) Qaqachaka seems at first surprising . . . the typical modern rectangular and gabled house of rude stone or adobe mud brick, with its tiny doorway and makeshift door, with its overgrown thatched roof topped by a cracked cooking pot and a cross, belies its symbolic richness.[34]

Arnold tells us that for the Bolivian Aymara in Qaqachaka, every element of this "Mother-Nest" is infused with symbolic significance. The house is an integrating template for cosmos, kinship, body, gender and property. Similarly, Mayer tells us that in the Mantaro Valley region of Peru, different categories of kinsmen supply different structural elements for the roof of a newlywed couple's house. The completed building represents the harmonious joining of the spouses' families.[35] I did not find this kind of explicit symbolism associated with structural elements in Sonqo's houses, but I did find the same overall equivalences between house, mother, nest, and cosmos.

Whether or not architecture explicitly encodes conscious ideas and values of a culture, it always serves—to use Bourdieu's oddly memorable phrase—as a "structuring structure of structures." Domestic architecture, in particular, imposes its structure on the most routine activities and thus informs our unconscious habits of body and mind.

Inhabited space—and above all the house . . . through the intermediary of the divisions and hierarchies it sets up between things, persons and practices . . . continuously inculcates and reinforces the taxonomic principles underlying . . . (a) culture.[36]

The old nest-like houses are rapidly being relegated to the ñawpa pacha by the new two-story tile-roofed houses. These more open multiroom structures—with glass-paned windows and six-foot-high doors—restructure their inhabitants' relationship to their activities and environment. The low doors in the old-style houses force you to bend over as you cross the threshold, whereas you enter the new ones standing upright. Entering the old house implied a qualitative change in consciousness, an experience confirmed every time one crossed the threshold, straightened up, and readjusted the senses to different light, temperature, smells, and spatial dimensions. The perceptual contrast was strong and definite, confirming the cultural salience of the opposition between "inside" and "outside."[37] This is less true with the new-style houses. Occupants are not as "hidden" in the interior, for the big windows allow insiders to look out and outsiders to look in. Old houses are stuffier and smokier while the new ones are colder. They have more interior space to heat, and the windows and doors that let in light and fresh air also let in the cold wind.

Indigenous Andean culture is an outdoor culture. Houses are for eating, sleeping, and storage. Andean cultures at the time of the Spanish conquest had not developed a tradition of furniture other than the occasional thronelike seat for high status persons, nor did European furniture take hold after the conquest, for Runakuna continued to live close to the ground. The new houses, in contrast, are more spacious and can accommodate activities like weaving and potato sorting that were previously done outdoors. If (as Sonqueños expect)

236

Plan International provides tables and chairs, household activities will be conducted away from the ground, placing distance between a family and its *wasitira*. If electricity ever comes to Sonqo (as it eventually should), families will be able to stay up at night doing chores, watching TV, reading, doing homework.

Plan International's building program presents Sonqueños with an important choice about how they will live. It's hardly a difficult decision, for who would pass up the opportunity to build oneself a bigger, better house? Harsh historical experience, moreover, has taught Sonqueños social and political advantages to building more substantial houses. In 1948, for example, four men and a woman from Sipaskancha Alta courageously took a neighboring *hacendado* to court, claiming that he had stolen the roofs from their houses and caused other damage to their property. The case was part of an ongoing lawsuit over land rights, for the *hacendado* claimed title to the land where the houses were located. The court found in favor of the *hacendado's* claim and dismissed the lawsuit. Anyway, the opinion stated, the so-called houses were "not to be considered serious buildings, but only little huts *(no se trata de edificios serios, sino pequeñas chozas)*."[38] It's hard to be taken seriously when one lives in a "primitive unhygienic hut" (page 13). Nevertheless, although no one wants to refuse Plan International's offer, some were faster to start building than others:

"I still live in a warm house" *(q'uñi wasi)*, Vicente announced with a defensive air, as I entered his small thatched house.

I wasn't sure whether it was an apology or a boast. While he assured me that he had plans to build a big new house nearer to the road, he also confided that he liked his cozy house and wasn't in any hurry to change it. He's comfortable and already enjoys his amenities—running water and a battery powered television set. He enjoys curling up next to his sleeping family and watching the nature programs that come on at 10 P.M.

"I've got no choice but to keep living here," grumbled Don Luis. "They don't give me anything because my children are all grown up." But when his sons offered to build him a new-style house he preferred to stay in his old *q'uñi wasi*. "Why should I change at my age?" he said.

Although not every Sonqueño is in a hurry to change, it's inevitable that new-style houses will eventually replace the old thatched-roofed dwellings of the *Runakuna*. The shift will transform their lives in manifold ways—affecting the rhythm of their daily activities, their bodily habitus, and their use of personal space. Equally significant, the shift is a harbinger of land privatization. Building a house makes a statement about one's right to live on the land. The Sipaskancha lawsuit of 1948 shows how even "huts" threatened the *hacendado's* land claims, so much so that he carried off the roofs and demolished the buildings. The new houses in Sonqo are "serious buildings" *(edificios serios)*, indicating a new kind of permanence. Because the old simple houses were more easily built they were also more easily abandoned. When a family decided it would be more convenient to live elsewhere in Sonqo's large territory, they left their old house and built another, often taking the thatch and roof beams with them. This strategy won't work with the new "serious" houses, which are not only more laborious to build, but represent a one-time infusion of construction materials from Plan International. A couple moving to a new location would face a significant (and probably impossible) expenditure of money in order to replace the house they left behind. They surely would not want to abandon their old house, but rather would sell or rent it. In this context it only makes sense that they be able to sell the *lote*, or parcel of land on which it stands, as well.

Two-story tile-roofed houses are not the only new architectural feature in Sonqo's landscape. There are also the outhouses. These too were built with the help of a development agency, and would be difficult to replace.

Who Needs Hygiene?

The FONCODES latrine program was the first development project to reach Sonqo. The latrines were brand new when I visited in 1995 and they took me by surprise. In my earlier experience the *Runakuna* found the idea repulsive. I recalled that in 1975 the gringo grapevine in Cuzco told of an expatriate couple who had nearly been expelled from a community for building themselves an outhouse. In 1995 the new latrines seemed unused except as storerooms for firewood or protection against wind and rain. Children liked to play in them. Several people commented that the seats were too cold. When I returned in 2000 the latrines did show evidence of use; however, I did not actually see anybody enter one. As far as I could tell, children were not directed to them as part of toilet training. Nevertheless, there was a general sense of pride in the *"baños,"* as they called them. The outhouses were a tangible mark of modernization and progress.

In some ways these latrines epitomize the Sonqueños' relationship to modernity. Their presence in Sonqo brings to the fore a tangle of social, biological, and cultural issues associated with "hygiene." The dictionary defines this term as "a condition or practice conducive to the preservation of health, as cleanliness." The problem in a multicultural society is that systems of hygiene are culturally constituted. Cultures vary in their conceptualization of the human body, of the conditions that promote health, and of the body's relation to the physical world outside itself. Understandings of cleanliness and filth are culturally defined; as are the consequences—physical and moral—of being in one state or the other. Because cleanliness and health are so deeply connected in our thinking, keeping clean becomes a duty, a moral imperative. "Cleanliness is next to godliness," and people who don't keep clean are experienced as morally reprehensible and physically distasteful.

Writing of highland Ecuador, Rudi Colloredo-Mansfield mentions "the white-mestizo fixation on the 'dirtiness of the Indians,'" ponchos stained with soil or a kitchen blackened with smoke and reeking of guinea pigs demonstrated not just the hard realities of peasant life but a moral and national failing.[39]

In the Introduction I quote a Colquepata Mestizo who describes the Indians' "huts" as "unhygienic" *(antihigiénicas)*. Furthermore, he associates these living conditions with an "Indian character" that is overwhelmingly negative: sullen, distrustful, timid, yet vengeful and dangerous. This is an example of what Colloredo-Mansfield calls "hygienic racism":

If "dirt is matter out of place" as Mary Douglas puts it (1966:35), then "dirty Indians" have been bodies, homes, and material cultures out of place in a modernizing Ecuador.[40]

One has to wonder how much of the push to improve hygiene in communities like Sonqo is motivated by an exaggerated abhorrence of dirt in Euro-American culture. Yet it would be disingenuous to indulge in cultural critique without acknowledging (since we do believe in germ theory) that rural farmers benefit from keeping excrement out of their water supply. As I commented with regard to coca chewing in Chapter 9, it is hard to sort out scientific opinion from social attitudes toward Indians. Concerns about cholera are real as well, although cholera is more typical of urban settings. Sanitation is a greater problem in rural towns that lack running water, where excretion takes place in the gutter or in chamber pots that are emptied into the street. But the rural mountain streams are hardly pure and clean; runoff from the steep hillside fields inevitably carries human and animal excrement, chemical fertilizer and pesticides into streams and irrigation canals. The priority would seem to be a functioning, sustainable system of piped water rather than outhouses—yet the outhouses were first to reach Sonqo. Teaching the "dirty Indians" to clean up and use the toilet seems to have been considered the prerequisite to further modernization.

The English words "dirt" and "soil" give rise to our negative adjectives, "dirty" and "soiled." We translate the Quechua words *map'a* and *qelli* as "dirty" but they don't actually have this reference to dirt. Something is *map'a* or *qelli* because it's gotten mixed up; its parts are not clearly differentiated. Dirt itself carries a positive valence; there's nothing intrinsically wrong with being dirty.[41]

People normally don't bathe in Sonqo. One reason for this is clear enough: it's cold! People sometimes take advantage of the warm midday sun to wash face, hands, and feet in a basin of water. Women unbraid their long hair and clean it with a wet comb. Seriously ill persons may be sponged all over with warm herbal concoctions. Bathing the whole body is reserved for ritually charged contexts. During his visit in 1999, David Edwards took Don Luis to visit the Island of the Sun in Lake Titicaca. They stayed on the way in a hotel in the city of Puno, where Luis was interested by the plumbing but had no interest in bathing. But on the Island of the Sun, greatly moved, he bathed naked in the frigid waters of Lake Titicaca.

The relationship to water is a careful one; drinking or washing directly from streams and springs is thought to cause *wiqsa nanay* (stomach ache) and *qopu* (rash). Water is not consumed "raw" (that is, unboiled), but rather in soups and teas. A woman preparing dinner on the dirt floor next to her *q'uncha* washes her potatoes in a pan of water, peels them, and then washes them again before tossing them in the cooking pot. To our sensibilities preparing food on a dirt surface seems a dubious practice, but it needn't lead to contaminated food.

The tricky issue is not dirt but excrement. As Sarah Lund Skar writes, "excrement is viewed pragmatically and not only as an object of aversion."[42] When not confined to the latrines, defecation *(akay)* takes place discreetly, usually under cover of darkness, in corral or field. At these high altitudes the feces dry up or are scavenged by pigs and dogs. Prior to the introduction of chemical fertilizers, animal excrement was a crucial link between the agricultural and pastoral economies of the household. It was also "an essential element in the system of reciprocal exchanges that characterizes the *warmi-qhari*'s married relationship" (page 144). Now that chemical fertilizer is used to "doctor" the fields this link is less crucial than it once was.[43]

Excrement carries powerful significance in any culture. Excremental symbolism is pervasive in Andean ritual and carries a positive valence that most "Westerners" find surprising and strange. As I wrote in Chapter 6, animal manure *(wanu)* falls under the category of *hampi,* medicine. Getting covered with sheep and llama droppings in animal fertility rituals feels appropriate, for the manure is "*hampi* for the potatoes." In some Andean communities participants in these rituals drink *chicha* garnished with their animals' droppings.[44] As fertilizer and fuel, excrement has transformative power; the animal's body that produces manure through its digestive and excretory processes achieves a kind of transubstantiation. The significance of this transformation carries over into other ritual practices like forced feeding, when the saturated body passes *samincha* to ancestors and Sacred Places.

In spite of the cultural importance of excrement in the Andes, there is little written on the subject. The exception is a fine paper by Sarah Lund Skar on "The Role of Urine in Andean Notions of Health and the Cosmos." Urination, unlike defecation, is treated fairly casually and is not a cause of embarrassment. Men simply turn away and women squat in their many heavy skirts. As far as I could see, people never use the outhouses for this purpose. Urine *(hisp'ay)* has manifold uses. It serves as a fixative in dyes and is mixed with ash to make the *llipt'a* that is chewed with coca leaves. It treats skin problems and is also mixed with chewed coca leaves to make an anesthetic compress for bruises and broken bones. Fermented urine is thought to ward off disease-carrying winds, and may be sprinkled as "Holy Water" around a house compound. Urine is an important element in the hydraulic cycle that regulates the relationship of the living and dead, and produces personal health and well-being. Skar writes,

Because it is replaceable, is not a static element but clearly is in motion, and regularly breaks the boundaries between the internal and the external, urine has a singular ability to convey harmony. These characteristics give it the power to correct relationships of imbalance at many levels and ultimately to unite the individual with the cosmos through the flow of water.[45]

Human bodies, mountains, and the Earth herself are conceived as analogous hydraulic systems.[46] A good example comes from Apurimac. Peter Gose describes men there drinking *chicha* while they work their fields. As the day passes they pour out their energy, sweat, and (as anyone who has drunk *chicha* knows) urine, likening themselves to their powerful Mount Qoropuna, who contains the land of the dead. The dead produce a subterranean lake from the flesh of their bodies, and Qoropuna "copiously urinates" forth this water in a life-supporting river. In Sonqo, too, they say "the dead travel in water."

Why did the people of Sonqo accept the outhouse project? I think it felt like an offer they couldn't refuse if they wanted to shed their Indianness. They like their *baños* because they indicate a modern orientation, yet their reticence in using them signals their ambivalence. Outhouses seemed repulsive twenty-five years ago, back in the *ñawpa timpu*. *Runakuna* were disgusted by the idea of gathering all that smelly human *aka* (shit) in one place instead of letting it disperse and dry up. Furthermore, their culture oriented them to a world moved by reciprocity. Excretion was just another kind of participation in the circulating cosmos—why should it be withheld? Now the outhouses stand like signposts indicating that this orientation has changed.

Coca and Cultural Identity

One thing that hasn't changed since the mid-1980s is the coca scarcity—still a side-effect of the interminable "war on drugs."

After their meal of salad and gruel the men of Mama Samana go outside to chew coca. I join them for a while, enjoying the warm sunshine as we sit in a line against the whitewashed wall of the community center. Searching in my small plastic coca bag for good leaves, I begin to prepare k'intus. Two of the younger men get to their feet and approach me with hands cupped in front of them, asking me for coca leaves. The older men, Luis and Melcanor, glance at me, embarrassed. It feels awkward to me too—I have never before seen anyone ask for coca. I give each of the young men a small handful. They accept gratefully and sit down to prepare k'intus.

Don Melcanor offers me a k'intu. We smile, remembering how we danced during Carnival many years ago. He asks me how much I paid for the coca. Five and a half soles per pound in Cuzco. He tells me that it's six soles per pound in Colquepata. And they get only two soles for an arroba (approximately twenty-five pounds) of potatoes.

241

Who can afford more than a little bit of coca? Anyway, they don't let you carry more than a pound. He looks over the hills to the east and tells me how he used to go work in the coca plantations and then walk back to Sonqo with an arroba of coca on his back. You can't do that anymore because the police will catch you and take it away. And hardly anyone comes through selling coca anymore, because they're afraid of getting caught.

"We're grieving for our coca" ("Lakikushayku cocaykumanta"), *he says.*

In the year 2000, *hallpay* was falling out of the regular routine and people did not always carry coca with them. This was not their choice. Ironically in a country that supplies so much of the world's coca, these traditional users of the leaf can't maintain their customs. One might have expected that, given their rapid reorientation toward urban values and the difficulty of obtaining the leaf, Sonqueños would just let coca go the way of thatched houses and knitted *chullu*s. Yet, when presented with a choice, Sonqo's evangelical Protestants chose the Maranata sect because it allowed them to keep chewing coca leaf.

Sonqueños may not be "Indians" anymore, but that doesn't mean that coca will disappear from their lives. As Sonqo's Catholic traditionalists become increasingly urban in their orientation, they may become more like their kinsmen who live in cities. These urban migrants chew coca sparingly and seldom exchange *k'intu*s as part of their daily routine; yet—as a visit to Cuzco's *hampi qhatu* (medicine market) attests—their city life includes a thriving mestizo tradition of curing and divination with coca leaves. It is possible that ten years from now, scarce coca will be saved for the *despacho* in August and special occasions like the first hair-cutting ceremony. The small routine *hallpay* ceremonies will have faded like other *Runa* life ways into the *ñawpa timpu*. An occasional *k'intu* exchange may remind these "indigenous mestizos" of their cultural roots, but *hallpay* will no longer frame the daily routine and provide a paradigm for reciprocity in human relations. The relationship with the Earth and Sacred Places will continue to provide a backdrop for rural life, but it will be experienced as less immediate and intimate, a bond to be invoked mainly in times of stress and need. If so, *despacho* and *coca qhaway* will be used mainly to address individual problems like theft, illness, bad luck, and marital strife.

The cold, high altitude Andean environment is stressful for the human organism and, even if material conditions improve significantly in Sonqo, life there will always be hard. Coca is valued for its energizing and comforting effects, and its scarcity is keenly felt. Is it coincidental that alcoholism became a critical problem in Sonqo when access to coca leaf became more difficult? It would be hard to prove a causal connection, but I think that the coca scarcity was probably a contributing factor (along with easier access to alcohol, a cultural predisposition to binge drinking, the collapse of aspirations raised during the Agrarian Reform, and the despairing realization that *"Nuestro trabajo no vale"*).

This brings me to Sonqo's Maranata Protestants, who are trying to radically rebuild a ritual framework that gives meaning and purpose to their lives. Is this a passing phase, or will they be able to interpret Pentecostal beliefs and practices in ways that make cultural sense to them? There are many ways this process could play itself out. Jeffrey Gamarra, who studied evangelical Protestant communities in Ayacucho, writes, "One probable scenario is the development of a popular evangelism that . . . combines elements of evangelical Protestantism, Catholicism and native Andean culture."[47] The *Hermanos'* shift from Adventism to the culturally more tolerant Maranata sect indicates that this is a likely scenario for Sonqo. Already they are incorporating traditions like the San Juan's Day sheep celebrations *(uwiha ch'uyay)* into their ritual practice. They emphasize, however, that they hold these celebrations "separately" not on June Twenty-fourth. Will they continue to maintain this separateness? Will Sonqo *Ayllu* will continue to crumble, with the *sectores* emerging as independent and possibly hostile communities? What happens will depend as much on social processes—factions, feuds, marriage alliances, relationships with development programs—as on changes in religious belief.

While the new Maranata framework excludes alcohol, it includes coca leaf as a positive choice. Clearly, *Hermanos* feel a need to keep coca and the ceremony of *hallpay* in their lives. So too, have they retained *tomay,* the ceremonial forms for drinking, without the alcoholic content. They use the charismatic intensity of group prayer rather than alcoholic inebriation to achieve an experience of *comunitas* and to connect themselves with the sacred. The ceremonies of *hallpay* and *tomay* continue to express and structure social bonds within the group, but they have lost their sacramental function.

While both Catholics and Protestants continue to value coca, they do so in ways that are curiously reversed. Catholic traditionalists in 2000 seemed less concerned with *hallpay* in the daily routiine, but they continued to value coca as a channel for communication with the Earth and Mountain Lords. The close-knit *Hermanos,* on the other hand, had segregated themselves as a social group from the larger community. During my short visit, they emphasized coca's traditional role as a facilitator of harmonious social bonds, and liberally exchanged *k'intus*. Their cermonial drinking, too, continued to stress the group's unity and internal hierarchy. Interestingly, alcohol-free drinking retained its *puchu* aspect, the "too muchness" of ritual forced feeding. But at the same time, both ceremonies were radically altered: there was no blowing over the coca leaves, no libations to the *Tirakuna.*

"Manan samichanku!" exclaim the Catholic traditionalists. "They don't offer the *samincha!"* This, indeed, is the great divide. What kind of entity is the Earth? If she is an animate person, who contains within herself all the hierarchy of localized Places, she needs to be sustained.

"Pero es espiritual!" counters Hipolito. No, he insists, they haven't forgotten *Pachamama* and *Tirakuna*. "But it's spiritual!" What does he mean by this? *Diosninchis* (Our God) is everywhere, he explains; when you pray to God you pray to everything.

I wish there had been more opportunity to discuss all this with Hipolito who, like his father, is quick-witted, thoughtful, and analytically minded. But there was too much going on and we were unable to continue talking. How does he understand this new charismatic practice of *risay* (prayer, from Spanish *rezar*)? What are its effects? How does it accomplish them? In what sense does this "spiritual" prayer substitute (as he implies) for the *samincha*?

With Protestant conversion *Diosninchis* (God) changes from a distant being—a kind of absentee landlord—to an approachable deity. As One Single Father God draws nearer and subsumes *Pacha Mama*, will the outpouring of spirit in *risay* come to resemble *samincha*? What kind of reciprocity can *risay* entail? What kind of gender complementarity exists within this unilateral male divinity? Will *Pacha Mama* and female Saints—now banished from religious observance—find their way back in another guise? And what of Mama Coca, Santísima María, the comforting mother?

Coda

"Adios Pueblos de Ayacucho! Kawsaspaqa topasunchis, wañuspaqa manan."

One still hears these lyrics to a popular *wayno* from the '70s wafting through grimy battery-powered radios in *campesino* households. *"Farewell towns of Ayacucho! If we live we'll meet again, and if we die we won't."* Erasmo liked the song and often paraphrased the words, especially when he said goodbye. For years I have been listening to Erasmo's recorded voice, smiling at his words and sometimes answering back. I have played and replayed the tapes, sifted through notes and memories of our conversations, written about them, talked about them. "Erasmo" has become both more and less than the flesh-and-blood person I left behind in Sonqo; the person who bade me his usual, slightly amused farewell, *"Kawsaspaqa, topakusunchis. Manan kawsaspachu, manan."*

I think there are no dialogues with the dead, only the constructions we put on them. These constructions inform our living awareness, as do imagined conversations we might yet have (and yet might not) with those who are absent. Like the *machukuna* they are always with us, so we had better make the best of it.

I made a tape recording with Basilia before I left Sonqo in March 1976. Making it was her idea. *"Yuyanaykipaq,"* she said. "So that you may remember." I did remember the occasion, but for many years I paid no attention to the tape. When I popped it in the tape deck while doing a long overdue inventory, I was startled to realize what a gift I had overlooked. Twenty-five years my senior, Basilia had understood far more clearly than I that my departure was an irrevocable ending. Although I would return some day, the leisurely time we had spent getting to know each other possessed its own quality that would never be reproduced. Our friendship would stay with me throughout my life and return sometimes to my thoughts with great poignancy. But its immediacy, the *kay pacha* of the lived-in moment, was about to end.

We were out in the sheep pasture when we made the tape. Basilia particularly planned that we should spend the day together, just the two of us. I realize now that she envisioned the recording as a joint effort, a dialogue stylized in the manner of Quechua responsive singing. This practice had almost died out in Sonqo and it took me awhile to catch on to what she wanted. (She tried to teach me weaving that way, too: Swish, swish, swish, there it is! now *you* do it!) I tried to sing as she sang but she grew impatient and took over both our parts. Here is part of the tape, which is too long to reproduce in its entirety. My line-by-line translation does not catch the music and delicacy of the original:

Basilia: *Pasapunkipuni, kunan noqapis, imaynan kirasaq?*
You're going, and now I, how am I going to stay behind?
Me: *Imayna?*
How?
Basilia: *Imaynan kirasaq? Qanpas ima nispan ripunki?*
How can I stay behind? And what will you say as you go away?

I should have burst into song at this point but I only said:

Ima nispa?
What indeed?

. . . .

Basilia: *Imallaman imallaman hamuranki kay llatata riqsichikuwanaykipaq?*
Imallan hamuranki kay llaqtata?
Why oh why did you come here to know this place? Why did you come here?
Me: *Yachaq . . .*
To learn . . .

She gave up on me and started in with her own song:

Pin yuyasunki	Who will remind you,
may willasunki	who will tell you
kay llaqtachata purirunayki	how you traveled to this little town,
kay llaqtachata hamuranayki?	how you came to this little town?
Imachallatan haywayurayki,	just what they gave you,
hayk'achallatan haywayurayki?	and how much they served you?
Unuchallatan mihuchirayki,	I only gave you water to drink
q'achuchallatan mihuchirayki,	I only gave you grass to eat
wasichallayta chayamoqtiyki,	when you came to my little house,
toqtuchallayta chayamoqtiykin.	when you came to my little nest.
. . . . . .	
Taytamamaykin chayayuspari	And when you arrive to your father-and-mother

245

Mamataytaykin chayayuspari	when you arrive to your mother-and-father
kay llaqtatan yuyarimunki,	you'll remember this town,
kay llaqtatan yuyarimunki.	you'll remember this town.
. . . . . .	
Imataraqsi qanri yuyawaq,	And what might you remember,
imataraqsi qanri yuyawaq?	what might you recall?
Hak'u hinachan sonqochallayoq,	With a heart like fine flour,
yawlli hinachan salwayushanki.	happy as a thorn bush?
. . . . . .	
Mayta mayta rishanki?	Where oh where are you going?
Mayta mayta rishanki?	Where oh where are you going?
Maytan pasashanki?	Where are you headed?
Me: *Ah, llaqtayman!*	Ah, to my country!

Basilia took over my part:

Ripuy niwaqtiykin,	You told me to go away, so I'm going.
ripushani.	
Pasay niwaqtiykin, pasashani.	You told me to leave, so I'm leaving.
Kunallan kunallan kutiramusaq,	But I'll turn back, turn back right away!
Kunallan kunallan wiltaramusaq!	I'll come back, come back right away!
Imataraqsi kutiramuspari	Yet it may not be to your house,
wasiykimanchus,	
Imataraqsi kutiramuspari	Yet it may not be to your village.
llaqtaykimanchus.	
Mananas kutispaqa	I may not ever turn back toward your village,
llaqtachaykimanchu.	
Mananas wasichaykimanchu	I may not ever come back to your house.
kutiramuspaqa.	
Mananas hinachu, hoq hinañasyá!	Things just won't be the same!
Mananas hinachu, hoq hinañasyá!	Things won't ever be the same!

She paused:

Nispa aqnata takiwaq . . .	That's the way you should sing it . . .

and continued:

Kutimuytaqa kutimusaqmi,	I'll return, return again.
weltamuytaqa weltamusaqmi.	I'll come back, come back again.
Manañasyari hinañachuri,	But not ever like this,
manañasyari hinañachuqa.	it won't ever be the same.
Hoq hinachañas kutiramusaqqa	I'll return different,
hoq hinachañas weltaramusaqqa.	I'll come back changed.

In whose voice did she sing these last phrases, hers or mine? I think it is her own.

246

Nispallachari llaqtachaykipi,	It's by talking like this in your little village
yacharuwanki, sawiruwanki.	that you'll get used to me, learn about me.
Sawiruwaspa yacharuwaspan	Learn about me, know about me,
hiñuchallayta yacharukunki,	you'll discern my inner self
sawiruwanki mañachallayta.	and comprehend my ways.
Ya'sta.	That's all.

It was sort of a homework assignment. After I returned home it would still take me time to understand her ways. More than that, it would take "talking like this." Understanding comes through give-and-take, through dialogue. Erasmo, too, gave me a homework assignment. Even back in my country, he said, I could study *coca qhaway* by dreaming deeply during thunderstorms. I never got the knack of it.

I did better with Basilia's assignment, although I wouldn't claim to comprehend the "inner self" of Basilia or her way of life. I have come to understand some things and I've tried to convey them in this book. I've found some "Andean" attitudes helpful in my own idiosyncratic orientation to life. One of these is *pacha. Pacha* the world as a living moment, a configuration of place, time and living human awareness. *Pacha* is immediate, material, concrete as the earth itself; yet *pacha* is ephemeral, for the moment is constantly reconfigured. My awareness brings *pacha* into existence, and *pacha* locates my awareness. Mind/body in the world: *"No ideas but in things!"*

So Basilia was right about the time and talk, and of course she was right that things would never be the same. I think the conversations are over now, but then you never know.

Adios Sonqo Ayllu! Alillaña Runakuna! Kawsaspaqa topasunchis, wañuspaqa manan.

Appendix A
A Note on Orthography

Orthography for the most part follows that used in Antonio Cusihuamán's *Diccionario Quechua Cuzco-Collao* (1976). For many place names I follow customary spelling rather than proper orthography. For example, I spell "Colquepata" as it appears on most maps and correspondence, although the word would be rendered more correctly as "Qolqepata." Personal names follow the Spanish spelling rather than the Quechua pronunciation (e.g., "Crisologo" rather than "Risulugu"). I have also followed the Spanish spelling of words that appear frequently in the ethnographic literature (e.g., *cargo* rather than *kargu; faena* rather than *phayna; trago* rather than *tragu*). Similarly, when referring to the fermented corn beverage indigenous to the Andes, I use *chicha* (used by Spanish speakers) rather than *aha* (used by Quechua speakers). Except where indicated otherwise, stress is always placed on the penultimate syllable.

The Quechua plural suffix *-kuna,* which indicates a collection of several similar things, is not strictly equivalent to English *-s.* When possible I use *-kuna* to indicate the plural form of a word (for example, *Runakuna,* "people"). Where *-kuna* would be unsuitable, I indicate the plural with English *-s* (for example, *kukuchi*s).

The Quechua language is rich in consonants. Some consonants have three forms—simple, aspirated, and glottalized—that are phonemically distinct from each other. A list of consonants follows below. Aspiration is indicated when "h" follows a consonant; " ' " indicates a voiceless glottal stop (i.e., the flow of air is stopped momentarily).

/ch/ *ch* in *china*
/chh/ *ch* in *chew*
/ch'/ no equivalent
/h/ *h* in *hat* but slightly more gutteral
/k/ *c* in *cut*
/kh/ *c* in *can't*
/k'/ no equivalent
/l/ *l* in *lean*
/ll/ like Spanish *ly*
/m/ *m* in *mat*
/n/ *n* in *not*
/ñ/ like Spanish *ny*
/p/ *p* in *pat*
/ph/ *p* in *pin*
/p'/ no equivalent
/q/ pronounced like /k/, but in the back of the throat
/qh/ no equivalent
/q'/ no equivalent
/r/ *r* in *rat*
/s/ *s* in *sit*
/sh/ *sh* in *shut*
/t/ *t* in *tin*
/t'/ *t* in *tsk! tsk!*
/w/ *w* in *went*
/y/ *y* in *yet*

Quechua vowels are far fewer in number. They are:

/a/ *ah* in *ah!*
/e/ *e* in *edible;* variant of /i/
/i/ *i* in *hit*
/o/ between *o* in *mop* and *mope*
/u/ *oo* in *hoop*

The following consonants appear only in words derived from Spanish:

/d/ *d* in *dog*
/f/ *f* in *fine*
/g/ *g* in *goat*
/v/ *v* in *vine*

Appendix B
What Should I Call You?
An Introduction to
Kinship Terminology

These tables show the terms one must know and understand in order to operate socially in a community like Sonqo. It is not respectful to address individuals directly by their proper names; good manners call for the appropriate kinship term. Adults unrelated by kinship politely address one another as *mamáy* (mother) and *taytáy* (father). Grownups call children *wawáy* (child) or use a nickname. Children address adults with the appropriate kin term and address one another with nicknames or sibling terms.

In the tables below, the left-hand column shows the term of address. The middle column gives an English gloss for the term and a brief explanation of its use. The right-hand column indicates the reciprocal term, that is, the term the recipient would use to address the speaker. Terms of address are formed from the kin term by adding the first-person possessive suffix *-y* (like *my* in English) and placing stress on the final syllable. For example, *"Imaynallan, Wayqíy?"* means "How are you, Brother?" (*imaynallan* = how are you; *wayqi* = brother). Sibling terms are gender specific; men and women use different terms. Thus my brother would call me *panáy* (sister of a man) and my sister would call me *ñañáy* (sister of a woman).

The middle column also indicates where terminological changes took place between 1985 and 2000. The distinction between cross and parallel cousins seems to be losing its significance as Quecha kinship terminology converges with Spanish usage.

Abbreviations

M = mother
F = father
B = brother
Z = sister
Ch = child
S = son
D = daughter
H = husband
W = wife
MB = mother's brother
MBD = mother's brother's daughter, etc.

For terms that are gender specific,

♀ = the speaker is female
♂ = the speaker is male

Table 1

My Generation Mates

If I call you	English translation and explanation	You call me
Wayqíy ♂	**My brother.** (I am male.) *Wayqi* refers to a man's <u>brother</u> and to his <u>male parallel cousins</u> (MZS, FBS). Also see *primu ermanu* (below).	*Wayqíy* ♂
Panáy ♂	**My sister.** (I am male.) *Pana* refers to a man's <u>sister</u> and to his <u>female parallel cousins</u> (MZD, FBD). Also see *prima ermana* (below).	*Turáy* ♀
Turáy ♀	**My brother.** (I am female.) *Tura* refers to a woman's <u>brother</u> and to her <u>male parallel cousins</u> (MZS, FBS). Also see *primu ermanu* (below).	*Panáy* ♂
Ñañáy ♀	**My sister.** (I am female.) *Ñaña* refers to a woman's <u>sister</u> and to her <u>female parallel cousins</u>, (MZD, FBD). Also see *prima ermana* (below).	*Ñañáy* ♀
Primu ermanúy or *Primúy*	**My male cousin.** In 1985, *primu* or *primu ermanu* (Sp. *primo,* male cousin, and *hermano,* brother) referred to <u>male cross cousins</u>, (MBS, FZS) and extended to more distant cousins (e.g., MMBSS). In 2000, the terms *primu* and *primu ermanu* referred to any male cousin. This included parallel cousins (MZS, FBS), who were less often called by sibling terms *wayqi* and *tura*.	*Primu ermanúy/-áy* or *Primúy/-áy*
Primu ermanáy or *Primáy*	**My female cousin.** In 1985, *prima* and *prima ermana* (Sp. *prima,* female cousin, and *hermana,* sister) referred to <u>female cross cousins</u> (MBD, FZD) and extended to more distant cousins (e.g., MMBDD). In 2000, the terms *prima* and *primu ermana* referred to any female cousin. This included parallel cousins (MZD, FBD) who were less often called by sibling terms *pana* and *ñaña*.	*Primu ermanúy/-áy* or *Primúy/-áy*
(not a term of address)	In 1985, ***ermanuntin*** (Sp. *hermano,* brother, and Quechua *-ntin,* together with) referred to a <u>group of siblings</u> who worked land and herded livestock in common; this could include <u>parallel cousins</u> (children of MZ and FB).In 2000, the term was being replaced by ***primuntin****,* a <u>group of cousins</u>, reflecting the loss of the cross-parallel distinction.	(not a term of address)

Table 2
Ascending Generations
My Parents and Grandparents

If I call you	English translation and explanation	You call me
Mamáy	**My mother.** In 1985, *mama* referred to both <u>mother</u> (M) and <u>mother's sister</u> (MZ). In 2000, it usually referred only to mother; one's mother's sister was called **tiáy** (Sp. *tia*, aunt).	*Wawáy* or *Churíy* or *Ususíy*
Taytáy	**My father.** In 1985, *tayta* referred to both <u>father</u> (F) and <u>father's brother</u> (FB). In 2000, it usually referred only to father; father's brother was called *tiúy* (Sp. *tio*, uncle).	*Wawáy* or *Churíy* or *Ususíy*
Ipáy	**My paternal aunt.** In 1985, *ipa* referred exclusively to <u>father's sister</u> (FZ). *Tiáy* (Sp. *tia*, aunt) sometimes replaced *ipáy*. In 2000, *tia* and *ipa* were used interchangeably in reference to both the paternal and maternal aunts (FZ and MZ).	*Subrinu wawáy*
Tiúy	**My maternal uncle.** In 1985, *tiu* (Sp. *tio*, uncle) referred to <u>mother's brother</u> (MB) and <u>mother's mother's brother</u> (MMB) but not to FB, who was called *tayta*. In 2000, *tiu* referred to father's brother (FB) as well as mother's brother's (MB), wife's brother (WB) and all four grandparents' male siblings (MMB, FFB, FMB, FMB). Also see *tiu* as an affine term in Table 4.	*Subrinu wawáy*
Auldy	**My grandmother.** *Aula* (Sp. *abuela*) refers to <u>father's mother, mother's mother, father's mother's sister</u>, and <u>mother's mother's sister</u> (FM, MM, FMZ, MMZ). In 2000, the preferred term for father's mother and mother's mother was *mama grande*.	*Hawayniy*
Aulúy or *Machuláy*	**My grandfather.** *Aulu* (Sp. *abuelo*) refers to <u>father's father, mother's father, father's father's brother</u>, and <u>mother's father's brother</u> (FF, MF, FFB, MFB). The more affectionate *Machuláy* (Grandpa) is often substituted for *Aulúy*. In 2000, the preferred term for FF and MF was *papa grande*.	*Hawayníy*

Table 3

Descending Generations
My Children and Grandchildren

If I call you	English translation and explanation	You call me
Wawáy*	**My child.** *Wawa* means <u>child</u>, and *wawáy* (my child) refers to my own <u>child</u> (Ch). If I am female, *wawáy* also applies to my <u>sister's child</u> (ZCh); if I am male, it also refers to my <u>brother's child</u> (Bch). Also see *subrinu wawáy* (below).	*Mamáy* or *Taytáy*
Churíy*	**My son.** *Churi* refers to one's <u>male child</u> (S).	*Mamáy* or *Taytáy*
Ususíy*	**My daughter.** *Ususi* refers to one's <u>female child</u> (D).	*Mamáy* or *Taytáy*
Subrinu wawáy or Subrinúy	**My nephew.** In 1985, *subrinu* (Sp. *sobrino,* nephew) referred to a <u>woman's brother's son</u> (BS) and to a <u>man's sister's son</u> (ZS). This usage emphasized the distinction between cross and parallel cousins. In 2000, it could refer to the son of any sibling (male or female).	*Ipáy* or *Tiúy*
Subrináy or Subrinu wawáy	**My niece.** In 1985, *subrina* (Sp. *sobrina,* niece) referred to a <u>woman's brother's daughter</u> (BD) and to a <u>man's sister's daughter</u> (ZD). This usage emphasized the distinction between cross and parallel cousins. In 2000, it could refer to the daughter of any sibling (male or female).	*Ipáy* or *Tiúy*
Hawayníy	**My grandchild.** *Haway* refers to one's own <u>child's child</u> (ChCh) and to one's <u>sibling's child's child</u> (ZChCh, BChCh).	*Auláy* or *Aulúy* or *Machuláy*

*In some central Andean communities, the term *Wawáy* (Child) is used only by women, while only men use the terms *Churíy* (Son) and *Ususíy* (Daughter). I did not find this distinction in Sonqo; individuals of both sexes are comfortable using all three terms.

Table 4
Affines and Fictive Kin
My Relatives by Marriage and *Compadrazgo*

If I call you	English translation and explanation	You call me
Qatayníy	**My son-in-law** or **my brother-in-law.** *Qatay* refers to <u>daughter's husband</u> (DH) and <u>sister's husband</u> (ZH).	*Swigrúy /-áy;* *Tiúy /-áy*
Qhachuníy	**My daughter-in-law** or **my sister-in-law.** *Qhachun* refers to <u>son's wife</u> (SW) or <u>sister's wife</u> (ZW).	*Swigrúy /-áy;* *Tiúy /-áy*
Qataymasíy ♂	**My fellow son-in-law or my fellow brother-in-law.** <u>Wife's sister's husband</u> (WZH).	*Qataymasíy* ♂
Qhachun-masíy ♀	**My fellow daughter-in-law or my fellow sister-in-law.** <u>Husband's brother's wife</u> (HBW).	*Qhachun-masíy* ♀
Swigrúy	**My father-in-law.** *Swigru* (Sp. *suegro*, father-in-law) refers to <u>wife's father</u> (WF) and <u>husband's father</u> (HF).	*Qatayníy* or *Qhachuníy*
Swigráy	**My mother-in-law.** *Swigra* (Sp. *suegra*, mother-in-law) refers to <u>wife's mother</u> (WM) and <u>husband's mother</u> (HM).	*Qatayníy* or *Qhachuníy*
Swigru-masíy ♂	**My fellow father-in-law.** <u>Daughter's husband's father</u> (DHF) or <u>son's wife's father</u> (SWF).	*Swigru-masíy* ♂
Swigra -masíy ♀	**My fellow mother-in-law.** <u>Daughter's husband's mother</u> (DHM) or <u>son's wife's mother</u> (SWM).	*Swigra-masíy* ♀
Tiúy	**My brother-in-law.** Also see Table 2. In an affinal context, *tiu* (Sp. *tio*, uncle) refers to <u>wife's brother</u> (WB).	*Qatayníy* or *Qhachuníy*
Tiáy	**My sister-in-law.** Also see Table 2. In an affinal context, *tia* (Sp. *tia*, aunt) refers to <u>husband's sister</u> (HZ).	*Qatayníy* or *Qhachuníy*
Comadríy *Compadríy*	**My comadre. My compadre.** This term is used not only by the individuals who created the tie of *compadrazgo*, but by their entire extended families. See the discussion of *compadrazgo* in Chapter 2.	*Comadríy* *Compadríy* **(or *Wawáy* if addressing a child)**

Notes

Introduction

1. *Ch'uño* is a kind of dehydrated potato that can be stored for long periods. It has a shriveled, mummified appearance and is believed by the *Runakuna* to exist in an ambiguous life-in-death state of being (see Allen 1982).

2. Coca chewing is called *pikchay* or *chakchay* in other regions of the Andes. For more information about coca's properties, see Chapter 9; for bibliographic references, see Chapter 9 Notes.

3. Malinowski [1922] 1961:25.

4. The dates of this fieldwork are April–March 1975–76; June–July 1978; June–July 1980; July–August 1984; and two weeks in November 1985.

5. Sontag 1970:185.

6. Malinowski [1922] 1961:25.

7. By invoking intersubjectivity to characterize the relationship between ethnographer and "informants," I do not intend to imply wholesale adherence to the phenomenological position (concerning, for instance, the transcendental ego). Both Husserl (e.g., 1970) and Schutz (e.g., 1967, 1970), who developed the notion of intersubjectivity, argued that intersubjectivity is central to all social sciences and that social scientists themselves are subjects studying the subjectivity of others. As I read him, Schutz was interested in elucidating the nature of intersubjectivity among members of a given society and was little concerned with the intersubjective relationship between the members of that society and the social scientist who studies them (see, for example, Schutz 1970:275–76). For ethnographers, however, the latter issue takes on great importance, as we try to come to terms with the intense face-to-face "we-relationships" that provide the context for our fieldwork. It is increasingly recognized that, since an ethnographer's dialogue with "the Other" is central in the

practice of anthropological fieldwork, this dialogue should maintain a comparable centrality in anthropological writing (e.g., D. Tedlock 1983:331–38,).

Clifford Geertz's application of Ryle's "thick description" to ethnographic writing (1973:3–30), and his forceful arguments for the interpretive nature of anthropology, opened a new space in the discipline for criticism and for experimental ethnography. Among other anthropologists who use the concept of intersubjectivity are Johannes Fabian (1983), who writes of "coevalness" (intersubjective time); Barbara Tedlock (1982); and Dennis Tedlock (1983). Also relevant to this subject are Renato Rosaldo (1983, 1989) on the "positioned subject," Marcus and Fischer (1986), and contributors to Clifford and Marcus, eds. (1986). Since the first edition of this book in 1988, "reflexivity" has become a central and much debated issue in extensive anthropological theory and practice (e.g., Behar and Gordon 1995, Scheper-Hughes 1995, Tedlock and Mannheim 1995).

8. D. Tedlock 1983:323.

9. I prefer to use the Sonqueños' own term for themselves rather than refer to them as Indians or peasants. Like other Quechua-speaking people, the inhabitants of Sonqo refer to themselves as *Runakuna,* "people." Although the word *Runakuna (Runa,* person, plus the plural suffix *-kuna)* may refer to human beings in a generic sense, it was commonly used in a more specific way to refer to indigenous Quechua-speaking people who adhere to native Andean cultural values. The Afterword discusses changes in this usages of the year 2000.

In 1969 the Velasco regime banned official use of the words *indígena* (native) and *Indio* (Indian) and substituted the word *campesino* (peasant). Skar (1982:75–78) provides an analysis of the policy. I am in agreement with his conclusion that the change in terms has been neither successful nor desirable. The word *campesino* has acquired the same derogatory connotations that were previously associated with the word *Indio.* I think it preferable to use a term that recognizes ethnic differences and to work on changing the negative connotations associated with these differences.

10. A bus service was added in the mid-1990s, providing a faster and incomparably more comfortable trip for those able to pay a higher fare.

11. The main street was paved as far as the plaza in the late 1990s.

12. In Colquepata I have heard this joke leveled at the neighboring district of Huancarani. Potatoes have been lower class food since preconquest times; the poor man in the Huarochiri myths (Salomon and Urioste 1991) is named *Watiacuri,* Baked Potato Gleaner (see also Murra 1973). In every community, people like to believe that their neighbors are even more dependent on potatoes than they are themselves. Cuzqueños, of course, are aware that from the perspective of the warm rice-eating coast, they themselves are cold potato eaters. In the year 2000 I found the presiding mayor of Colquepata, Sr. Gregorio Puma Chilo, making a virtue of necessity. His business card proudly announces, "Municipalidad Distrital de Colquepata, Capital de la Papa y del Chuño" (District Municipality of Colquepata, Potato and Chuño Capital).

13. The original Spanish is rather idiosyncratic: "Los indios viven dispersos en las comunidades 'Ayllus,' sus chozas distantes unas de otras, son antihigiénicas muy primitivas. No usan cama i si tienen está compuesta de unos cueros sucias de llama o cordero . . . Los indios no han constituido aldeas i mucho menos pequeños pueblos, aislamiento que contribuye aún más a su insociabilidad i a hacer su carácter uraño [*sic*]" (Abrill A. 1959:6).

14. "*Caracteristicas más sobresalientes del Indio del Ccolquepata:* Como todo indio es tímido, esceptico; no espera nada de nadie, desconfia de todo i de todos, su respuesta es siempre dubitativa, observa, espera, sin alterar su fisonomía en los momentos de peligro, parece insensible sin necesidades fisiológicas; soporta las penas, los castigos más crueles, con estoicismo sorprendente. Pasa de la desgracia a sus ocupaciones ordinarias con indiferencia; parece tener desprecio por la vida; parece sin embargo, la ama tan intensamente como a su terruño [*sic*]. El indio no es (sencillo) suicida odio al mestizo

sus eternos verdugos [sic]. En las rebeliones en masa es feroz, cruel i sanguinario" (Abrill A. 1959:4).

15. I am grateful to Enrique Mayer for his helpful information and for his insights concerning data collected in Colquepata by the late Cesar Fonseca. Leonidas Concha, an agronomist working with Fonseca and Mayer during my 1985 visit to Sonqo, was also very helpful.

16. See José María Caballero (1981) on this "commercial revolution."

17. During the 1950s, the situation in Colquepata apparently was similar to that in the neighboring district of P'isaq, described by Oscar Núñez del Prado (1973).

18. Mayer summarizes Fonseca's insightful comments: "The peasants, due to insecurity, ignorance of alternatives, and long-standing investments in social relations, constantly seek to personalize economic relations by cultivating alliances with *Misti*s. The *Misti*s, while they speak deprecatingly of the peasants, continue to utilize these networks of contacts and personal transactions. The *Misti*s' economic activities are enmeshed in an endless net of gift-giving and personal favors that reach maximum expression in *compadrazgo*. The town *Misti*s often say that 'the Indian has to die Indian; the Indian is Indian.' Sadly, the Indians will keep on trying to socialize mercantile relations, whereas the *Misti*s will try by all means to mercantilize relations of kinship and *compadrazgo*" (1988; my translation).

19. Cesar Fonseca made the same observation. In his opinion the police station had been promoted by Colquepata Mestizos to counter the perceived threat posed by the Indians' new assertiveness. See Mayer (1988:86).

20. See Mayer (1988:82) for a somewhat more pessimistic analysis of changing *Runa-Misti* relations in the Colquepata region since the agrarian reform.

21. Historical information in this section is derived from archival research that I carried out primarily during November and December 1985 in the Archivo General de la Nación and the Archivo de la Biblioteca Nacional (both in Lima); and the Archivo Histórico (Departamental) del Cuzco, the Archivo Arzobispal del Cuzco, the Ministerio de Agricultura (Sub-dirección: Comunidades Campesinas y Nativas), and the Fuero Privativo Agrario (all in Cuzco). I am grateful to the personnel of these various archives for their assistance and interest, as well as to the staff of the Centro de Estudios Rurales Andinos ("Bartolomé de las Casas") for the use of its library. I also received access to documents from the private files of the late Dr. Julio Frisancho, for which I extend my thanks to the Frisancho family and in particular to Sr. Armando Guevara Gil.

22. "de que se pudiesen sustentar y pagar su tasa las que para ello y para acudir a las demás obligaciones que tienen fuesen nesesarias." From the *Visita de Diego Maravier en el Pueblo de San Geronimo de Colquepata, 1595,* Archivo Arzobispal del Cuzco, cat. no. G.26.274.1. Transcription by Henrique Urbano and Laura Hurtado. I am grateful to Dr. Urbano for bringing this document to my attention and for providing me with a copy of his transcription.

23. The *ayllu*s listed in the 1595 *visita* are Miscaora Conchuco, Hanansaya Collana, Chocopía, Hurinsaya, Payan, Miscaora, Tucra, Tiobamba *(yanacona que fueron del Capitán Diego Maldonado),* Guaranca, Umasbamba *(de la encomienda de Don Antonio Peyreyra),* Cotani, Sayllapata, and Accha. Also listed is the *Repartimiento* of Sayllapata *(de la Corona Real que fueron de Mama Chimbo Coya de Cuzco).* A 1792 census lists the *ayllu*s Calla, Toca-aylla, Soncco, Miscahura, Tocra, Sipaskancha, Coata, Guaranca, Micaycotani, Sayllapata, Accha, Pampacuyo, and Cuyo Chico, as well as the *hacienda*s Umasbamba, Orconpuquio, Viscachoni, Cotatoclla, Paucona, and San Juan de Buena Vista (Archivos de la Biblioteca Nacional, cat. no. C3269, f/20–30). In 1959 Abrill listed the following *ayllu*s: Colquepata (formerly Calla), Chocopía, Sonqo, Sipaskancha Baja, T'oqra, Miskawara, Accha, Mik'a, Qotani, Ninamarca, and Sayllapata (1959:3). These *ayllu*s are now recognized *comunidades campesinas,* with the addition of Pajapata and Q'oja. Sipaskancha consists of two separate communities, Sipaskancha Baja (the former Sipaskancha) and Sipaskancha Alta, a former *hacienda*. Colquepata (Calla), Chocopía,

Sonqo, the Sipaskanchas, Toqra, and Miskawara share the same watershed and form a closely knit subunit within the district's communities.

24. Lartaún's *visitas*, which provided the legal basis for land titles held by many indigenous communities in the department of Cuzco, are now lost. Fortunately, in 1926 an extract of the *visita* concerning Sonqo was included in legal documents recognizing Sonqo as a *"comunidad indígena"* (Fuero Privativo Agrario, Expediente nos. 457–78). In the 1940s this extract was included in lawsuits brought against the neighboring *hacienda* Paucona (personal archive of Dr. J. Frisancho), and they are reproduced in part in documents concerning a border dispute between Sonqo and Sipaskancha in 1978 (Fuero Privativo Agrario, Expediente nos. 227–78). However, to understand how Colquepata's *ayllu*s were transformed in the early seventeenth century, it would be necessary to compare the document from 1595 with Lartaún's complete 1658 *visita* of Colquepata—a potentially fascinating study, but impossible until Lartaún's *visita* is recovered.

25. Zimmerer 1996:57.

26. "nuestra comunidad que tiene trecientos ventiun años de vida legal y real y que mucho antes existía desde la época de los Incas" (Fuero Privativo Agrario, Expediente nos. 227–78 (1980), f/20).

27. Duviols 1971.

28. See Bourdieu (1977).

29. Bateson 1972: 134–50.

30. On the interface between acting and ethnographic fieldwork see Turnbull (1979), Schechner (1985), Allen and Garner (1996).

Chapter 1. Water, Stones, and Light

1. Geertz 1973:5.

2. See Urton (1981).

3. The *Apukuna* are well discussed in Andean ethnography. For example, see Arguedas ([1958] 1978); Bastien ([1978] 1985); Casaverde (1970); Earls (1969); Gose (1994); D. Gow (1976); Isbell ([1978] 1985b); Marzal (1971); Martínez 1989; Mishkin ([1946] 1963); Morissette and Racine (1973); and J. Núñez del Prado Bejar (1970).

4. On the hierarchy of the *Apukuna*, see in particular Earls (1969, 1981); Gose (1994), Martínez 1989; Morissette and Racine (1973); and Urton (1981).

5. See also Juvenal Casaverde (1970:145) for similar data from neighboring P'isaq.

6. On the cognitive organization of space, see Martínez (1989); Poole (1984); Rappaport (1985); Urbano (1974); and Zuidema (1985).

7. See also R. Gow and Condori (1976:5–19), Rasnake (1988:231–37) on *Pacha Mama*.

8. See Albó (1982) and Urton (1981:174–77).

9. The predominantly male class of *Tirakuna* does include some female members. The *Wasitira* of each house compound is thought to be female, as are certain hills. Erasmo said that these are the small, insignificant ones; Basilia, on the other hand, thought that the great Sawasiray-Pitusiray is *mamapuni,* "definitely a mama." Rasnake (1988:236) reports from Bolivia that mountain peaks are categorized as male *(mallku)* or female *(t'alla).*

10. I discuss this point, and its connection with Protestant conversion, in the Afterword to this second edition.

11. Chirinos and Maque recount a similar belief (1996: 168–69).

12. Basilia did not specify which of the two saints—Santa Rosa and Santa Inés— invented spinning and which invented weaving. She seemed to consider the question irrelevant. She told me a *kwintu* (story) about them: Santa Rosa and Santa Inés were traveling together when they came to an impassable river. They decided to make a bridge. One of the saints spun while the other wove, until the threads formed a bridge

that Basilia likened to the long, narrow skirt border she herself was weaving on a backstrap loom. Other women say that the *awaq mamachas* (weaver saints) are Mama Sinakara (also called La Virgen de Fatima) and Mama Consebida. Basilia insisted that these saints were *musuq* (new)—not from the *Kwintu Timpu* (Story Era)—and did not consider them to be as important as Rosa and Inés.

13. See Gerald Taylor's (1976) insightful discussion of the word *kamay* as used by colonial sources

14. For example, see Murra (1973).

15. This idea is widespread in the Andes (e.g., Bastien ([1978] 1985). The circulatory cosmos plays an important part in Urton's (1981) book on Andean astronomy, and shorter discussions can be found in Silverblatt and Earls (1976) and Allen (2002). The theme of circulation runs through the work of Arguedas ([1958] 1978). See also Sherbondy (1979a and 1979b) and Zuidema (1978, 1980).

16. See Urton's (1981) description of Andean cosmology.

17. The feast of Santa Barbara, 5 December, is dedicated to Apu Qhaqha.

18. See Lumbreras 1974:203–205.

19. My thanks go to Prof. Jaime Pantigoso, who transcribed the tape.

20. The same belief is described by Juan Núñez del Prado Bejar (1970:57–120).

21. Ritual drinking for the dead is discussed in Chapter 6.

22. Guaman Poma de Ayala [1614] 1936:287.

23. Duviols 1971:254.

24. In Ayacucho, the word *khuyaq* refers to the network of *compadres* and kinsmen upon whom one can call for help. See Isbell ([1978]1985b:168–76). On *enqas* see Bolin (1998); Flores Ochoa (1977a, 1977b).

25. I am grateful to the staff of the Museo Inka of the University of San Antonio Abad del Cuzco, who cooperated in this project with much interest and enthusiasm.

26. See also Sallnow (1978:128).

27. The *Machukuna* are described as living together in a community including male and female members; in contrast, *Machula Aulanchis* are always described as male.

28. The *Machukuna* are also said to have fled to springs. Springs, too, have a dual aspect. They support human well-being by providing water for people, crops, and animals, but they also cause skin diseases and intestinal problems by entering the body's orifices. See also Núñez del Prado (1970).

29. This afterworld is also called *bulgun,* a word whose origins I have not been able to determine.

30. The following account is summarized from my notes, as Basilia was not speaking for the tape recorder.

31. For detailed studies of Andean pilgrimages, see Poole (1984, 1991) and Sallnow (1982, 1987).

Chapter 2. The Web of Reciprocity

1. I am much obliged to Sra. Ernestina Monroy, then director of Sonqo's primary school, for her interested and supportive reception.

2. *"Urpicháy,"* literally "my little dove," is a term of polite endearment and often used as a casual form of thank-you.

3. *Ruki papa* (also called *luki papa*) is a type of frost-resistant bitter potato that will not grow below 8,200 feet and cannot propagate itself without human intervention (Skar 1982:155; Zimmerer 1996:128). *Ruki* is edible only when processed as *moraya,* a type of fine *ch'uño* (freeze-dried potato).

4. A woman recruits her *ayni* partners independently from her husband. In other words, they need not be the wives, sisters, or daughters of the men who are working with her husband.

5. Julia Meyerson (personal communication) reports a similar attitude in the community of Pacariqtambo (province of Paruro). When she examined and handled a foot plow during a work break, the men were embarrassed and insisted that she stop.

6. This comment was not recorded on tape and has been reconstructed from fieldnotes.

7. See Isbell ([1978] 1985b:114) on the role of the *masa* (son-in-law in the Ayacucho dialect of Quechua).

8. For example, see Arguedas ([1958] 1978); Lobo (1982).

9. Tristan Platt (1986) provides a most succinct and suggestive study of *yanantin.*

10. See Isbell ([1978] 1985b); Skar (1982).

11. The relationship between these kin-based groups and the *ayllu* will be discussed in Chapter 3. The words *ermanu* and *phamilya* are both derived from Spanish (*hermano,* brother; *familia,* family). I did not hear, nor could I elicit, Quechua terminology for either sibling group or kindred. Susan Lobo (1982) describes the persistence of sibling groups in the squatter settlements of Lima. As women may bear children over approximately a twenty-five-year period, siblings may be separated in age by many years. Siblings separated by a span of twenty years, for example, feel a sense of obligation to each other but, for obvious reasons, seldom develop the strong affective bonds characteristic of siblings closer in age. It is not infrequent for uncles (or aunts) to be closer in age and affection to their nephews (or nieces) than to their own brothers and sisters.

12. Affinal kin terms are listed in Table 4 of Appendix B. *Qatay* (DH or ZH) refers to the husband of one's daughter or sister; *qhachun* (SW or BW) refers to the wife of one's son or brother. A *qataymasi* is a fellow *qatay;* in other words, *qataymasi*s stand in the *qatay* relationship to the same group of people.

13. I have never had the opportunity to witness this private "marriage" ceremony. See Oscar Núñez del Prado (1958) on a comparable ceremony in Q'ero.

14. *Rutuchikuy* is described by some of the earliest Spanish chroniclers, including Betanzos (1996[1551]:179) and Molina (1943[1573]:90).

15. This speech was not recorded on tape and has been reconstructed from fieldnotes.

16. For example, see Alberti and Mayer (1974); Brush (1977); Gose (1994); Isbell ([1978] 1985b); Mannheim (1986a); Mayer (1974, 1975, 1977, 2002); O. Núñez del Prado (1973); D. Núñez del Prado Bejar (1972); Skar (1982); among others.

17. Isbell provides a similar definition from the community in Chuschi in the department of Ayacucho: "According to the Chuschino definition, *minka* is when an individual calls for aid, usually in the form of labor of some kind, and those who respond to his call are 'lending *ayni*,' for which they expect repayment in comparable labor service" ([1978] 1985b:167).

18. Mayer emphasizes this aspect of *mink'a* in his groundbreaking analysis of reciprocity relations in Tangor (department of Pasco). He describes *mink'a* as a form of exchange in which goods are given in recompense for services. He comments, "Essentially, *minka* exchanges are not seen as exchanges between related people but rather as a reciprocal relationship that serves to create social bonds rather than expressing them" (1977:67). In Sonqo I found that *mink'a* (equivalent to *minka* in the central Peruvian dialects) did not refer to a relationship per se, but to a quality of asymmetry inherent in certain relationships.

19. Gonzalez Holguín [1608] 1989:240.

Chapter 3. "And Then in That Sun"

1. Molina [1573] 1943:1243. See also Sherbondy (1979a).

2. Notice the use of the word *pacha* in this sentence to indicate a moment in time.

3. Uppercase type indicates that the word was spoken with heightened emphasis and volume.

4. Murúa [1605] 1962, 2:3.

5. See Stern (1982) and Wachtel (1977).

6. Here Luis switches to the present tense with past intent. Previously his narrative alternated between "mythic" past *(-sqa)* and simple past *(-ra)*.

7. "To them they paid thirty-five centavos in kitchen service *(kusinera mañay)*." In other words, the Anton Quispes would pay the tax of thirty-five centavos for their poorer *ayllu*-mates in return for kitchen service. The word *mañay* means "to lend" in a generalized sense; used in a more restricted sense, *mañay* refers to services owed to the community by its members or, conversely, to services owed *by* the community *to* its members (as in *chakra mañay*, the "lending" to individuals of usufruct rights to community lands). The word is also used to refer to governmental taxation.

8. Davies 1974.

9. I have not been able to locate the Anton Quispes in the historical record, so I cannot say which, if any, historical figures correspond to them. It is worth noting that Miguel Quispe, a significant indigenous political leader in the 1920s, came from the Sayllapata near Sonqo. Quispe is a very common surname, and none of my respondents in Sonqo made a connection between Miguel Quispe and the Three Anton Quispes. De la Cadena (2000:306–308) provides an interesting analysis of a journalist's interview with Miguel Quispe in 1922.

10. See Sahlins (1981); Salomon (1982); Zuidema (1982); on the intersection of oral and wirtten traditions in the Andes see Lund (1997), Rappaport (1985, 1990, 1994), Urton (1990).

11. The epidemic of the 1720s is mentioned in the following documents concerning Colquepata: Archivo Departamental del Cuzco, *Corregimientos Provincias*, Legajo 62, f/246, years 1711–37; Archivo Arzobispal del Cuzco, *Colquepata* 21 (cat. no. LXV11,2,22) and *Paucartambo* 14–15 (cat. no. LXXV,1,15, f/38). See also Kubler ([1945] 1963). A serious epidemic decimated the lower reaches of Paucartambo in 1809, but it is not clear from the sources how this affected higher regions of the province like Colquepata (Biblioteca Nacional del Perú, *Virreynato: Indios Trabajo*, cat. no. D10588, year 1809).

12. Biblioteca Nacional del Perú, *Indios*, cat. no. C3269, f/20–30, year 1792; Archivo General de la Nación, *Tributos* (Real Hacienda: contribución de indígenas), Legajo 5, Cuaderno 120, year 1801; Archivo Departamental del Cuzco, *Padroncillo de contribuyentes: Colquepata*, year 1850.

13. See Zuidema (1990); also Spalding (1984:28–34).

14. See, for example, Ossio (1981); Rostworowski (1981:42–43); Skar (1982); Zuidema (1964).

15. See Isbell ([1978] 1985b).

16. See, among many others, Isbell ([1978] 1985b); Palomino (1971).

17. Skar 1982:170, 215.

18. On the sectorial fallowing system in the province of Paucartambo see Mayer (1988) and Zimmerman (1996). For other works on sectorial fallowing in the Andes see, among others, Fonseca (1972); Mayer (1979, 1985, 2002); Mayer and Fonseca (1979); Orlove and Godoy (1986). In Sonqo, a second system of *surt'is* operated in the high *puna* fields (also called *loma* or *hawan hallpa*, outer land) where bitter *ruki* potatoes are cultivated. See the Afterword to the Second Edition.

19. See Platt's (1986:230–31) description of similarly nested *ayllus* within a moiety system.

20. Don Luis described the *ayllu* hierarchy (neighborhood → community → district → province → department → nation) in accordance with the hierarchy of Peruvian political organization. This description ignores the way that the provinces of Paucartambo and Quispikanchis form an ethnic unit within the department of Cuzco, a unity expressed through the joining of their community-level *ayllus* in the Qoyllur Rit'i pilgrimage. Nevertheless, Luis's account need not be seen as contradicting my

interpretation of the Qoyllur Rit'i pilgrimage as the expression of a regional *ayllu*. Luis was explaining the principle of the *ayllu*, a flexible term that may be applied equally well in different contexts. Nationally imposed political units may be conceptualized as a hierarchy of *ayllus*; this hierarchy does not coincide precisely with the hierarchy of *ayllus* produced in the context of spatial and religious organization. Under the Incas these three contexts (political, spatial, and religious) were closely integrated (see the work of R. T. Zuidema passim).

21. Avila ([1598] 1966:257), as quoted by Rostworoski (1981:42); my translation.

22. Zuidema (1977:257, 266); Isbell ([1978] 1985b:105), quoting a Quechua speaker from Ayacucho; Skar (1982:169).

23. Without external constraints, the fluidity characteristic of neighborhood-level *ayllus* would probably characterize community-level *ayllus* as well. Indeed, in the year 2000, the community-level *ayllu* appeared to be in the process of fissioning into smaller neighborhood-based sectors. See my discussion of this point in the Afterword.

24. The *saqra* is similar to the *kukuchi* and the *condenado,* and in some contexts the terms are interchangeable.

25. This shift from *saqra llaqta* to *saqra tinda* is reminiscent of the thesis put forward by Taussig in *The Devil and Commodity Fetishism in South America* (1980).

26. I have not witnessed this New Year's Day investiture. As it was described to me, contingents from Colquepata's *ayllus* run from the town plaza straight back to their home communities.

27. I deliberately use the word "power" rather than "influence" (cf. Bourque and Warren 1984) to avoid overemphasizing the distinction between formal and informal processes, which I think is unwarranted here.

28. See Irene Silverblatt (1987).

29. The ethnographer-novelist Arguedas describes this with great effect in his novel, *Los Rios Profundos* (Deep Rivers [1958] 1978), in which market women of Abancay lead an uprising against local officials and *hacendados.*

30. Reminiscing in 1995, Crisologo commented that "Alcides ate his own mother." He explained that when a person dies it is said, "The *alcalde* ate him or her." Alcides was Alcalde at the time of his mother's death.

Chapter 4. Coca Knows

1. See Bastien ([1978] 1985:112).

2. Coca's pharmacological properties are discussed in Chapter 9.

3. See my discussion of this problem in Chapter 9.

4. Douglas 1973:74.

5. *Llipt'a* (compressed ash chewed with coca leaves) is called *"Mamanchispa ñawin,"* which may be translated as "Our Mother's eyes." The word *ñawin* also means wellspring, or first and essential part (see Lira 1982:211; Cusihuamán 1976:96; Isbell [1978] 1985b:253). Thus, the phrase *Mamanchispa ñawin* probably refers to *llipt'a*'s capacity to release coca's stimulating alkaloids. Coca chewed without *llipt'a* has no effect.

6. See Goffman (1967:50).

7. I first published this interpretation in Allen (1981).

Chapter 5. Drinking Together

1. Studies of alcohol consumption in the Andes include Bunker (1986); Carter (1977); Doughty (1971); Gomez Huamán (1966); Heath (1959, 1971, 1974, 1975);

Holmberg (1971); Mangin (1957); Roderiguez Sandoval (1945); Saignes (1993), Simmons (1959, 1960); Vasquez (1967). See also Abercrombie (1998); Arnold (1991); Meyerson 1990; Rasnake (1988)on the ritual meanings of alcohol; see Hill (1985) on alcohol and ethnography.

2. This speech, not recorded on tape, has been reconstructed from fieldnotes.

3. Valderrama and Escalante 1997:54–55.

4. I develop this theme further in Allen (1998).

Chapter 6. Rites of the Household

1. See Sándor's (1986) critique of approaches that treat all ritual behavior as metaphorical.

2. Salomon (1983) describes buried *despachos* in colonial Ecuador as "buried messages."

3. See Veronica Cereceda (1986) for a semiotic analysis of these woven sacks; also Arnold (1997).

4. I have not observed any pattern in the placement of these *k'intus* on the paper.

5. In 1995 Erasmo's brother Julian told me that the folding process that produces , "two heads and one foot," applies only to the *despacho* and not to the *unkhuña* (coca cloth). Indeed, *unkhuña*s are sometimes folded with all four corners protruding. Nevertheless, I have retained Figure 7 in the second edition because it it illustrates this folding process well, and Erasmo so was emphatic in his comparison.

Double-headedness is characteristic of power objects. *Enqa*s representing domestic animals are often carved with two heads or with the attributes of both sexes. Like *enqa*s, double ears of corn are called *illa,* implying a connection with light. *Enqa*s should be set standing on the ritual table facing the sunrise; similarly the *despacho* should be burned with its head pointing to the sunrise. See Allen (1997).

6. Lira (1982:334) defines *wiraq'oya* as *"cierto zahumerio contra el viento"* ("a kind of fumigant against the wind"). Evil wind is thought to bring various diseases.

7. This rejection of *fixyu* illustrates how, in Erasmo's view of the world; the thing and the word are intrinsically connected. On related subjects, see Bruce Mannheim (1982 and 1987b).

8. Gifford and Hoggarth (1976:79); informant from Sicuani.

9. Double-*qero*s with a passage connecting the two chambers are considered ideal for *ch'uyay,* Carnival, and weddings, but I did not see them in use. See my interpretation of these vessels in Allen (2002).

10. I was not present when Don Luis stored his *ch'uño* and am grateful to Rick Wagner for his description of the ritual.

11. Luis's two bins were on the family's bed in the main house. His storeroom had no raised platform, and *ch'uño* cannot be stored on the ground, for dampness ruins dehydrated potatoes. I asked him where the family would sleep, and he answered, "On the other half of the bed, of course."

12. This vessel was partially destroyed by robbers in 1994.

13. *"Llama fistapí/Yanayki waqachíq."* Luis recalled bits of this ritual song from his childhood, remarking that it was seldom sung anymore. He explained that the *yana* (lover or helpmate) weeps to see blood running from the llamas' ears. According to the chronicler Molina ([1574]1943:80), the Incas' llama celebration coincided with the young nobleman's ear piercing ceremony: *"sacaban a los dichos caballeros a las chacras y a otros en sus casas y les horadaban las orejas, que era la postrera ceremonía que hacian en armarlos caballeros . . . Metíanlos en los agueros de la oreja unos hilos de algodón, y cada dia se le ponían mayor para que el aguero de la oreja se le fuese haciendo grande. Concluido lo cual, . . . empezaban este día las fiestas que hacían por el ganado . . . Asperjaban con chicha el ganado . . . "* (They

took the young knights to the fields, and others in their houses, and pierced their ears, which was the last ceremony they did to make them knights . . . They put some strands of wool in the [newly pierced] ear lobe and every day they made it bigger so that it would become large. When this [ear piercing] was over, they began the festivals for the herds . . . They sprinkled the herds with *chicha*"). Interestingly, it seems that the ear piercing, as a ritual practice, has been carried over from the noble youths to the llamas. This song may express a symbolic equation between the llamas and unmarried youths.

14. Dalle 1971:59.

15. Marzal (1971) reports this practice from the vicinity of Urcos.

Chapter 7. Rites of the *Ayllu*

1. See, for example, Isbell ([1978] 1985b); Ossio, ed. (1981); Palomino (1971); Platt 1986; Rasnake 1998; and Skar (1982).

2. Transcribed from a rendition recorded for me by Basilia Gutiérrez. It is impossible to convey in translation the mesmerizing quality of the song's repetitive rhythm. Men and women divide into two choruses, one of which sings every other line while the other interjects *"Puqllay!"* Once the song is finished, they reverse parts and repeat it. Doña Basilia sang both parts for the tape recorder. In the last line *("Kirilla yachará!"),* *kirilla* probably derives from *guerilla,* an interpretation that is supported by the fact that Carnival dancers describe themselves as warriors. *Yachará* seems to derive from Quechua *yachay* (to know or to learn) combined with a Spanish future tense ending. On the other hand, Basilia may have committed a slip of the tongue, rendering *yachaná* ("one must learn"; final emphasis due to song rhythm) as *yachará.* At any rate, *"kirilla yachará!"* seems to mean that the dancers must "learn about" Carnival fighting.

3. Gutiérrez de Santa Clara ([1548] 1905:563), quoted in Hopkins (1982:170).

4. *". . . como estuvieron vivos . . ."* (Molina [1574]1943:82).

5. Bolin (1998) provides a vivid description of Carnival in a herding community.

6. The following excerpts are from a tape of Carnival songs that a group of Sonqueños, calling themselves *Reinos de Sullumayo* (Lords of the Sullo River), recorded in 1995 on their own "low tech" equipment to sell in the Colquepata market. Cirilo Gutiérrez helped me with the transcription.

7. See Roca et al. (1966). Roca's group accompanied a contingent from P'isaq to the encounter at Chiwchillani. Curiously, they described the *tinkuy* as an encounter between the districts of P'isaq and San Salvador, and did not mention dance groups from the Colquepata *ayllus.* Sallnow also describes this *tinku* (1987:136–46). His Qamawara informants stressed the fact that, although members of each community fought as a team, the *tinku* also provided an opportunity for individuals to settle old scores and pursue personal quarrels (1987:136). This is consistent with my interpretation of the *tinku* as a ritual frame that both allows and limits the expression of violence.

8. Simforoso, who knows Spanish fairly well, speaks here in an amusing mixture of Quechua and Spanish.

9. Excerpt from a song taped on the same occasion as the previous transcription.

10. *Waqankilla* might be translated as "You'll just cry out," and I was told that women should chew it, like coca, to "open their throats for singing."

11. Sung by Basilia Gutiérrez, March 1976. *"Sapa runachawan/saminman churaspa,"* a problematic phrase, is rather freely translated as "Now that it's tossed its *sami*/to each little man." Prof. Jaime Pantigoso transcribed this passage and translated it into Spanish as, *"Con cada uno de los hombrecitos / poniendolos en regocijo."*

12. From a hymn recorded during a candlelight vigil in Sonqo; it is sung during vigils and on the Qoyllur Rit'i pilgrimage.

13. See, among others, D. Gow (1976); Flores Ochoa (1990); Ramirez (1969).

14. British anthropologist Michael Sallnow describes this process metaphorically as "recharging the *taytacha*'s batteries" (Sallnow 1974:127). See also Sallnow (1987).

15. In some communities, the *arariwa* is defined mainly in terms of his duties as the guardian of agricultural fields, and his role as ritual dance leader is deemphasized. In his autobiography, Gregorio Condori gives this description of the *arariwa*'s duties in the community of Acopía: "Every year on Carnival Monday a Cropkeeper *(arariwa)* was chosen, and it was like taking on a *cargo* that lasted for the entire year. The Cropkeeper *(arariwa)* had to guard over the potato patches, protecting them from hail, pests, and frost. To do so he'd build a small hut on a hill near the potato fields. And he'd have to stay there, watching the sky, every single day of the rainy season . . . If the hail still seemed bent on destroying the potatoes, the Cropkeeper would quickly strip, and naked as the day he came out of his mother's womb, he'd insult the hail, slinging dirt clods sprinkled with holy water and kerosene toward it" (Valderrama, Escalante, Gelles and Martínez 1996:44). Sallnow (1974), who studied a community near Sonqo, and D. Gow (1974), who studied near Qoyllur Rit'i, give similar descriptions of the *arariwa*'s functions.

16. Panpipes are not part of Sonqo's regular repertoire of instruments and figure only in the *ch'unchu* dancer's costume, apparently as a sign of the tropical forest. The dancers do not know how to play the panpipes and only blow across them to produce a rippling sequence of notes.

17. See Ellen Leichtman (1987) for a discussion of structural dualism in Andean music.

18. The differences in *ch'unchu* melody for each district are slight but distinctive. In 1980, for example, I arrived at the sanctuary independently and waited for the contingent of pilgrims from Sonqo to arrive. I lay awake in a tent listening to the *ch'unchu* music of the arriving delegations and could tell immediately when pilgrims from Colquepata began arriving. See Wissler (1999).

19. For further works on Qoyllur Rit'i dancers see Flores Ochoa (1990:73–94); D. Gow (1976); Poole (1984, 1990, 1991); Randall (1982); Sallnow (1974 and 1987), Wissler (1999). There are several ethnographic films about Qoyllur Rit'i, including *In the Footsteps of Taytacha* by Getzels and Gordon (1985), and *Qoyllur Rit'i: A Woman's Journey* by Gabriela Martínez Escobar and Holly Wissler.

20. I discuss this "pebble game" further in my article, "When Pebbles Move Mountains: Iconicity and Symbolism in Quechua Ritual" (Allen 1997).

21. The *ukukus* are lectured on the responsibilities of manhood and receive a *bautismo* (baptism) in the form of three whip lashes administered by members of the *Hermandad* or by more senior *ukukus* (Getzels and Gordon1985; Wissler 1999:27).

22. On the *ukuku* story, see Allen (1983); Morote Best (1956).

23. In 1980 I returned with them, for I had been in Peru less than two weeks and was suffering from altitude sickness. I found a seat in a bus crowded with market vendors and shopkeepers, who were speaking more Spanish than Quechua. After a few hours, the bus climbed to a high pass and stopped. The driver turned to his passengers and said quietly, "Now let us say goodbye to Our Lord." The people removed their hats and twisted around in their seats for a last glimpse of the snow-capped peaks. As the bus crossed the pass, the Qoyllur Rit'i range disappeared from view, and only near Cuzco could we again see Ausangati's squarish crest.

24. Quoted in Ramirez (1969:77); my translation.

25. *Alcalde* and *arariwa* complement each other in their roles as, respectively, the *ayllu*'s internal and external ritual leaders. Saints' Days and Carnival Week, festivities contained within the *ayllu,* contrast with occasions like *Comadres P'unchay* and Corpus Christi, which bring Sonqo into ritual contact with other *ayllus*. These latter rituals, which emphasize Sonqo's boundedness as well as its integration within a larger social unit, are led by the *arariwa,* the guardian of community boundaries.

26. See Rappaport's (1985) insightful development of a similar theme in a Colombian community.

Chapter 8. *Yawar Mayu:* Blood River

1. David Gow (1974; 1976) discusses the close association of *Apu* and saint at Qoyllur Rit'i.

2. D. Gow (1976) and Ramirez (1969) report that the *ch'unchu*s and the *qolla*s fought a final ritual battle in Ocongate.

3. The term *"comunitas"* is taken from Turner (1969). D. Gow (1976) and Wissler (1999) describe the experience of *comunitas* during the Qoyllur Rit'i pilgrimage.

4. Diane Hopkins (1982) discusses the word *puqllay* from this perspective. Sonqo *Runakuna* often use the word *topay* (to meet; derived from Spanish *topar*) almost synonymously with *tinkuy*. Things *topay* when they fit together exactly, like two halves of a pin or the seams of a garment. Medicine and coca leaves *topay* when they take effect. Although *tinkuy* and *topay* share similar semantic fields, *tinkuy* connotes a mixture whose ingredients lose their separate identities in a new whole, whereas *topay* connotes a coming together of parts that maintain their integrity within the whole.

5. Skar 1982.

6. Zuidema 1976.

7. Mayer 1977.

8. Fonseca 1974:11.

9. See G. Taylor (1976).

10. Isbell [1978] 1985b; Platt (1986).

11. According to some of the older townspeople in Colquepata, such a dual organization once existed but is no longer operative or even well remembered.

12. The role of asymmetrical dualism in Sonqo's mythic history is discussed in my article "Patterned Time" (1984). Also see Lévi Strauss's classic article "Do Dual Organizations Exist?" (1963); and Olivia Harris (1986) on the relationship of binary and triadic organization in Andean societies. In terms of social organization, Andean *ayllu*s often display tripartite as well as dual organization. In Inca Cuzco, for example, members of each of the four subsections were further subdivided into three groups (Zuidema 1964). In Chuschi, the two sets of authorities corresponding to the two moieties are subsumed under a third overarching set of authorities (Isbell [1978] 1985b). The triads in Sonqo's mythic history are thus only another variation of an Andes-wide theme: the *ayllu* is represented in its social organization, ritual symbolism, and myth through the interplay of binary and triadic principles, either of which may predominate, and which may sometimes be interpreted as variants of each other. Exactly how this general theme finds expression depends on the social, historical, and environmental context of the given *ayllu*. For more extended discussions of dual and triadic organization see, among others, Bastien ([1978] 1985); Earls (1972); Harris (1986); Isbell ([1978] 1985b); Mannheim (1986b, 1986c, 1987a); Platt (1986); Skar (1982); Urton (1981, 1997); and Zuidema (1964, 1982, 1985).

13. See Goffman ([1974] 1986).

14. Geertz 1973: 113–14. On violence as cultural performance see Isbell (1985a, 1995).

15. See also Isbell and Roncalla's article on Quechua riddles (1977).

16. Geertz 1973:412–53.

17. Bateson 1972:139.

18. *Chullo*s are knitted hats with ears flaps worn mainly by Indians. Mestizos occasionally wear plain knitted *chullo*s, but are never seen in ones decorated with buttons, tiny beads, and tassels. These ornate *chullo*s serve to display the maker's wealth and knitting skill and are prized by *Runakuna* in the region of Sonqo.

Chapter 9. Coca and Cultural Identity

1. On Andean "messianism," see, among others, Burga (1988); Flores Galindo (1986); R.Gow (1981); Kapsoli (1977, 1984); Millones, ed.(1990); Ossio, ed. (1973); Stern, ed. (1987); Urbano (1993a).

2. For works on coca leaf, see Boldó i Climent, ed. (1986); Cabieses (1992); Carter, Mamani, Morales, and Parkerson, ed. (1980); Cotlear (1999); Estremadoyro (1991); Gironda (2000); Henman, Anthony (1992); Pacini and Franquemont, ed. (1986); Spedding (1994); Weil (1995). See also Gelles (1985) and other contributions to the *Cultural Survival Quarterly* 9:4. An early classic work on coca is Mortimer's *History of Coca: The "Divine Plant" of the Incas* ([1901] 1974). *Mama Coca*, "an on-line academic journal on complexity, conflict and drugs in the American region," is available at www.mamacoca.org.

3. Among the many sources on the Spanish conquest of Peru are Hemming (1970), Stern (1982), and Wachtel (1977).

4. Murra 1986.

5. Masuda 1984:15.

6. See Gelles (1985).

7. Bray and Dollery 1983; Fuchs 1978; Gagliano 1994; Monge 1948, 1952.

8. See Plowman (1986).

9. Burchard 1979; Vitti 1979.

10. For example, Gutiérrez Noriega (1949).

11. The terms "hot" and "cold" refer to intrinsic qualities of a substance; potatoes are "cold" even when ladled steaming from the cooking pot.

12. Hanna 1974.

13. On medicinal uses of coca leaf see, among others, Carter, Morales and Mamani (1981); Bastien (1981). See also Bolton (1976).

14. Grinspoon and Bakalar 1976.

15. Kendall 1985:10.

16. See Grinspoon and Bakalar (1976:76–77).

17. Nieschulz 1971; Burchard 1975.

18. See Grinspoon and Bakalar (1976:Chapter 2); Plowman (1986).

19. Gutiérrez Noriega dedicated himself, at great personal sacrifice, to the attempt to prove scientifically that long-term coca chewing had serious negative effects on intelligence and physical health (e.g., Gutiérrez Noriega and Zapata Ortíz 1948). However, his studies have long been dismissed as inconclusive (see Grinspoon and Bakalar 1976:92,120).

20. The commission's report was based on a two month fact-finding tour, most of which was spent talking to Mestizo officials—the very segment of Andean society most antagonistic to coca-chewing Indians and most eager to show their superiority to them. It seems not to have occurred to the commission to talk to the coca chewers themselves. See my commentary in Allen ([Wagner] 1978:6–11).

21. Careful studies by Negrete and Murphy (1967) suggest that long-term coca chewing causes a mild psychological deficit not observable in normal interaction, but which shows up on intelligence tests designed to show ability for abstract thinking and the kind of memory associated with literacy. Grinspoon and Bakalar (who cannot in any sense be described as "pro-coca") consider these studies "ambiguous and inconclusive" owing to "confusing environmental variables and difficulties in interpreting the tests" (1976:124). I would add that the cultural variables are probably as problematic as the environmental ones. Grinspoon and Bakalar remark, "With a few minor exceptions, no one contends that coca causes any significant crime, violence, loss of psychomotor control, acute illness, or severe withdrawal reactions. The harm imputed to it almost always falls into the categories of chronic psychological or physical

deterioration and general social deficit . . . the evidence that coca does any damage of this kind is inconclusive" (1976:218).

22. Malinowski [1922] 1961:25.

23. See, for example, Amnesty International's report on Peru (1985).

24. See Chapter 3. For a similar tradition from Ayacucho see Silverblatt and Earls (1976).

Afterword to the Second Edition

1. In July and August of the year 2000, I spent just over two weeks in Sonqo and three more weeks in Cuzco, much of it with Sonqueños.

2. This quotation is excerpted from a longer statement David Edwards recorded on video in August 1999. Mr. Edwards took Don Luis to visit Lake Titicaca and recorded his commentary while visiting the Island of the Sun. I am grateful to him for sharing the video with me.

3. Don Luis refers here to *qeros*, ceremonial drinking vessels made of wood.

4. Readers may feel confused by this use of the Spanish word *hermano* (brother) to denote individuals who have converted to evangelical Protestantism. In Chapter 2, I introduced the word *ermanu*, derived from the same Spanish word, as a term denoting the sibling group. Sonqueños pronounce the two words *(Hermano* and *ermanu)* identically and distinguish their meanings according to context. In hopes of minimizing confusion I have used different spellings, *ermanu* for the sibling group and *Hermano* for the Protestants. All Sonqueños, Protestant and Catholic, use the word *Hermano* when speaking of Protestant converts. It is the most commonly used term (rather than *Protestante, Advenitsta,* or *Maranata*).

5. Linda Seligmann (1995) provides a detailed and insightful analysis of the Agrarian Reform and its aftermath in Huanoquite, a Cuzco community more affected by the *Sendero Luminoso* movement than Sonqo.

6. Spanish *suerte,* from which *surt'i* is derived, is usually translated in English as *luck* but can also mean *lot,* as in *casting lots.*

7. See Mayer 2002, Chapters 8–9.

8. It's interesting that, when projected onto a grid, the cyclical movement of upper-zone crop rotation produces diagonal patterns. The lower zone, which included several crops and varying cycles, produces more complex designs. Although I never heard weavers make explicit comparisons between the weaving process and crop rotation, it seems possible that planning an eight-year planting cycle was conceptually similar to warping the loom for a patterned textile. In Andean warp-faced weaving, the weaver lays out her pattern in vertical stripes and then "picks out" the pattern within the different stripes with each pass of the shuttle. Although Sonqo weavers never made explicit comparisons between the weaving process and crop rotation, it seems that they share a similar mental process.

9. Zimmerer 1996:169. Also see Brush and Taylor (1992), Mayer and Glave (1999).

10. Barley often replaced beans and *tarwi,* crops that replenish nitrogen in the rotational cycle; this further exacerbated soil degradation (Zimmerer 1996:168).

11. This may be an exaggeration, but it is clear that the population of Colquepata District did increase significantly. Between 1961 and 1981 it rose from 5,327 to 6,873 (Zimmerer 1996:237). Zimmerer attributes this "demographic leap" in Paucartambo (ibid.:152) to immigration during the post-reform period (ibid.:76).

12. Zimmerer's *Changing Fortunes: Biodiversity and Peasant Livelihood in the Andes* (1996) provides an in-depth study of the reconfiguration of land-use areas in Colquepata.

13. See Zimmerer 1996:166–68 for a detailed discussion of these labor requirements.

14. See Mayer 2002:229.

15. On the ideological significance of changing diet see Weismantel's chapter on "Food in Discourse: Everyday Symbols in Ideological Conflict" in her book, *Food, Gender and Poverty in the Ecuadorean Andes* (1998:143–67). Zimmerer makes interesting observations about a decline in the remarkable diversity of potato types cultivated in Paucartambo. Many of the less commercially viable types—small, variegated, with many eyes—were particularly prized in the farmers' traditional cuisine. Ironically, these potato types have become a luxury enjoyed by more prosperous farmers, who can afford to devote some land and labor to please their own palates. The poorest farmers, with marginal land, also continue to cultivate a more diverse array: "Their poor farmland pressed them to grow potato and ulluco landraces in order to furnish nearly the sole source of everyday subsistence" (1966:93). Farmers who compose the large middle portion of the spectrum are usually too strapped for cash to devote their resources to the very crops they traditionally enjoyed eating.

16. Mayer 2002:220.

17. The problem of massive poverty in Peru is a very complex issue that goes far beyond the scope of this chapter. Mayer's Chapter 10 in *The Articulated Peasant* (2002) provides a good overview of issues affecting rural poverty, as well as an insightful critique of assumptions hidden in the *Mapa de la Pobreza*.

18. I encountered considerable variation in *surt'i* names. In 1995 Julian listed the *Uray Hallpa surt'i*s as: Qhalipampa, Qotoni, Yutukalli, Chakayuqpampa, Wanakauri, Towlakancha, Añas Wachana, and Pikimachay. In 2000, Don Luis gave me the following list of uray *surt'i* names: Mama Samana, Uray Wanakawri, Urqukancha Urayman, Yutukalli Surt'i, Hatun Pampa, Qhalipampa, Pikimachay, Churuwamba, and Qhalipampa. Only two of these, Mama Samana and Qhalipampa, coincide with the current *sectores*. He said that Pikimachay included Qoyapuqru. He only remembered five *Hawa Hallpa* names: Hatun Ñan Wayk'u, T'uqra Kancha, Surayuq, Q'uncha Rumi, Palta Rumi.

19. Enrique Mayer (2002:213).

20. This is one of three projected reservoirs in Sonqo. The second, a smaller construction above Qoyapuqru, was almost complete when I visited in 2000. Work on the third, in Qhalipampa, had barely begun. It surely is not coincidental that the new *sector* organization was galvanized by hydraulic projects, given the great social, cultural, and economic significance of water.

21. Mayer 2002:224.

22. Quecha makes an important grammatical distinction between two kinds of first-person plural, inclusive and exclusive. The inclusive form includes the person being spoken to; the exclusive does not. For example, if I use the inclusive form of the verb *riy* (to go), "*Rishanchis,*" I'm saying that "We (including you) are going." If I use the exclusive form, "*Rishayku,*" I'm saying that "We (but not you) are going." Curiously, Apolinar's exclamation, "*Allinmi kanchis kunan!*" used the inclusive *kanchis,* even though it was addressed to me, a non-Protestant. Possibly this reflects evangelical rhetoric to draw the respondent into the fold by implication.

23. On the rapid spread of Protestantism in Latin America see, e.g., David Martin, ed. (1990).

24. His story was confirmed later by Don Luis and others in Mama Samana who were not sympathetic to Protestantism.

25. I did not record the conversation, so this quotation is reconstructed from my notes. I was struck by his phrase, "I was lazy, I lied, I stole," which evokes the Inca adage (often repeated by school teachers) "Don't be lazy, don't lie, don't steal" ("*Ama qilla, ama llulla, ama suwa*").

26. Coleman 2000:98. Although several Maranata congregations maintain websites, I found it difficult to obtain background information about the history and organization of the movement.

27. The website is http://members.truepath.com/Maranata.

28. According to Erasmo's identification document, he was born in 1940. This would make him only fifty-eight at the time of his death in 1996. However, these documents are not particularly reliable. Individuals of Erasmo's generation often did not know their ages and could not give accurate information when the documents were originally issued.

29. Mendoza 2000:4. There is a wealth of current scholarship on Peruvian dance. See, among others, Poole (1990, 1991); Mendoza (2000); De la Cadena (2000); Romero (2001); and the essays in Romero, ed. (1993).

30. Poole 1991:152.

31. De la Cadena 2000:286.

32. A few Sonqueños joined delegations from Chocopia and Miskawara.

33. For example, see Panofsky (1957) and MacCormack (1998). For a vivid description and analysis of Amazonian house villages see David Guss (1989). Also see Hugh-Jones (1979) and Reichel-Dolmatoff (1971, 1984) on the house symbolism in tropical South America.

34. Arnold 1991:5.

35. Enrique Mayer 1977:78.

36. Bourdieu 1977:89.

37. See Mary Weismantel's (1998:197–201) insightful discussion of this opposition.

38. Resolucion, September 11, 1948, Ministerio de Justicia y Trabajo, Cuzco. The late Dr. Julio Frisancho represented the claimants; my thanks to Armando Guevara Gil for bringing the case to my attention.

39. Rudi Colloredo-Mansfield (1999:59)

40. Rudi Colloredo-Mansfield (1999:84–85). Also see Marisol De la Cadena's analysis of sanitation campaigns in Cuzco (2000:68–72). Kevin Healy's chapter, "The Biases of Western Aid" (in Healy 2001:17–38), provides a general critique of international development programs.

41. Benjamin Orlove (1998) provides an interesting discussion of this point as it relates to understandings of race in the Andes.

42. Sarah Lund Skar 1987:275.

43. Excrement is occasionally used to treat human illness. According to Lira (1985), pig or dog feces may help colic, guinea pig droppings combat *susto* (illness caused by a sudden fright), hummingbird droppings help heal broken bones and minimize night sweats, and smoke from burning human feces wards off measles and chicken pox.

44. Roger Rasnake, personal communication (May 1979).

45. Sarah Lund Skar 1987:284–85.

46. Gose 1994:134. On the body as a hydraulic system see Bastian 1985.

47. Jeffrey Gamarra 1998:155

Glossary

All words are Quechua except where indicated as Spanish.

A

achakáw!: expression of horror or disgust
aha: fermented corn beverage; see *chicha*
ahijado: (Spanish) godchild
alawaru: musical phrase used to demarcate stages of a ritual (from Spanish *alabado,* prayer)
alcalde: (Spanish) mayor, ritual leader of the *ayllu*
allin: good
allin kawsay: well-being
alma: soul or bones of the dead (from Spanish *alma*)
altumisa: divination ritual of the highest order (from Spanish *alto* plus *misa* or *mesa*)
altumisayuq: diviner of the highest order; see *altumisa*
amaru: large subterranean dragonlike serpent; may incorporate feline characteristics
animu: spirit animating a living being (from Spanish *animo*)
apu: lord, a term usually reserved for the most powerful Sacred Places
ayllu: indigenous community or other social group whose members share a common focus
ayni: neighborly aid, to be reciprocated in kind

C

cargo: (Spanish) community office or other duty owed to the community by its members *carguyuq:* a person who holds a *cargo* (derived from Spanish *cargo* plus Quechua suffix *-yuq*)

comadre: (Spanish) spiritual comother; reciprocal term of address between parent and godmother of a child

compadrazgo: (Spanish) spiritual coparenthood; bond of fictive kinship

compadre: (Spanish) spiritual cofather; reciprocal term of address between parent and godfather of a child

condenado: (Spanish) soul of the damned; see *kukuchi*

copita: (Spanish) shot glass for serving *trago*

costal: (Spanish) cloth sack woven in stripes of brown and black, used to store and transport produce; in ritual, provides surface upon which ritual objects are placed

CH

chakitaklla: foot plow

chansanakuy: stylized humorous repartee; literally, joking together

chicha: fermented corn beverage; called *chicha* by Spanish speakers, *aha* by Quechua speakers

chirawa: dry season, late May through August

chullpa: ruined tower, thought to be the abode of *Machukuna*

churi: son

CH'

ch'allay: libation of a beverage poured onto the ground

ch'aska: bright star

ch'unchu: ritual dancers thought to represent wild men from the jungle

ch'uño: dehydrated potatoes, made by a process of alternate freezing and thawing

ch'uyay: libation of a beverage thrown over the recipient, usually in animal fertility rituals

D

despacho: (Spanish) offering bundle, usually burned

despedida: (Spanish) goodbye party

dokumentuyuq: person who possesses documents (derived from Spanish *documento* plus the Quechua suffix *-yuq*)

E

enqa, also *enqaychu:* small stone model, considered the repository of well-being for the animal or household it represents; see *illa*

ermanu: sibling or group of siblings (from Spanish *hermano*)

F

faena: (Spanish) communal work party

forastero: (Spanish) outsider to the community; see *hawamanta runa*

G

gaseosa: (Spanish) sweet carbonated beverage

H

hacendado: (Spanish) owner of an *hacienda*
hachu: wad of chewed coca
hacienda: (Spanish) privately owned rural estate
hallpay: to chew coca
hampi: medicine, anything with special animating properties
hampi akllay: preparation of *despacho;* literally, to choose medicine
hanan pacha: upper world, sometimes refers to Christian heaven
hatun: large, great
hawamanta runa: person from outside the community; see *forastero*
Hermano: a convert to Protestantism.
hispay: to urinate.
hucha: sin

I

illa: synonym of *enqa*
illariy: to shine
imayna: how
inti: sun
istrilla: a small found-object, thought to impart well-being to the finder (from Spanish *estrella,* star)

K

kamachikuq: authority, one who commands
kamay: to create, in the sense of imparting order
Kawsasqanchis: All Souls' Day, 1 November
kawsaqkuna: literally, living ones; usually refers to *enqa*s
kawsay: to live
kay pacha: this world, the terrestrial sphere between *hanan pacha* and *ukhu pacha*
kukuchi: cannibalistic soul of the damned trapped in a rotting corpse
-kuna: pluralizing suffix
kuraq: elder; may be used either as noun or adjective, as in English
kuraq tayta: community elder; literally, elder father

KH

khuyaq: a caring protector, a loving guardian
khuyay: to care for, to protect

K'

k'intu: a prestation of coca leaves, often three in number, with the leaves carefully placed one on top of the other and offered with the right hand
k'uychi: rainbow

L

layqa: sorcerer
layqasqa: bewitched
leon: any large feline (from Spanish *leon,* lion)

LL

llaqta: town characterized by nucleated rather than dispersed settlement
lliklla: a woman's woven shawl
llipt'a: compressed ash chewed with coca to release the stimulating alkaloids

M

machu: old
Machu: Old One, quasidemonic survivor of a previous race; plural, *Machukuna*
Machula Aulanchis: "Our Old Grandfathers," benevolent aspect of the *Machukuna*
   (*Aulanchis* derives from Spanish *abuelo,* grandfather, plus the Quechua possessive
   suffix *-nchis,* our)
Machuláy: "Grand-daddy"; affectionate term of address
mama: mother, adult woman
mamacha: female saint; image of the Virgin Mary or other female saint; literally, little
   mother
Mamanchispa q'apaynin: literally, Our Mother's fragrance; refers to coca leaves
maqt'a: boy
maypichá!: "Who knows where?" or "Where indeed!"
mayu: river
mihuq: one who eats; in ritual, one who eats for the dead
mink'a: a request for labor; a collective labor party
Mishi: Mestizo town dweller (from Spanish *Mestizo*); plural, *Mishikuna*
montera: flat fringed hat
Musuq Wata: New Year
muyuy: to circulate, to rotate

Ñ

ñak'aq: nocturnal demon who extracts the heart or body fat from its sleeping victim;
   literally, slaughterer
ñawin: eye; principle or essential part
ñawpa: anterior, previous
nawsa: blind; illiterate

O

oca: (Oxalis tuberosa) sweetish white Andean tuber

P

pacha: world; earth; a moment in time
Pacha: personal name of the animate Earth
pachakuti: apocalypse; literally, world reversal
Pacha Mama: Mother Earth
Pacha Tira: malevolent aspect of *Pacha Mama* (*tira* derives from Spanish *tierra*)
papa: potato
paqo: diviner, ritual specialist
paseo: (Spanish) round of ritual visits paid to officials of the community
Pisti Timpu: Era of the Plague
pollera: (Spanish) full skirt
poqoy: to ripen; rainy season, season of maturation, December through March

puchu: enough, plenty
puchuela: low ceramic bowl used for ritual drinking of *chicha*
puchullaña: "That's enough."
puchusayki: "I'll satiate you."
puna: high grasslands
puqllay: play
Puqllay: Carnival Week
pututu: conch shell trumpet

PH

phamilia: close consanguineal kinsmen including first cousins; may extend to second
    cousins (from Spanish *familia*)
phukuy: to blow; ritual offering in which one blows over coca or food in order to
    share it with deities

P'

p'acha: clothing
p'asna: girl
p'unchay: day

Q

qatay: son-in-law or brother-in-law
qataymasi: fellow sons-in-law or fellow brothers-in-law, those who stand in the *qatay*
    relationship to the same people; literally, fellow *qatay*
qayqa: evil atmosphere surrounding a corpse
qero: wooden goblet or tumbler, used for ritual drinking of *chicha*
qoyllur: star
Qoyllur Rit'i: chain of sacred snow-covered peaks, object of a regional pilgrimage prior
    to Corpus Christi; literally, Star-Snow
quinoa: (Chenopodium quinoa) high-protein Andean grain

QH

qhachun: daughter-in-law or sister-in-law
qhachunmasi: codaughter-in-law or cosister-in-law, those who stand in the *qhachun*
    relationship to the same people; literally, fellow *qhachun*
qhaqha: place that has been struck by lightning
qhari: man, husband
qhapaq: mighty, powerful, wealthy.
qhaway: to watch; to perform divination by watching certain signs

Q'

q'uncha: low adobe fireplace used for cooking

R

rayu: lightning (from Spanish *rayo*)
regidor: (Spanish) town crier
runa: human being; culturally, an indigenous Andean person; plural, *runakuna*

runa p'acha: indigenous costume
rutuchikuy: ritual first haircutting

S

sami: animating essence
saminchay: to offer a blessing
samlyuq: possessing *sami*
santu: holy (from Spanish *santo*)
santuyuq: possessing skills invented by specific saints
saqra: demon (noun); demonic (adjective)
segundo: (Spanish) assistant mayor
sullka: younger
surt'i: sector of community lands in the traditional system of crop rotation (from Spanish *suerte*)

T

tayta: father, adult man
taytacha: male saint, crucifix; literally, little father
Taytakuna: Fathers; often refers to the mountain lords
Taytanchis: Our Father; Christian God
timpu: an era (from Spanish *tiempo*)
tinku: encounter; confluence of two or more streams; ritual battle
tinkuy: to join through a violent meeting, to encounter
Tirakuna: Sacred Places (from Spanish *tierra* plus the Quechua plural suffix *-kuna*)
tiyana: seat or living place
tomay: to drink (from Spanish *tomar*); see *ukyay*
trago: (Spanish) low-grade cane alcohol

T'

t'inka: libation made by flicking drops of beverage into the air with the thumb and the forefinger

U

uchu: hot pepper
ukyay: to drink

W

wanu: manure

References

Archives

Archivo Arzobispal del Cuzco.

Archivo Departamental de Cuzco.

Archivo General de la Nación.

Biblioteca Nacional del Perú.

Fuero Privativo Agrario (Segundo Juzgado de Tierras, Cuzco).

Books and Articles

Abercrombie, Thomas A. 1998. *Pathways of Memory and Power: Ethnography and History among an Andean People*. Madison: University of Wisconsin Press.

Abrill A., Victor. 1959. *El Indio del Ccolquepata*. Paper written for Geografía Humana General y del Perú, a course given at the University of Cuzco. Entered in the Archivo Departamental del Cuzco under course title, paper no. 22.

Adorno, Rolena, ed. 1982. *From Oral to Written Expression: Native Andean Chronicles of the Early Colonial Period*. Syracuse: University of Syracuse Press.

Ahlqvist, Anders, ed. 1982. *Papers from the Fifth International Conference of Historical Linguistics*. Amsterdam: John Benjamins.

Alberti, Giorgio, and Enrique Mayer, eds. 1974. *Reciprocidad e intercambio en los Andes peruanos*. Perú Problema, no. 12. Lima: Instituto de Estudios Peruanos.

Albó, Xavier. 1982. *Pachamama y Q'ara:* El Aymara ante la opresión de la naturaleza y de la sociedad. Paper presented at the 44th Congress of Americanists in Manchester, England, September 1982.

Allen, Catherine J. 1978. See Wagner, Catherine Allen, 1978.

———. 1982. Body and Soul in Quechua Thought. *Journal of Latin American Lore* 8 (2): 179–96.

———. 1983. Of Bear-Men and He-Men: Bear Metaphors and Male Self-Perception in a Peruvian Community. *Latin American Indian Literatures* 7 (1): 38–51.

———. 1984. Patterned Time: The Mythic History of a Peruvian Community. *Journal of Latin American Lore* 10 (2): 151–74.

———. 1997. When Pebbles Move Mountains: Iconicity and Symbolism in Quechua Ritual. In Howard-Malverde 1997:73–94.

———. 1998. When Utensils Revolt: Mind, Matter and Modes of Being in the Pre-Columbian Andes. *Res: Anthropology and Aesthetics* 33:18–27.

———. 2002. The Incas Have Gone Inside: Pattern and Persistence in Andean Iconography. *Res: Anthropology and Aesthetics* 40 (fall 2002).

Allen, Catherine J., and Nathan Garner. 1996. *Condor Qatay: Anthropology in Performance.* Prospect Heights, Ill.: Waveland Press, Inc.

Amnesty International. 1985. *Peru: Amnesty International Briefing.* London: Amnesty International Publications.

Arguedas, José María. [1958] 1978. *Deep Rivers.* Frances Horning Barraclough, trans. Austin: University of Texas Press. Originally published as *Los rios profundos.* Buenos Aires: Editorial Losada.

———. [1956] 1985a. Puquio, a Culture in Process of Change. Frances Horning Barraclough, trans. In Arguedas 1985b:149–92. Originally published as Puquio, una cultura en proceso de cambio. *Revista del Museo Nacional de Lima* 25:184–232.

———. [1941] 1985b. *Yawar Fiesta.* Frances Horning Barraclough, trans. Austin: University of Texas Press.

Arnold, Denise. 1991. The House of Earth-bricks and Inka-stones: Gender, Memory, and Cosmos in Qaqachaka. *Journal of Latin American Lore* 17:3–69.

———. 1997. Making Men in Her Own Image: Gender, Text, and Textile in Qaqachaka. In Howard-Malverde 1997:99–134.

Arnold, Denise Y., Domingo Jiménez, and Juan de Dios Yapita, eds. 1992. *Hacia un orden andino de las cosas.* La Paz: IIISBOL.

Avila, Francisco de. [1598] 1966. *Dioses y hombres de Huarochirí.* José María Arguedas, trans. Lima: Museo Nacional de la Historia/Instituto de Estudios Peruanos.

Bastien, Joseph W. 1981. Metaphorical Relations between Sickness, Society, and Land in a Qollahuaya Ritual. In Bastien and Donahue, eds 1981

———. [1978] 1985. *Mountain of the Condor: Metaphor and Ritual in an Andean Ayllu.* Prospect Heights, IL.: Waveland Press. Originally published as American Ethnological Society Monograph no. 64. St. Paul: West Publishing Co.

Bastien, Joseph W., and John M. Donahue, eds. 1981. *Health in the Andes.* American Anthropological Association Special Publication, no. 12. Washington, D.C.

Bateson, Gregory. 1972. *Steps to an Ecology of Mind.* New York: Ballantine Books.

Behar, Ruth, and Deborah A. Gordon, eds. 1995. *Women Writing Culture.* Berkeley: University of California Press.

Betanzos, Juan de. 1996 [1551]. *Narrative of the Incas.* Trans. and ed. by Roland Hamilton and Dana Buchanan. Austin: University of Texas Press.

Boldó i Climent, Joan. 1986. *La coca andina: Visión de una planta satanizada.* Mexico City: Instituto Indigenista Interamericano. Originally published as *América Indígena* vol. 38, no. 4 (1978), Enrique Mayer, ed.

Bolin, Inge. (1998). *Rituals of Respect: The Secret of Survival in the High Peruvian Andes.* Austin: University of Texas Press.

Bolton, Ralph. 1976. Andean Coca Chewing: A Metabolic Perspective. *American Anthropologist* 78:630–33.

Bolton, Ralph, and Enrique Mayer, eds. 1977. *Andean Kinship and Marriage.* American Anthropological Association Special Publication, no. 7. Washington, D.C.

Bourdieu, Pierre. 1977. *Outline of a Theory of Practice*. Richard Nice, trans. Cambridge Studies in Social Anthropology no. 16. Cambridge: Cambridge University Press.

Bourque, Susan C., and Kay B. Warren. 1981. *Women of the Andes: Patriarchy and Social Change in Two Peruvian Towns*. Ann Arbor: University of Michigan Press.

Bouysee-Casagne, Thérèse et al. (eds), 1987:61–132. *Trés Reflexiones sobre el Pensamiento Andino*, La Paz: HISBOL.

Bray, Warwick, and Colin Dollery. 1983. Coca Chewing and High-Altitude Stress: A Spurious Correlation. *Current Anthropology* 24 (3): 269–82.

Brown, Jonathan. 1998. *The Word Made Image: Religion, Art and Architecture in Spain and Spanish America, 1500–1600*. Boston: Trustees of the Isabella Stewart Gardner Museum.

Bruner, Edward M., ed. 1983. *Text, Play and Story: The Construction and Reconstruction of Self and Society*. 1983 Proceedings of the American Ethnological Society. Washington, D.C.

Brush, Stephen B. 1977. *Mountain, Field and Family: The Economy and Human Ecology of an Andean Village*. Philadelphia: University of Pennsylvania Press.

Brush, Stephen B., and J. Edward Taylor. 1992. Technology Adoption and Biological Diversity in Andean Potato Agriculture. *Journal of Development Economics* 39:365–387.

Bunker, Stephen G. 1986. Ritual, Respect and Refusal: Drinking Behavior in an Andean Village. *Human Organization* 46, no. 4: 334–42.

Burchard, Roderick. 1975. Coca Chewing: A New Perspective. In V. Rubin, ed.1975:463–84.

———. 1979. Recent Anthropological Research on the Metabolic Effects of Coca Use in the Andes. Manuscript, Department of Anthropology, University of Manitoba.

Burga, Manuel. 1988. *Nacimiento de una utopía: Muerte y resurrección de los incas*. Lima: Instituto de Apoyo Agarario.

Caballero, José María. 1981. *Economía agraria de la sierra peruana antes de la Reforma Agraria de 1969*. Lima: Instituto de Estudios Peruanos.

Cabieses, Fernando. 1992. *La coca: Dilemma trágico?* Lima: Enaco.

Carter, William E. 1977. Ritual, the Aymara, and the Role of Alcohol in Human Society. In Du Toit, ed. 1977:101–10.

Carter, William E., Mauricio Mamani P., José V. Morales, and P. Parkerson. 1980. *Coca in Bolivia*. La Paz: U.S. National Institute of Drug Abuse.

Carter, William E., José V. Morales, and Mauricio Mamani. 1981. Medicinal Uses of Coca in Bolivia. In Bastien and Donahue, eds. 1981:119–49.

Casaverde Rojas, Juvenal. 1970. El mundo sobrenatural de una comunidad. *Allpanchis* (Cuzco) 2:121–244.

Castelli, Amalia, Marcia Koth de Paredes, and Mariana Mould de Pease, eds. 1981. *Etnohistoria y antropología andina*. Lima: Museo Nacional de Historia.

Cereceda, Veronica. 1986. The Semiology of Andean Textiles: The Talegas of Isluga. In Murra, Wachtel, and Revel, eds. 1986:149–73.

Chirinos Rivera, Andrés, and Alejo Maque Capira. 1996. *Eros Andino: Alejo Khunku willawanchik*. Cusco: Centro de Estudios Regionales Andinos "Bartolomé de Las Casas."

Clifford, James, and George E. Marcus, eds. 1986. *Writing Culture: The Poetics and Politics of Ethnography*. Berkeley: University of California Press.

Coleman, Simon. 2000. *The Globalisation of Charismatic Christianity: Spreading the Gospel of Prosperity*. Cambridge: Cambridge University Press.

Colloredo-Mansfield, Rudi. 1999. *The Native Leisure Class: Consumption and Cultural Creativity in the Andes*. Chicago: University of Chicago Press.

Cotlear, Julio. 1999. *Drogas y política en el Perú: La conexión norteamericana*. Lima: Instituto de Estudios Peruanos.

Cusihuamán, Antonio. 1976. *Diccionario Quechua: Cuzco collao.* Lima: Ministerio de Educación/Instituto de Estudios Peruanos.

Dahlgren, C. 1982. *Maranata: En Sociolgisk Studie av en Sektörelses Uppkomst och Utveckling.* Vänersborg: Plus Ultra.

Dalle, Luis. 1971. Kutipay. *Allpanchis* (Cuzco) 3:59–65.

Davies, Thomas M. 1974. *Indian Integration in Peru: A Half-Century of Experience, 1900–1948.* Lincoln: University of Nebraska Press.

De la Cadena, Marisol. 2000. *Indigenous Mestizos: The Politics of Race and Culture in Cuzco, Peru, 1919–1991.* Durham, N.C.: Duke University Press.

Doughty, Paul L. 1971. The Social Uses of Alcoholic Beverages in a Peruvian Community. *Human Organization* 30:187–97.

Douglas, Mary. 1966. *Purity and Danger: An Analysis of the Concepts of Pollution and Taboo.* London: Routledge & Kegan Paul.

———. 1973. *Natural Symbols: Explorations in Cosmology.* New York: Random House.

Du Toit, Brian, ed. 1977. *Drugs, Ritual, and Altered States of Consciousness.* Rotterdam: Balkema.

Duviols, Pierre. 1971. *La Lutte contre les religions autochtones dans le Pérou colonial.* Paris and Lima: Institut Français d'Études Andines.

Earls, John. 1969. The Organization of Power in Quechua Mythology. *Journal of the Steward Anthropological Society* 1 (1): 63–82.

———. 1972. *Andean Continuum Cosmology.* Ann Arbor, Mich.: University Microfilms.

———. 1981. Patrones de jurisdicción y organización entre los Qaracha Wankas: Una reconstrucción arqueológica y etnohistórica de una época flúida. In Castelli, Koth de Paredes, and Mould de Pease, eds. 1981.55–91.

Earls, John, and Irene Silverblatt. 1976. La realidad física y social en la cosmología andina. *Proceedings of the 42nd Congress of Americanists* (Paris) 4:299–325.

Estremadoyro, J. M. 1991. *La coca.* Lima: Surmedsa.

Fabian, Johannes. 1983. *Time and the Other: How Anthropology Makes Its Object.* New York: Columbia University Press.

Flores Galindo, Alberto. 1986. *Buscando un Inca: Identidad y Utopía en los Andes.* Cuba: Casas de las Americas.

Flores Ochoa, Jorge A. 1977a. Enqa, enqaychu, illa y khuya rumi. In Flores Ochoa 1977b: 211–237.

———, ed. 1977b. *Pastores de la puna: uywamichiq punarunakuna.* Lima: Instituto de Estudios Peruanos.

———. 1990. *El Cuzco: Resistencia y Continuidad.* Cusco, Peru: Editorial Andina, S.R.Ltda.

Fonseca Martel, César. 1972. Sistemas económicos en la comunidades campesinas del Perú. Ph.D. diss., Universidad Nacional Mayor de San Marcos, Lima

———. 1974. Modalidades de la minka. In Alberti and Mayer, eds. 1974:86–109.

Fuchs, Andrew. 1978. Coca Chewing and High-Altitude Stress: Possible Effects of Coca Alkaloids on Erythropoiesis. *Current Anthropology* 19 (2): 277–92.

Gagliano, Joseph A. 1994. *Coca Prohibition in Peru: The Historical Debates.* Tucson: University of Arizona Press.

Gamarra C., Jeffrey. 1998. Entre la Biblia y la espada: Respuestas andinas a los nuevos movimientos religiosos. In Millones, Tomoeda and Fujii 1998:143–160.

Garner, Nathan C., and Colin M. Turnbull. 1979. *Anthropology, Drama and the Human Experience.* Washington, D.C.: Division of Experimental Programs, The George Washington University.

Geertz, Clifford. 1973. *The Interpretation of Cultures.* New York: Basic Books.

Gelles, Paul. 1985. Coca and Andean Culture: The New Dangers of an Old Debate. *Cultural Survival Quarterly* 9 (4): 20–23.

———. 2000. *Water and Power in Highland Peru: The Cultural Politics of Irrigation and Development.* New Brunswick: Rutgers University Press.

Getzels, Peter, and Harriet Gordon. 1985. *In the Footsteps of Taytacha.* Watertown, Mass.: Documentary Educational Resources. Film.

Gifford, Douglas, and Pauline Hoggarth. 1976. *Carnival and Coca Leaf: Some Traditions of the Peruvian Quechua Ayllu.* New York: St. Martin's Press.

Gironda C., Eusebio. 2001. *Coca Inmortal.* La Paz: Plural Editores.

Goffman, Erving. 1967. *Interaction Ritual: Essays on Face-to-Face Behavior.* New York: Anchor Books.

———. [1974] 1986. *Frame Analysis: An Essay on the Organization of Experience.* Boston: Northeastern University Press. Originally published by Harper and Row, New York.

Gomez Huamán, N. 1966. Importancia social de la chicha como bebida popular en Huamanga. *Wamani* 1 (1): 33–57.

Gonzalez Holguín, Diego. [1608] 1989. *Vocabulario de la lengua general de todo el Perú.* Lima: Instituto de Historia, Universidad Nacional Mayor de San Marcos.

Gose, Peter. 1994. *Deathly Waters and Hungry Mountains: Agrarian Ritual and Class Formation in an Andean Town.* Toronto: University of Toronto Press.

Gow, David. 1974. Taytacha Qoyllur Rit'i. *Allpanchis* (Cuzco) 7:49–100.

———. 1976. *The Gods and Social Change in the High Andes.* Ann Arbor, Mich.: University Microfilms.

Gow, Rosalind. 1981. *Yawar Mayu:* Revolution in the Southern Andes, 1860–1980. Ph.D. diss., University of Wisconsin-Madison.

Gow, Rosalind, and Bernabé Condori. 1976. *Kay Pacha.* Biblioteca de la Tradición Oral Andina no. 1. Cuzco: Centro de Estudios Rurales Andinos "Bartolomé de las Casas."

Grinspoon, Lester, and James B. Bakalar. 1976. *Cocaine: A Drug and Its Social Evolution.* New York: Basic Books.

Gross, Daniel, ed. 1973. *Peoples and Cultures of Native South America.* New York: Natural History Press.

Guaman Poma de Ayala, Felipe. [1614] 1936. *Nueva corónica y buen gobierno.* Paris: Institut d'Ethnologie.

Guss, David M. 1989. *To Weave and Sing: Art, Symbol and Narrative in the South American Rain Forest.* Berkeley: University of California Press.

Gutiérrez de Santa Clara, Pedro. [1548] 1905. *Historia de las guerras civiles del Perú,* vol. 3. Madrid: Libreria General de Victorian Suárez.

Gutiérrez Noriega, Carlos. 1949. El hábito de la coca en el Perú. *América Indígena* 9 (2): 143–222.

Gutiérrez Noriega, Carlos, and Vicente Zapata Ortiz. 1948. Observaciones fisiológicas y patológicas en sujetos habituados a la coca. *Revista de la Farmacología y Medicina Experimental* (Lima) 1:1–31.

Hanna, Joel M. 1974. Coca Leaf Use in Southern Peru: Some Biosocial Aspects. *American Anthropologist* 76:281–96.

Harris, Olivia. 1986. From Asymmetry to Triangle: Symbolic Transformations in Northern Potosí. In Murra, Wachtel, and Revel, eds. 1986:260–79.

Hayes, E. Nelson, and Tanya Hayes, eds. 1970. *Claude Lévi-Strauss: The Anthropologist as Hero.* Cambridge: MIT Press.

Healy, Kevin. 2001. *Llamas, Weaving, and Organic Chocolate: Multicultural Grassroots Development in the Andes and Amazon of Bolivia.* Notre Dame, Ind.: University of Notre Dame Press.

Heath, Dwight B. 1959. Drinking Patterns among the Bolivian Campa. *Quarterly Journal of Studies on Alcohol* 19 (3): 491–508.

———. 1971. Peasants, Revolution and Drinking: Interethnic Drinking Patterns in Two Bolivian Communities. *Human Organization* 30:179–86.

———. 1974. Perspectivas socioculturales del alcohol en América Latina. *Acta Psiquátrica y Psicológica de América Latina* 20:99–111.

———. 1975. A Critical Review of Ethnographic Studies of Alcohol Use. *Research Advances in Alcohol and Drug Problems* 2:1–92.

Hemming, John. 1970. *The Conquest of the Incas.* Cambridge: Harvard University Press.

Henman, Anthony. 1992. *Mama Coca.* La Paz: HISBOL.

Hill, Thomas W. 1985. On Alcohol and Ethnography: A Problem in the History of Anthropology. *Current Anthropology* 26 (2): 282–83.

Homburg, Alan R. 1971. The Rhythms of Drinking in a Peruvian Coastal Community. *Human Organization* 30:198–202.

Hopkins, Diane. 1982. Juego de Enemigos. *Allpanchis* (Cuzco) 20:167–87.

Howard-Malverde, Rosalind, ed. 1997. *Creating Context in Andean Cultures.* Oxford and New York: Oxford University Press.

Hugh-Jones, Christine. 1979 *From the Milk River: Spatial and Temporal Processes in Northwest Amazonia.* Cambridge: Cambridge University Press.

Husserl, Edmund. 1970. *The Crisis of European Sciences and Transcendental Phenomenology.* Evanston, Ill.: Northwestern University Press.

Isbell, Billie Jean. 1982. Culture Confronts Nature in the Dialectical World of the Tropics. *Annals of the New York Academy of Sciences* (1982):353–63.

————. 1985a. Languages of Domination and Rebellion in Highland Peru. *Social Education* 49 (29): 119–21.

————. [1978] 1985b. *To Defend Ourselves: Ecology and Ritual in an Andean Village.* Prospect Heights, Ill.: Waveland Press. Originally published as Latin American Monograph no. 47. Austin: University of Texas Press.

————. 1995. Women's Voices: 1975. In Tedlock and Mannheim 1995:54–74.

Isbell, Billie Jean, and Fredy Roncalla. 1977. The Ontogenesis of Metaphor: Riddle Games among Quechua Speakers Seen as Cognitive Discovery Procedure. *Journal of Latin American Lore* 3 (1): 19–49.

Kapsoli, Wilfredo. 1977. *Los Movimientos Campesinos en el Perú, 1879–1965.* Lima: Delva.

————. 1984. *Ayllus del Sol: Anarquismo y utopía andina.* Lima: Tarea.

Kendall, Sarita. 1985. South American Cocaine Production. *Cultural Survival Quarterly* 9 (4): 10–11.

Kubler, George. [1946] 1963. The Quechua in the Colonial World. In Steward, ed. 1963:331–410.

Leichtman, Ellen. 1987. The Bolivian Huayño: A Study in Musical Understanding. Ph.D. diss., Brown University.

Lévi-Strauss, Claude. 1963. *Structural Anthropology.* Claire Jacobson and Brooke Grundfest Schoepf, trans. New York: Basic Books.

Lira, Jorge. 1982. *Diccionario Kkechuwa-Español.* Cuadernos Culturales Andinos no. 5 Bogotá: Secretaria Ejecutiva del Convenio "Andres Bello."

Lobo, Susan. 1982. *A House of My Own: Social Organization in the Squatter Settlements of Lima* Tucson: University of Arizona Press.

Lumbreras, Luis G. 1974. *The Peoples and Cultures of Ancient Peru.* Betty J. Meggers, trans. Washington, D.C.: Smithsonian Institution Press.

MacCormack, Sabine. 1998. Art in a Missionary Context: Images from Europe and the Andes in the Church of Andahuaylillas near Cuzco. In Brown 1998.

Malinowski, Bronislaw. [1922] 1961. *Argonauts of the Western Pacific.* New York: E. P. Dutton.

Mangin, William. 1957. Drinking among Andean Indians. *Quarterly Journal of Studies on Alcohol* 18 (1): 55–65.

Mannheim, Bruce. 1982. Iconicity in Phonological Change. In Ahlqvist, ed. 1982.

————. 1986a. The Language of Reciprocity in Southern Peruvian Quechua. *Anthropological Linguistics* 28:267–73.

————. 1986b. Poetic Form in Guaman Poma's *Wariqsa Arawi. Amerindia* 11:41–67.

————. 1986c. Popular Song and Popular Grammar: Poetry and Metalanguage. *Word* 37:45–75.

————. 1987a. Couplets and Obliqueness: The Social Organization of a Folk Song. *Text* 7:265–88.

————. 1987b. A Semiotic of Andean Dreams. In B. Tedlock, ed. 1987:132–53.

Marcus, George E., and Michael M. J. Fischer. 1986. *Anthropology as Cultural Critique: An Experimental Moment in the Human Sciences*. Chicago: University of Chicago Press.

Martin, David, ed. 1990. *Tongues of Fire: The Explosion of Protestantism in Latin America*. Oxford: Blackwell.

Martínez, Gabriel. 1989. *Espacio y pensamiento*. La Paz: HISBOL.

Martínez Escobar, Gabriela. 2000. *Qoyllur Rit'i: A Woman's Journey*. Ethnographic Film produced by Holly Wissler.

Marzal, Manuel. 1971. *El mundo religioso de Urcos*. Cuzco: Instituto de Pastoral Andina.

Masuda, Shozo. 1984. *Contribuciones a los estudios de los Andes centrales*. Tokyo: University of Tokyo Press.

Masuda, Shozo, Izumi Shimada, and Craig Morris, eds. 1985. *Andean Ecology and Civilization: An Interdisciplinary Perspective on Andean Ecological Complementarity*. Tokyo: University of Tokyo Press

Matos Mendieta, R., ed. 1988. *Sociedad andina, pasado y presente: Contribuciones en homenaje a la memoria de César Fonseca*. Lima: FOMENCIAS.

Maybury-Lewis, David, and Uri Almagor. 1989. *The Attraction of Opposites: Thought and Society in the Dualistic Mode*. Ann Arbor: University of Michigan Press.

Mayer, Enrique. 1974. Las reglas del juego en la reciprocidad andina. In Alberti and Mayer, eds. 1974:37–65.

————. 1975. *Reciprocity, Self-Sufficiency and Market Relations in a Contemporary Community in the Central Andes of Peru*. Latin American Studies Dissertation Series no. 72. Ithaca: Cornell University.

————. 1977. Beyond the Nuclear Family. In Bolton and Mayer, eds. 1977:60–80.

————. 1979. *Uso de la tierra en los Andes: Ecología y agricultura en el valle de Mantaro, con referencia especial a la papa*. Lima: International Potato Center.

————. 1985. Production Zones. In Masuda, Shimada, and Morris, eds. 1985.

————. 1988. De hacienda a comunidad: El impacto de la Reforma Agraria en la provincia de Paucartambo, Cusco. In Matos Mendieta, 59–100.

————. 2002. *The Articulated Peasant: Household Economies in the Andes*. Boulder, Colo.: Westview Press.

Mayer, Enrique, and César Fonseca. 1979. *Sistemas agrarios en la Cuenca del Río Cañete (Depto. de Lima)*. Lima: Oficina Nacional de Evaluación de Recursos Naturales.

Mayer, Enrique, and Manuel Glave. *Aguito para Ganar* (A Little Something to Earn): Profits and Losses in Peasant Economies. *American Ethnologist* 26 (2): 344–69.

Mendoza, Zoila S. 2000. *Shaping Society through Dance: Mestizo Ritual Performance in the Peruvian Andes*. Chicago: University of Chicago Press.

Meyerson, Julia. 1990. *Tambo*. Austin: University of Texas Press.

Míguez Bonino, José. 1997. *Faces of Latin-American Protestantism*. Stockwell trans. Grand Rapids, Mich.: W.B. Eerdsman.

Millones, Luis, ed. 1990. *El Retorno de las Huacas: Estudios y documentos sobre el* Taki Onqoy, *Siglo XVI*. Lima: Instituto de Estudios Peruanos.

Millones, Luis, Hiroyasu Tomoeda, and Tatsuhiko Fujii, eds. 1998. *Historia, religíon y ritual de los pueblos ayacuchanos*. Senri Ethnological Reports 9. Osaka: National Museum of Ethnology.

Mishkin, Bernard. [1946] 1963. The Contemporary Quechua. In Steward, ed. 1963:411–70.

Molina, Cristóbal de. [1573] 1943. *Relación de las fábulas y ritos de los Incas*. Serie 1, Tomo 4. Lima: Los Pequeños Grandes Libros de Historia Americana.

Monge, Carlos. 1948. *Acclimatization in the Andes*. Baltimore: Johns Hopkins University Press.

————. 1952. The Need for Studying the Problem of Coca-leaf Chewing. *Bulletin on Narcotics* 4:13–15.

Montoya Rojas, Rodrigo. 1997. *El Tiempo del Descanso*. Lima: SUR.

284

Morales, Edmundo. 1989. *Cocaine: White Gold Rush in Peru.* Tucson: University of Arizona Press.

Morissette, Jacques, and Luc Racine. 1973. La Hiérarchie des wamani: Essai sur la pensée classificatoire quechua. *Signes et Languages de Ameriques* 3 (1–2): 167–88.

Morote Best, Efraín. 1958. El oso raptor. *Archivos Venezolanos de Folklore* (Caracas) 5:135–78.

Mortimer, W. Golden. [1901] 1974. *History of Coca: "The Divine Plant" of the Incas.* San Francisco: And/Or Press.

Murra, John V. 1973. Rite and Crop in the Inca State. In D. Gross, ed. 1973:377–94.

———. 1986. Notes on Pre-Columbian Cultivation of Coca Leaf. In Pacini and Franquemont, eds. 1986:49–52.

Murra, John V., Nathan Wachtel, and Jacques Revel, eds. 1986. *Anthropological History of Andean Polities.* Cambridge: Cambridge University Press.

Murúa, Martin de. [1605] 1962. *Historia general del Perú. Origin y genealogía real de los reyes Incas.* Madrid: Biblioteca Americana Vetus.

Negrete, J. C., and H. B. M. Murphy. 1967. Psychological Deficit in Chewers of Coca Leaf. *Bulletin on Narcotics* 19 (4): 11–17.

Nieschulz, Otto. 1971. Psychopharmacologische Untersuchugen über Cocain und Ecgonin, e in Beitrag sum Problem Cocaismus und Cocainismus. *Arzneimittel-Forschung* 21:275–83.

Núñez del Prado, Oscar. 1958. El hombre y la familia: Su matrimonio y organización político-social en Q'ero. *Revista Universitaria* (Cuzco) 47 (144).

———. 1973. *Kuyo Chico: Applied Anthropology in an Indian Community.* Lucy Whyte Russo and Richard Russo, trans. Chicago: University of Chicago Press.

Núñez del Prado Bejar, Daisy. 1972. La reciprocidad como ethos de la cultura quechua. *Allpanchis* (Cuzco) 4:135–65.

Núñez del Prado Bejar, Juan Victor. 1970. El mundo sobrenatural de los Quechuas del sur del Perú, a través de la comunidad de Qotabamba. *Allpanchis* (Cuzco) 2:135–56.

Orlove, Benjamin. 1998. Down to Earth: Race and Substance in the Andes. *Bulletin of Latin American Research* 17(2):207–22.

Orlove, Benjamin, and Ricardo Godoy. 1986. Sectorial Fallowing Systems in the Andes. *Journal of Ethnobiology* 6 (1): 169–204.

Ossio, Juan M., ed. 1973. *Ideología mesiánica del mundo andino.* Lima: Edición de Ignacio Prado Pastor.

———. 1981. Expresiones simbólicas y sociales de los ayllus andinos: El caso de los ayllus de la comunidad de Cabana y del antiguo repartimiento de los Rucanas-Antamarcas. In Castelli, Koth de Paredes, and Mould de Pease, eds. 1981:189–214.

Pacini, Deborah, and Christine Franquemont, eds. 1986. *Coca and Cocaine: Effects on People and Policy in Latin America.* Cultural Survival Report no. 23. Cambridge: Cultural Survival, Inc.

Palomino, Salvador. 1971. Duality in the Socio-cultural Organization of Several Andean Populations. *Folk* 13:63–88.

Panofsky, Erwin. 1957. *Gothic Architecture and Scholasticism.* New York: Meridian Books.

Platt, Tristan. 1986. Mirrors and Maize: The Concept of *Yanantin* among the Macha of Bolivia. In Murra, Wachtel, and Revel, eds. 1986:228–59.

———. 1987. Entre *Chaxwa* y *Mucsa:* Para una historia de la pensamiento político aymara. In Bouysee-Casagne et al. (eds), 1987:61–132.

Plowman, Timothy. 1986. Coca Chewing and the Botanical Origins of Coca (*Erythroxylum* sp.) in South America. In Pacini and Franquemont, eds. 1986:5–34.

Poole, Deborah. 1984. *Ritual-Economic Calendars in Paruro: The Structure of Representation in Andean Ethnography.* Ann Arbor, Mich.: University Microfilms.

———. 1990. Accommodation and Resistence in Andean Ritual Dance. *Drama Review* 32 (1): 98–126.

———. 1991. Miracles, Memory and Time in an Andean Pilgrimage Story. *Journal of Latin American Lore* 17 (1–2):131–64.

Ramirez, Juan Andrés. 1969. La novena al Señor de Qoyllur Rit'i. *Allpanchis* (Cuzco) 1:61–88.

Randall, Robert. 1982. Qoyllur Rit'i, an Inca Fiesta of the Pleiades: Reflections on Time and Space in the Andean World. *Boletín del Instituto Francés de Estudios Andinos* (Lima) 11 (1–2):37–81.

Rappaport, Joanne. 1985. History, Myth and the Dynamics of Territorial Maintenance in Tierradentro, Colombia. *American Ethnologist* 12 (1):27–45.

———. 1990. *The Politics of Memory: Native Historical Interpretation in the Colombian Andes.* Cambridge: Cambridge University Press.

———. 1994. *Cumbe Reborn: An Andean Ethnography of History.* Chicago: University of Chicago Press.

Rasnake, Roger Neil. 1988. *Domination and Cultural Resistance: Authority and Power among an Andean People.* Durham, N.C.: Duke University Press.

Reichel-Dolmatoff, Gerardo. 1971. *Amazonian Cosmos: The Sexual and Religious Symbolism of the Tukano Indians.* Chicago: University of Chicago Press.

———. 1984. Some Kogi Models of the Beyond. *Journal of Latin American Lore* 10 (1): 63–86.

Roca, Demetrio, J. Casaverde Rojas, J. Sánchez Farfán, and T. C. Cevallos. 1966. Wifala o p'asña capitán. *Folklore* (Cuzco) 1:83–102.

Roderiguez Sandoval, L. 1945. Drinking Motivations among the Indians of the Ecuadorean Sierra. *Primitive Man* 18:39–46.

Rosaldo, Renato. 1983. Grief and a Headhunter's Rage. In Bruner, ed. 1983:178–95.

———. 1989. *Culture and Truth.* Boston: Beacon Press.

Romero, Raúl R., ed. 1993. *Música, Danzas y Mascaras en los Andes.* Lima: Pontifícia Universidad Católica del Perú, Instituto Riva-Aguero.

Romero, Raúl R. 2001. *Debating the Past: Music, Memory and Identity in the Andes.* Oxford: Oxford University Press.

Rossi, Ino, ed. 1982. *The Logic of Culture: Advances in Structural Theory and Methods.* New York: J. F. Bergin.

Rostworowski de Diez Canseco, María. 1981. La voz *parcialidad* en su contexto en los siglos XVI y XVII. In Castelli, Koth de Paredes, and Mould de Pease, eds. 1981:35–45.

Rubin, Vera, ed. 1975. *Cannibis and Culture.* Chicago: Aldine.

Sahlins, Marshall. 1981. *Historical Metaphors and Mythical Realities: Structure in the Early History of the Sandwich Islands Kingdom.* Ann Arbor: University of Michigan Press.

Saignes, Thierry, ed. 1993. *Borrachera y memoria: la experiencia de lo sagrado en los Andes.* La Paz: HISBOL.

Sallnow, Michael J. 1974. La peregrinación andina. *Allpanchis* (Cuzco) 7:101–42.

———. 1982. A Trinity of Christs: Cultic Processes in Andean Catholicism. *American Ethnologist* 9 (4): 730–49.

———. 1987. *Pilgrims of the Andes: Regional Cults in Cusco.* Washington, D.C.: Smithsonian Institution Press.

Salomon, Frank. 1982. Chronicles of the Impossible: Notes on Three Peruvian Indigenous Historians. In Adorno, ed. 1982:9–40.

———. 1983. Shamanism and Politics in Late Colonial Ecuador. *American Ethnologist* 10 (3): 413–28.

———. 1991. Introductory Essay: The Huarochirí Manuscript. In Salomon and Urioste 1991:1–38.

Salomon, Frank, and George L. Urioste. 1991. *The Huarochirí Manuscript: A Testament of Ancient and Colonial Andean Religion.* Austin: University of Texas Press.

Sándor, András. 1986. Metaphor and Belief. *Journal of Anthropological Research* 42 (2): 101–22.

Schechner, Richard. 1985. *Between Theater and Anthropology*. Philadelphia: University of Pennsylvania Press.

Scheper-Hughes, Nancy. 1995. The Primacy of the Ethical: Propositions for a Militant Anthropology. *Current Anthropology* 36 (3): 409–20.

Schutz, Alfred. 1967. *The Phenomenology of the Social World*. Evanston, Ill.: Northwestern University Press.

———. 1970. *On Phenomenology and Social Relations: Selected Writings*. Helmut R. Wagner, ed. Chicago: University of Chicago Press.

Seligmann, Linda J. 1995. *Between Reform and Revolution: Political Struggles in the Peruvian Andes, 1969–1991*. Stanford: Stanford University Press.

Sherbondy, Jeanette. 1979a. Los lagos y la hydrología en la cosmología andina. Paper presented at the 43rd Congress of Americanists in Vancouver, British Columbia, August 1979.

———. 1979b. Les Réseaux d'irrigation dans la géographie politique de Cuzco. *Journal de la Société des Américanistes* 66:45–66.

Sigmund, Paul E., ed. 1999. *Religious Freedom and Evangelization in the Challenge of Religious Pluralism*. Maryknoll, N.Y.: Orbis Books.

Silverblatt, Irene. 1987. *Moon, Sun and Witches: Gender Ideologies and Class in Inca and Colonial Peru*. Princeton: Princeton University Press.

Silverblatt, Irene, and John Earls. 1976. Mito y renovación: El caso de Moros y los Aymaraes. *Allpanchis* (Cuzco) 10:93–104.

Simmons, Ozzie G. 1959. Drinking Patterns and Interpersonal Performance in a Mestizo Peruvian Community. *Quarterly Journal of Studies on Alcohol* 20:103–11.

———. 1960. Ambivalence and the Learning of Drinking Behavior in a Peruvian Community. *American Anthropologist* 68:1018–27.

Skar, Harald O. 1982. *The Warm Valley People: Duality and Land Reform among the Quechua Indians of Highland Peru*. Oslo Studies in Social Anthropology no. 2. Oslo: Universitetsforlaget.

Skar, Harald O., and Frank Salomon. *Natives and Neighbors in South America: Anthropological Essays*. Göteborg, Sweden: Göteborgs Etnografiska Museum.

Skar, Sarah Lund. 1987. The Role of Urine in Andean Notions of Health and the Cosmos. In H. Skar and F. Salomon, eds. 1987:267–69.

———. 1997. On the Margin: Letter Exchange among Andean Non-Literates. In Howard-Malverde 1997:185 95.

Sontag, Susan. 1970. The Anthropologist as Hero. In Hayes and Hayes, eds. 1970:184–96.

Spalding, Karen. 1984. *Huarochirí: An Andean Society Under Inca and Spanish Rule*. Stanford: Stanford University Press.

Spedding, Alison. 1994. *Wachu wachu: Cultivo de coca e identidad en los Yunkas de La Paz*. La Paz: HISBOL/CIPCA/Cocayapu.

Stern, Steve J. 1982. *Peru's Indian Peoples and the Challenge of the Spanish Conquest: Huamanga to 1640*. Madison: University of Wisconsin Press.

———. 1987. *Resistence, Rebellion and Consciousness in the Andean Peasant World*. Madison: University of Wisconsin Press.

Steward, Julian H., ed. [1946] 1963. *Handbook of South American Indians*. Vol. 2, *The Andean Civilizations*. Smithsonian Institution Bureau of American Ethnology Bulletin 143. New York: Cooper Square.

Sullivan, Lawrence. 1988. *Icanchu's Drum: An Orientation to Meaning in South American Religions*. New York: Macmillan Publishing Company.

Taussig, Michael. 1980. *The Devil and Commodity Fetishism in South America*. Chapel Hill: University of North Carolina Press.

Taylor, Gerald. 1976. Camay, Camac et Camasca dans le manuscrit quechua de Huarochirí. *Journal de la Société des Américanistes* 63.231–44.

Tedlock, Barbara. 1982. *Time and the Highland Maya*. Albuquerque: University of New Mexico Press.

———, ed. 1987. *Dreaming: Anthropological and Psychological Interpretations*. Cambridge: Cambridge University Press.

Tedlock, Dennis. 1983. *The Spoken Word and the Work of Interpretation*. Philadelphia: University of Pennsylvania Press.

Tedlock, Dennis, and Bruce Mannheim, eds. 1995. *The Dialogic Emergence of Culture*. Urbana: University of Illinois Press.

Turnbull, Colin M. 1979. Anthropology and Drama: The Anthropological Perspective. In Garner and Turnbull, eds. 1979:1–13.

Turner, Victor W. 1969. *The Ritual Process: Structure and Anti-Structure*. Ithaca: Cornell University Press.

United Nations Economic and Social Council. 1950. *Report of the Commission of Inquiry on the Coca Leaf*. 5th year, 12th session, special supplement, vol. I. Lake Success, N.Y.: UNESCO Official Records.

Urbano, Henrique-Oswaldo. 1974. La representación andina del tiempo y del espacio en la fiesta. *Allpanchis* (Cuzco) 7:9–49.

———. 1993a. Las tres edades del mundo: La idea de utopía y de historia en los Andes. In Urbano 1993b:283–304.

———. 1993b. *Mito y Simbolismo en los Andes: la figure y la palabra*. Cuzco: Centro de Estudios Regionales Andinos "Bartolomé de Las Casas."

Urton, Gary D. 1981. *At the Crossroads of the Earth and the Sky: An Andean Cosmology*. Austin: University of Texas Press.

———. 1990. *The History of a Myth: Pacariqtambo and the Origin of the Incas*. Austin: University of Texas Press.

———. 1997. *The Social Life of Numbers*. Austin: University of Texas Press.

Valderrama Fernández, Ricardo, and Carmen Escalante Gutiérrez, eds. 1977. *Gregorio Condori Mamani: Autobiografía*. Biblioteca de la Tradición Oral Andina no. 2. Cuzco: Centro de Estudios Rurales Andinos, "Bartolomé de las Casas."

——— and Carmen Escalante Gutiérrez. 1988. *Del Tata Mallku a la Pachamama: Riego, sociedad y ritos en los andes peruanos*. Cuzco: Centro de Estudios Regionales Andinos Bartolomé de Las Casas.

——— and Carmen Escalante Gutiérrez, Paul H. Gelles, and Gabriela Martínez Escorbar. 1996. *Andean Lives: Gregorio Condori Mamani and Asunta Quispe Huamán*. Translation by Gelles and Martínez of Valderrama y Escalante 1977, with an introduction by Paul H. Gelles. Austin: University of Texas Press.

Vasquez, Mario C. 1967. La chicha en los paises andinos. *América Indígena* 27:265–82.

Vitti, Trieste. 1979. Recent Biochemical Research on Coca Alkaloid: Metabolic Implications. Manuscript, Department of Pharmacy, University of Manitoba.

Wachtel, Nathan. 1977. *The Vision of the Vanquished: The Spanish Conquest of Peru through Indian Eyes*. New York: Barnes and Noble.

Wagner, Catherine Allen. 1978. *Coca, Chicha and Trago: Private and Communal Rituals in a Quechua Community*. Ann Arbor, Mich.: University Microfilms.

Weil, Andrew. 1995. Letter from the Andes: The New Politics of Coca. *The New Yorker*, May 15: 70–80.

Weismantel, Mary J. [1988] 1998. *Food, Gender and Poverty in the Ecuadorean Andes*. Prospect Heights, Ill.: Waveland Press. Originally published by the University of Pennsylvania Press, Philadelphia.

———. 2001. *Cholas and Pishtacos: Stories of Race and Sex in the Andes*. Chicago: University of Chicago Press.

Wissler, Holly. 1999. *An Outsider Inside: Ritual, Music and Dance in the Qoyllur Rit'i Festival of the Peruvian Andes*. M.A. thesis, University of Idaho, Department of Music.

Zimmerer, Karl S. 1996. *Changing Fortunes: Biodiversity and Peasant Livelihood in the Peruvian Andes*. Berkeley: University of California Press.

Zuidema, R. T. 1964. *The Ceque System of Cuzco: The Social Organization of the Capital of the Inca*. Leiden: E. J. Brill.

———. 1978. Lieux sacrés et irrigation: Tradition, historique, mythes et rituels au Cuzco. *Annales* 5–6:1036–1238.

———. 1980. El Ushnu. *Revista de la Universidad Complutense de Madrid* 38 (117): 317–62.

———. 1982. Myth and History in Ancient Peru. In Rossi, ed. 1982:150–75.

———. 1985. L'Organisation andine du savoir rituel et technique en termes d'espace et de temps. *Techniques et Culture* 6:43–66.

———. 1990. *Inca Civilization in Cuzco*. Austin: University of Texas Press.

Index

administration of community, 92–96, 207, 215, 220, 226, 242; assemblies, 89–92, 97–98, 221; decision-making process, 95–97, 209–10; and schoolteachers, 93; *sectores*, 207, 214, 216, 233; Velasco regime's reorganization, 89

affines, 64, 66–67, 212, 216, 260n4; in oral history, 79; terminology, 255, 261n12

agrarian reform, 14–15, 208, 209–10, 215, 220, 242, 258n19, 258n20, 269n5. *See also* Velasco regime

agriculture, 24, 25, 179, 207, 209–10, 260n3; cash crops, 15, 20–21, 54, 84–85, 208, 209, 211–12, 214, 220; sectoral fallowing, 84, 179, 204, 208–12, 214–16, 257n9, 262n18, 269n6, 269n8, 270n18; subsistence, 212–13

agustu (first days of August), 41, 143, 218, 242

alcalde (mayor), 93–95, 210, 232, 263n30; as compared with *arariwa*, 171, 266n16, 266n25; election of, 89–92; as power object, 173

alcoholic beverages, 114–26; alcoholism, 204, 213, 218–21, 242; *alkul*, 219; attitudes toward intoxication, 122–24, 219–20; beer, 33, 118; compared to coca, 19, 118–21, 242; and community, 9; mar-

ket-day drinking, 116, 123; and Protestantism, 208, 221–22, 243; red wine, 118; and sacred places, 124–25, 218; substitution of carbonated beverages, 33, 224, 228–29, 243. *See also* chicha; trago

All Souls' Day. *See* Day of the Dead

alma (soul; plural, *almakuna*): as bones, 40, 225; deindividualized concept, 43–44; malevolence, 43–44, 227; personal, 4, 227; and *qayqa*, 43; return on Day of the Dead, 139–40, 151, 218

amaru (giant serpent), 36, 46, 176

ancestors: the dead as, 9, 218–19; and elders, 99; and *enqas*, 43; invocation in coca chewing, 108; *Machula Aulanchis*, 40–41, 99; mummies of, 41–42; origin, 76; reciprocity with, 73 218–19, 240; and sacred places, 41, 76, 79, 80–81, 99; and water, 35, 240. See also *Machu*

animal husbandry/herding, 52, 203, 218, 240; and collapse of sectoral fallowing, 211–12; diminished importance, 204, 208–11, 216, 218, 229; liver flukes, 208, 209, 210–12; manure, 49, 144–45, 211, 240; and reciprocal labor, 57, 211; and school, 57, 211; and sexual division of labor, 55, 211; small animal, 50, 218. *See also* fertility rituals

291

animu (spirit), 43
Apu (Mountain Lord; plural, *Apukuna*),
26–28. *See also* places, sacred
arariwa: compared with *alcalde*, 171,
266n25; as guardian of boundaries, 158,
266n16; pilgrimage duties, 163–64, 171,
175, 266n25
Arnold, Denise, 203, 221, 235–36
ayllu (community), 9, 18, 75–104; ancestors, 76; and coca chewing, 108–9; colonial history, 15–17, 89; compared to
household and cosmos, 99; definition of,
18, 86–87, 108, 207–8, 214; in district of
Colquepata, 15, 205, 258n23; fissioning,
214–15, 263n23; formation, 87, 214; and
hacienda system, 89, 208; and inheritance,
83, 215; legal recognition as community,
16, 259n24; nested quality, 85, 214,
262n20; and reciprocity, 49, 84, 208; and
sacred places, 17, 28; *sectores*, 207, 214–17,
222, 227, 243, 270n18; topography, 85,
156, 214; in year 2000, 207–18
ayni (reciprocal aid), 23, 71, 72–74, 120,
151, 160; diminished importance,
212–13. See also *mink'a*

Bateson, Gregory, 18, 182
battle, annual *(tinku)*, 155–59, 160, 174,
176–78, 183, 231, 265n5, 265n7, 267n4,
267n5
birds, 43, 143, 148, 158, 231, 271n43
blood river *(yawar mayu)*, 44, 169, 174, 176
Bourdieu, Pierre, 18, 232

cargo system, 32, 47, 90–96, 179, 220, 226;
alcalde (mayor), 89–92, 93–95, 171, 173;
Carnival, 89–93, 160; Corpus Christi,
163–64, 220; Santa Cruz, 151–52
Carnival *(Puqllay)*, 19, 41, 114–15, 142,
154–62, 210, 218, 219, 224, 225, 230,
231, 232, 241
Chakra Mañay ceremony (Distribution of
the Fields), 80, 210
chansanakuy (stylized joking), 180–83
chicha, 114–15, 117, 122, 148, 152, 205,
210, 240
childbearing, 5–6, 196–97, 261n11
Christ: Christ Child, 162; images carried to
Qoyllur Rit'i, 153, 163, 168, 170, 172,
175; second coming of, 232; as sun, 36
chullpa, 54–59. See also *Machu*
ch'uño (dehydrated potatoes), 2, 23, 55, 63,
75, 114, 224, 256n1, 260n3; storage ritual, 143, 146–47
circulation: in Andean worldview, 194–95,
241; in Inca ritual vessel, 145–46; in reci-

procity relationships, 73; of cultivated
fields, 209; of rivers, 36, 195, 209; of
sami, 36, 195
coca: in *despacho*, 64–65, 129, 130–31, 135,
179; *llipt'a* (ash), 105, 240, 263n5;
offered to the dead, 41; plant, 7, 190;
properties of, 7, 190, 240, 242; social
contract, 68, 105, 108, 109, 242; sup-
pression of, 192, 208, 218, 239, 242; and
U.N. Commission of Enquiry, 192,
268n20; vehicle for communication with
deities, 9, 110; and Virgin Mary *(Maman-
chis)*, 7, 244, 263n5
coca chewing *(hallpay):* to allay grief, 4, 7,
242; and bond with land, 9, 18, 19, 109;
compared to drinking, 19, 118–21, 193;
debate concerning, 188–93; denigration
of, 3, 20; distribution during festivals,
115, 210, 233, 241; etiquette,1, 2, 19, 51,
56, 104–6, 227; history, 188–89; mytho-
logical origin, 7, 244; nutrition, 190; orientation in space and time, 107–8, 205;
as ritual frame, 183, 193; as sacrament,
109, 218, 242, 243; and socialization, 3,
112, 242. *See* ritual techniques
cocaine, 190–93
Colloredo-Mansfield, Rudi, 238–39
Colquepata: agriculture, 209–12, 232;
*ayllu*s, 15, 258n23; development projects,
216; history, 16–17, 258n21–24; patronal
feast, 15, 231–32, 241; population, 9,
269n11; town, 9–15, 203, 205–6, 221,
227, 230
Comadres, Feast of. *See* battle, annual
compadrazgo (godparent relationship),
13–14, 28–31, 45, 67–71, 137, 151, 219,
220, 222, 229, 242
conch shell trumpet *(pututu)*, 93, 152, 198
condenado. See *kukuchi*
Connerton, Paul, 232
Corpus Christi sponsorship, 20, 50, 95, 162,
171, 220
corn beer. See *chicha*
crop rotation. *See* sectoral fallowing
cross, Christian *(taytacha)*, 3, 224, 225, 228,
236; and Feast of Santa Cruz, 151–54;
male symbolism of, 152–53; at Qoyllur
Rit'i sanctuary, 167, 175; sign of, 37, 55,
135

dances: *awka chileno,* 231; *ch'unchu,*164–65,
167, 175, 220, 231, 266n18; llamas, 212;
majeño, 231; *p'asñacha,* 232–33; *qhapaq
negro,* 231, 232; *qolla,* 168, 175, 231;
saqra, 231; *sargento,* 156–58, 161, 174,
176, 231; *ukuku,* 24, 164–65, 231